P9-DHE-901

CompTIA® A+
Practice
Questions
Third Edition

Patrick Regan

CompTIA® A+ Practice Questions Exam Cram, Third Edition

Copyright © 2010 by Pearson Education, Inc.

ISBN-13: 978-0-7897-4257-5

ISBN-10: 0-7897-4257-8

Library of Congress Cataloging-in-Publication Data:

Regan, Patrick E.

CompTIA A+ practice questions : exam cram / Patrick Regan. – 3rd ed.

p. cm.

ISBN 978-0-7897-4257-5 (pbk. w/cd)

1. Electronic data processing personnel—Certification. 2. Computer technicians—Examinations, questions, etc. 3. Microcomputers—Maintenance and repair—Examinations—Study guides. I. Title.

QA76.3.R4553 2010

004.165—dc22

2009038381

Printed in the United States of America

Third Printing: October 2010

Trademarks

Warning and Disclaimer

Bulk Sales

Que Publishing offers excellent discounts on this book when ordered in quantity for bulk purchases or special sales. For more information, please contact

U.S. Corporate and Government Sales
1-800-382-3419
corpsales@pearsontechgroup.com

For sales outside the United States, please contact

International Sales
international@pearson.com

Publisher
Paul Boger

Associate Publisher
David Dusthimer

Acquisitions Editor
Betsy Brown

Senior Development Editor
Christopher Cleveland

Managing Editor
Patrick Kanouse

Technical Editor
Chris Crayton

Senior Project Editor
Tonya Simpson

Copy Editor
The Wordsmithery, LLC

Proofreader
Dan Knott

Publishing Coordinator
Vanessa Evans

Multimedia Developer
Dan Scherf

Book Designer
Gary Adair

Compositor
TnT Design, Inc.

Contents at a Glance

Table of Contents

About the Author

Patrick Regan has been a PC technician, network administrator/engineer, design architect, and security analyst for the past 16 years. He has a bachelor's degree in physics from the University of Akron. He has taught many computer and network classes at Sacramento local colleges (Heald Colleges and MTI Colleges) and has participated in and led many projects for Heald Colleges, Intel Corporation, Miles Consulting Corporation, and Pacific Coast Companies. For his teaching accomplishments, he received the Teacher of the Year award from Heald Colleges and has received several recognition awards from Intel Corporation. Previously, he worked as a product support engineer for Intel Corporation Customer Service, a senior network engineer for Virtual Alert—where he supported the BioTerrorism Readiness suite and as a senior design architect/engineer—and training coordinator for Miles Consulting Corporation (MCC), a premiere Microsoft Gold partner and consulting firm. He is currently a senior network engineer at Pacific Coast Companies where he supports a large enterprise network.

He holds many certifications including the Microsoft MCSE, MCSA, MCT; MCITP; CompTIA A+, Network+, Server+, Linux+, Security+ and CTT+; Cisco CCNA; and Novell CNE and CWNP Certified Wireless Network Administrator (CWNA).

During the past several years, he has written several textbooks for Prentice Hall, including *Troubleshooting the PC*; *Networking with Windows 2000 and 2003*; *Linux*, *Local Area Networks*, *Wide Area Networks* and the Acing Series (*Acing the A+*, *Acing the Network+*, *Acing the Security+*, and *Acing the Linux+*). He has also co-authored the *MCSA/MCSE 70-290 Exam Cram: Managing and Maintaining a Microsoft Windows Server 2003 Environment*, Second Edition and written *MCTS 70-620 Exam Cram: Microsoft Windows Vista, Configuring*; *MCTS 70-642 Exam Cram: Windows Server 2008 Network Infrastructure, Configuring*; and *MCTS 70-643 Exam Cram: Windows Server 2008 Applications Infrastructure, Configuring*. In addition, he has completed the study guides for the A+ certification exams for Cisco Press.

You can write with questions and comments to the author at Patrick_Regan@hotmail.com. (Because of the high volume of mail, every message might not receive a reply.)

Dedication

I dedicate this book to my mother.

Acknowledgments

Publishing a book takes the collaboration and teamwork of many individuals. Thanks to everyone involved in this process at Pearson Education, especially Betsy and Chris. To the editorial and technical reviewers, thank you for making sure that my work was sound and on target.

We Want to Hear from You!

As the reader of this book, *you* are our most important critic and commentator. We value your opinion and want to know what we're doing right, what we could do better, what areas you'd like to see us publish in, and any other words of wisdom you're willing to pass our way.

As an associate publisher for Que Publishing, I welcome your comments. You can email or write me directly to let me know what you did or didn't like about this book—as well as what we can do to make our books better.

Please note that I cannot help you with technical problems related to the topic of this book. We do have a User Services group, however, where I will forward specific technical questions related to the book.

When you write, please be sure to include this book's title and author as well as your name, email address, and phone number. I will carefully review your comments and share them with the author and editors who worked on the book.

Email: feedback@quepublishing.com

Mail: David Dusthimer
                Associate Publisher
                Pearson Education, Inc.
                800 East 96th Street
                Indianapolis, IN 46240 USA

Reader Services

Visit our website and register this book at www.examcram.com/register for convenient access to any updates, downloads, or errata that might be available for this book.

Introduction

Welcome to *CompTIA A+ Practice Questions Exam Cram*. The sole purpose of this book is to provide you with practice questions that are complete with answers and explanations to help you learn, drill, and review for the CompTIA A+ certification exam. The book offers many questions that will help you practice each exam objective and will help you assess your knowledge before you write the real exam. The detailed answers to every question will help you reinforce your knowledge about different issues involving the concepts associated with the A+ exam (2009 edition).

Who This Book Is For

If you have studied the content for both the 220-701 and 220-702 exam and feel you are ready to put your knowledge to the test, but you are not sure that you want to take the real exam yet, this book is for you! If you have answered other practice questions or unsuccessfully taken the real exam, and want to do more practice questions before going to take the real exam, this book is for you, too! Even when the exam is done and you have passed with flying colors and have the A+ certificate in your pocket, keep the book handy on your desktop to look for answers to your everyday security issues.

What You Will Find In This Book

This book is all about practice questions! The practice questions in the book, some very easy and others with a little complicated problem scenario, all are intended to raise your confidence level before you take the real exam. You will find questions that you will face in real life.

This book is organized according to the objectives published by CompTIA for the 220-701: CompTIA A+ Essentials and 220-702: CompTIA A+ (2009 Edition) exams. Each chapter corresponds to an exam objective and in every chapter you will find the following three elements:

▶ **Practice Questions:** These are the numerous questions that will help you learn, drill, and review exam objectives. All of the questions in this section are multiple-choice type. Choose the correct answer based on your knowledge of security.

▶ **Quick-Check Answer Key:** After you have finished answering the questions, you can quickly grade your exam from this section. Only correct answers are given in this section. No explanations are offered yet!

Even if you have answered a question incorrectly, do not be discouraged. Just move on! Keep in mind that this is not the real exam. You can always review the topic and do the questions again.

▶ **Answers and Explanations:** This section provides you with correct answers as well as further explanations about the content posed in that question. Use this information to learn why an answer is correct and to reinforce the content in your mind for the exam day.

Note

It is not possible to reflect a real exam on a paper product. As mentioned earlier, the purpose of the book is to help you prepare for the exam and not provide you with real exam questions. Neither the author nor the publisher can guarantee that you will pass the exam only by memorizing the practice questions given in this book.

Hints for Using This Book

Because this book is a paper practice product, you might want to complete your exams on a separate piece of paper so that you can reuse the practice questions again and again without having previous answers in your way. Also, a general rule of thumb across all practice questions products is to make sure that you are scoring in the high 80% to 90% range for all topics before attempting the real exam. The higher percentages you score on practice question products, the better your chances for passing the real exam. Of course, we cannot guarantee a passing score on the real exam, but we can offer you plenty of opportunities to practice and assess your knowledge level before you enter the real exam.

When you have completed the exam on paper, use the companion CD to take a timed exam. This will further help you gain confidence and make a self-assessment in case you need more study. Your results will indicate the exam objectives in which you need further study or hands-on practice.

Need Further Study?

Are you having a hard time correctly answering these questions? If so, you probably need further review of all exam objectives. Be sure to see the following sister products to this book:

CompTIA Security+ Exam Cram, Fourth Edition by David L. Prowse; (ISBN: 0-7897-4242-X)

CompTIA A+ Cert Flash Cards Online (220-701, 220-702), Retail Packaged Version 2/e by Scott Honeycutt (ISBN: 9780789742636)

1

CHAPTER ONE

Hardware

The first domain for the A+ Essentials (220-701) exam is hardware, which focuses on teaching you to identify components and to demonstrate a basic knowledge of hardware technology. This domain is essential because it gives you a background for the other domains and also counts as 27% of the test score, the largest percentage of all the domains. It also includes the most objectives because today's PCs have such a wide variety of hardware and technology:

The objectives for this domain are as follows:

- ▶ 1.1—Categorize storage devices and backup media
- ▶ 1.2—Explain motherboard components, types, and features
- ▶ 1.3—Classify power supplies types and characteristics
- ▶ 1.4—Explain the purpose and characteristics of CPUs and their features
- ▶ 1.5—Explain cooling methods and devices
- ▶ 1.6—Compare and contrast memory types, characteristics, and their purpose
- ▶ 1.7—Distinguish between the different display devices and their characteristics
- ▶ 1.8—Install and configure peripherals and input devices
- ▶ 1.9—Summarize the function and types of adapter cards
- ▶ 1.10—Install, configure, and optimize laptop components and features

1.1 Categorize storage devices and backup media

- ▶ FDD
- ▶ HDD
  - ▶ Solid state vs. magnetic
- ▶ Optical drives
  - ▶ CD/DVD/RW/Blu-Ray
- ▶ Removable storage
  - ▶ Tape drive
  - ▶ Solid state (e.g. thumb drive, flash, SD cards, USB)
  - ▶ External CD-RW and hard drive
  - ▶ Hot swappable devices and non-hot swappable devices

1. Which of the following are considered legacy devices?

   ○ **A.** FDD

   ○ **B.** HDD

   ○ **C.** CD/DVD drive

   ○ **D.** Blu-Ray drive

Quick Answer: **40**
Detailed Answer: **41**

2. How much disk space does a standard DS/HD 3 1/2" floppy disk hold?

   ○ **A.** 1.2 MB

   ○ **B.** 1.44 MB

   ○ **C.** 2.5 MB

   ○ **D.** 5.0 MB

Quick Answer: **40**
Detailed Answer: **41**

3. Which of the following are drives that are hot swappable? (Choose two answers.)

   ○ **A.** USB hard drive

   ○ **B.** IDE hard drive

   ○ **C.** Internal tape drive

   ○ **D.** USB CD-RW drive

Quick Answer: **40**
Detailed Answer: **41**

4. Which has the greatest storage capacity?

   ○ **A.** CD

   ○ **B.** CD-RW

   ○ **C.** DVD

   ○ **D.** Blu-Ray

Quick Answer: **40**
Detailed Answer: **41**

5. How much disk space can you store on a CD-RW disk?

   ○ **A.** Usually between 650 and 700 MB

   ○ **B.** 4.7 GB

   ○ **C.** 8.5 GB

   ○ **D.** 17.1 GB

   ○ **E.** 25 GB

Quick Answer: **40**
Detailed Answer: **41**

6. Which of the following does not have any mechanical moving parts? (Choose all that apply.)

   ○ **A.** USB thumb drive

   ○ **B.** SD card

   ○ **C.** CD-RW drive

   ○ **D.** Hard drive

Quick Answer: **40**
Detailed Answer: **41**

7. Which of the following is not true when discussing the advantages of a solid state drive over a magnetic drive?

  - ○ **A.** Faster start-up
  - ○ **B.** Faster random access for reading
  - ○ **C.** Quieter
  - ○ **D.** Lower power
  - ○ **E.** Unlimited read and writes

8. Which of the following is the smallest in physical size?

  - ○ **A.** USB thumb drive
  - ○ **B.** SD card
  - ○ **C.** CD-RW drive
  - ○ **D.** Hard drive

9. Which of the following devices would you use primarily to back up data and which must be read sequentially to access the data?

  - ○ **A.** Floppy disk drive
  - ○ **B.** Tape drive
  - ○ **C.** Hard drive
  - ○ **D.** Rewritable DVD drive

10. How much data does a Standard SD memory card store?

  - ○ **A.** Up to 4 GB
  - ○ **B.** Up to 32 GB
  - ○ **C.** Up to 2 TB
  - ○ **D.** Up to 18 GB

11. Where can you find a Standard SD memory card?

  - ○ **A.** A USB thumb drive
  - ○ **B.** A cellular/smart phone
  - ○ **C.** A digital camera
  - ○ **D.** A PDA
  - ○ **E.** All of the options provided are correct

12. Which of the following are not valid formats for the SD memory cards?

Quick Answer: **40**
Detailed Answer: **42**

- ○ **A.** Mini SD card
- ○ **B.** Micro SD card
- ○ **C.** Standard SD card
- ○ **D.** Compact SD card

13. What do you call the technology that allows you to connect and disconnect a device to a computer while the computer is running?

Quick Answer: **40**
Detailed Answer: **42**

- ○ **A.** Hot-swappable
- ○ **B.** Power-charged
- ○ **C.** Plug and play
- ○ **D.** Compact

1.2 Explain motherboard components, types, and features

- ▶ Form Factor
  - ▶ ATX/BTX
  - ▶ Micro ATX
  - ▶ NLX
  - ▶ I/O interfaces
  - ▶ Sound
  - ▶ Video
  - ▶ USB 1.1 and 2.0
  - ▶ Serial
  - ▶ IEEE 1394/Firewire
  - ▶ Parallel
  - ▶ NIC
  - ▶ Modem
  - ▶ PS/2
- ▶ Memory slots
  - ▶ RIMM
  - ▶ DIMM
  - ▶ SODIMM
  - ▶ SIMM

▶ Processor sockets

▶ Bus architecture

▶ Bus slots

    ▶ PCI

    ▶ AGP

    ▶ PCIe

    ▶ AMR

    ▶ CNR

    ▶ PCMCIA

▶ PATA

    ▶ IDE

    ▶ EIDE

▶ SATA, eSATA

▶ Contrast RAID (levels 0, 1, 5)

▶ Chipsets

▶ BIOS/CMOS/Firmware

    ▶ POST

    ▶ CMOS battery

▶ Riser card/daughterboard

14. Which motherboard is designed to replace the ATX motherboard?

    ○ **A.** LPX

    ○ **B.** NLX

    ○ **C.** BTX

    ○ **D.** CTX

Quick Answer: **40**
Detailed Answer: **42**

15. Which motherboard form factor is the most commonly used form factor in today's computers?

    ○ **A.** ATX

    ○ **B.** BTX

    ○ **C.** NLX

    ○ **D.** PCI

Quick Answer: **40**
Detailed Answer: **42**

16. What type of motherboard form factor is shown in Figure 1.1?

Quick Answer: **40**
Detailed Answer: **42**

FIGURE 1.1

- ○ **A.** LPX
- ○ **B.** NLX
- ○ **C.** BTX
- ○ **D.** ATX

17. Under what circumstances can you install an NLX system board in a Micro ATX case?

Quick Answer: **40**
Detailed Answer: **42**

- ○ **A.** None; the two form factors are incompatible with each other.
- ○ **B.** Always; the NLX is backward-compatible with the Micro ATX case.
- ○ **C.** When you install an NLX-to-ATX adapter kit.
- ○ **D.** Only in PC versions that use a universal tower case.

Quick Check
Quick Answer: **40**
Detailed Answer: **43**

18. Look at Figure 1.2. Identify the letter shown in Figure 1.2 that identifies the expansion slots.

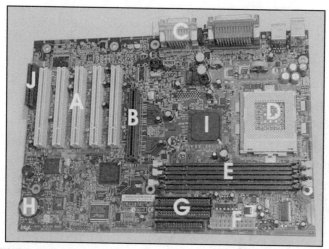

FIGURE 1.2

- ○ **A.** A
- ○ **B.** C
- ○ **C.** E
- ○ **D.** G

19. Look at Figure 1.2. Which letter shown in Figure 1.2 identifies the power connector?

Quick Answer: **40**
Detailed Answer: **43**

- ○ **A.** C
- ○ **B.** D
- ○ **C.** F
- ○ **D.** G

20. Look at Figure 1.2. Which letter shown in Figure 1.2 identifies the chipset?

Quick Answer: **40**
Detailed Answer: **43**

- ○ **A.** D
- ○ **B.** I
- ○ **C.** H
- ○ **D.** B

21. What port is shown in Figure 1.3?

FIGURE 1.3

- ○ **A.** Game port
- ○ **B.** VGA port
- ○ **C.** PS/2 port
- ○ **D.** Serial port
- ○ **E.** Parallel port

22. What port is shown in Figure 1.4?

FIGURE 1.4

- ○ **A.** Game port
- ○ **B.** VGA port
- ○ **C.** PS/2 port
- ○ **D.** Serial port
- ○ **E.** Parallel port

23. What port is shown in Figure 1.5?

FIGURE 1.5

- ○ **A.** Game port
- ○ **B.** VGA port
- ○ **C.** DVI port
- ○ **D.** Serial port
- ○ **E.** Parallel port

Quick Check

Quick Answer: **40**
Detailed Answer: **43**

24. What port is shown in Figure 1.6?

FIGURE 1.6

- ○ **A.** USB port
- ○ **B.** VGA port
- ○ **C.** DVI port
- ○ **D.** Serial port
- ○ **E.** Firewire port

25. What port is shown in Figure 1.7?

Quick Answer: **40**
Detailed Answer: **43**

FIGURE 1.7

- ○ **A.** USB port
- ○ **B.** VGA port
- ○ **C.** DVI port
- ○ **D.** PS/2 port
- ○ **E.** Firewire port

Quick Check

26. What port is shown in Figure 1.8?

Quick Answer: **40**
Detailed Answer: **43**

FIGURE 1.8

- ○ **A.** Game port
- ○ **B.** VGA port
- ○ **C.** PS/2 port
- ○ **D.** Serial port
- ○ **E.** Parallel port

27. What port is shown in Figure 1.9?

Quick Answer: **40**
Detailed Answer: **43**

FIGURE 1.9

- ○ **A.** RJ-45
- ○ **B.** VGA port
- ○ **C.** PS/2 port
- ○ **D.** Serial port
- ○ **E.** Parallel port

28. You are looking at the various ports in the back of your computer. What color would the keyboard port be?

Quick Answer: **40**
Detailed Answer: **44**

- ○ **A.** Purple
- ○ **B.** Green
- ○ **C.** Pink
- ○ **D.** Blue

29. You are looking at the ports on your new sound card. Which color is used to connect speakers or headphones?

Quick Answer: **40**
Detailed Answer: **44**

- ○ **A.** Pink
- ○ **B.** Light blue
- ○ **C.** Lime green
- ○ **D.** Gold

30. Which type of memory slots are found in laptop computers?

Quick Answer: **40**
Detailed Answer: **44**

- ○ **A.** RIMM
- ○ **B.** DIMM
- ○ **C.** SODIMM
- ○ **D.** SIMM

31. Which type of memory slots are the most common type of slot found in desktop computers?

Quick Answer: **40**
Detailed Answer: **44**

- ○ **A.** RIMM
- ○ **B.** DIMM
- ○ **C.** SODIMM
- ○ **D.** SIMM

32. Which of the following has 184 pins and is 16 bits wide? (Choose the best answer.)

Quick Answer: **40**
Detailed Answer: **44**

- ○ **A.** SIMMs
- ○ **B.** DIMMs
- ○ **C.** RIMMs
- ○ **D.** SODIMMs

33. Which two of the following describes the number of pins normally associated with Dual Inline Memory Modules (DIMMs)? (Select two answers.)

Quick Answer: **40**
Detailed Answer: **44**

- ○ **A.** 30
- ○ **B.** 72
- ○ **C.** 144
- ○ **D.** 168
- ○ **E.** 184

34. Which of the following is 64 bits wide? (Select all that apply.)

Quick Answer: **40**
Detailed Answer: **44**

- ○ **A.** 72-pin SIMM
- ○ **B.** 168-pin DIMM
- ○ **C.** 184-pin DIMM
- ○ **D.** 184-pin RIMM

Quick Check

35. Which type of expansion slot is specifically made for video adapters?

Quick Answer: **40**
Detailed Answer: **44**

○ **A.** PCI

○ **B.** AGP

○ **C.** AMR

○ **D.** CNR

36. Which type of slots will you find in a laptop?

Quick Answer: **40**
Detailed Answer: **44**

○ **A.** PCI

○ **B.** AGP

○ **C.** PCMCIA

○ **D.** CNR

37. Which of the following components on the motherboard usually houses the IDE connectors?

Quick Answer: **40**
Detailed Answer: **44**

○ **A.** PCI bus

○ **B.** North Bridge

○ **C.** PCMCIA bus

○ **D.** South Bridge

38. What is the clock speed for a PCI slot?

Quick Answer: **40**
Detailed Answer: **44**

○ **A.** 33 MHz

○ **B.** 66 MHz

○ **C.** 133 MHz

○ **D.** 533 MHz

39. What is clock speed of the AGPx8 expansion slot?

Quick Answer: **40**
Detailed Answer: **44**

○ **A.** 66 MHz

○ **B.** 133 MHz

○ **C.** 266 MHz

○ **D.** 533 MHz

40. Which is the fastest interface?

Quick Answer: **40**
Detailed Answer: **44**

○ **A.** PCI

○ **B.** PCIe

○ **C.** AGP

○ **D.** PCMCIA

41. Which hard drive interfaces use gray ribbon cables?

- ○ **A.** Parallel ATA
- ○ **B.** Serial ATA
- ○ **C.** PCMCIA
- ○ **D.** CNR

Quick Answer: **40**
Detailed Answer: **45**

42. Which is the newest type of printer interface?

- ○ **A.** Serial
- ○ **B.** DVI
- ○ **C.** USB
- ○ **D.** Parallel

Quick Answer: **40**
Detailed Answer: **45**

43. Which offers the fastest interface for hard drives?

- ○ **A.** IDE
- ○ **B.** EIDE
- ○ **C.** SATA
- ○ **D.** USB

Quick Answer: **40**
Detailed Answer: **45**

44. How many devices can an ATX Pentium system board support if it employs EIDE technology with ATA-2 enhancements?

- ○ **A.** 2
- ○ **B.** 4
- ○ **C.** 7
- ○ **D.** 8

Quick Answer: **40**
Detailed Answer: **45**

45. What do you call the SATA drive connected through an external interface?

- ○ **A.** PATA
- ○ **B.** eSATA
- ○ **C.** IEEE 1394
- ○ **D.** USATA

Quick Answer: **40**
Detailed Answer: **45**

46. What is the maximum cable length for eSATA?

- ○ **A.** 1 m
- ○ **B.** 2 m
- ○ **C.** 4 m
- ○ **D.** 8 m

Quick Answer: **40**
Detailed Answer: **45**

47. What is the transfer speed for the initial release of eSATA?

Quick Answer: **40**
Detailed Answer: **45**

- ○ **A.** 100 Mbps
- ○ **B.** 200 Mbps
- ○ **C.** 300 Mbps
- ○ **D.** 400 Mbps

48. Which of the following forms of RAID is used for disk mirroring?

Quick Answer: **40**
Detailed Answer: **45**

- ○ **A.** RAID-0
- ○ **B.** RAID-1
- ○ **C.** RAID-5
- ○ **D.** RAID-10

49. Which component is considered the brains of the computer that performs mathematical calculations and performs comparisons?

Quick Answer: **40**
Detailed Answer: **45**

- ○ **A.** Processor
- ○ **B.** RAM
- ○ **C.** Chipset
- ○ **D.** ROM

50. What is used to keep the internal clock running while the computer is not turned on or has no power?

Quick Answer: **40**
Detailed Answer: **45**

- ○ **A.** Switching power supply
- ○ **B.** Processor
- ○ **C.** PCMCIA
- ○ **D.** CMOS battery

51. What do you call the process that makes sure everything is running fine and finds a boot device when the computer is first turned?

Quick Answer: **40**
Detailed Answer: **46**

- ○ **A.** CMOS
- ○ **B.** Firmware
- ○ **C.** POST
- ○ **D.** ROM

1.3 Classify power supplies types and characteristics

- ▶ AC adapter
- ▶ ATX proprietary
- ▶ Voltage, wattage and capacity
- ▶ Voltage selector switch
- ▶ Pins (20, 24)

52. What device is used to convert AC into clean DC power to be used by the PC?

- ○ **A.** Power supply
- ○ **B.** Power inductor
- ○ **C.** Power resistor
- ○ **D.** Power conversion kit

53. In which of the following is the output from a power supply rated?

- ○ **A.** Voltage
- ○ **B.** Watts
- ○ **C.** Hertz
- ○ **D.** Ohms

54. What voltage is used in the United States?

- ○ **A.** 60
- ○ **B.** 110
- ○ **C.** 220
- ○ **D.** 400

55. What voltage is used in Europe?

- ○ **A.** 60
- ○ **B.** 110
- ○ **C.** 220
- ○ **D.** 400

56. For power supplies found in today's desktop computer, what is the most common form factor?

- ○ **A.** ATX
- ○ **B.** BTX
- ○ **C.** LPX
- ○ **D.** AT

57. How many pins are used to connect an ATX power supply to the motherboard? (Choose all that apply)

- ○ **A.** 4
- ○ **B.** 6
- ○ **C.** 20
- ○ **D.** 24
- ○ **E.** 40

58. What is the voltage supplied by an ATX power supply? (Choose all that apply.)

   ○ **A.** −12 VDC

   ○ **B.** −5 VDC

   ○ **C.** −3.3 VDC

   ○ **D.** +3.3 VDC

   ○ **E.** +5 VDC

   ○ **F.** +12 VDC

Quick Answer: **40**
Detailed Answer: **46**

59. What voltages are present on the power supply's 4-pin Auxiliary (disk drive) power connector?

   ○ **A.** +5 and +12 VDC

   ○ **B.** +3.3 and +5 VDC

   ○ **C.** +5 VDC and −5 VDC

   ○ **D.** +12 VDC and −12 VDC

Quick Answer: **40**
Detailed Answer: **46**

60. Which of the following describe the front side bus?

   ○ **A.** The bus that carries data between the processor and the main memory (RAM)

   ○ **B.** The bus that connects the front of the case

   ○ **C.** The bus that connects the front of the motherboard

   ○ **D.** The bus that connects the processor to the Level 2 cache

Quick Answer: **40**
Detailed Answer: **46**

1.4 Explain the purpose and characteristics of CPUs and their features

▶ Identify CPU types

   ▶ AMD

   ▶ Intel

▶ Hyper threading

▶ Multi core

   ▶ Dual core

   ▶ Triple core

   ▶ Quad core

▶ Onchip cache

   ▶ L1

   ▶ L2

▶ Speed (real versus actual)

▶ 32 bit versus 64 bit

61. Which component is considered the brains of the computer that performs mathematical calculations and performs comparisons?

Quick Answer: **40**
Detailed Answer: **46**

- ○ **A.** Processor
- ○ **B.** RAM
- ○ **C.** Chipset
- ○ **D.** ROM

62. Which of the following sockets are used for a 3.8 GHz Pentium 4 processor?

Quick Answer: **40**
Detailed Answer: **47**

- ○ **A.** Socket 423
- ○ **B.** Socket 462
- ○ **C.** Socket 478
- ○ **D.** Socket 754
- ○ **E.** Socket A

63. You are looking at a processor socket that has 426 pins. Which processors can be inserted into it?

Quick Answer: **40**
Detailed Answer: **47**

- ○ **A.** Intel Pentium 4 processor
- ○ **B.** AMD Athlon processor
- ○ **C.** AMD Athlon 64 processor
- ○ **D.** Intel Core2 processor

64. What socket does the Intel Core i7 use?

Quick Answer: **40**
Detailed Answer: **47**

- ○ **A.** Socket 478
- ○ **B.** Socket 754
- ○ **C.** Socket A
- ○ **D.** Socket B

65. What socket does the AMD Phenom processor use?

Quick Answer: **40**
Detailed Answer: **47**

- ○ **A.** Socket A
- ○ **B.** Socket B
- ○ **C.** Socket AM2+
- ○ **D.** Socket 1

66. What type of socket is used for an AMD Athlon XP microprocessor?

Quick Answer: **40**
Detailed Answer: **47**

- ○ **A.** Socket 462
- ○ **B.** Socket 423
- ○ **C.** Socket 370
- ○ **D.** Slot 1

67. What technology used in Intel processors allows the processor to act like two logical processors so that it can utilize the processor resources more efficiently and improve performance?

- ○ **A.** MMX technology
- ○ **B.** Hyper-threading technology
- ○ **C.** SSE
- ○ **D.** Multi-core

Quick Answer: **40**
Detailed Answer: **47**

68. Because the clock speed of a processor cannot be scaled dramatically, what is the best way to increase the power of your processor?

- ○ **A.** Increase the RAM
- ○ **B.** Use multiple processors or a processor with multiple cores
- ○ **C.** Add a cache chip on the motherboard
- ○ **D.** Put the processor in Turbo mode

Quick Answer: **40**
Detailed Answer: **47**

69. What can you do to increase the link between RAM and the processors?

- ○ **A.** Increase the RAM
- ○ **B.** Increase the L1 and L2 cache
- ○ **C.** Use faster disks
- ○ **D.** Use larger paging files

Quick Answer: **40**
Detailed Answer: **47**

70. Older processors can see up to 4 GB or 64 GB of memory. What would allow you to see above 64 GB of memory?

- ○ **A.** A 32-bit processor
- ○ **B.** A 64-bit processor
- ○ **C.** A motherboard with a North Bridge or South Bridge chipset
- ○ **D.** Flash the motherboard

Quick Answer: **40**
Detailed Answer: **47**

71. You have an older motherboard that can support dual processors. You decide to only use one processor. You think that something needs to go into the empty processor socket. What component would that be?

- ○ **A.** A resistor pack
- ○ **B.** A termination pack
- ○ **C.** An inverter
- ○ **D.** Voltage regulator module (VRM)

Quick Answer: **40**
Detailed Answer: **47**

72. Today, processor clock speed is expressed in what unit of measurement?

    ○ **A.** GigaHertz (GHz)

    ○ **B.** Voltage (V)

    ○ **C.** Amps (A)

    ○ **D.** Ohms (Ω)

Quick Answer: **40**
Detailed Answer: **48**

73. Which of the following architectures allows you to run both 64-bit and 32-bit programs?

    ○ **A.** x64

    ○ **B.** IA-64

    ○ **C.** MMX

    ○ **D.** SSE2

Quick Answer: **40**
Detailed Answer: **48**

74. The Athlon 64 processor uses what architecture?

    ○ **A.** x64

    ○ **B.** IA-64

    ○ **C.** x86

    ○ **D.** PowerNow

Quick Answer: **40**
Detailed Answer: **48**

1.5 Explain cooling methods and devices

▶ Heat sinks

▶ CPU and case fans

▶ Liquid cooling systems

▶ Thermal compound

75. What provides cooling to the system? (Choose all that apply.)

    ○ **A.** Case fan

    ○ **B.** Processor heat sink

    ○ **C.** Processor fan

    ○ **D.** Power supply fan

Quick Answer: **40**
Detailed Answer: **48**

76. When installing a new processor, what should you apply directly to the processor? (Choose all that apply.)

    ○ **A.** Cooling liquid

    ○ **B.** Thermal compound

    ○ **C.** A heat sink

    ○ **D.** A fan

Quick Answer: **40**
Detailed Answer: **48**

77. What are the two disadvantages of using a liquid cooling system? (Choose two answers.)

Quick Answer: **40**
Detailed Answer: **48**

- ○ **A.** Requires a large amount of space within the computer case
- ○ **B.** Condensation can occur
- ○ **C.** Needs more technical knowledge to install
- ○ **D.** Requires a special torque wrench

78. What cooling technology do you normally find in laptop computers that moves heat away from the processor?

Quick Answer: **40**
Detailed Answer: **48**

- ○ **A.** Heat sink and fan
- ○ **B.** Heat pipe and fan
- ○ **C.** Liquid nitrogen system
- ○ **D.** Sprinkler cooling

79. What technology is used to cool a component by applying voltage to two dissimilar materials that have been connected together?

Quick Answer: **40**
Detailed Answer: **48**

- ○ **A.** Water-cooled processor
- ○ **B.** Heat sink
- ○ **C.** Mister
- ○ **D.** Peltier cooling

1.6 Compare and contrast memory types, characteristics and their purpose

- ▶ Types
  - ▶ DRAM
  - ▶ SRAM
  - ▶ SDRAM
  - ▶ DDR/DDR2/DDR3
  - ▶ RAMBUS
- ▶ Parity vs. Non-parity
- ▶ ECC vs. non-ECC
- ▶ Single-sided vs. double-sided
- ▶ Single channel vs. dual channel
- ▶ Speed
  - ▶ PC100
  - ▶ PC133
  - ▶ PC2700

▶ PC3200

▶ DDR3-1600

▶ DDR2-667

80. When accessing data, which of the following has the fastest throughput?

 ○ **A.** A flash drive

 ○ **B.** RAM

 ○ **C.** A hard disk drive

 ○ **D.** A CD-ROM

Quick Answer: **40**
Detailed Answer: **49**

81. Which type of RAM is used for RAM cache?

 ○ **A.** DRAM

 ○ **B.** VRAM

 ○ **C.** SRAM

 ○ **D.** SDRAM

Quick Answer: **40**
Detailed Answer: **49**

82. Which of the following RAM modules required 8 ns DRAM chips and was capable of operating at 125 MHz?

 ○ **A.** PC-66

 ○ **B.** PC-100

 ○ **C.** PC-133

 ○ **D.** PC-800

Quick Answer: **40**
Detailed Answer: **49**

83. Which package does Synchronous DRAM use?

 ○ **A.** SIMMs

 ○ **B.** DIMMs

 ○ **C.** RIMMs

 ○ **D.** SIPPs

Quick Answer: **40**
Detailed Answer: **49**

84. What is the MOST common video RAM technology on video cards?

 ○ **A.** DDR SDRAM

 ○ **B.** SODIMM

 ○ **C.** SIMM

 ○ **D.** DIMM

Quick Answer: **40**
Detailed Answer: **49**

85. If the DDR module is rated at PC3200 and 400 MHz, what is the memory bus speed?

- ○ **A.** 100 MHz
- ○ **B.** 200 MHz
- ○ **C.** 400 MHz
- ○ **D.** 800 MHz

Quick Answer: **40**
Detailed Answer: **49**

86. What is the minimum RAM type that should be used with a 133-MHz FSB?

- ○ **A.** PC133
- ○ **B.** PC166
- ○ **C.** DDR133
- ○ **D.** PC100

Quick Answer: **40**
Detailed Answer: **49**

87. Which of the following are error-detecting technologies used with RAM? (Choose all that apply.)

- ○ **A.** Parity
- ○ **B.** Static
- ○ **C.** ECC
- ○ **D.** Recharging

Quick Answer: **40**
Detailed Answer: **49**

88. DDR-2 offers which of the following data rates?

- ○ **A.** 800 GBps
- ○ **B.** 3.2 GBps
- ○ **C.** 6.4 GBps
- ○ **D.** 12.8 GBps

Quick Answer: **40**
Detailed Answer: **50**

89. What advantages does DDR-2 have over DDR-1? (Choose two answers.)

- ○ **A.** Faster bandwidth
- ○ **B.** Lower latency
- ○ **C.** Cache mode
- ○ **D.** Lower power consumption

Quick Answer: **40**
Detailed Answer: **50**

90. What characteristic allows a memory chip to be divided into two banks, which are accessed one bank at a time?

- ○ **A.** Double-rated
- ○ **B.** Double-sided
- ○ **C.** Turbo cached
- ○ **D.** Dynamic

Quick Answer: **40**
Detailed Answer: **50**

91. Which DDR-3 uses modules called PC3-12800?

- ○ **A.** DDR3-800
- ○ **B.** DDR3-1066
- ○ **C.** DDR3-1333
- ○ **D.** DDR3-1600

1.7 Distinguish between the different display devices and their characteristics

- ▶ Projectors, CRT, and LCD
- ▶ LCD technologies
  - ▶ Resolution (e.g. XGA, SXGA+, UXGA, WUXGA)
  - ▶ Contrast ratio
  - ▶ Native resolution
- ▶ Connector types
  - ▶ VGA
  - ▶ HDMI
  - ▶ S-Video
  - ▶ Component/RGB
  - ▶ DVI pin compatibility
- ▶ Settings
  - ▶ Refresh rate
  - ▶ Resolution
  - ▶ Multi-monitor
  - ▶ Degauss

92. From the following display types, which takes up the least space on a desk?

- ○ **A.** Terminal
- ○ **B.** LCD
- ○ **C.** CRT
- ○ **D.** LED

93. What is the resolution for the standard VGA monitor?

- ○ **A.** 320×240
- ○ **B.** 640×480
- ○ **C.** 800×600
- ○ **D.** 1024×768

94. What is the maximum resolution of an Extended Graphics Array (XGA) monitor?

Quick Answer: **40**
Detailed Answer: **50**

- ○ **A.** 320×240
- ○ **B.** 640×480
- ○ **C.** 800×600
- ○ **D.** 1024×768
- ○ **E.** 1200×1024

95. What is the maximum resolution of an Ultra Extended Graphics Array (UXGA)?

Quick Answer: **40**
Detailed Answer: **50**

- ○ **A.** 800×600
- ○ **B.** 1024×768
- ○ **C.** 1200×1024
- ○ **D.** 1600×1200

96. What is the maximum resolution of Wide Extended Graphics Array (WUXGA)?

Quick Answer: **40**
Detailed Answer: **50**

- ○ **A.** 1366×768
- ○ **B.** 1790×1050
- ○ **C.** 1920×1200
- ○ **D.** 2560×1600

97. Which of the following determine how many different colors a video system can display?

Quick Answer: **40**
Detailed Answer: **50**

- ○ **A.** Resolution
- ○ **B.** Refresh rate
- ○ **C.** Color depth
- ○ **D.** Size of the pixels

98. What describes the ratio of the luminance of the brightest color (white) to that of the darkest color (black) that the system is capable of producing?

Quick Answer: **40**
Detailed Answer: **50**

- ○ **A.** Resolution
- ○ **B.** Refresh rate
- ○ **C.** Contrast ratio
- ○ **D.** Color depth

99. What describes the distance between pixels?

- ○ **A.** Resolution
- ○ **B.** Contrast ratio
- ○ **C.** Color depth
- ○ **D.** Dot pitch

100. What type of connector connects digital audio/video sources to Blu-Ray players, PCs, video game consoles, and AV receivers and is a compact audio/video interface for transmitting uncompressed digital data?

- ○ **A.** DVI
- ○ **B.** HDMI
- ○ **C.** VGA
- ○ **D.** SVGA

101. Which video connectors are compatible for video?

- ○ **A.** SVGA and DVI
- ○ **B.** DVI and HDMI
- ○ **C.** SVGA and HDMI
- ○ **D.** S-Video and DVI

102. Which DVI standards support both digital and analog transfers?

- ○ **A.** DVI-I
- ○ **B.** DVI-D
- ○ **C.** DVI-A
- ○ **D.** DVI-B

1.8 Install and configure peripherals and input devices

- ▶ Mouse
- ▶ Keyboard
- ▶ Bar code reader
- ▶ Multimedia (for example, web and digital cameras, MIDI, microphones)
- ▶ Biometric devices
- ▶ Touch screen
- ▶ KVM switch

103. What should you do after connecting a standard USB keyboard or mouse?

Quick Answer: **40**
Detailed Answer: **51**

- ○ **A.** Load the drivers from the CD.
- ○ **B.** Reboot the computer.
- ○ **C.** Shut down the computer. Turn the computer back on.
- ○ **D.** Nothing.

104. What is plug and play?

Quick Answer: **40**
Detailed Answer: **51**

- ○ **A.** A technology used in game controllers to visually detect motion
- ○ **B.** A power saving technology that quickly turns on when needed
- ○ **C.** An autodetect feature for game controller/MIDI interface
- ○ **D.** A characteristic that discovers a hardware component in a system without the need to configure the physical device

105. USB devices, PCMCIA/PC cards, and PCI-X use what type of technology?

Quick Answer: **40**
Detailed Answer: **51**

- ○ **A.** Turbo feature
- ○ **B.** Plug-and-play
- ○ **C.** Encrypting component
- ○ **D.** Caching technology

106. You just connected a new USB network adapter to your computer. What is the next thing you need to do?

Quick Answer: **40**
Detailed Answer: **51**

- ○ **A.** Make sure that you are running Windows XP
- ○ **B.** Make sure that the device is turned on
- ○ **C.** Make sure the driver is loaded
- ○ **D.** Make sure you connect power to the device

107. You work as a technician at Acme.com. You need to install a fingerprint reader on a computer running Windows Vista. What should you do next? (Choose two answers.)

Quick Answer: **40**
Detailed Answer: **51**

- ○ **A.** Make sure that the application that uses the fingerprint reader is digitally signed
- ○ **B.** Make sure that the driver that you are installing is digitally signed
- ○ **C.** Connect the device before you load the driver
- ○ **D.** Load the driver before you connect the device

108. You just installed a touch screen device and the associated drivers. What should you do next?

  ○ **A.** Enable the touch screen in the device manager.

  ○ **B.** Link the touch screen to a printer.

  ○ **C.** Calibrate the touch screen.

  ○ **D.** Link the touch screen to a pointing device such as a mouse.

109. You have two computers but only one monitor. You want to easily share the monitor between the two computers. What should you do?

  ○ **A.** Use a wireless card for your monitor and a wireless card for your second computer.

  ○ **B.** Use a split video cable for the two computers.

  ○ **C.** Connect a USB cable between the second computer and the monitor.

  ○ **D.** Use a KVM to connect the two computers and one monitor.

1.9 Summarize the function and types of adapter cards

▶ Video

  ▶ PCI

  ▶ PCIe

  ▶ AGP

▶ Multimedia

  ▶ Sound card

  ▶ TV tuner cards

  ▶ Capture cards

▶ I/O

  ▶ SCSI

  ▶ Serial

  ▶ USB

  ▶ Parallel

▶ Communications

  ▶ NIC

  ▶ Modem

110. Which of the following is based on a serial interface?

   ○ **A.** AGP

   ○ **B.** PCI

   ○ **C.** PCI-X

   ○ **D.** PCI-E

Quick Answer: **40**
Detailed Answer: **52**

111. PCI-X is directly backward-compatible with which of the following devices?

   ○ **A.** 3.3 v standard PCI devices

   ○ **B.** 5.0 v standard PCI devices

   ○ **C.** AGP devices

   ○ **D.** PCI-E devices

Quick Answer: **40**
Detailed Answer: **52**

112. How many lanes can PCI Express support? (Choose all that apply.)

   ○ **A.** 1

   ○ **B.** 2

   ○ **C.** 4

   ○ **D.** 8

   ○ **E.** 18

Quick Answer: **40**
Detailed Answer: **52**

113. Which of the following types of connectors are usually associated with speaker and microphone ports?

   ○ **A.** 25-pin, D-shells

   ○ **B.** 1/8" mini plugs and jacks

   ○ **C.** RJ-11 jacks and plugs

   ○ **D.** 15-pin, D-shells

Quick Answer: **40**
Detailed Answer: **52**

114. What is the recommended maximum length of an RS-232 cable?

   ○ **A.** 100 feet (30 meters)

   ○ **B.** 30 feet (9 meters)

   ○ **C.** 10 feet (3 meters)

   ○ **D.** 50 feet (15 meters)

Quick Answer: **40**
Detailed Answer: **52**

115. How many devices can be attached to a single Universal Serial Bus (USB) host?

   ○ **A.** 32

   ○ **B.** 64

   ○ **C.** 127

   ○ **D.** 255

Quick Answer: **40**
Detailed Answer: **52**

116. What is the data transfer speed of a USB 1.1 interface?

    ○ **A.** 100 Mbps

    ○ **B.** 480 Mbps

    ○ **C.** 1 Gbps

    ○ **D.** 12 Mbps

Quick Answer: **40**
Detailed Answer: **52**

117. What is the data transfer speed of a USB 2.0 interface?

    ○ **A.** 100 Mbps

    ○ **B.** 480 Mbps

    ○ **C.** 1 Gbps

    ○ **D.** 12 Mbps

Quick Answer: **40**
Detailed Answer: **52**

118. How many devices can 1394 support?

    ○ **A.** 1

    ○ **B.** 7

    ○ **C.** 16

    ○ **D.** 63

Quick Answer: **40**
Detailed Answer: **52**

119. What is the maximum distance for a single cable for USB 2.0?

    ○ **A.** 1 meter

    ○ **B.** 2 meters

    ○ **C.** 3 meters

    ○ **D.** 5 meters

Quick Answer: **40**
Detailed Answer: **53**

120. What interface is associated with RS-232?

    ○ **A.** Parallel

    ○ **B.** Serial

    ○ **C.** USB

    ○ **D.** Firewire

Quick Answer: **40**
Detailed Answer: **53**

121. What connector would you use to connect your modem to the phone line?

    ○ **A.** RJ-11

    ○ **B.** RJ-45

    ○ **C.** RS-1284

    ○ **D.** RS-90

Quick Answer: **40**
Detailed Answer: **53**

122. Parallel ports are usually denoted with?

Quick Answer: **40**
Detailed Answer: **53**

    ○ **A.** LPTx

    ○ **B.** COMx

    ○ **C.** Printerx

    ○ **D.** PARx

123. Look at Figure 1.10. What kind of USB connector would you use?

Quick Answer: **40**
Detailed Answer: **53**

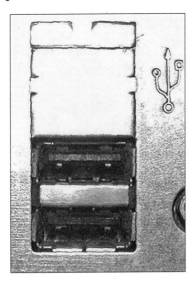

FIGURE 1.10

    ○ **A.** USB-A

    ○ **B.** USB-B

    ○ **C.** Mini-USB

    ○ **D.** Micro-USB

1.10 Install, configure, and optimize laptop components and features

▶ Expansion devices

    ▶ PCMCIA cards

    ▶ PCI Express cards

    ▶ Docking station

▶ Communication connections

    ▶ Bluetooth

    ▶ Infrared

    ▶ Cellular WAN

    ▶ Ethernet

    ▶ Modem

▶ Power and electrical input devices

    ▶ Auto-switching

    ▶ Fixed input power supplies

    ▶ Batteries

▶ Input devices

    ▶ Stylus/digitizer

    ▶ Function keys

    ▶ Point devices (e.g. touch pad, point stick/track point)

124. Which of the following types of PC Card slots would be able to accommodate all the other physical PC Card types?

    ○ **A.** Type I

    ○ **B.** Type II

    ○ **C.** Type III

    ○ **D.** All of the options provided are correct

Quick Answer: **40**
Detailed Answer: **53**

125. Which of the following technologies are used for a short-range communication connection to a wireless keyboard and mouse?

    ○ **A.** Cellular

    ○ **B.** Ethernet

    ○ **C.** Firewire

    ○ **D.** Bluetooth

Quick Answer: **40**
Detailed Answer: **53**

126. What should you do to determine the right amperage of the alternating current (AC) adapter for a laptop? (Select two answers.)

    ○ **A.** Check the Power Options applet in Control Panel

    ○ **B.** Consult the user's manual

    ○ **C.** Use a multimeter

    ○ **D.** Consult the vendor's website

Quick Answer: **40**
Detailed Answer: **53**

127. Which of the following battery types are not recommended for use in laptops because they have a short battery life?

    ○ **A.** Nickel Metal-Hydride (NiMH)

    ○ **B.** Nickel Cadmium (NiCD)

    ○ **C.** Nickel-Lithium (Ni-Li)

    ○ **D.** Lithium-Ion (Li-Ion)

Quick Answer: **40**
Detailed Answer: **53**

128. What is the thickness of a Type II PC/PCMCIA Card?

Quick Answer: **40**
Detailed Answer: **53**

- ○ **A.** 0.13 inches (3.3 millimeters)
- ○ **B.** 0.40 inches (10 millimeters)
- ○ **C.** 0.20 inches (5 millimeters)
- ○ **D.** Thicker than 0.40 inches (10 millimeters)

129. What is a PC Card also known as?

Quick Answer: **40**
Detailed Answer: **53**

- ○ **A.** A PC Bus card
- ○ **B.** A smart card
- ○ **C.** PCMCIA
- ○ **D.** A PCI adapter

130. What is the thickness of the Type III PCMCIA card?

Quick Answer: **40**
Detailed Answer: **54**

- ○ **A.** 0.13 inches (3.3 millimeters)
- ○ **B.** 0.40 inches (10 millimeters)
- ○ **C.** 0.20 inches (5 millimeters)
- ○ **D.** Thicker than 0.40 inches (10 millimeters)

131. What would happen when you press the Fn key on a laptop?

Quick Answer: **40**
Detailed Answer: **54**

- ○ **A.** You would refresh the desktop.
- ○ **B.** You would enable the numeric keypad.
- ○ **C.** You would enable additional features on the keyboard.
- ○ **D.** You would close the active window.

132. Which of the following different types of power sources can be used to power a laptop or notebook computer? (Select all that apply.)

Quick Answer: **41**
Detailed Answer: **54**

- ○ **A.** Standard AA batteries
- ○ **B.** AC power
- ○ **C.** Docking station through DC power
- ○ **D.** Batteries

133. Which of the following laptop or notebook pointing devices looks like an opto-mechanical mouse turned upside down?

Quick Answer: **41**
Detailed Answer: **54**

- ○ **A.** Mouse
- ○ **B.** Trackball
- ○ **C.** Touch screen
- ○ **D.** Drawing tablet

134. What is the typical range of a wireless IrDA device?

- ○ **A.** 1 meter
- ○ **B.** 10 meters
- ○ **C.** 50 meters
- ○ **D.** 100 meters

135. What is the easiest way that you can prevent a laptop from over-heating?

- ○ **A.** Do not place a laptop next to a wall
- ○ **B.** Keep the laptop in the carrying case while not being used
- ○ **C.** Shut down the laptop for 15 minutes
- ○ **D.** Use the laptop on a hard surface

1.11 Install and configure printers

- ▶ Differentiate between printer types
  - ▶ Laser
  - ▶ Inkjet
  - ▶ Thermal
  - ▶ Impact
- ▶ Local vs. network printers
- ▶ Printer drivers (compatibility)
- ▶ Consumables

136. What printer type produces print by spraying ink at the page?

- ○ **A.** Laser
- ○ **B.** Thermal
- ○ **C.** Inkjet
- ○ **D.** Dot matrix

137. What printer type melts a toner onto the paper, similar to a copy machine?

- ○ **A.** Laser
- ○ **B.** Thermal
- ○ **C.** Inkjet
- ○ **D.** Dot matrix

138. Which of the following printers can produce photographic-quality, continuous-tone images?

Quick Answer: **41**
Detailed Answer: **54**

- ○ **A.** Dot matrix printer
- ○ **B.** Dye sublimation printer
- ○ **C.** Direct thermal printer
- ○ **D.** Thermal wax transfer printer

139. What type of printer uses small heated pins to transfer multicolor images onto the paper?

Quick Answer: **41**
Detailed Answer: **54**

- ○ **A.** Dye sublimation printer
- ○ **B.** Thermal wax printer
- ○ **C.** Solid ink printer
- ○ **D.** Laser printer

140. Which of the following printer types requires special paper?

Quick Answer: **41**
Detailed Answer: **54**

- ○ **A.** Laser
- ○ **B.** Thermal
- ○ **C.** Dot matrix
- ○ **D.** Inkjet

141. You have been asked to install a new desktop PC in a customer's front office. A laser printer was attached to the parallel port of the old computer and is supposed to be moved up to the new system. However, no one can find the old signal cable. What type of cable must you get to connect the old printer to the new PC?

Quick Answer: **41**
Detailed Answer: **54**

- ○ **A.** RS-232
- ○ **B.** IEEE-1394
- ○ **C.** IEEE-1284
- ○ **D.** HDMI

142. In a laser printer, a thermal fuse is used to prevent which of the following?

Quick Answer: **41**
Detailed Answer: **54**

- ○ **A.** Heat-sink failure
- ○ **B.** A fuser from overheating
- ○ **C.** A high-voltage power supply from overheating
- ○ **D.** A low-voltage power supply from overheating

143. What is the major purpose of a tractor-feed mechanism, and where is it most commonly used?

- ○ **A.** It is used on color laser printers that handle single sheet forms.
- ○ **B.** It is used on inkjet printers that handle multipart forms.
- ○ **C.** It is used on laser printers that handle continuous, multipart forms.
- ○ **D.** It is used on dot matrix printers that handle continuous, multipart forms.

144. What does the primary corona wire found in a laser printer do?

- ○ **A.** Transfers toner to the paper
- ○ **B.** Applies a uniform negative charge to the drum
- ○ **C.** Presses toner into the paper
- ○ **D.** Transfers characters to the paper

145. What component melts the toner to the paper in a laser printer?

- ○ **A.** Corona wire
- ○ **B.** Drum
- ○ **C.** Print head
- ○ **D.** Fuser

146. What are the two functions of the two corona wires in a laser printer? (Choose two answers.)

- ○ **A.** They transfer toner from the drum to the paper.
- ○ **B.** They fuse the toner to the paper.
- ○ **C.** They condition the drum to be written on.
- ○ **D.** They clean the drum.

147. What is the order of operations of a laser printer?

- ○ **A.** Conditioning, cleaning, writing, developing, fusing, transferring
- ○ **B.** Cleaning, conditioning, writing, developing, transferring, fusing
- ○ **C.** Writing, conditioning, cleaning, developing, fusing, transferring
- ○ **D.** Conditioning, cleaning, writing, developing, transferring, fusing

148. Which component of a laser printer transfers toner to the paper?

    ○ **A.** The drum

    ○ **B.** The transfer corona wire

    ○ **C.** The fuser assembly

    ○ **D.** The platen

Quick Answer: **41**
Detailed Answer: **55**

149. What is the main circuit board in a dot-matrix printer called?

    ○ **A.** Main control board

    ○ **B.** Print head board

    ○ **C.** Control panel

    ○ **D.** Sensor board

Quick Answer: **41**
Detailed Answer: **55**

150. Which interface is widely used to connect a variety of wireless devices to wireless printers?

    ○ **A.** Bluetooth

    ○ **B.** IrDA

    ○ **C.** 802.11x

    ○ **D.** USB

Quick Answer: **41**
Detailed Answer: **55**

151. Which of the following is TRUE about the impact printer? (Choose two answers.)

    ○ **A.** It has a print-head.

    ○ **B.** It has toner powder.

    ○ **C.** It has an ink ribbon.

    ○ **D.** It has an ink cartridge.

Quick Answer: **41**
Detailed Answer: **56**

152. Which of the following printers use ink cartridges?

    ○ **A.** Laser printers

    ○ **B.** Bubble jet printers

    ○ **C.** Impact printers

    ○ **D.** None of the above

Quick Answer: **41**
Detailed Answer: **56**

153. Which of the following substances in the toner cartridge makes the toner "flow" better?

    ○ **A.** Ink supply

    ○ **B.** Polyester resins

    ○ **C.** Iron oxide particles

    ○ **D.** Carbon substance

Quick Answer: **41**
Detailed Answer: **56**

154. Which part of the laser printer gives the voltage for the charge and the transfer corona assemblies?

- ○ **A.** Controller circuitry
- ○ **B.** High-voltage power supply (HVPS)
- ○ **C.** DC power supply (DCPS)
- ○ **D.** Transfer corona

Quick Answer: **41**
Detailed Answer: **56**

155. What is used to drain the charge in the paper when printing with a laser printer?

- ○ **A.** Static-charge eliminator strip
- ○ **B.** The rubber cleaning blade
- ○ **C.** The iron particles in the toner
- ○ **D.** The developer

Quick Answer: **41**
Detailed Answer: **56**

156. Which is the slowest printer interface?

- ○ **A.** Serial
- ○ **B.** SCSI
- ○ **C.** USB
- ○ **D.** Parallel

Quick Answer: **41**
Detailed Answer: **56**

157. The fastest printing from a workstation would be provided by which of the following?

- ○ **A.** USB 2.0
- ○ **B.** Bluetooth
- ○ **C.** IEEE 802.11a
- ○ **D.** IEEE 802.11g

Quick Answer: **41**
Detailed Answer: **56**

158. Which of the following specifications describes the Extended Capabilities Port (ECP) used for printers?

- ○ **A.** IEEE 1284
- ○ **B.** IEEE 802.15
- ○ **C.** IEEE 802.3
- ○ **D.** IEEE 802.11i
- ○ **E.** IEEE 1394

Quick Answer: **41**
Detailed Answer: **56**

Quick-Check Answer Key

1. A	34. B, C	66. A	99. D
2. B	35. B	67. B	100. B
3. A, D	36. C	68. B	101. B
4. D	37. D	69. B	102. A
5. A	38. A	70. B	103. D
6. A, B	39. D	71. D	104. D
7. E	40. B	72. A	105. B
8. B	41. A	73. A	106. C
9. B	42. C	74. A	107. B and C
10. A	43. C	75. A, B, C, D	108. C
11. E	44. B	76. B, C, D	109. D
12. D	45. B	77. A, C	110. D
13. A	46. A	78. B	111. B
14. C	47. C	79. D	112. A, B, C, D
15. A	48. B	80. B	113. B
16. D	49. A	81. C	114. D
17. D	50. D	82. B	115. C
18. A	51. C	83. B	116. D
19. C	52. A	84. A	117. B
20. B	53. B	85. B	118. D
21. D	54. B	86. A	119. D
22. B	55. C	87. A, C	120. B
23. C	56. A	88. C	121. A
24. A	57. C, D	89. A, D	122. A
25. D	58. A, B, D, E and F	90. B	123. A
26. A		91. D	124. C
27. A	59. A	92. B	125. D
28. A	60. A	93. B	126. B and D
29. C	61. A	94. D	127. B
30. C	62. C	95. D	128. C
31. B	63. D	96. C	129. C
32. C	64. D	97. C	130. B
33. D, E	65. C	98. C	131. C

132. B, D	**139.** B	**146.** A and C	**153.** B
133. B	**140.** B	**147.** B	**154.** B
134. A	**141.** C	**148.** B	**155.** A
135. D	**142.** B	**149.** A	**156.** C
136. C	**143.** D	**150.** A	**157.** A
137. A	**144.** B	**151.** A and C	**158.** A
138. B	**145.** D	**152.** B	

Answers and Explanations

1. **Answer: A.** You would have to look for an older system to find a floppy disk drive in a computer. Answers B and C are incorrect because most computers today have HDD and CD/DVD drives, and answer D is incorrect because Blu-Ray is a newer form of an optical drive.

2. **Answer: B.** Answer B is correct because a DS/HD 3 1/3" disk can hold 1.44 MB of formatted data. DS is short for double-sided and HD is short for high density. Therefore, answers A, C, and D are incorrect.

3. **Answer: A and D.** Answers A and D are correct because USB devices are considered to be hot swappable devices. Answers B and C are not typically hot swappable.

4. **Answer: D.** Answer D is correct because a Blu-Ray disk can hold 25 GB on a single-layer disk and 50 GB on a double-layer disk. Answers A, B, and C are incorrect because a CD including CD-RW can store anywhere from 640 to 800 MB, and a DVD can store up to 8.5 GB.

5. **Answer: A.** Answer A is correct because a CD-RW disk will usually store between 650 MB and 700 MB depending on the disk and disk burning CD drive. Answers B, C, and D are incorrect because they describe the storage space for a DVD based on single-sided versus double-sided and single-layer versus double-layer. E is incorrect because 25 GB is the size for a Blu-Ray disk.

6. **Answer: A and B.** Answers A and B are correct because the USB thumb drive and SD card are solid state electronic devices. Therefore, they do not have any mechanical moving parts. CD-RW drives (answer C) and hard drives (answer D) have mechanical parts, which make them high failure items compared to components that do not have mechanical parts.

7. **Answer: E.** Answer E is correct because solid state drives have a limited amount of writes for a disk area. Answers A, B, C, and D are incorrect because solid state devices typically have a faster start-up type because there is no spin-up. They have a fast random access for reading because there are no read-write heads. They are also quieter and consume less power because there are no movable mechanical parts.

8. **Answer: B.** Answer B is correct because SD cards (short for Secure Digital) is smaller than a USB thumb drive, which is smaller than a CD-RW drive and hard drive. Therefore, the other answers are incorrect.

9. **Answer: B.** Answer B is correct because a tape drive uses magnetic tapes to store data in a sequential fashion. Answers A, C, and D are incorrect because floppy disk drives, hard drives, and rewritable DVD drives use random access, which means they can jump to the spot where the data is to start reading or writing without having to read the data before or after the desired data.

10. **Answer: A.** A standard Secure Digital (SD) memory card can store anywhere from 4 MB to 4 GB. Therefore, answers B, C, and D are incorrect. An SDHC memory card can store from 4 GB to 32 GB while an SDXC can store from 32 GB to 2 TB.

11. **Answer: E.** Answer E is correct because standard SD memory cards are widely used in digital cameras (answer C), handheld computers, PDAs (answer D), media players, mobile phones (answer B), GPS receivers, and video game consoles. They can also be inserted into a USB thumb device (answer A) which can be moved between various devices and your PC.

12. **Answer: D.** The common format for SD memory cards is the standard SD card, Mini SD card, and Micro SD card. There is no such thing as a compact SD card. Therefore answer D is correct and the other answers are incorrect.

13. **Answer: A.** Answer A is correct because hot swappable means that a device can be connected and disconnected while the computer is running. Answer B is incorrect because there is no such thing as power-charged technology. Answer C is incorrect because plug-and-play devices are devices that can be connected without needing to be configured. Answer D is incorrect because compact technology does not refer to power or hot-swappable technology.

14. **Answer: C.** Answer C is correct because the BTX motherboard is designed to take over the aging ATX specification. Answers A and B are incorrect because the LPX and NLX are older designs used in slimline computers. Answer D is incorrect because the CTX is a form factor that does not exist.

15. **Answer: A.** Answer A is correct because the ATX is an aging motherboard form factor that is still commonly used today. Answer B is incorrect because the BTX was designed to replace the ATX design but still has not quite caught on. Answer C is incorrect because the NLX is an older design used in slimline computers. Answer D is incorrect because PCA is not a motherboard form factor. The BTX motherboard establishes a straighter path of airflow with few obstacles.

16. **Answer: D.** Answer D is correct because the figure shows an ATX motherboard. The ATX motherboard has the processor and memory slots at right angles to the expansion cards, which puts the processor and memory in line with the fan output of the power supply, allowing the processor to run cooler. The ATX motherboard has a 20-pin power connector that accepts a single power connector.

17. **Answer: D.** The new low-profile extended (NLX) form factor became a legitimate standard for cases, power supplies, and system boards. However, manufacturers have chosen to produce low-profile units based on microATX and miniATX designs. These form factors followed the ATX design specification but reduced the size of the unit (and its associated costs) by limiting the number of expansion slots. Unless you obtain a universal case design specifically to handle both the NLX and MicroATX form factors, you cannot install the NLX system board.

18. **Answer: A.** Answer A is correct because the expansion slots are identified as A. Answer B is incorrect because the expansion ports are identified as C. Answer C is incorrect because the memory slots are identified as E. Answer D is incorrect because the disk connectors are identified as G.

19. **Answer: C.** Answer C is correct because the power connector is identified as F. Answer A is incorrect because the expansion ports are identified as C. Answer B is incorrect because the processor socket is identified as D. Answer D is incorrect because the disk connectors are identified as G.

20. **Answer: B.** Answer B is correct because the chipset is identified as I. Answer A is incorrect because the processor socket is identified as letter D. Answer C is incorrect because the CMOS battery is identified as H. Answer D is incorrect because the AGP slot is identified as B.

21. **Answer: D.** Answer D is correct because a serial port is a two-row 9-pin male connector. Answer A is incorrect because a game port is a two-row 9-pin female connector. Answer B is incorrect because the VGA port is a three-row 15-pin female connector. Answer C is incorrect because a PS/2 is a four-pin connector. Answer E is incorrect because the parallel port is a two-row 25-pin female connector.

22. **Answer: B.** Answer B is correct because the VGA port is a three-row 15-pin female connector. Answer A is incorrect because a game port is a two-row 9-pin female connector. Answer C is incorrect because a PS/2 is a four-pin connector. Answer D is incorrect because a serial port is a two-row 9-pin male connector. Answer E is incorrect because the parallel port is a two-row 25-pin female connector.

23. **Answer: C.** Answer C is correct because a DVI port used in video systems is shown in Figure 1.5. Answer A is incorrect because a game port is a two-row 9-pin female connector. Answer B is incorrect because the VGA port is a three-row 15-pin female connector. Answer D is incorrect because a serial port is a two-row 9-pin male connector. Answer E is incorrect because the parallel port is a two-row 25-pin female connector.

24. **Answer: A.** Answer A is correct because Figure 1.6 shows a USB port. Therefore, answers B, C, D, and E are incorrect.

25. **Answer: D.** Answer D is correct because Figure 1.7 shows a PS/2 port used for keyboards and mice. Therefore, answers A, B, C, and E are incorrect.

26. **Answer: A.** Answer A is correct because a game port is a two-row 15-pin female connector. Answer B is incorrect because the VGA port is a three-row 15-pin female connector. Answer C is incorrect because a PS/2 is a four-pin connector. Answer D is incorrect because a serial port is a two-row 9-pin male connector. Answer E is incorrect because the parallel port is a two-row 25-pin female connector.

27. **Answer: A.** Answer A is correct because an RJ-45 connector resembles a phone connector but is a little bit larger because it has eight connectors instead of four. A game port is a two-row 15-pin female connector. Answer B is incorrect because the VGA port is a three-row 15-pin female connector. Answer C is incorrect because a PS/2 is a four-pin connector. Answer D is incorrect because a serial port is a two-row 9-pin male connector. Answer E is incorrect because the parallel port is a two-row 25-pin female connector.

28. **Answer: A.** Answer A is correct because the keyboard port is purple. Answers B, C, and D are incorrect because green is used for the PS/2 mouse, pink is used for the parallel port, and blue is used for the VGA port.

29. **Answer: C.** Lime green identifies analog line level audio output used for front speakers or headphones. Answer A is incorrect because pink identifies analog microphone audio input. Answer B is incorrect because light blue identifies analog line level audio input. Answer D is incorrect because gold identifies a game port or MIDI port.

30. **Answer: C.** Answer C is correct because Small-Outline DIMMs (SODIMM) are used in laptops while RIMMs, DIMMs, and SIMMs are used in desktop computers.

31. **Answer: B.** Answer B is correct because Dual In-line Memory Modules (DIMMs) are the most common form of memory. RIMMs and SIMMs are obsolete forms of memory and SODIMMs are usually found in laptops.

32. **Answer: C.** A RIMM, short for Rambus Inline Memory Module, has 184-pins and 16-bit–wide bus. DIMMs (Answer B) come with 168 pins, 184 pins, or 240 pins. SODIMMs (Answer D) have 72, 100, 144, 200, or 204 pins. DIMMs have a 64-bit data path. The 72- and 100-pin SODIMM packages support 32-bit data transfer, while the 144-, 200-, and 204-pin SODIMM packages support 64-bit data transfer.

33. **Answer: D and E.** DIMMs, short for Dual In-line Memory Module come with 168 pins or 184 pins. A RIMM, short for Rambus Inline Memory Module, has 184-pins and 16-bit–wide bus. SODIMMs have 72, 100, 144, 200, or 204 pins.

34. **Answer: B and C.** DIMMs have a 64-bit–wide data paths. SIMMs and RIMMs have 32-bit–wide data paths.

35. **Answer: B.** AGP is short for Accelerated Graphics Port. It was created when the PCI could not be pushed any further. Instead of a shared bandwidth, the AGP is a dedicated bus that runs at a faster speed. Answers C and D are incorrect because AMR (short for Audio/Modem Riser) is made for sound cards and modems while a CNR (Communications and Networking Riser) is made for audio, networking, and modem cards.

36. **Answer: C.** Answer C is correct because the PCMCIA is short for Personal Computer Memory Card International Association. PCMCIA cards (also known as PC Cards) are used to store data or to expand the capabilities of a laptop computer or notebook computer. Answers A, B, and D are incorrect because PCI, AGP, and CNR are primarily found on desktop computers.

37. **Answer: D.** The South Bridge is generally used for slower devices such as USB ports, IDE drives, and ISA slots. The North Bridge (Answer B) is for faster components on the motherboard such as graphics and memory. PCI Bus (Answer A) and PCMCIA (Answer C) are incorrect because the PCI bus and PCMCIA bus are used to expand your system.

38. **Answer: A.** PCI slots are 32-bit and 64-bit slots that operate at 33.33 MHz clock speed. On a 32-bit bus, they transfer up to 133 Mbps. Therefore, the other answers are incorrect.

39. **Answer: D.** The AGPx8 has a clock speed of 533 MHz and has a transfer rate of approximately 2.1GBps. Therefore, the other answers are incorrect.

40. **Answer: B.** The PCIe, short for PCI Express, is designed to replace the older PCI, PCI-X, and AGP standards. V1.x runs at 250 Mbps per lane while v3.0 runs at 1 GBps per

lane. An eight-lane PCIe slot will transfer at a rate faster than the fastest version of AGP (Answer C), which only runs at 66 MHz and has a bandwidth of 266 Mbps for a 64-bit slot. PCI (Answer A) runs at 33 MHz and transfers 133 Mbps for a 32-bit slot and 266 Mbps for a 64-bit slot. The slowest of these is the PCMCIA interface.

41. Answer: A. Answer A is correct because parallel ATA uses 40-pin gray ribbon cables. Answer B is incorrect because the serial ATA uses 7-pin cables. Answer C is incorrect because the PCMCIA is an expansion standard for laptop computers. Answer D is incorrect because CNR is used for audio, modems, and network interfaces.

42. Answer: C. The serial, parallel, and USB interfaces can all be used for printers, but the USB interface is the newest interface. Answer B is incorrect because DVI is a video interface.

43. Answer: C. While serial ATA (SATA) use only four wires to transmit data, it transmits them at a far faster speed. Serial ATA transmits up to 6.0 GBps while IDE/EIDE can transmit up to 133 Mbps. Answer D is incorrect because USB 2.0 can transmit up to 480 Mbps, which is equal to 60 MBps.

44. Answer: B. In systems that support parallel ATA, you can connect up to four IDE devices, two on each of the two cables. Therefore, the other answers are incorrect.

45. Answer: B. eSATA provides a variant of Serial ATA (SATA) meant for external connectivity. PATA (Answer A), short for parallel ATA, is the first ATA standard. The IEEE 1394 (Answer C), sometimes referred to as Firewire, is an external interface usually used for digital audio, digital video, and other similar applications. Answer D is incorrect because there is no USATA interface.

46. Answer: A. The maximum cable length for eSATA, short for External SATA, is 1 M. Therefore, the other answers are incorrect.

47. Answer: C. The transfer speed for the initial release of eSATA is 300 Mbps. Therefore, the other answers are incorrect.

48. Answer: B. RAID is short for Redundant Array of Inexpensive Disks. RAID-1 is used for disk mirroring in which two disks are copies of each other. If one disk fails, you will keep on working. In RAID-0, multiple disks act together as one for faster performance. Unfortunately, RAID-0 is not true RAID because if one disk fails, the entire set fails. Answer C is incorrect because RAID-5 uses a set of disks that act as one. Different from RAID-0, RAID-5 uses part of the disks to hold parity information. If one disk fails, you can keep working and rebuild the failed disk when it is replaced. RAID-10 combines both striping and mirroring.

49. Answer: A. Processors are considered the brain of the computer. RAM (Answer B) is considered the short-term memory for the computer. The chipset (Answer C) is the electronic devices that control the other devices with your PC. The ROM (Answer D), short for Read-Only Memory, can be used to store the most basic commands for the computer. You can think of the ROM as the instincts of the computer.

50. Answer: D. The CMOS battery will keep the clock running even when the computer is not running. The switching power supply (Answer A) is the component that converts AC into clean DC power. The processor (Answer B) is the brains of the computer that requires the computer to be running to operate. PCMCIA (Answer C) is a technology used to expand laptop and notebook computers.

51. **Answer: C.** POST is short for Power-on Self Test. It resides in the firmware. When the computer is first turned on, the computer must do basic diagnostics to make sure everything is running fine. It then looks for a boot device to boot or load an operating system. Answer A is incorrect because CMOS is a type of chip that is typically used to store computer configurations. This information is usually managed through the BIOS setup program. The firmware (Answer B) is the instincts or basic instructions that the computer follows. ROM (Answer D), short for Read-Only Memory, is a type of memory that remembers its content even when the computer is turned off.

52. **Answer: A.** The power supply is used to convert AC into clean DC power. While there are no such things as power inductors and power resistors, inductors and resistors are electronic components used in most electronic devices, including power supplies. Answer D is incorrect because the power conversion kit is not an official PC component but would be used to convert electricity from one format to another.

53. **Answer: B.** Power supply is measured in watts, which determines how much power can be supplied at one time. Voltage (Answer A) is used to measure the pressure in an electrical line and the resistance of the electrical line is measured in ohms (Answer D). Hertz (Answer C) is used to measure the frequency of an electrical signal.

54. **Answer: B.** The voltage used in the United States is 110 VAC, and Europe uses 220 VAC. Of course, the other answers would be incorrect.

55. **Answer: C.** The voltage used in the United States is 110 VAC, and Europe uses 220 VAC. Of course, the other answers would be incorrect.

56. **Answer: A.** ATX is overwhelmingly the most commonly used power supply. The BTX (Answer B) and LPX (Answer C) are not form factors used for power supplies; they only describe motherboard form factors. The AT form factor (Answer D) is an obsolete form factor only found in older computers.

57. **Answer: C and D.** The original form for the ATX power supply included a 20-pin connector. Later, it was revised and 4 pins were added for a total of 24-pins. Answer A is incorrect because the power cable to power disk drives used four pins (Answer A). The older AT power supplies had two 6-pin (Answer B) connectors known as P8 and P9. Forty pins (Answer E) is the number of pins used for IDE cables.

58. **Answer: A, B, D, E, and F.** The ATX power supply supplies +/– 5 volts, +/– 12 volts, and +3.3 volts. It does not supply –3.3 volts (Answer C).

59. **Answer: A.** A power supply's 4-pin auxiliary connector is a +5 and +12 VDC connector. Therefore, the other answers are incorrect.

60. **Answer: A.** The front-side bus (FSB) is the bus that carries data between the processor and the primary memory or RAM, usually through the Northbridge or equivalent. There is no name for the wires that connect to the front of the case (Answer B). Because motherboards vary greatly, there is no rule on what is placed on the front of the motherboard; therefore, no special name is given to the front of the motherboard. The bus that connects the processor to the Level 2 cache (Answer D) is the back side bus.

61. **Answer: A.** Processors are considered the brain of the computer. RAM (Answer B) is considered the short-term memory for the computer. The chipset (Answer C) is the electronic chips located on the motherboard that controls and coordinates the other devices within your PC. The ROM (Answer D), short for Read-Only Memory, can be

used to store the most basic commands for the computer. You can think of the ROM as the instincts of the computer.

62. **Answer: C.** The 3.8 GHz Pentium 4 processor used the Socket 478. The Socket 478 has 478 pins. Therefore, the other answers are incorrect.

63. **Answer: D.** The 426 socket was used by the Intel Core2 processor. The Pentium 4 processors (Answer A) used a Socket 423, Socket 478, or Socket T. The AMD Athlon processor (Answer B) used a Socket A, which has 426 pins, and the Athlon 64 (Answer C) used a Socket 939 or Socket 940.

64. **Answer: D.** The Intel Core i7 uses the Socket B, which has 1,366 pins. The Pentium 4 processors use the Socket 478 (Answer A), and the Athlon 64 uses the Socket 754 (Answer B). Athlon and Duron processors use Socket A (Answer C), which has 426 pins.

65. **Answer: C.** The AMD Phenom processors with 3 or 4 core use the Socket AM2+, which has 940 contacts. The Socket A sockets (Answer A) are used for AMD Athlon and Duron processors. The Socket B (Answer B) is used for the Intel Core i7 processor. There is no such thing as a Socket 1 (Answer D).

66. **Answer: A.** The AMD Socket 462/Socket A specification has been used with Athlon, Duron, Athlon XP, Athlon XP-M, Athlon MP, and Sempron processors. Therefore, the other answers are incorrect.

67. **Answer: B.** Hyper-Threading Technology, used in newer Intel processors, allows the processor to act like two processors (logical processors) so that it can utilize the processor resources more efficiently and improve performance. MMX technology (Answer A) consists of 57 instructions that improve the performance of multimedia tasks. SSE (Answer C), short for Streaming SIMD Extensions, is an instruction set that contains 70 instructions to process multiple numbers in one transaction. A processor that has multiple cores (Answer D) means it has more than one physical core, not logical core.

68. **Answer: B.** By having multiple processors or multiple core, you can process several items at the same time. Increasing the RAM (Answer A) would most likely increase the performance of the computer but would not increase the power of the processor. Today, you cannot add a cache chip (Answer C) to your motherboard. Processor cache is part of the processor. Lastly, there is no such thing as Turbo mode (Answer D) on today's processors.

69. **Answer: B.** The L1 and L2 cache is used to cache instructions and data kept in the RAM. While increasing the RAM (Answer A) and using faster disks (Answer C) will not increase the link between the RAM and processors. Lastly, using larger paging files (Answer D) will increase the amount of available memory but would most likely not increase the speed of the computer.

70. **Answer: B.** A 64-bit processor can theoretically see as many as 18 exa-bytes because it has a 64-bit address bus. A 32-bit processor (Answer A) with a 32-bit address bus can only see as many as 4 GB of RAM and a 32-bit processor with a 36-bit address bus can see up to 64 GB. A motherboard with an updated BIOS (done by flashing the motherboard—Answer D) and a motherboard with a North Bridge or South Bridge (Answer C) will not physically increase the amount of memory that the system can see.

71. **Answer: D.** A voltage regulator is required on some motherboards to make sure that the motherboard is electrically balanced if the only one of the two processor sockets is

used. While the VRM might include resistors (Answer A), and inverters (Answer C), they are not connected directly into the processor sockets. Answer D is incorrect because the termination pack is usually a resistor pack. Note that some dual-processor motherboards do not require a VRM. The only way to know is to read the manual that comes with the motherboard.

72. **Answer: A.** Processor clock speed is expressed in hertz. Because processors run much faster these days, they are expressed in Gigahertz (GHz). Therefore, the other answers are incorrect.

73. **Answer: A.** Today's 64-bit processors sold by Intel and AMD use the x86 (also known as x86-64 and AMD64) instruction set architecture. The IA-64 (Answer B) is used by Intel's Itanium processors. Unfortunately, the IA-64 architecture will only run 64-bit applications that were written for the IA-64 architecture and will not run x86 pro-grams. MMX (Answer C) and SSE2 (Answer D) are added instructions that allow the processor to manipulate multiple values using a single transaction.

74. **Answer: A.** The Athlon 64 processor uses the x64 (also known as x86-64) architec-ture. The IA-64 architecture (Answer B) is used by the Itanium processor. The x86 (Answer C) is the older 32-bit architecture used in the Pentium, Pentium Pro, Pentium II, Pentium III, and Pentium 4 processors. PowerNow (Answer D) is a technology used by AMD to conserve power.

75. **Answer: A, B, C, and D.** Today, virtually all computers require a processor heat sink and fan to keep the processor cool. In addition, to prevent the case from overheating, the power supply fan and sometimes other case fans will push air through the system. Some chipsets and memory chipsets might also have heat sinks or other additional cooling components.

76. **Answer: B, C, and D.** To keep a processor cool you must use a heat sink and fan or some other cooling system. The thermal compound will increase the thermal conduc-tivity between the processor and heat sink so that it can dissipate heat more efficiently. When you replace a processor, you should replace the thermal compound. Cooling liq-uid (Answer A) would be incorrect because any type of liquid is a bad idea inside an electronic device unless it is sealed.

77. **Answer: A and C.** To work effectively, liquid cooling kits require a large amount of space within the computer case. In addition, liquid cooling is a relatively new technol-ogy that usually requires a higher level of technical knowledge to install. Condensation (Answer B) is not an inherent problem with liquid cooling and does not require a spe-cial torque wrench (Answer D).

78. **Answer: B.** A heat pipe is a hollow tube containing a heat transfer liquid. As the liquid evaporates, it carries heat to the cool end, where it condenses and then returns to the hot end. Heat pipes are used when space is tight (as in small form-factor PCs) or absolute quiet is needed. The disadvantage of using a heat pipe is cost. Heat sinks (Answer A) provide a larger surface area to dissipate heat faster. A liquid nitrogen sys-tem (Answer C) can dissipate large amounts of energy but requires special installation to prevent insulation and it must be refilled often. Answer D is incorrect because sprinkler cooling is bad for any electrical system.

79. **Answer: D.** The Peltier Effect takes place when an electrical current is sent through two dissimilar materials that have been connected to one another at two junctions.

One junction between the two materials becomes warm while the other becomes cool in what amounts to an electrically driven transfer of heat from one side of the device to the other. A mister would mean liquid on electronic components, which would be bad for any electronic component.

80. **Answer: B.** Of the components listed, RAM has the fastest throughput. The slowest devices are the hard disk drive (Answer C) and CD-ROM (Answer D) because they are mechanical devices. Of course, the CD-ROM drive is much slower than a hard drive. A flash drive is an electronic device that is still slower than RAM.

81. **Answer: C.** SRAM, short for static RAM, is faster than DRAM and doesn't require refreshing like DRAM does. Therefore, it is used for RAM cache. VRAM (Answer B) is short for video RAM and allows for simultaneous reading and writing. DRAM (Answer A) is used for memory chips and requires refreshing. SDRAM (Answer D), short for Synchronization Dynamic RAM, is an improved version of the original DRAM.

82. **Answer: B.** PC-100 Synchronization DRAM (SDRAM) requires 8 ns DRAM chips that can operate at 125 MHz. Therefore, the other answers are incorrect.

83. **Answer: B.** Synchronous DRAM (SDRAM) uses Dual-Inline Memory Modules (DIMMs) while Rambus DRAM uses the Rambus inline memory module (RIMM— Answer C). SIMM (Single In-Line Memory Module—Answer A) is used in older systems. SIPPs (Answer D) are obsolete packages that were used before SIMMs.

84. **Answer: A.** Double-data-rate synchronous dynamic random access memory (DDR SDRAM) is the most common form of memory used for RAM and video memory. DDR SDRAM comes in DDR (its original form), DDR2, and DDR3. The other answers are incorrect because SODIMM, SIMM, and DIMM are memory package types.

85. **Answer: B.** The PC3200 (3.2GBps/400MHz) Double Data Rate (DDR) module is designed for use with a double-pumped front-side bus that runs on a 400 MHz effective FSB. This means that the memory bus speed runs at 200 MHz and the memory transfer data on both the rising and falling edges of the memory bus's square wave clock signal. This means that these devices transfer data at a rate of twice the actual bus speed frequency. Therefore, the other answers are incorrect.

86. **Answer: A.** Using RAM slower than the FSB speed would create a significant overclocking situation for the RAM modules and cause the system to fail. Using PC166 RAM (Answer B) would be wasteful because the system reduces its operation to 133MHz. There are no DDR133 devices (Answer C); there are, however, PC-2100 modules that are constructed using DDR 266 chips that operate with a 133MHz bus clock. PC133 devices are backward-compatible with PC100 (Answer D) devices, but the reverse is not so.

87. **Answer: A and C.** Parity and ECC (short for Error-Correcting Code) are both used to detect errors. Parity (Answer A) uses an extra bit for every byte that indicates if the bit within the byte is odd or even. From time to time, the bits within the byte are checked again to see if the parity bit still holds true. If it does not, one of the bits has changed. The ECC (Answer C) uses several bits to perform and store a mathematical calculation. At a later time, the same mathematical calculation is done again and checked with the ECC bits. If they are different, an error has occurred. Different from parity, ECC can also correct single-bit errors. Static memory (Answer B) is incorrect because static memory is a type of memory, not an error-detecting technology. Recharging (Answer D) is incorrect because it is the technique through which dynamic RAM is regularly recharged so that the capacitors within a memory chip remember its values.

88. **Answer: C.** DDR-1 can provide up to 3.2 GBps while DDR-2 can provide up to 6.4 GBps. DDR-3 can theoretically go up to 12.8 GBps.

89. **Answer: A and D.** DDR-2 has a faster bandwidth. DDR-1 can run up to 3.2 GBps and DDR-2 can run up to 6.4 GBps. DDR-2 also consumes less power. DDR-2 is faster because of its faster bandwidth, not because of lower latency.

90. **Answer: B.** Double-sided RAM has its chips divided into two sides (called "banks"), only one of which can be seen at a time by the computer. To use the second half of the storage available, the computer must switch to the second bank and can no longer read or write to the first half until it switches back again. It accesses one bank while the other bank prepares to be accessed. DDR uses double-rated technology (Answer A) where it reacts with rise and fall of each clock cycle, which doubles its performance. Dynamic RAM uses capacitor technology to store a bit of data. Dynamic RAM constantly needs to be refreshed to remember its content (Answer D). There is no such thing as turbo cached (Answer C).

91. **Answer: D.** DDR3-1600 has a peak transfer rate of 12,800 Mbps (12.8 GBps), which gives the name PC3-12800. It also uses 200 MHz memory clock and 800 MHz I/O bus clock. Of course, the data rate is 1600 Mbps because it reacts on the rise and fall of the clock cycle, doubling its throughput.

92. **Answer: B.** Screens are divided into two types, CRT and LCD. LCD screens are thin while CRT screens (Answer C) are large and bulky. LED (Answer D) is a technology used in LCD. A terminal (Answer A) is a generic term in video systems and does not indicate the technology used.

93. **Answer: B.** VGA is the basis for all modern video systems used in today's computers. While today's computer systems run at a much higher resolution than VGA, VGA mode can still be useful when troubleshooting certain problems. VGA uses a resolution of 640×480. Therefore, the other answers are incorrect.

94. **Answer: D.** The initial version of XGA expanded upon IBM's VGA, adding support for two resolutions: 800×600 pixels with high color (16 bits per pixel; that is, 65,536 colors) and 1024×768 pixels with a palette of 256 colors (8 bits per pixel). Therefore, the other answers are incorrect.

95. **Answer: D.** UXGA has a standard monitor resolution of 1600×1200 pixels, which is quadruple the default resolution of SVGA (800×600). Therefore, the other answers are incorrect.

96. **Answer: C.** WUXGA has a display resolution of 192×1200. Wide XGA has a resolution of 1366×768. Therefore, the other answers are incorrect.

97. **Answer: C.** The color depth expresses how many bits describe the colors of a single pixel. Because 8 bits can give you 256 different options, it can display 256 different colors. 16 bits can display 65,536 colors and 24 bits can display 16,777,216 colors. The resolution (Answer A) describes the number of pixels on the screen. The refresh rate (Answer B) describes how often a screen refreshes per second. The size of the pixel (Answer D) has no effect on how many colors it can display.

98. **Answer: C.** The contrast ratio is a measure of a display system, defined as the ratio of the luminance of the brightest color (white) to that of the darkest color (black) that the system is capable of producing. A high contrast ratio is a desired aspect of any display

since the whites look white and the blacks look black. The color depth (Answer D) expresses how many bits describe the colors of a single pixel. The resolution (Answer A) describes the number of pixels on the screen at one time. The refresh rate (Answer B) expresses how often the screen redraws itself each second.

99. **Answer: D.** The dot pitch, usually measured in millimeters, describes the distance between pixels. A smaller number means the pixels are closer together, which means a sharper image. The resolution (Answer A) describes the number of pixels on the screen at one time. The refresh rate expresses how often the screen redraws itself each second. The contrast ratio (Answer B) is a measure of a display system, defined as the ratio of the luminance of the brightest color (white) to that of the darkest color (black) that the system is capable of producing. The color depth (Answer C) expresses how many bits describe the colors of a single pixel.

100. **Answer: B.** HDMI (High-Definition Multimedia Interface) is a compact audio/video interface for transmitting uncompressed digital data. HDMI connects digital audio/video sources such as set-top boxes, Blu-ray disc players, personal computers (PCs), video game consoles (such as the PlayStation 3 and Xbox 360), and AV receivers to compatible digital audio devices, computer monitors, and digital televisions. DVI (Answer A), short for Digital Visual Interface, is a video interface standard designed to maximize the visual quality of digital display devices such as LCD computer displays and digital projectors. VGA (Answer C), short for Video Graphics Array, is an older video interface for computer displays. Answer D, Super VGA (SVGA) is an improved version of VGA.

101. **Answer: B.** DVI and HDMI Video are compatible with each other provided both devices are HDCP compatible. Therefore, the other answers are incorrect.

102. **Answer: A.** DVI-I is short for DVI-Integrated, which supports both digital and analog signals. DVI-D (Answer B) supports digital only and DVI-A (Answer C) supports analog only. There is no such thing as DVI-B (Answer D).

103. **Answer: D.** When you add a USB mouse or keyboard, drivers are automatically loaded. And because they are plug-and-play devices, you can plug them in while the computer is on. Because you don't have to do anything, the other answers are incorrect.

104. **Answer: D.** Plug-and-play technology allows you to connect a device without configuring the device. Some common plug-and-play devices used today include USB devices, modern PCI expansion cards, PCI-X and PCI-E expansion cards, and PCMCIA/PC cards. Therefore, the other answers are incorrect

105. **Answer: B.** Plug-and-play technology allows you to connect a device without configuring the device. Some common plug-and-play devices used today include USB devices, modern PCI expansion cards, PCI-X and PCI-E expansion cards, and PCMCIA/PC cards.

106. **Answer: C.** Plug-and-play technology allows you to connect a device without configuring the device. Some common plug-and-play devices used today include USB devices, modern PCI expansion cards, PCI-X and PCI-E expansion cards, and PCMCIA/PC cards. Typically after you connect a plug-and-play device, the only thing that you need to ensure is that a driver is loaded. Many drivers are included with Windows. If a driver is not included with Windows, you will have to load the driver manually. The other answers are incorrect because there is no type of device or technology that has these features.

107. **Answer: B and C.** To load drivers, you must have the device connected first. Then it is always recommended that you use signed drivers. Answer A is incorrect because the

driver, not the application, should be digitally signed. Answer D is incorrect because the driver might not load if it does not detect that the device is actually connected.

108. **Answer: C.** When you have a touch screen, you must physically install the device, load the appropriate drivers, and load the appropriate software that comes with the touch screen. You then need to calibrate it so that when you touch the touch screen, it will respond properly. If you installed the driver, you won't have to enable the driver (Answer A); it should be enabled by default. You do not need to link the touch screen (Answer B) to the printer or a pointing device (Answer D).

109. **Answer: D.** KVM is short for Keyboard, Video Mouse. It is a hardware device that enables a user to control multiple computers from a single keyboard, monitor, and mouse. Monitors do not support wireless cards (Answer A) and they do not support USB connections (Answer C). Although some monitors may actually support two video connections, which also will have controls on the monitor to change between the two systems, you cannot purchase a split video cable to connect two PCs to a single monitor.

110. **Answer: D.** PCI-E, short for PCI-Express, is a serial bus with a different physical interface that was designed to replace both PCI and PCI-X. PCI, PCI-X, and AGP are all based on parallel interface. Since the PCI, PCI-X, and AGP are based on parallel-signal technology, Answers A, B, and C are incorrect.

111. **Answer: B.** PCI-X is a parallel interface that is directly backward-compatible with all but the oldest (5-volt) standard PCI devices. It is not compatible with 3.3 v standard PCI devices (Answer A), AGP devices (Answer C), and PCI-E devices (Answer D).

112. **Answer: A, B, C, and D.** PCI Express can support up to 32 lanes (1, 2, 4, 8, 16, and 32). It does not support 18 lanes (Answer E).

113. **Answer: B.** The microphone (audio in) and speakers (audio out) are plugged into the appropriate 1/8" mini-jacks on the back of the sound card. The 25-pin D-Shells (Answer A) are used for parallel cables. The RJ-11 jacks and plugs (Answer C) are used for phone connections/modems. The 15-pin D-shells (Answer D) are used for game ports (two rows) or VGA (three rows).

114. **Answer: D.** The recommended maximum length of an RS-232 cable is 50 feet (15 meters). However, some references use 100 feet as the acceptable length of an RS-232C serial cable. Serial connections are tricky enough without problems generated by the cable being too long. Make the cable as short as possible.

115. **Answer: C.** The Universal Serial Bus (USB) provides a fast, flexible method of attaching up to 127 peripheral devices to the computer. The peripherals can be daisy chained, or networked together, using connection hubs that enable the bus to branch out through additional port connections.

116. **Answer: D.** Full-speed USB devices that operate under the USB 1.1 specification operate at 12 Mbps. Therefore, the other answers are incorrect.

117. **Answer: B.** Full-speed USB devices that operate under the USB 2.0 specification (also referred to as high-speed USB) support data rates up to 480 Mbps. USB 1.0 operates up to 12 Mbps. Therefore, the other answers are incorrect.

118. **Answer: D.** 1394, sometimes referred to as Firewire, can support up to 63 devices. Therefore, the other answers are incorrect.

119. Answer: D. The maximum distance for a single cable for USB 2.0 is 5 meters. Therefore, the other answers are incorrect.

120. Answer: B. RS-232, short for Recommended Standard 232, is a standard for serial binary data signals used in computer serial ports. Parallel ports (Answer A) use the IEEE 1284 standard. Firewire (Answer D) uses the IEEE 1394 interface. Answer C is incorrect because the USB uses its own standardization.

121. Answer: A. RJ-11 is a physical interface often used for terminating telephone wires. RJ-45 (Answer B) is a physical interface used for network cables such as Ethernet. RS-1284 (Answer C) and RS-90 (Answer D) do not exist.

122. Answer: A. Parallel ports are usually associated with printers and are denoted as LPT1, LPT2, and LPT3. LPT is short for line print terminal. COMX (Answer B) is associated with the serial ports COM1, COM2, COM3, and COM4. The others do not exist.

123. Answer: A. The larger port found on a computer uses the Type A connectors. The Type-B connectors (Answer B), mini-USB (Answer C), and Micro-USB (Answer D) are usually used on USB devices.

124. Answer: C. Type III can also accommodate Type I and II. Type II (Answer B) can only accommodate Types I and II cards. Type I (Answer A) cards can only accommodate Type I cards.

125. Answer: D. Bluetooth is a wireless technology that was developed as a short-range communication for wireless keyboard and mice. Cellular (Answer A) is usually used with cell phones and wireless access points. Ethernet (Answer B) is a wired network standard. Firewire is a high-speed interface for devices.

126. Answer: B and D. To find the right amperage of an AC adapter for a laptop, you must contact the manufacturer by phone or email support or by visiting the website. You can also refer to the owner manual that comes with that laptop. Answer A is incorrect because the Control Panel cannot show the right amperage. Answer C is incorrect because a multimeter is used to measure voltage or resistance but cannot tell you the proper amperage setting.

127. Answer: B. Of the batteries shown, the Nickel Cadmium (NiCD) batteries have a short battery life and have other drawbacks including memory effect that cause the battery to suffer a sudden drop in voltage. Today, Lithium-Ion (Li-Ion—Answer D) is a much more popular battery because it is lighter and does not suffer from memory effect. Answers A and C are incorrect because Nickel Metal-Hybride and Nickel-Lithium are popular batteries used with laptops that do not suffer from the memory effect that you find with Nickel Cadmium batteries.

128. Answer: C. A Type II PCMCIA card has a thickness of .20 inches or 5 millimeters. Type II PCMCIA cards are used for a wide range of expansion cards such as network cards, modems, and wireless cards. Therefore, the other answers are incorrect.

129. Answer: C. PC Cards are also known as PCMCIA. PCMCIA is short for Personal Computer Memory Card International Association, named after the international standards body that defines and promotes the PC cards. The first version of the cards—Type I cards—are memory cards used in laptop computers. Because they are not limited to memory devices, the cards were renamed to PC Cards. Therefore, the other answers are incorrect.

130. Answer: B. Type III PCMCIA cards are 0.40 inches or 10 millimeters thick. Type III PCMCIA cards are used for small hard drives. Therefore, the other answers are incorrect.

131. Answer: C. The Fn keys give you additional features on the keyboard, such as brightness controls, sleep functions, display controls, and others. Therefore, the other answers are incorrect.

132. Answer: B and D. Laptop and notebook computers can be powered by AC power via an adapter and built-in batteries. Answer C is incorrect because a docking station expands a laptop, but the laptop still gets its power from batteries and AC power. Answer A is incorrect because laptops use their own type of batteries, not standard AA batteries.

133. Answer: B. A trackball is basically a mouse turned upside down. Instead of moving the mouse back and forth, you roll the ball while the socket remains stationary. Therefore, the other answers are incorrect.

134. Answer: A. IrDA, which uses infrared light, only has a range of approximately 1 meter. Therefore, the other answers are incorrect.

135. Answer: D. If you use a laptop on a hard surface the vents underneath the laptop have room for airflow, which will help keep the system cool. While most of the other methods might help keep the computer cooler, they are not always practical. It does not matter if you keep the laptop in the carrying case (Answer B) while it is not being used.

136. Answer: C. Inkjet printers spray or squirt small droplets of ink onto the paper. Laser printers (Answer A) use toner that is melted onto paper. Thermal printers (Answer B) use special paper that is heat sensitive. Dot matrix printers (Answer D) use ribbons that include ink or film that is transferred by pressure.

137. Answer: A. A laser printer works similarly to a copy machine that uses a laser to charge a surface that can be used to place toner onto a piece of paper. A fuser then melts the toner onto the paper. Therefore, the other answers are incorrect.

138. Answer: B. In the dye sublimation printer, a heating element strip is used to transfer the color substance on a plastic film to the paper. The heating element contains thousands of small heat points that create fine patterns of color dots. By adjusting the temperature, you can produce different shades. Therefore, the other answers are incorrect.

139. Answer: B. A thermal printer uses a thermal print head to melt dots of wax-based ink from the transfer ribbon onto the paper. Therefore, the other answers are incorrect.

140. Answer B. Thermal printers use special heat-sensitive or chemically reactive paper to form characters on the page. Heat elements then burn or melt dot patterns on special paper. Thermal printers can be further broken into direct thermal printers and thermal wax transfer printers. Therefore, the other answers are incorrect.

141. Answer: C. Parallel ports use the IEEE-1284 standard. Therefore, you should connect with an IEEE-1284 cable. RS-232 (Answer A) is used for serial ports. IEEE-1394 (also known as Firewire—Answer B) is used for high-speed devices. Answer D is incorrect because HDMI is used as a high-definition video interface.

142. Answer: B. A thermal fuse will blow when a component is too hot. In this case, the thermal fuse makes sure the fuser assembly does not overheat. Without it, there could be severe damage to the printer or a potential fire hazard. Therefore the other answers are incorrect.

143. Answer: D. Tractor feeds are used with very heavy forms, such as multi-part continuous forms. Tractor feeds are usually found on dot-matrix printers. Therefore, the other answers are incorrect.

144. Answer: B. The primary corona wire prepares/charges the drum with a uniform negative charge (–600 V). Therefore the other answers are incorrect.

145. Answer: D. Toner is a fine powder that forms the printed text and images on the paper. The fuser melts or fuses the toner onto the paper. The transfer corona wire (or transfer roller—Answer A) is responsible for transferring the toner from the drum to the paper. The toner is transferred to the paper because of the highly positive charge the transfer corona wire applies to the paper. The primary corona wire creates a highly charged negative field that conditions the drum to be written on by applying a uniform negative charge (<600V) to it. The drum (Answer B) is the component where an image is drawn out with lasers discharging parts of the drum. Answer C is incorrect because there is no print head in a laser printer.

146. Answer: A and C. The transfer corona wire (or transfer roller) is responsible for transferring the toner from the drum to the paper. The toner is transferred to the paper because of the highly positive charge the transfer corona wire applies to the paper. The primary corona wire creates a highly charged negative field that conditions the drum to be written on by applying a uniform negative charge (<600V) to it. Therefore the other answers are incorrect.

147. Answer: B. Before the laser writes on the drum, it is cleaned and conditioned. The laser is used to create a charged image on the drum, which attracts toner expelled by the developer roller. The toner is attracted to the drum and is then transferred to paper that has been given a different charge. After being transferred from the drum to the paper, the toner is pressed and fused into the paper. Therefore, the other answers are incorrect.

148. Answer: B. The transfer corona wire (transfer roller) is responsible for transferring the toner from the drum to the paper. The toner is transferred to the paper because of the highly positive charge the transfer corona wire applies to the paper. The drum (Answer A) is the component where an image is drawn out with lasers discharging parts of the drum. The fuser assembly (Answer C) is the component that melts the toner onto the paper. The platen (Answer D) does not exist in laser printers.

149. Answer: A. The primary component of a dot-matrix printer is a main control board. It contains the logic circuitry required to convert the signals, received from the computer's adapter card, into character patterns, as well as to generate the control signals to position the print head properly on the page. The print head board (Answer B) is usually associated with dot-matrix and ink-jet printers to control the print head. The Control Panel (Answer C) is a program, not an electronic component. Answer D is incorrect because the sensor board is used to detect a signal or state of something.

150. Answer: A. The Bluetooth option enables users to print directly from notebook PCs, PDAs, or cell phones. Bluetooth can be added to an existing USB or parallel port printer through a small Bluetooth receiver that plugs into the port. It also makes printer placement a simple and dynamic activity. You need only to position the printer within the specified range (generally, 20 feet—the maximum range for low power Bluetooth is 10 meters or 32 feet) of the Bluetooth device to achieve connectivity. Also, you can pick up the printer and relocate it to another room or office. IrDA (Answer B) is a wire-less technology based on infrared but is not as common or as fast as Bluetooth. 802.11x (Answer C) is an authentication protocol and USB (Answer D) is an interface connected through a USB cable.

151. **Answer: A and C.** The impact printer uses a print head that hits the surface of the ink ribbon, which presses the ink onto the paper. Toner powder (Answer B) is used in laser printers, and ink cartridges (Answer D) are used in ink-jet printers.

152. **Answer: B.** The bubble jet uses an ink cartridge, which consists of the print head and ink supply. Laser printers (Answer A) use toner, and impact printers (Answer C) use ink ribbons.

153. **Answer: B.** The polyester resin makes the "flow" of the toner better. Ink (Answer A) is not used in toner or toner cartridges. Iron oxide particles (Answer C) allow the laser printer to move toner into the necessary spots. Today, carbon substance (Answer D) is not a main component used in toner.

154. **Answer: B.** The high-voltage power supply supplies the voltages for the charge and transfer corona assemblies. Controller circuitry (Answer A) is used to control the oper-ations of the laser printer. The DC power supply (Answer C) is used to convert AC into clean DC power so that it can be used by the electronics and mechanical devices of the laser printer. The transfer corona wire (or transfer roller— Answer D) is responsi-ble for transferring the toner from the drum to the paper. The toner is transferred to the paper because of the highly positive charge the transfer corona wire applies to the paper. The primary corona wire creates a highly charged negative field that conditions the drum to be written on by applying a uniform negative charge (<600V) to it.

155. **Answer: A.** In the corona assembly is a static-charge eliminator strip that drains away the charge imparted to the paper by the corona. If you do not drain away the charge, the paper would stick to the EP cartridge and jam the printer. The rubber cleaning blade (Answer B) removes excess toner. The iron particle in the toner (Answer C) allows the toner to be moved and properly placed. The developer (Answer D) is used to collect small, negatively charged magnetic beads (toner) and attach the toner to the rotating metal roller.

156. **Answer: C.** The slowest of the listed printer interfaces is the serial port, which can communicate at 115,200 bits per second. The IEEE 1284 standard allows for faster throughput and bidirectional data flow with a theoretical maximum throughput of 4 megabits per second (4,000,000 bits per second). USB 2.0 can communicate up to 480 Mbps and SCSI can even go faster than that.

157. **Answer: A.** USB 2.0 can communicate at 480 Mbps. Bluetooth version 1.2 can com-municate at 1 Mbps and Bluetooth version 2.0 can communicate at 3 Mbps (Answer B). 802.11a (Answer C) and 802.11g (Answer D) can communicate up to 54 Mbps.

158. **Answer: A.** IEEE 1284 is the specification for the Extended Capabilities Port (ECP) which is also known as the parallel port. IEEE 802.15 (Answer B) is the standard for Wireless Personal Area Network. IEEE 802.3 (Answer C) is a collection of IEEE standards defining the physical layer, and the media access control (MAC) sublayer of the data link layer, of wired Ethernet. IEEE 802.11i (Answer D) is a security mechanism for wireless networks. IEEE 1394 (Answer E) is a high-speed interface, also known as Firewire.

C H A P T E R T W O

Troubleshooting, Repair, and Maintenance

Now that you have had an introduction to hardware, you are ready to look at the basics of troubleshooting. As you go through this chapter and future chapters, you can apply the basics of troubleshooting to understand how a computer works and how to quickly fix any problem.

Of course, any time a computer breaks down or degrades is a bad time. Therefore, you need to learn how a little maintenance can make a computer last longer so that you avoid problems before they occur and before you lose data.

This domain for the 220-701 exam counts as 20%. The given objectives for this domain are as follows:

- ▶ 2.1—Given a scenario, explain the troubleshooting theory
- ▶ 2.2—Given a scenario, explain and interpret common hardware and operating system symptoms and their causes
- ▶ 2.3—Given a scenario, determine the troubleshooting methods and tools for printers
- ▶ 2.4—Given a scenario, explain and interpret common laptop issues and determine the appropriate basic troubleshooting method
- ▶ 2.5—Given a scenario, integrate common preventative maintenance techniques

2.1 Given a scenario, explain the troubleshooting theory

- ▶ Identify the problem
  - ▶ Question the user and identify user changes to computer and perform backups before making changes
- ▶ Establish a theory of probable cause (question the obvious)
- ▶ Test the theory to determine cause
  - ▶ Once theory is confirmed determine next steps to resolve problem
  - ▶ If theory is not confirmed re-establish new theory or escalate
- ▶ Establish a plan of action to resolve the problem and implement the solution
- ▶ Verify full system functionality and, if applicable, implement preventative measures
- ▶ Document findings, actions, and outcomes

1. You have a computer with Windows XP and you want to upgrade to Windows Vista. What should you do before you perform the upgrade?

   ○ **A.** You should upgrade the RAM.

   ○ **B.** You should add a new hard drive.

   ○ **C.** You should upgrade the virus checker.

   ○ **D.** You should back up the computer.

2. Which of the following questions would you ask clients when troubleshooting their systems? (Select all that apply.)

   ○ **A.** Can you show me the problem?

   ○ **B.** How much did your computer cost?

   ○ **C.** Has any new software been installed recently?

   ○ **D.** Where did you buy your computer?

   ○ **E.** Have any other changes been made to the computer recently?

3. Which of the following troubleshooting steps usually takes place while you are talking to the user who is experiencing the problem?

   ○ **A.** Gathering information on the issue

   ○ **B.** Isolating possible causes of the issue

   ○ **C.** Eliminating possibilities

   ○ **D.** Documenting your findings and solutions

4. Which of the following troubleshooting steps requires you to have knowledge of the different system and configuration areas and the utilities needed to troubleshoot these areas?

   ○ **A.** Gathering information on the issue

   ○ **B.** Talking to the user who is experiencing the problem

   ○ **C.** Isolating possible causes of the issue and eliminating possibilities

   ○ **D.** Documenting your findings and solutions

5. After you understand what the problem is, what would be the next thing to check?

   ○ **A.** Establish a plan to resolve the problem.

   ○ **B.** Perform preventative maintenance

   ○ **C.** Check the obvious

   ○ **D.** Document your findings

6. Which of the following two questions would you first ask a customer when he reports a blank monitor? (Choose two answers.)

Quick Answer: **81**
Detailed Answer: **82**

- ○ **A.** Is the monitor on?
- ○ **B.** Did you check the color settings?
- ○ **C.** Have you checked whether the contrast or brightness is turned down?
- ○ **D.** What type of computer do you have?

7. Before you can test a solution, you must first do which of the following?

Quick Answer: **81**
Detailed Answer: **82**

- ○ **A.** Back up the system
- ○ **B.** Document the findings, actions, and outcomes
- ○ **C.** Establish a theory of probably cause
- ○ **D.** Verify full system functionality

8. What should you do after you resolve the problem and implement the solution?

Quick Answer: **81**
Detailed Answer: **83**

- ○ **A.** Verify full system functionality
- ○ **B.** Document findings, actions, and outcomes
- ○ **C.** Clean up after yourself
- ○ **D.** Do a full system scan to look for other problems

9. Using the troubleshooting theory, the last thing you should do is which of the following?

Quick Answer: **81**
Detailed Answer: **83**

- ○ **A.** Clean up after yourself
- ○ **B.** Do a full system scan to look for other problems
- ○ **C.** Document findings, actions, and outcomes
- ○ **D.** Verify full system functionality

10. What should you do when you have checked your theory and have found out that it did not correct the problem?

Quick Answer: **81**
Detailed Answer: **83**

- ○ **A.** Come up with a new theory
- ○ **B.** Do a full system scan to look for other problems
- ○ **C.** Document findings, actions, and outcomes
- ○ **D.** Verify full system functionality

2.2 Given a scenario, explain and interpret common hardware and operating system symptoms and their causes

▶ OS related symptoms

  ▶ Bluescreen

  ▶ System lock-up

  ▶ Input/output device

  ▶ Application install

  ▶ Start or load

  ▶ Windows-specific printing problems

    ▶ Print spool stalled

    ▶ Incorrect/incompatible driver

▶ Hardware related symptoms

  ▶ Excessive heat

  ▶ Noise

  ▶ Odors

  ▶ Status light indicators

  ▶ Alerts

  ▶ Visible damage (e.g. cable, plastic)

▶ Use documentation and resources

  ▶ User/installation manuals

  ▶ Internet/web based

  ▶ Training materials

11. When you are using Windows, your GUI interface turns into text mode with a blue background. What is this referred to as?

  ○ **A.** A kernel excursion

  ○ **B.** A stop error

  ○ **C.** An unrecoverable application error

  ○ **D.** A virus warning

Quick Answer: **81**
Detailed Answer: **83**

12. You are using Windows and your system freezes up. The keyboard and mouse do not respond and nothing is changing on the screen. What is this known as?

  ○ **A.** System lock-up

  ○ **B.** Blue Screen of Death

  ○ **C.** Overheating

  ○ **D.** Killdump

Quick Answer: **81**
Detailed Answer: **83**

13. Which of the following are typical indications of a boot process fail situation?

- ○ **A.** An automatic reboot
- ○ **B.** Complete lock-up
- ○ **C.** A blank screen
- ○ **D.** A blue error screen
- ○ **E.** All of the above

14. You just installed a new data-scanning software package. Now the computer never finishes booting Windows. What is most likely the cause of the failure?

- ○ **A.** The new data-scanning software
- ○ **B.** Corruption of the boot sector
- ○ **C.** A corrupt driver
- ○ **D.** Corruption of the volume boot sector

15. What is most likely the cause of the problem when you print a document and it prints strange characters and/or printing code?

- ○ **A.** Incorrect print driver
- ○ **B.** Bad cable
- ○ **C.** Bad printer
- ○ **D.** Electromagnetic interference

16. What cold be a cause if a machine starts locking up after being on for approximately 15 minutes?

- ○ **A.** Virus
- ○ **B.** Electromagnetic interference
- ○ **C.** Overheating
- ○ **D.** Electrical spike

17. What would you check when your documents are not printing, although they printed with no problem yesterday? (Choose all that apply.)

- ○ **A.** The print spool stalled.
- ○ **B.** The printer is not on.
- ○ **C.** The system is overheating.
- ○ **D.** Electromagnetic interference.

18. What components can cause a loud-pitched whining sound? (Choose two components.)

- ○ **A.** Hard drive
- ○ **B.** RAM
- ○ **C.** Motherboard
- ○ **D.** Fan

19. What are some of the symptoms of overheating? (Choose all that apply.)

- ○ **A.** Computer locking up
- ○ **B.** Computer generating strange errors
- ○ **C.** A burned smell
- ○ **D.** Files from the hard drive start to disappear

20. What would you suspect as the problem if a system's power-on light is not on?

- ○ **A.** The machine is not turned on or is not plugged in.
- ○ **B.** Virus.
- ○ **C.** Blue Screen of Death.
- ○ **D.** Bad startup program.

21. You have a drive light that is always on and is hardly ever shutting off. What does this indicate?

- ○ **A.** The hard drive has power most of the time.
- ○ **B.** The drive is constantly reading and writing, which usually indicates the disk system cannot keep up.
- ○ **C.** The hard drive intermittently gets disconnected.
- ○ **D.** The hard drive is running so fast that the computer cannot keep up.

22. During boot-up, how are problems commonly identified before the video system is activated?

- ○ **A.** POST numeric codes
- ○ **B.** POST electrical signals
- ○ **C.** POST beep codes
- ○ **D.** POST software diagnostic package

23. If you turn on the computer and you hear a single beep while the computer starts up, what is the problem?

Quick Answer: **81**
Detailed Answer: **84**

- ○ **A.** There is a memory problem.
- ○ **B.** There is a processor problem.
- ○ **C.** There is no problem.
- ○ **D.** The OS fails to start.

24. What can you use to diagnose a computer that does not boot and does not generate an audio or video error code?

Quick Answer: **81**
Detailed Answer: **85**

- ○ **A.** Power LED
- ○ **B.** POST card
- ○ **C.** Software diagnostic package
- ○ **D.** RAM tester

25. When a user turns on his computer, the computer makes several beeps and the power-on self test (POST) does not complete. Which of the following components might be at fault? (Choose two answers.)

Quick Answer: **81**
Detailed Answer: **85**

- ○ **A.** RAM
- ○ **B.** The hard drive
- ○ **C.** The CD-ROM drive
- ○ **D.** The power supply
- ○ **E.** The processor

26. If you have a system with AMI BIOS codes, what does two or three beeps indicate?

Quick Answer: **81**
Detailed Answer: **85**

- ○ **A.** Processor problem
- ○ **B.** RAM problem
- ○ **C.** Video card problem
- ○ **D.** Power problem

27. Which device produces several beeps and causes the system to fail during the POST?

Quick Answer: **81**
Detailed Answer: **85**

- ○ **A.** Hard disk drive
- ○ **B.** USB adapter
- ○ **C.** Power supply
- ○ **D.** Video display

28. If you receive the "Non-system disk or disk error" error message, what issue should you troubleshoot?

   ○ **A.** The computer failed to locate a boot sector with an operating system installed.

   ○ **B.** A memory size error.

   ○ **C.** A missing or malfunctioning keyboard.

   ○ **D.** A video card driver cannot be found.

29. Which of the following would cause a Windows XP system not to boot up? (Choose all that apply.)

   ○ **A.** A missing or corrupt NTLDR

   ○ **B.** An accidentally deleted CONFIG.SYS file

   ○ **C.** A missing or corrupt BOOT.INI

   ○ **D.** An accidentally deleted AUTOEXEC.BAT file

30. You just installed a hard drive and you notice that your system is not recognizing the hard drive. You notice that there are some jumpers on the hard drives. Where should you check on how to set the jumpers? (Choose all that apply.)

   ○ **A.** User or installation manuals

   ○ **B.** Manufacturer's website

   ○ **C.** Training material

   ○ **D.** Diagnostic software

2.3 Given a scenario, determine the troubleshooting methods and tools for printers

▶ Manage print jobs

▶ Print spooler

▶ Printer properties and settings

▶ Print a test page

31. You are troubleshooting a printing problem. When you examine the print queue of the local printer, you see three files in print queue and nothing is coming out of the printer. What is the first step you should take to correct this problem?

   ○ **A.** Turn the printer on and off until the print queue clears.

   ○ **B.** Right-click on the printer's icon, click Properties, and then select Details. Select Spool Settings and select the Print Directly to the Printer option to bypass the spooler to get your print job.

○ **C.** Delete all the files from the print spooler queue and resend your print job to the printer.

○ **D.** Double-click on the printer's icon and select the Restart option from the Documents menu.

32. Which of the following can you use to start the print spooler from the command prompt?

○ **A.** Start/Spooler

○ **B.** Run/Spooler

○ **C.** Net start spooler

○ **D.** Spooler.com

Quick Answer: **81**
Detailed Answer: **86**

33. What Windows structure allows multiple files to be loaded to a printer for printing?

○ **A.** Print Manager

○ **B.** Print Spooler

○ **C.** Print Buffer

○ **D.** Print Queue

Quick Answer: **81**
Detailed Answer: **86**

34. In a network printing environment, what Windows structure controls printing for everyone on the network?

○ **A.** Print Spooler

○ **B.** Print Manager

○ **C.** Print Buffer

○ **D.** Printer Queue

Quick Answer: **81**
Detailed Answer: **86**

35. In Windows, how do you test the print spooler if the printer won't print?

○ **A.** Use Scandisk to check the disk integrity

○ **B.** Print directly to the printer port (LPTx)

○ **C.** Change the printer cable

○ **D.** Print directly to the printer using the Advanced tab of the printer's properties page

Quick Answer: **81**
Detailed Answer: **86**

36. A user is having problems printing to his local printer. It was working fine until he sent several documents to the printer one after the other. The printer turned out a few pages but then stopped printing. The user can no longer print to that printer from his computer. When you attempt to print a test page from the printer, it prints successfully. What item should you check next?

- ○ **A.** The printer signal cable
- ○ **B.** The Windows Print spooler
- ○ **C.** The printer driver
- ○ **D.** The printer port enabling in the CMOS Setup

37. A user reports that she can't print to her local inkjet printer; no paper comes out and nothing is printed. When you examine the Printers and Faxes page of the Windows XP system, you see that only an HP Laser 1100 printer is showing on the page. What is the most likely cause of this problem?

- ○ **A.** The printer is not installed in the system.
- ○ **B.** The print spooler has been disabled on the system.
- ○ **C.** The wrong printer driver has been installed in the system.
- ○ **D.** The default printer setting has been set incorrectly on the printer.

38. What is the last step in installing a new laser printer at a customer's office?

- ○ **A.** Run a test page from the printer
- ○ **B.** Reset the printer's page counter
- ○ **C.** Run a test page from the host computer
- ○ **D.** Give the customer the bill

39. How do you send a test page to the printer in Windows Vista?

- ○ **A.** Open Printers in the Control Panel. Right-click the printer and select Properties. On the General tab, click Print Test Page.
- ○ **B.** Open Printers in the Control Panel. Right-click the printer and select Print Test Page.
- ○ **C.** Right-click the desktop and choose the printer. Then open the file menu and select Print Test Page.
- ○ **D.** Open an application. Open the file menu and select Print. Then with the selected printer, click Print Test Page.

40. What is the minimum permission need to print a document?

Quick Answer: **81**
Detailed Answer: **87**

- ○ **A.** Print
- ○ **B.** Manage Documents
- ○ **C.** Change Documents
- ○ **D.** Read Printers

41. What is the minimum permission needed to delete any print job from the print queue?

Quick Answer: **81**
Detailed Answer: **87**

- ○ **A.** Print
- ○ **B.** Manage Documents
- ○ **C.** Change Documents
- ○ **D.** Read Printers

42. Which of the following devices have light indicators? (Choose two answers.)

Quick Answer: **81**
Detailed Answer: **87**

- ○ **A.** Modem
- ○ **B.** Serial port
- ○ **C.** Parallel port
- ○ **D.** Network interface card

2.4 Given a scenario, explain and interpret common laptop issues and determine the appropriate basic troubleshooting method

- ▶ Issues
  - ▶ Power conditions
  - ▶ Video
  - ▶ Keyboard
  - ▶ Pointer
  - ▶ Stylus
  - ▶ Wireless card issues
- ▶ Methods
  - ▶ Verify power (e.g. LEDs, swap AC adapter)
  - ▶ Remove unneeded peripherals
  - ▶ Plug in external monitor
  - ▶ Toggle Fn keys or hardware switches
  - ▶ Check LCD cutoff switch
  - ▶ Verify backlight functionality and pixilation
  - ▶ Check switch for built-in WIFI antennas or external antennas

43. You are working on a laptop computer. While you are typing, your pointer in Windows seems to jump often to a different location while you are typing. As a result, every time you jump, you start typing in that location. What can you do to overcome this problem?

- ○ **A.** Make sure you turn on the track pad
- ○ **B.** Make sure you load the proper driver for the track pad
- ○ **C.** Make sure you load the proper driver for the keyboard
- ○ **D.** Replace the keyboard

Quick Answer: **81**
Detailed Answer: **87**

44. What is a main difference between the processor on a laptop and on a desktop?

- ○ **A.** Power consumption and heat production
- ○ **B.** Size and clock speed
- ○ **C.** L2 Cache and clock speed
- ○ **D.** Power consumption and front side bus speed
- ○ **E.** L2 Cache and front side bus speed

Quick Answer: **81**
Detailed Answer: **87**

45. You have a 2.2-GHz processor in a laptop computer. However when you use diagnostic software, you find out it is only running at 1.6 GHz. What is most likely the problem?

- ○ **A.** Processor throttling technology is being used.
- ○ **B.** The incorrect processor is installed.
- ○ **C.** The jumper settings are incorrect.
- ○ **D.** Hyper-Threading technology is being used.

Quick Answer: **81**
Detailed Answer: **88**

46. When you purchase a spare battery for your laptop computer, what should you do with the battery when you don't need it for long periods of time?

- ○ **A.** Store it fully charged in a refrigerator
- ○ **B.** Store it fully charged at room temperature
- ○ **C.** Fully discharge it in a refrigerator
- ○ **D.** Fully discharge it at room temperature

Quick Answer: **81**
Detailed Answer: **88**

47. Which battery type has the highest electrochemical potential and which usually offers the lightest batteries?

- ○ **A.** NiCD
- ○ **B.** NiMH
- ○ **C.** Lithium-Ion
- ○ **D.** Alkaline

Quick Answer: **81**
Detailed Answer: **88**

48. You notice that the length of time that your portable computer can run on the battery before it shuts down is significantly shorter than it used to be and appears to be getting shorter and shorter. What can you do to restore some additional usage to the battery?

Quick Answer: **81**
Detailed Answer: **88**

    ○ **A.** Place the battery in a commercial battery charger overnight to build the level of charge in the battery backup.

    ○ **B.** Keep the external AC power adapter plugged into the notebook whenever possible to increase the amount of charge in the battery.

    ○ **C.** You must fully discharge the battery and then recharge it over repeated cycles.

    ○ **D.** Take the battery out of the computer and warm it in an oven on low heat for an hour.

49. Which of the following is the best way to detect a bad battery in a Windows Vista–based laptop PC?

Quick Answer: **81**
Detailed Answer: **88**

    ○ **A.** Check the voltage with a multimeter.

    ○ **B.** Check the battery indicator in the systray portion of the taskbar.

    ○ **C.** Disconnect the AC adapter and measure the time it takes for the system to fail.

    ○ **D.** Check the battery level in the Control Panel's ACPI applet.

50. Which of the following are functions of the Fn key on a notebook PC? (Select all that apply.)

Quick Answer: **81**
Detailed Answer: **88**

    ○ **A.** To access hidden functions on the hard drive

    ○ **B.** To access additional functions from the keyboard

    ○ **C.** To access additional display devices attached to the system

    ○ **D.** To access additional Windows features from the keyboard

51. A user complains that the screen on his laptop remains blank when he turns on his laptop. You see that the power light comes on and that the laptop does boot up. What should you do to enable the display?

Quick Answer: **81**
Detailed Answer: **88**

    ○ **A.** Press the Fn and Screen keys until the display appears

    ○ **B.** Attach an external monitor to the laptop

    ○ **C.** Make sure that the screen's video cable is plugged into the laptop

    ○ **D.** Check that the monitor is powered on

52. How do you normally add an external monitor to a notebook PC?

Quick Answer: **81**
Detailed Answer: **88**

- ○ **A.** Plug the external monitor into the external VGA connector and press the appropriate function key combination.
- ○ **B.** Turn off the notebook and plug the monitor into the external VGA connector; then restart the system.
- ○ **C.** Plug the external monitor into the external VGA connector and reboot the notebook until the external monitor is recognized.
- ○ **D.** Simply plug the external monitor into the external VGA connector, and the system will detect it.

53. You have a notebook computer that is producing a fuzzy, blurry image. What is the most likely cause?

Quick Answer: **81**
Detailed Answer: **88**

- ○ **A.** The notebook's video is not working in its native resolution.
- ○ **B.** LCDs cannot produce fuzzy images.
- ○ **C.** The wrong drivers have been installed for the video display and need to be replaced.
- ○ **D.** The notebook's video resolution is set incorrectly.

54. What should you do first to troubleshoot a laptop computer that has no display on the built-in LCD panel?

Quick Answer: **81**
Detailed Answer: **89**

- ○ **A.** Plug an external video monitor into the external VGA connector and redirect the video output to that port.
- ○ **B.** Restart the system, enter CMOS Setup, and ensure that the default, onboard video option is enabled.
- ○ **C.** Press the Fn key and F5 function key to redirect the video output to the LCD display.
- ○ **D.** Reboot the notebook until the internal display is recognized.

55. You just started a computer with Windows XP. However, every time you press a key, you get foreign letters and numbers on the screen. What would the cause of this be?

Quick Answer: **81**
Detailed Answer: **89**

- ○ **A.** Num Lock is engaged.
- ○ **B.** Caps Lock is engaged.
- ○ **C.** F Lock is engaged.
- ○ **D.** Scroll Lock is engaged.

56. The fan in your system intermittently makes a loud whining noise and then stops. What should you do?

- ○ **A.** The fan is typically louder when you first turn on the computer, and should not be heard after it starts.
- ○ **B.** Something was blocking the fan, which was finally blown out.
- ○ **C.** The fan is switched on and off automatically as the laptop warms up.
- ○ **D.** The fan has stopped completely and the laptop should be serviced before there is heat damage.

57. You have a laptop computer that has a built-in wireless network card. However, you cannot connect to your wireless network. What is the first thing you should check?

- ○ **A.** To determine whether TCP/IP has been configured in Windows
- ○ **B.** To determine whether the 802.11x wireless adapter is turned on
- ○ **C.** To determine whether the 802.11x antenna has been installed
- ○ **D.** To determine whether the SSID and WEP functions have been established

2.5 Given a scenario, integrate common preventative maintenance techniques

- ▶ Physical inspection
- ▶ Updates
  - ▶ Driver
  - ▶ Firmware
  - ▶ OS
  - ▶ Security
- ▶ Scheduling preventative maintenance
  - ▶ Defrag
  - ▶ Scandisk
  - ▶ Check disk
  - ▶ Startup programs
- ▶ Use of appropriate repair tools and cleaning materials
  - ▶ Compressed air
  - ▶ Lint free cloth
  - ▶ Computer vacuum and compressors

▶ Power devices

　▶ Appropriate source such as power strip, surge protector or UPS

▶ Ensuring proper environment

▶ Backup procedures

58. When you upgrade the firmware on a motherboard, what are you actually doing?

　○ **A.** Flashing the BIOS

　○ **B.** Replacing the CMOS chip

　○ **C.** Replacing the BIOS

　○ **D.** Resetting the CMOS

Quick Answer: **81**
Detailed Answer: **89**

59. What is the Windows Update website used for?

　○ **A.** To locate hardware updates for a computer

　○ **B.** To allow a technician to update the computer remotely

　○ **C.** To locate and install critical updates for the Windows operating system

　○ **D.** To archive updates for the Windows operating system

Quick Answer: **81**
Detailed Answer: **89**

60. Periodically, software vendors will bundle many software patches together. What is this package known as?

　○ **A.** Service Pack

　○ **B.** Containment Pack

　○ **C.** Critical Bundle

　○ **D.** Release Pack

Quick Answer: **81**
Detailed Answer: **89**

61. How do you configure all Windows XP computers to download and install updates at the same time each day?

　○ **A.** Open Automatic Updates from the Control Panel, select the Automatic (Recommended) radio button, and specify the time.

　○ **B.** Open Windows Updates on the Start menu, select the Automatic (Recommended) radio button, and specify the time.

　○ **C.** Open Automatic Updates in the Administrative Tools menu, select the Automatic (Recommended) radio button, and specify the time.

　○ **D.** Open Windows Update Scheduler in System Tools, select the Automatic (Recommended) radio button, and specify the time.

Quick Answer: **81**
Detailed Answer: **89**

62. You just installed Windows Vista on a new computer. Which Windows service automatically delivers security updates, critical updates, and service packs to help protect computers against viruses and other security threats?

Quick Answer: **81**
Detailed Answer: **90**

- ○ **A.** Windows WQHL
- ○ **B.** Automatic Updates
- ○ **C.** Add Windows Components/Updates
- ○ **D.** Windows Security Center

63. You just downloaded and installed Service Pack 2 for Windows XP. Now programs that access network resources no longer work. How can you fix the problem?

Quick Answer: **81**
Detailed Answer: **90**

- ○ **A.** Configure the Windows Firewall setting to permit the applications to access the network
- ○ **B.** Stop and restart the operating system's networking services one at a time
- ○ **C.** Simply reinstall SP2
- ○ **D.** Use the Add or Remove Programs utility to remove the new service pack

64. You have just installed a 500 GB hard drive in a Windows XP Professional machine. Unfortunately, when you try to access the drive, it recognizes only 137 GB of drive space. What are the most likely causes of this problem? (Choose all that apply.)

Quick Answer: **81**
Detailed Answer: **90**

- ○ **A.** The system needs a new HDD driver for Windows XP to handle this size drive.
- ○ **B.** The firmware on the HDD needs to be updated to work with Windows XP Pro.
- ○ **C.** The system needs to have Service Pack 1 (SP1) or higher installed to handle this size drive.
- ○ **D.** The system needs to have the BIOS flashed with a version that can accommodate the new drive.

65. What is the component that acts as a translator between a hardware device and the operating system?

Quick Answer: **81**
Detailed Answer: **90**

- ○ **A.** Service pack
- ○ **B.** Driver
- ○ **C.** File converter
- ○ **D.** DLL file

66. How do you update a driver in Windows XP?

   ○ **A.** Navigate Start, All Programs, Accessories, System Tools, System Configuration and then select the Upgrade Driver option from the menu.

   ○ **B.** Navigate Start, Control Panel, Add Hardware. The Hardware Wizard then detects the new driver and installs it.

   ○ **C.** Navigate Start, My Network Places, Connections, Properties and then click on the Update Driver button.

   ○ **D.** Navigate Start, Control Panel, System, Hardware tab, Device Manager and then expand the Network Adapters node. Select the desired network adapter, click on the Driver tab, and then click on the Update Driver button.

67. Which of the following Windows XP/Vista utilities can be used to keep a disk drive free of problems?

   ○ **A.** Disk Defragmenter

   ○ **B.** Disk Cleanup

   ○ **C.** Check Disk

   ○ **D.** All of the options provided are correct.

68. Your computer has become sluggish after months of use. Although you use your computer every day, you have not made any significant changes since you first purchased the computer. What can you do to improve performance by fixing the problem that has made your system slow?

   ○ **A.** Add more RAM

   ○ **B.** Upgrade the CPU

   ○ **C.** Defragment the hard drive

   ○ **D.** All of the options provided are correct

69. Which of the following commands would you enter at the command prompt in Windows XP Professional Service Pack 2 when you want to defragment the C drive?

   ○ **A.** DEFRAG C:

   ○ **B.** FDISK

   ○ **C.** SCANDISK

   ○ **D.** CHKDSK C: /F

70. What commands can you use to look at the available options for DEFRAG?

Quick Answer: **81**
Detailed Answer: **91**

- ○ **A.** DEFRAG /HELP
- ○ **B.** DEFRAG -f
- ○ **C.** DEFRAG /?
- ○ **D.** DEFRAG /H

71. You need to delete unused files on a Windows XP computer in order to free up extra hard drive space with as little effort as possible. Which utility should you use?

Quick Answer: **81**
Detailed Answer: **91**

- ○ **A.** Disk Cleanup
- ○ **B.** DEL
- ○ **C.** Scandisk
- ○ **D.** Disk Defragmenter

72. Which of the following tools can be used to correct corrupt file problems or disk errors?

Quick Answer: **81**
Detailed Answer: **91**

- ○ **A.** Regedit
- ○ **B.** Attrib
- ○ **C.** Scandisk
- ○ **D.** Fdisk

73. Where should a user create a shortcut to a program so that the program starts automatically for every person that logs into Windows XP Professional?

Quick Answer: **81**
Detailed Answer: **91**

- ○ **A.** Documents and Settings, Programs, Startup, All Users
- ○ **B.** Documents and Settings, All Users, Start Menu, Programs, Startup
- ○ **C.** Documents and Settings, Programs, All Users, Startup
- ○ **D.** Documents and Settings, All Users, Programs, Startup

74. Where should a user create a shortcut to a program so that the program starts automatically for every person that logs into Windows Vista?

Quick Answer: **81**
Detailed Answer: **91**

- ○ **A.** C:\Documents and Settings\Programs\Startup\All Users
- ○ **B.** C:\Users\All Users\Start Menu\Programs\Startup
- ○ **C.** C:\Documents and Settings\Programs\All Users\Startup
- ○ **D.** C:\Users\All Users\Programs\Startup

75. Which of the following tools allows a user to manage her computer system's configuration?

○ **A.** REGEDIT.EXE

○ **B.** SCANREG.EXE

○ **C.** MSCONFIG.EXE

○ **D.** Disk Management

76. What should you use to clean an LCD screen?

○ **A.** Mild soap and water

○ **B.** Ammonia-based solvent

○ **C.** Bleach or hydrogen peroxide

○ **D.** Alcohol-free cleaning fluid

77. What should you do FIRST when you need to clean a CRT monitor?

○ **A.** Wipe the screen with anti static cloth

○ **B.** Unplug the computer

○ **C.** Unplug the monitor

○ **D.** Spray the glass with ammonia based cleaner

78. What is the best type of cleaning tool for use on the exterior of
computers and peripheral components?

○ **A.** A vacuum cleaner

○ **B.** A damp cloth

○ **C.** A soft brush

○ **D.** A can of antistatic spray

79. What type of cleaning solution should be used on the exterior of
computer components?

○ **A.** Bleach and water

○ **B.** Window cleaner

○ **C.** Soap and water

○ **D.** Citrus-based cleaners

80. Which of the following is a good preventive maintenance procedure for hard disk drives?

○ **A.** Ensure unobstructed airflow around the hard drives to
reduce overheating.

○ **B.** Increase the disk cache to allow for larger page swap-
ping.

   ○ **C.** Clean regularly with anti-static cloth.

   ○ **D.** Upgrade the RAM to improve read/write performance.

81. To remove dust from inside a computer, which of the options below should the technician use? (Select two.)

   ○ **A.** Alcohol swabs

   ○ **B.** Compressed air

   ○ **C.** Gently blow the dust out

   ○ **D.** Vacuum the dust out of the system

Quick Answer: **81**
Detailed Answer: **92**

82. What product is recommended for manual cleaning of tape drive R/W heads?

   ○ **A.** Soft cloths

   ○ **B.** Cotton swabs

   ○ **C.** A pencil eraser

   ○ **D.** Foam swabs

Quick Answer: **81**
Detailed Answer: **92**

83. You live in a house with electrical power that is unstable, including frequent spikes and brownouts. Which should you use to protect your computer?

   ○ **A.** A power conditioner

   ○ **B.** A surge protector

   ○ **C.** A generator

   ○ **D.** An Uninterruptible Power Supply (UPS)

Quick Answer: **81**
Detailed Answer: **92**

84. What surge-suppressor rating describes how quickly its protective circuitry can react to changes in the incoming line and limit the amount of current that passes through?

   ○ **A.** Clamping voltage

   ○ **B.** Clamping speed

   ○ **C.** Filter value

   ○ **D.** Surge limiting

Quick Answer: **81**
Detailed Answer: **92**

85. Which of the following is a passive device that protects electrical components from spikes in the power line?

   ○ **A.** A power conditioner

   ○ **B.** A surge protector

   ○ **C.** A generator

   ○ **D.** An Uninterruptible Power Supply (UPS)

Quick Answer: **81**
Detailed Answer: **92**

86. The output of a UPS should be which of the following?

    ○ **A.** DC voltage

    ○ **B.** Sine wave

    ○ **C.** Square wave

    ○ **D.** Saw wave

Quick Answer: **81**
Detailed Answer: **93**

87. Which device uses a battery to supply clean power to a computer?

    ○ **A.** Surge protector

    ○ **B.** Power conditioner

    ○ **C.** UPS

    ○ **D.** Generator

Quick Answer: **81**
Detailed Answer: **93**

88. You find water dripping from the ceiling in the server room. Which of the following should you do first?

    ○ **A.** Notify building maintenance

    ○ **B.** Notify the network administrator

    ○ **C.** Place a note in the server room logbook

    ○ **D.** Immediately turn off the servers

Quick Answer: **81**
Detailed Answer: **93**

89. You want to perform a hardware upgrade. What should you do before you do the upgrade?

    ○ **A.** Back up all the data

    ○ **B.** Determine the amount of RAM available

    ○ **C.** Scan the hard disk for errors

    ○ **D.** Download the Latest BIOS and drivers for the existing components

Quick Answer: **81**
Detailed Answer: **93**

90. Which of the following is valuable and irreplaceable user data that should be included in a data backup strategy? (Select two.)

    ○ **A.** E-mail

    ○ **B.** Program Files

    ○ **C.** System files

    ○ **D.** My Documents

Quick Answer: **81**
Detailed Answer: **93**

91. What utilities can you use to back up the Registry? (Select two.)

    ○ **A.** Windows Registry Checker

    ○ **B.** System File Checker

    ○ **C.** System Restore

    ○ **D.** Scan Disk

Quick Answer: **81**
Detailed Answer: **93**

92. What can you use to create a restore point in Windows XP?

Quick Answer: **81**
Detailed Answer: **93**

- ○ **A.** Run the Backup application in System Tools
- ○ **B.** Run the System Restore application in System Tools
- ○ **C.** Run the Backup and Restore application in System Tools
- ○ **D.** Run the Disk Defragmenter application in System Tools

93. What do you use to back up a computer running Windows Vista?

Quick Answer: **81**
Detailed Answer: **93**

- ○ **A.** NT Backup
- ○ **B.** Backup and Restore Center
- ○ **C.** WINBackup
- ○ **D.** BACKUP.EXE

94. Which attribute is used to indicate that a file has been backed up or not?

Quick Answer: **81**
Detailed Answer: **93**

- ○ **A.** R
- ○ **B.** A
- ○ **C.** D
- ○ **D.** S

95. Which type of backup provides the fastest restore in case of a hard drive crash?

Quick Answer: **81**
Detailed Answer: **94**

- ○ **A.** Normal (full)
- ○ **B.** Incremental with differential
- ○ **C.** Normal (full) with incremental
- ○ **D.** Normal (full) with differential

96. After backing up a drive, you should occasionally do which of the following?

Quick Answer: **81**
Detailed Answer: **94**

- ○ **A.** Restore a nonessential file to the hard drive
- ○ **B.** Reformat the hard drive
- ○ **C.** Shutdown the system
- ○ **D.** Reformat the tape

97. Which type of backup job backs up only the files that have changed since the last backup job of any kind?

Quick Answer: **81**
Detailed Answer: **94**

- ○ **A.** Full
- ○ **B.** Differential
- ○ **C.** Incremental
- ○ **D.** Partial

98. Which backup method requires you to provide the full backup and a tape for each day you want to go back and restore?

Quick Answer: **81**
Detailed Answer: **94**

    ○ **A.** Full

    ○ **B.** Incremental

    ○ **C.** Differential

    ○ **D.** Copy

99. Which backup method requires you to provide the full backup and a tape and the last smaller backup to restore?

Quick Answer: **81**
Detailed Answer: **94**

    ○ **A.** Full

    ○ **B.** Incremental

    ○ **C.** Differential

    ○ **D.** Copy

Quick-Check Answer Key

1. D
2. A, C, and E
3. A
4. C
5. C
6. A and C
7. C
8. A
9. C
10. A
11. B
12. A
13. E
14. A
15. A
16. C
17. A and B
18. A and D
19. A, B, and C
20. A
21. B
22. C
23. C
24. B
25. A and E
26. B
27. D
28. A
29. A and C
30. A and B
31. D
32. C
33. D

34. A
35. D
36. B
37. A
38. C
39. A
40. A
41. B
42. A and D
43. B
44. A
45. A
46. D
47. C
48. C
49. C
50. B and C
51. A
52. A
53. A
54. A
55. A
56. D
57. B
58. A
59. C
60. A
61. A
62. B
63. A
64. C and D
65. B
66. D

67. D
68. C
69. A
70. A, C, and D
71. A
72. C
73. B
74. B
75. C
76. A
77. C
78. B
79. C
80. A
81. B and D
82. D
83. D
84. B
85. B
86. B
87. C
88. A
89. A
90. A and D
91. A and C
92. B
93. B
94. B
95. A
96. A
97. C
98. B
99. C

Answers and Explanations

1. **Answer: D.** Before you make a major change to the system, including upgrading a system, you should back up the system. In case there is a problem, you can restore the system to the original state. To upgrade to Windows Vista, not all systems needed to have the RAM (Answer A) upgraded or a new hard drive (Answer B) added. Lastly, the virus checker (Answer C) might need to be upgraded but it will be done after you install Windows Vista.

2. **Answer: A, C, and E.** You first want to understand the problem, which can be done by seeing the problem. You should also ask if any changes have been made recently to see if this is the cause of the problem. You should not add a new hard drive (Answer B) or back up the system (Answer D) until you understand the problem.

3. **Answer: A.** After you talk to the user experiencing the problem, the next logical step would be to gather information, including asking if any hardware or software that might have caused the problem has been added or changed. You should try to replicate the problem and what the user was doing at the time when the error first occurred. After you gather the information, you can isolate possible causes (Answer B), eliminate possibilities (Answer C), and document your findings and solutions (Answer D).

4. **Answer: C.** Isolating possible causes of the issue and eliminating possibilities usually follow after you have gathered information on the problem. This is where your knowledge on the different systems and configuration areas is important, as well as knowing the various tools and utilities used to troubleshoot and debug issues pertaining to these areas. Before you try to isolate the problem, you gather the information (Answer A) on the issue, including talking to the user who is experiencing the problems (Answer B). After you understand the problem, you isolate the possible causes. At the end, you document your findings and solutions (Answer D).

5. **Answer: C.** When you identify the problem, you should always check the obvious. For example, if a monitor will not come on, make sure it is turned on and plugged in. After you check the obvious, you can establish a plan to resolve the problem (Answer A). After the solution is found (Answer D), you can document your findings. Performing preventative maintenance (Answer B) should be done before the problem occurs in an attempt to stop the problem from occurring.

6. **Answer: A and C.** While multiple things can cause a blank screen, you should always check the obvious first, including making sure it is turned on and that it is plugged in. You should also check to see if the contrast or brightness is turned down. Checking the color settings (Answer B) will not help if the monitor is on or off. Answer D is incorrect because the type of computer is almost irrelevant.

7. **Answer: C.** After you identify the problem, you need to establish a theory of probable cause before you can test the theory to determine cause. Of course you should always check the obvious first. Backing up the system (Answer A) should have been done on a regular basis before the problem occurred or before you make a significant change. When the problem is fixed, you verify full system functionality (Answer D) to make sure that the problem is truly fixed and that the solution did not break anything else. At the end, you document the findings, actions, and outcomes (Answer B).

8. **Answer: A.** After you resolve the problem, you should verify the full system functionality to make sure that the system is truly fixed or that the fix did not break something else. While you are verifying full system functionality, you might perform a full system scan looking for other problems. After the system has been verified as operating properly, you document findings, actions, and outcomes (Answer B). Of course, as you leave, you should clean up after yourself (Answer C).

9. **Answer: C.** To complete the troubleshooting model, you need to document your findings, actions, and outcomes. This documentation allows you to find trends over a period of time and can be used when similar problems occur in the future. Of course, as good customer service, you clean up after yourself (Answer A), which is not part of the troubleshooting model. Verifying full system functionality is done after a solution has been implemented (Answer D).

10. **Answer: A.** After your first or previous theory and its solution, you should come up with a new theory and then try to test that theory. You perform a full system scan (Answer B) as part of verifying full system functionality (Answer D). You document findings, actions, and outcomes (Answer C) after you have fixed the problem.

11. **Answer: B.** The Blue Screen of Death is known as a stop error displayed by Windows. It occurs when the kernel or a driver running in kernel mode encounters an error from which it cannot recover. It is caused by poorly written device drivers, malfunctioning hardware, or poorly written DLLs. An unrecoverable application error (Answer C) was produced in earlier versions of Windows, such as Windows 3.0. A kernel excursion relates to a Linux system. A virus warning (Answer D) might cause a wide range of symptoms and messages, and it is possible that a virus can cause a Blue Screen of Death.

12. **Answer: A.** When the computer freezes up, it becomes unresponsive. The only solution is to reboot the computer. Computer freezes can be caused by poorly written device drivers, malfunctioning hardware, poorly written DLLs, or poorly written software. It can also be caused because the processor is running at 100% processor utilization, which will usually release itself when its work is done. A Blue Screen of Death (BSOD—Answer B) is a basic text screen with a blue background. Overheating (Answer C) could cause the computer to freeze. A killdump is usually associated with UNIX machines.

13. **Answer: E.** Automatic reboot, complete lock/system lock-up, blank screen, and Blue Screen of Death are all typical indications of boot process failure.

14. **Answer: A.** Because you just installed the new software, it is most likely the cause of the problem. Most likely the software loads some component during start up that is causing a problem. A corruption of the boot sector (Answer B) or a volume boot sector (Answer D) would probably cause Windows not to boot up or even start. A corrupt driver (Answer C) could cause Windows to stop booting. However, because you made a recent change by installing the program, it would be your number one suspect.

15. **Answer: A.** The most likely cause of strange characters or programming code printed while printing a document is due to an incorrect print driver. A bad cable (Answer B), bad printer (Answer C), and electromagnetic interference (EMI—Answer D) can cause strange characters but not programming code.

16. **Answer: C.** When a system overheats, the machine might reboot, shut down, lock up, or starting given random errors. A virus (Answer A) can cause a range of symptoms, including locking up a computer after 15 minutes of being on, but the more likely cause is overheating, especially if it is always after 15 minutes. Electromagnetic interference (Answer B) and electrical spikes (Answer D) can cause the machine to lock up, but the more likely cause is still overheating, especially if it is always after 15 minutes.

17. **Answer: A and B.** If you look at your print queue, you will see the documents are still sitting in the print queue. Either the computer cannot communicate with the printer for some reason, including if the printer is shut off or the print spool is stalled. If the system is overheating (Answer C), there will be a few different symptoms, including it locking up or rebooting. Electromagnetic interference (EMI—Answer D) might cause system lock up or the system to reboot, but it would not cause the printer to stall or not communicate.

18. **Answer: A and D.** Because the hard drive and fan spin at a high number of revolutions per minute and they are mechanical parts, they can generate loud-pitched whining sounds when they start to wear out. The RAM (Answer B) and motherboard (Answer C) are electronic components without mechanical components. Therefore, they do not generate loud-pitched whining sounds.

19. **Answer: A, B, and C.** When a system starts to overheat, an excessively warm case or a burned smell can be a symptom of overheating. It can also cause the computer to lock up and to generate strange errors. While the overheating can cause problems with the hard drive, if files start to disappear (Answer D), you should suspect a virus.

20. **Answer: A.** The system power-on light indicates that the machine is on and it is receiving power. Therefore, if the light is not on, you should check to make sure the machine is turned on and receiving power. That would also mean making sure the machine is plugged in, any surge protector is turned on, and the AC wall plug is turned on. Viruses (Answer B), Blue Screen of Death (Answer C), and problems with the startup program are software problems, which would at least allow the computer to turn on.

21. **Answer: B.** When a hard drive is always running, your computer will probably act erratic or sluggish. Therefore, the disk system is working too hard. The hard drive light does not usually indicate if the hard drive has power most of the time (Answer A). If the hard drive does have a power problem, it would be disconnected and would not reconnect without a reboot. If the hard drive is connected intermittently (Answer C), it would probably cause the drive light to shut off. Lastly, by looking at the light, you cannot determine if the hard drive is running too fast (Answer D). It will only tell you if it is powered on or is reading/writing.

22. **Answer: C.** POST is short for Power-On Self Test. Before the video system is turned on, it will test basic functionality of the system. If a problem is found, it will give a series of beeps to identify the problem. While you can insert a POST card into an expansion slot that can be used to identify a problem, nothing will show up on the monitor to show the numeric codes (Answer A). You cannot read POST electrical signals except with the POST card (Answer B). Because the system has not booted, you cannot load a POST software diagnostic package if one did exist.

23. **Answer: C.** If the computer boots properly, it will give a single beep. The beep codes only indicate a problem when there is a problem found before the video system is activated. Because there is no problem, the other answers are incorrect.

24. **Answer: B.** If no video or audio codes appear, you can place a special expansion card into a socket called a POST card. Before every action is taken during bootup, a code is sent that can be read and displayed by the POST card. If the system fails during boot, the code will indicate which action it failed on. You can then look up the code based on the BIOS manufacturer to determine what the failure was. Therefore, the other answers are incorrect.

25. **Answer: A and E.** If the computer does not boot and there is nothing displayed on the screen, the problem is most likely with the motherboard, processor, or RAM. If a hard drive (Answer B) or the CD-ROM drive (Answer C) fails, usually something will be displayed on the screen unless one of those devices shorts out the system. If the power supply (Answer D) fails, usually you will not hear any beeps either.

26. **Answer: B.** Two short beeps on a system with AMI BIOS indicates a parity error and three short beeps indicate a base memory read/write error. Both of these beep codes indicate a memory problem. Therefore, the other answers are incorrect.

27. **Answer: D.** When a self-test failure or setup mismatch is encountered, the BIOS might indicate the error through a blank screen, a visual error message on the video display, or an audio response (beep codes) produced by the system's speaker. For example, the beep code message produced by one BIOS manufacturer's devices is "eight beeps indicate a video adapter memory error." Replace the video card. If the USB adapter (Answer B) or power supply fails (Answer C), you will usually not get a beep code. If the hard drive fails (Answer A), it will not cause a beep code to occur.

28. **Answer: A.** You have a missing operating system when the computer fails to locate a boot sector with an operating system installed on any of its disks. A memory size error (Answer B) or a missing or malfunctioning keyboard (Answer C) are POST errors that would show up before Windows loads. If a video card driver cannot be found (Answer D) while Windows loads it will not cause a non-system disk or disk error.

29. **Answer: A and C.** NTLDR is a file necessary during the boot process. If it is missing or corrupted, Windows XP will not be able to boot. The BOOT.INI determines which partition or volume to boot from and can be used to display a boot menu. The Config.sys (Answer B) and Autoexec.bat (Answer D) files are associated with the older DOS and Windows 9X operating systems.

30. **Answer: A and B.** When you need to know how to configure a device, you should always check the user or installation manual that came with the device or check the manufacturer's website. Training material (Answer C) and diagnostic software (Answer D) would not show specific jumper settings.

31. **Answer: D.** If the printer operation stalls during the printing operation, you should first access the print spooler's Document menu and try to restart the printer. If the printer still does not print, delete backed-up spool files (.SPL and .TMP) in the %SystemRoot%\System32\Spool\Printers directory. Begin by simply deleting the first print job to determine whether it is the source of the problem. If so, it is likely that the other print jobs will go ahead and print and allow your print job to process. Also, make sure that you have plenty of free disk space to handle the print jobs. If the printer is on, it should be ready to accept print jobs from the queue. Turning the printer on or off (Answer A) is not correct because for whatever the reason, the print jobs are not getting forwarded to the printer. Of course, you should see if the printer is on and con-

nected. Answer B is incorrect because sending print jobs directly to the printer will not fix the problem with the print queue and you do not get the benefits of using a print queue. Answer C is incorrect because deleting all print jobs and resending the print jobs will not fix the problem with the print queue.

32. **Answer: C.** You can attempt to restart a stalled print spooler by entering `net start spooler` at the command prompt or using the Run option (Click the Start button, select Run, type in the command, and pressing Enter). The other commands will not work.

33. **Answer: D.** The print queue structure allows multiple files to be loaded to a print server for printing (which might or might not be located with the physical print device). Closing the print window does not interrupt the print queue in Windows. The print jobs in the queue are completed unless they are deleted from the list. The print manager (Answer A) is a software component that allows you to access print jobs and manage them. The print spooler (Answer B) is the software component that queues the print jobs. The print buffer (Answer C) would be a component of the printer to hold and process print jobs.

34. **Answer: A.** Windows employs a print spooler processing architecture that controls the flow of information between the host computer and the physical printer. In a local printing operation, the spooler consists of the logical blocks between the client computer and the print device. These blocks process threads in the background and pass them to the printer when it is ready to receive data. In essence, the application prints to the Windows printer driver, the driver controls the operation of the spooler, and the driver prints to the printer from the spooler. In a network printing operation, the print spooler must run on both the local server and remote client systems. The information passes from the remote client spooler to the print server's spooler, which manages the local printing for everyone sending print jobs to that printer. The Print Manager (Answer B) provides an interface to manage the print jobs. The print buffer (Answer C) is a component of the printer to hold and process print jobs. Answer D is a storage area for print jobs in Windows.

35. **Answer: D.** If a printer is not printing in Windows, check the print spooler to see whether it causes the problem. Select the Print Directly to the Printer option on the Advanced tab of the printer's properties page. If the print job goes through, there is a spooler problem. If not, the hardware and printer driver are suspect. Scandisk (Answer A) will not print any reports. LPTx (Answer B) indicates parallel ports, which are not as commonly used today. Instead, most local printers are USB. Changing the printer cable (Answer C) will not send a print job to the printer.

36. **Answer: B.** From the printer's properties window, select Spool Settings and select the Print Directly to the Printer option. If the print job goes through, there is a spooler problem. If not, the hardware and printer driver are suspect. To check spooler problems, examine the system for adequate hard disk space and memory. Also try canceling the top print job in the spooler and then try to print again. If an Enhanced Metafile (EMF) Spooling option is selected in the Print Processor page, change it to a RAW format option and try printing again. The driver (Answer C) does not normally go bad in the middle of printing. In addition, the printer port does not disable itself (Answer D) in the middle of operations. The cable could have gone bad (Answer A); typically that happens if someone did something such as ran over it or accidentally pull it out.

37. **Answer: A.** Normally, if a printer is not producing anything in a Windows environment even though print jobs have been sent to it, you should check the print spooler to see whether any particular type of error has occurred. To view documents waiting to be printed, you double-click on the desired printer's icon. While viewing the print spooler queue, you should check to make certain that the printer has not been set to Pause Printing. In this scenario, the customer is trying to print to an inkjet printer, but only a laser printer has been defined for use. You must use the Add Printer Wizard to add and define the local inkjet printer in the local computer's Printers and Faxes list. Because the driver has not been loaded and the printer has not been defined, it will not know how to print to the printer. Therefore, the other answers are incorrect.

38. **Answer: C.** Because this is a new installation, before you leave the office, you should verify that the printer installation runs correctly from the host computer through to the printer. In the case of a network-ready printer, you should verify that the customer can print from different locations in the network. Running a test page from the printer (Answer A) will not test connectivity. Giving the customer a bill (Answer D) is not part of the installation process. Resetting the printer's page counter (Answer B) is not an installation step and is not an available option for many printers.

39. **Answer: A.** To print a test page using Windows, open the Printers in the Control Panel. Right-click the printer and select Properties. On the General tab, click the Print Test Page. The other options are not viable options to print test pages.

40. **Answer: A.** There are three main printer permissions: print, manage printer, and manage documents. To print documents, you only need the print permission. Therefore, the other answers are incorrect.

41. **Answer: B.** There are three main printer permissions: print, manage printers, and manage documents. To manage the print queue, including deleting any documents from the print queue, a user needs the manage documents permission. If you have the print permissions, you can delete your own print jobs, but you cannot delete other print jobs. Therefore, the other answers are incorrect.

42. **Answer: A and D.** Of the four devices listed, the modem and network interface card has multiple light indicators indicating that you have a connection. The serial port (Answer B) and parallel port (Answer C) do not have light indicators.

43. **Answer: B.** If you don't have the proper driver, if you accidentally press the track pad while typing, the cursor will jump to where the mouse pointer is, causing you to type in a different location. To avoid this, you need to load the proper driver for the track pad, which disables the tap feature of the track pad while you are typing. Answer A is incorrect because the track pad is already on. Because this is a track pad problem, you don't have to replace the keyboard driver (Answer C) or replace the keyboard (Answer D).

44. **Answer: A.** Laptop components are made to consume less power and produce less heat. As an end result, components that consume less power means longer battery life. Also, components that produce less heat means a smaller cooling system. While laptop components are sometimes smaller (Answer B) than their desktop equivalent, this is not always true. In addition, while lower clock speed (clock speed and front side bus speed) might consume less power and produce less heat, it is not always the goal of laptop components. The clock speed (Answer B), amount of L2 cache and clock speed (Answer C), and front side bus speed (Answer D) might be lower on laptop computers so that it will have lower power consumption and less heat production.

45. **Answer: A.** When a processor does not run at full speed, it usually means that it is being throttled so that it does not consume as much battery leading to longer battery life. While the jumpers (Answer C) could be wrong (a problem that is becoming less common) and the wrong processor (Answer B) could be installed, it is unlikely. Hyper-Threading (Answer D) deals with logical processors and does not affect processor clock speed.

46. **Answer: D.** If the battery is stored for long periods of time, you should fully discharge the battery and store it at normal room temperature. Therefore, the other answers are incorrect.

47. **Answer: C.** Lithium is a light metal that has high electrochemical potential. Because lithium itself is unstable, lithium-ion batteries are made from lithium ions produced from chemicals. Therefore, the other answers are incorrect.

48. **Answer: C.** To correct battery memory problems, you must start the portable computer using only the battery and allow it to run until it completely discharges the battery and quits. Then recharge the battery for at least 12 hours. Repeat this process several times, watching for consistently increasing operating times. Placing a battery in a charger (Answer A) or keeping it connected to AC will not fix the battery problem. Lastly, don't cook your batteries (Answer D).

49. **Answer: C.** The system shutting down earlier than normal indicates that either the battery is bad or that it is having a battery memory problem in which it becomes internally conditioned to run for less time than the designed capacity. You should check the battery with a multimeter (Answer A), but that would not tell you how well it holds the charge. Software (Answers B and D) cannot fully and reliably report if a battery is good or bad.

50. **Answers: B and C.** The portable keyboard normally contains an Fn function key. This key activates special functions in the portable, such as display brightness and contrast. Other common Fn functions include Suspend mode activation and LCD/external-CRT device selection. Therefore, the other answers are incorrect. The Fn key does not access hidden functions on the hard drive. Although the Fn key does not access Windows features, there are usually other keys on the keyboard such as the Windows key that can be used to access Windows features.

51. **Answer: A.** By pressing the Fn and screen keys, you can toggle between external monitor, LCD screen, and both. Because lights come on, the system looks like it is booting. Therefore, you are hoping that the screen is redirected. Because it looks like the laptop turns on, it just needs to have the laptop monitor activated. So you do not have to plug in an external monitor (Answer B). Because laptops have their monitors built in, you don't have to worry about if the screen's video cable is plugged in or if it is turned on.

52. **Answer: A.** Most portables offer standard connectors to enable full-size keyboards and VGA monitors to be plugged in. The portable's Fn key can be used to redirect the video output to the external VGA port. You do not need to turn off (Answer B) or reboot (Answer C) to connect a second monitor. Answer D is incorrect because when you need to connect an external monitor, you need to press the Fn key to activate it.

53. **Answer: A.** If the display image has more pixels than the display's actual number of pixels, it loses some of its picture information and sharpness. On the other hand, if the image has fewer pixels than the display, you see all the pixels displayed, but there is no

increased quality because of the additional resolution capabilities of the display. The additional picture elements added to fill in the image might make it look worse. If the wrong drivers are installed (Answer C), you would not be able to correctly access certain video modes, it would not turn on or you would get odd sizes. If you choose the wrong video resolution (Answer D), nothing appears on the screen or you get odd sizes.

54. **Answer: A.** If you are having problems with the built-in LCD display, you should plug an external monitor into the external VGA port and redirect the video output there to see if the system can display an image. This allows you to determine whether the video problem is in the LCD display or in the built-in video display adapter circuitry. You should also check the brightness and contrast settings. Entering the CMOS setup program (Answer B) could cause the problem but is highly unlikely. By pressing the Fn key (Answer C), you can toggle between internal and external monitors. Of course, you will have to connect the external monitor before you can test to see if the video portion of the laptop works. Rebooting (Answer D) will most likely not fix the problem and will not help you troubleshoot the problem.

55. **Answer: A.** When you start getting strange characters, you should always check to see if your Num Lock is engaged. If it is always enabled after you start your computer, you can usually disable it in the BIOS setup program. Caps Lock (Answer B) would give you uppercase characters instead of lowercase characters. F lock (Answer C) is used for special computer functions such as monitor brightness, toggling between internal monitor and external monitors and hardware volume. Scroll Lock (Answer D) is used with the numeric keypad.

56. **Answer: D.** If a fan makes a loud whining noise it means that it is about to fail. If the noise stops, it most likely means that the fan has completely failed. Although some systems might have thermal control, a fan should not make loud whining noises when it is turned on. Therefore Answers A and C are incorrect. Something blocking the fan (Answer B) would not typically cause a noise. Of course, your system would most likely be running hotter than normal.

57. **Answer: B.** You should make sure that the wireless adapter is turned on (check the obvious). Because it is built-in, you should look for an on-off switch for the wireless card or an Fn key. Some laptops might also have it enabled using the BIOS setup program. Therefore the other answers are incorrect.

58. **Answer: A.** Firmware is software that is contained within ROM chips. It generally can be thought of as the instincts of the computer because it has the lowest level of instructions for controlling hardware. When you upgrade firmware, you are flashing the BIOS. Therefore, the other answers are incorrect.

59. **Answer: C.** Although Windows Updates can have many updates, it is designed to locate and install critical updates including security patches. Therefore, the other answers are incorrect.

60. **Answer: A.** Service Packs are software packages that contain multiple patches that are released by manufacturers. Therefore, the other answers are incorrect.

61. **Answer: A.** By configuring Automatic Updates, you can specify the time to install the updates. Automatic Updates is accessed through the Control Panel. Therefore, the other answers are incorrect.

62. **Answer: B.** You can configure Windows to automatically check the Windows Update Service. Enabling the Automatic Updates feature causes Windows to routinely check for updates. These updates include Security Updates, Critical Updates, and Service Packs. Therefore, the other answers are incorrect.

63. **Answer: A.** Windows XP Service Pack 2 includes several new security features, including the Windows Firewall. By default, the Windows Firewall service blocks all connection requests initiated from outside its network. Therefore, the other answers are incorrect because the new firewall is most likely the cause of the problem.

64. **Answer: C and D.** When you install a new larger hard drive in a system, a BIOS might not recognize its full capacity. The most common reason for this is that the system's BIOS version does not support the size of the new drive and reverts to its maximum support capabilities. You might need to flash the BIOS with the latest upgrade version to support the new drive. You might also gain additional support by updating the operating system with the latest patches and service packs. In the case of Windows XP Professional, the move to Service Pack 1 (SP1) increased the capability of Windows to handle larger drives beyond 137 GB. Windows XP does not have to have a new driver to work with larger drives and the firmware should already work with Windows XP (Answer D).

65. **Answer: B.** A driver acts as a translator between hardware and software. However, you must have the correct driver for the hardware item to work. For example, a driver for one printer most likely won't work for another printer. Therefore, the other answers are incorrect.

66. **Answer: D.** You can use Device Manager to identify installed ports, update device drivers, and change I/O settings, as well as troubleshoot device driver issues. To update a driver in Device Manager, select the network adapter entry that needs to be updated, click its Driver tab, and click the Driver Update button. Therefore, the other answers are incorrect.

67. **Answer: D.** The Check Disk utility (Answer C) will check for errors with the disk. The Disk Defragmenter (Answer A) will optimize the disk by reorganizing files on the disk so that they will not be spread throughout the disk. The Disk Cleanup utility is used to help free up disk space. If the hard drive fills up, a wide range of problems can occur. The Disk Defragmenter is used to keep a drive performing well by keeping files together rather than spreading them throughout the disk. Disk Cleanup (Answer B) is used to keep the hard drive free of unnecessary files.

68. **Answer: C.** A disk becomes fragmented where files are spread throughout the drive. When the files are spread throughout a disk rather than being in a single place, the system becomes slower for read/writes. To overcome this problem, you should regularly defragment the hard drive. Adding more RAM (Answer A) or installing a faster processor (Answer B) will often make Windows run better, but because the system got slower over time the problem is most likely because the hard drive got defragmented.

69. **Answer: A.** The command to start a Defrag is the DEFRAG command. In addition to DEFRAG, you must also specify the drive letter. The FDISK command (Answer B) is used to partition a drive. Scandisk (Answer C) and Chkdsk (Answer D) are used to look for and fix disk errors.

70. Answer: A, C, and D. Explanation: DEFRAG /?, DEFRAG /H, and DEFRAG /HELP all display a list of switches that are used with the DEFRAG command. The list includes the correct switch that would allow the technician to force defragmentation even though the free space on the hard disk is low. The -f (Answer B) is used to force a defragment when you have low disk space.

71. Answer: A. The Disk Cleanup will search a hard drive looking for ways to free up disk space. The DEL command (Answer B) is used to manually delete files at a command prompt. Scandisk (Answer C) is used to find and fix errors on the disk. Disk Defragmenter (Answer D) is used to optimize the disk after files have been spread throughout a disk.

72. Answer: C. You can use the Windows Scandisk utility to correct corrupt file problems or disk errors, such as cross-linked files. Regedit (Answer A) is used to edit the Windows Registry. The ATTRIB command (Answer B) is used to change the file's attributes such as read-only or hidden. FDISK (Answer D) is used to partition a hard drive at the command prompt.

73. Answer: B. If a shortcut is placed in the Startup folder, it will automatically execute when a user logs in. For it to affect all users, it would have to be in the All Users start-up folder. To affect only one user, it would be placed under an individual user's startup folder. Therefore, the other answers are incorrect.

74. Answer: B. If a shortcut is placed in the Startup folder, it will automatically execute when a user logs in. For it to affect all users, it would have to be in the All Users start-up folder. To affect only one user, it would be placed under an individual user's startup folder. Because it is Windows Vista, the folder is located under the C:\Users folder. Windows XP uses the C:\Documents and Settings folder. Therefore, the other answers are incorrect.

75. Answer: C. The MSCONFIG.EXE tool can be used to manage a computer system's configuration. It can be used to configure what services and programs start when Windows starts. Regedit (Answer A) is used to manage the Windows registry. Scanreg (Answer B) is a legacy tool used to clean up and correct problems with the Windows registry. Disk Management (Answer D) is part of the Microsoft Management Console (MMC) that allows you to manage disks.

76. Answer: A. When cleaning an LCD screen, you should use mild soap and water, which will not damage the screen or leave a film on the screen. Ammonia-based solvents (Answer B), bleach, hydrogen peroxide (Answer C), and cleaning fluid (Answer D)—unless specifically made to clean an LCD screen—could damage the LCD screen or the film on it that reduces glare.

77. Answer: C. When doing maintenance, you should always think safety first. Therefore, you should unplug the monitor before you clean it to avoid electrocution. The other answers are incorrect.

78. Answer: B. A damp cloth is easily the best general-purpose cleaning tool for use with computer equipment. A vacuum cleaner (Answer A), soft brush (Answer C), and can of antistatic spray (Answer D) will not remove grime from the computer case or other components. Instead, they can only remove dust or small particles.

79. **Answer: C.** Outer-surface cleaning can be accomplished with a simple soap-and-water solution, followed by a wipe down with a damp cloth. Care should be taken to make sure that none of the liquid splashes or drips into the inner parts of the system. The other options—bleach, Window cleaner, and citrus-based cleaners—might ruin the finish of the exterior of computer components or the computer case.

80. **Answer: A.** When performing maintenance inside a computer, you should make sure there is good air flow throughout the system. If too much dust accumulates, air flow will be hampered, which causes heat backup. Increasing the disk cache (Answer B) is not usually done today because the disk cache is built into the hard drive. An anti-static cloth (Answer C) might be one of the tools you use but you will most likely use a can of compressed air. Answer D is incorrect because although RAM might make the system faster, it might also make the drives last longer or run more reliably indirectly by decreasing overall disk reads and writes because less paging is needed. Keeping the hard drive from overheating is the best answer.

81. **Answer: B and D.** To remove dust from inside the computer, you should use compressed air or a vacuum. If you choose a vacuum, you need to choose one that is designed not to emit electrostatic discharge. Anything with liquid is a bad idea, including alcohol (Answer A). Gently blowing the dust out (Answer C) will be more efficiently done with a special vacuum cleaner or a can of compressed air.

82. **Answer: D.** To manually clean read/write heads, use isopropyl alcohol on a foam swab. Soft cloths (Answer A) and cotton swabs (Answer B) can shed fibers that can contaminate the drive and damage portions of its R/W head. Answer C is incorrect because a pencil eraser could damage the head and would not remove the dirt and grime that needs to be removed.

83. **Answer: D.** An Uninterruptible Power Supply (UPS) system is a backup power system that utilizes batteries to provide short-term power when power losses such as a black out or a brownout are detected. It also will protect against spikes because it provides clean power. A power conditioner (Answer A) will only protect against brownouts. A surge protector (Answer B) will only protect against spikes and not protect against brownouts. A generator (Answer C) is used to provide power after a blackout. To use the generator, you need to start the generator so that it starts providing power. In addition, generators are typically more expensive.

84. **Answer: B.** The surge suppressor's clamping speed rating describes how quickly it can react to changes in the incoming power level and act to minimize it. The clamping voltage (Answer A) is the maximum amount of voltage that a surge protector will allow through before it will suppress the power surge. The filter value (Answer C) specifies how much noise it filters. Surge limiting (Answer D) is the maximum amount that the surge protector will suppress or protect against.

85. **Answer: B.** Surge protectors are passive devices that are used to protect electrical components from spikes in the power line. Surge protectors usually utilize Metal Oxide Varistors (MOVs) to shunt the voltage spike to ground. A power condition (Answer A) will protect against noise and brownouts. A generator (Answer C) is used to provide backup after a blackout has occurred. A UPS (Answer D) is used to provide clean AC power and is used to protect against blackouts.

86. **Answer: B.** The UPS should output the same power that it gets from an AC outlet. Therefore, it should be a sine wave. The other answers are incorrect.

87. **Answer: C.** A UPS uses a battery connected in series (AC power is connected to UPS, which is connected to the computer) so that it is always supplying power to the computer. If power goes out or fluctuates, the battery will still supply clean power. A surge protector (Answer A) protects against a spike while a power conditioner (Answer B) is used to eliminate noise and protect against brownouts. Generators (Answer D) are used to provide power after a blackout has occurred.

88. **Answer: A.** The presence of water from any kind of leak should always be a concern. Therefore, you should contact building maintenance to get the leak fixed and possibly shutdown and move any systems that could be damaged. Notifying the network administrator (Answer B), placing a note in the server room logbook (Answer C), or turning off the servers (Answer D) will not help fix the leak.

89. **Answer: A.** You should always back up data to ensure that no user data would be lost if a major problem occurs. Therefore, the other answers are incorrect.

90. **Answer: A and D.** When you need to back up a Windows computer, you should back up My Documents and E-mail. You should also check your Desktop to see if anything is there that you need to back up. Although program files (Answer B) and system files (Answer C) are important, they don't change as much as data files and emails, and program files and system files can always be reinstalled.

91. **Answer: A and C.** The Windows Registry contains configuration settings for Windows and most of the Windows applications. While the Windows Registry Checker can be used to check the Registry for consistency, you can also back it up. You can use the System Restore to create restore points, which would include the Registry. System File Checker (Answer B) is used to check certain Windows system files used with the Windows File Protection feature and not the registry. Scan Disk (Answer D) is used to find and fix disk problems.

92. **Answer: B.** System restore takes a snapshot of all Windows configurations including the registry. If a problem occurs when installing a driver or program, you could restore to the Restore Point. Backups (Answers A and C) are used to back up an entire system or certain folders or files. The Disk Defragmenter (Answer D) application is used to optimize a disk by keeping files together instead of spreading them through the disk.

93. **Answer: B.** The Backup and Restore Center is a backup/restore application found on Windows Vista that can be easily configured to periodically back up files on users' computers. NT Backup (Answer A) is used in Windows 2000 and Windows XP. WINBackup (Answer C) and Backup.exe (Answer D) are not included with current Windows systems.

94. **Answer: B.** When you back up a program, it usually shuts off the archive (A) attribute to indicate it has been backed up. When a file is changed or a new file is added, the archive attribute is turned off. The read-only (R) attribute (Answer A) indicates if a file is read-only. The Directory (D) attribute (Answer C) indicates if an entry is a directory or not. The System (S) attribute (Answer D) indicates whether a file is a system file.

95. Answer: A. The normal (full) backup contains a single backup of everything. Therefore, if you need to do a restore, you only need the normal (full) backup. The normal with incremental backup (Answer C) needs two or more restore tapes (the full plus each incremental in sequential order) to get a system up and running. A normal with differential (Answer D) requires two restore tapes (the full plus the last differential). You should not mix incremental with differentials (Answer B).

96. Answer: A. You should occasionally restore a nonessential file so that you can test the backups and the backup hardware to make sure they are working properly. Reformatting the hard drives (Answer B), reformatting the tapes (Answer D), or shutting down the system (Answer C) does not allow the tapes or tape backups to run any better.

97. Answer: C. An incremental backup only backs up the files with the archive attribute on. Therefore, it backs up only files that are new or changed since the last backup. A full backup (Answer A) backs up all files regardless of whether they have been backed up or not. A differential backup (Answer B) backs up any files that have changed since the last full backup. There is no such thing as partial backup (Answer D).

98. Answer: B. When you use incremental backups, you perform a full backup, followed by several incremental backups. The incremental backups only back up the files that have the archive attribute on. When you need to do a restore, you need to restore the full backup followed in order by each incremental backup since the full was last done. When you use only full backups (Answer A), you just need to restore the single full backup. If you use differential backups with full backup (Answer C), you need to restore the full backup and the most recent differential backup. The copy backup (Answer D) backs up all files specified, but it does not change the attributes that would change the backup schemes you already have in place. A copy backup is usually done when you are about to upgrade or change a system.

99. Answer: C. When you use differential backups, you perform a full backup followed by differential backups. The differential backups only back up the files with the archive attribute on. In this way it is different from incremental backup because it does not shut off the archive attribute. When you do another differential backup, it will back up those files previously backed up with a differential backup. When you need to do a restore, you need to restore the full backup followed by the most recent differential backup. When you use only full backups (Answer A), you just need to restore the single full backup. When you use incremental backups (Answer B), you perform a full backup, followed by several incremental backups. The incremental backups only back up the files with the archive attribute on. When you need to do a restore, you need to restore the full backup followed in order by each incremental backup since the full backup was last done. The copy backup (Answer D) will back up all files specified, but it does not change the attributes that would change the backup schemes you already have in place. It is usually done when you are about to upgrade or change a system.

CHAPTER THREE

Operating System and Software

The previous domains covered basic hardware. While hardware is what makes a computer run, you need an operating system to put it all together. It is the operating system that coordinates all the hardware components and gives you an interface to tell the computer what you want to do. Therefore, you need to understand the most common operating system, Microsoft Windows.

This domain for the 220-701 exam counts as 20%. The given objectives for this domain are as follows:

▶ 3.1—Compare and contrast the different Windows Operating Systems and their features

▶ 3.2—Given a scenario, demonstrate proper use of user interfaces

▶ 3.3—Explain the process and steps to install and configure the Windows OS

▶ 3.4—Explain the basics of boot sequences, methods, and startup utilities

3.1 Compare and contrast the different Windows Operating Systems and their features

▶ Windows 2000, Windows XP 32-bit vs. 64-bit, Windows Vista 32-bit vs. 64-bit

  ▶ Side bar, Aero, UAC, minimum system requirements, system limits

  ▶ Windows 2000 and newer upgrade paths and requirements

  ▶ Terminology (32-bit vs. 64-bit, x86 vs. x64)

  ▶ Application compatibility, installed program locations (32-bit vs. 64-bit), Windows compatibility mode

▶ User interface, start bar layout

1. What is the minimum amount of RAM needed to install Windows XP Professional?

Quick Answer: **122**
Detailed Answer: **123**

- ○ **A.** 64 MB
- ○ **B.** 128 MB
- ○ **C.** 256 MB
- ○ **D.** 512 MB

2. What is the minimum amount of RAM needed to install Windows Vista Home Basic Edition?

Quick Answer: **122**
Detailed Answer: **123**

- ○ **A.** 256 MB
- ○ **B.** 512 MB
- ○ **C.** 1 GB
- ○ **D.** 2 GB

3. What is the minimum amount of RAM needed to install Windows Vista Ultimate Edition?

Quick Answer: **122**
Detailed Answer: **123**

- ○ **A.** 256 MB
- ○ **B.** 512 MB
- ○ **C.** 1 GB
- ○ **D.** 2 GB

4. What is the minimum free disk space you need to install Windows XP?

Quick Answer: **122**
Detailed Answer: **123**

- ○ **A.** 1.5 GB
- ○ **B.** 5 GB
- ○ **C.** 10 GB
- ○ **D.** 20 GB

5. What is the minimum free disk space required to install Windows Vista?

Quick Answer: **122**
Detailed Answer: **123**

- ○ **A.** 5 GB
- ○ **B.** 10 GB
- ○ **C.** 15 GB
- ○ **D.** 20 GB

6. What is the maximum amount of RAM that Windows XP Professional supports?

Quick Answer: 122
Detailed Answer: 123

- ○ **A.** 1 GB
- ○ **B.** 2 GB
- ○ **C.** 4 GB
- ○ **D.** 8 GB

7. What is the maximum amount of memory that Windows Vista Home Basic (32-bit) recognizes?

Quick Answer: 122
Detailed Answer: 123

- ○ **A.** 1 GB
- ○ **B.** 2 GB
- ○ **C.** 4 GB
- ○ **D.** 8 GB

8. What is the maximum amount of memory that Windows Home Basic (64-bit) recognizes?

Quick Answer: 122
Detailed Answer: 123

- ○ **A.** 1 GB
- ○ **B.** 2 GB
- ○ **C.** 4 GB
- ○ **D.** 8 GB

9. Which of the following is not a user interface for Windows Vista? (Choose the best answer.)

Quick Answer: 122
Detailed Answer: 123

- ○ **A.** Basic
- ○ **B.** Classic
- ○ **C.** Standard
- ○ **D.** X
- ○ **E.** Aero

10. Which of the following are new features or updates that have been added to Windows Vista? (Choose all that apply.)

Quick Answer: 122
Detailed Answer: 123

- ○ **A.** Sidebar with gadgets
- ○ **B.** Internet Explorer 7
- ○ **C.** Media Player 11
- ○ **D.** Full support for IPv6

11. Which of the following are new features of Windows Vista? (Choose all that apply.)

Quick Answer: **122**
Detailed Answer: **123**

  - ○ **A.** Enables users to be more productive
  - ○ **B.** Makes it easier to carry out common tasks
  - ○ **C.** Provides a more secure desktop environment
  - ○ **D.** Provides a higher level of reliability

12. Which of the following does Windows Vista include to make it easier for users to quickly find information such as documents and emails? (Choose the best answer.)

Quick Answer: **122**
Detailed Answer: **124**

  - ○ **A.** Windows Search (also known as Instant Search), which searches as you type
  - ○ **B.** A new index service that indexes 25% faster then previous versions
  - ○ **C.** A new folder structure to help better organize documents and emails
  - ○ **D.** All of the provided options are correct

13. Which of the following describes Windows Aero?

Quick Answer: **122**
Detailed Answer: **124**

  - ○ **A.** A new hardware-based graphical user interface intended to be cleaner and more aesthetically pleasing than those of previous versions of Windows
  - ○ **B.** A special theme that is based on the Aerospace industry
  - ○ **C.** A background theme that shows the blue skyline
  - ○ **D.** A search-oriented desktop interface

14. Which of the following does not support adding Windows Vista to a Windows domain? (Choose all that apply.)

Quick Answer: **122**
Detailed Answer: **124**

  - ○ **A.** Windows Vista Starter
  - ○ **B.** Windows Vista Home Basic
  - ○ **C.** Windows Vista Home Premium
  - ○ **D.** Windows Vista Business
  - ○ **E.** Windows Vista Enterprise
  - ○ **F.** Windows Vista Ultimate

15. Which of the following describes the Windows Sidebar?

Quick Answer: **122**
Detailed Answer: **124**

  - ○ **A.** An abbreviated start menu of commonly used programs
  - ○ **B.** A mini browser used to open favorite websites quickly
  - ○ **C.** A virtual PC environment that allows you to run older software packages
  - ○ **D.** A transparent panel where a user can place Desktop gadgets

Quick Check

Quick Answer: **122**
Detailed Answer: **124**

16. You work as a desktop support technician at Acme.com. Because you need to connect to the domain, you need to install Windows Vista Business Edition on a new computer for the graphics department. The new computer has the following specifications:

- ▶ 1.4 GHz Intel processor
- ▶ 384 MB of RAM
- ▶ 15 GB disk space
- ▶ Super VGA video card
- ▶ Integrated sound card
- ▶ Intel 10/100 network adapter.

Which hardware does not meet the minimum requirements to install Windows Vista? (Choose all that apply.)

- ○ **A.** The processor
- ○ **B.** The amount of RAM
- ○ **C.** The hard drive
- ○ **D.** The video card
- ○ **E.** The network adapter

Quick Answer: **122**
Detailed Answer: **124**

17. Because you need to connect to the domain, you need to install Windows Vista Business Edition on a computer for the graphics department. The computer has the following specifications:

- ▶ 1.5-GHz AMD processor
- ▶ 512 MB of RAM
- ▶ Drive C (system drive) has 8 GB of free disk space.
- ▶ Drive D (program drive) has 25 GB of free disk space.
- ▶ Integrated sound card
- ▶ Intel 10/100 network adapter.

Which hardware does not meet the minimum requirements to install Windows Vista?

- ○ **A.** You should add a faster processor to the computer.
- ○ **B.** You should add more memory to the computer.
- ○ **C.** You need to free up space on Drive C.
- ○ **D.** You should install Windows Vista on Drive D.

18. You have a computer that has a 120 GB hard drive divided into two partitions. Each partition is 60 GB. Windows XP Professional has been installed on the first partition. The second partition has not been defined. You want to set up the computer to dual boot between Windows XP Professional and Windows Vista Business Edition. What do you need to do to set this up?

- ○ **A.** Format the second partition with the NTFS file system, boot from the Windows Vista DVD, and install Windows Vista on the second partition.

- ○ **B.** Format the first partition with the NTFS file system, boot from the Windows Vista DVD, and install Windows Vista on the first partition.

- ○ **C.** Boot from the Windows Vista DVD and upgrade the Windows XP partition to Windows Vista.

- ○ **D.** Install Windows XP on the first partition, boot from the Windows Vista DVD, and install Windows Vista on the second partition.

19. Which versions of Windows can be upgraded to Windows Vista Home Basic Edition?

- ○ **A.** Microsoft Windows XP Professional
- ○ **B.** Microsoft Windows XP Home
- ○ **C.** Microsoft Windows XP Tablet PC
- ○ **D.** Microsoft Windows 2000 Professional SP3

20. Which version of Windows XP is eligible for an in-place upgrade to Windows Vista Business?

- ○ **A.** Windows XP Home
- ○ **B.** Windows XP Professional
- ○ **C.** Windows XP Tablet PC Edition
- ○ **D.** All of the above

21. While all editions of Windows Vista can support multiple core processors, which of the following cannot support dual processors?

- ○ **A.** Windows Vista Business Edition
- ○ **B.** Windows Vista Home Premium Edition
- ○ **C.** Windows Vista Ultimate Edition
- ○ **D.** Windows Enterprise Edition

22. Which versions of Windows Vista are eligible to be upgraded to Windows Vista Enterprise? (Choose two answers.)

Quick Answer: **122**
Detailed Answer: **124**

- ○ **A.** Vista Home Premium
- ○ **B.** Vista Business
- ○ **C.** Vista Home Basic
- ○ **D.** Vista Ultimate

23. You are the network administrator for Acme.com. You have ordered some new computers, and the new computers only have one partition with Windows Vista Home Basic. Unfortunately, each computer must run Windows Vista Business Edition so that they can connect to the Windows domain. When you upgrade Windows Vista, which directory will hold the old operating system files and directories in case you need to access the Documents and Settings folders and Program Files folder?

Quick Answer: **122**
Detailed Answer: **125**

- ○ **A.** Windows\panther folder
- ○ **B.** Windows folder
- ○ **C.** Windows.OLD folder
- ○ **D.** Files and Settings folder
- ○ **E.** Explorer folder

24. You work as a helpdesk technician for Acme.com. You have a Windows XP computer that you need to upgrade, but you are not sure if the older sound card and video card are compatible. What should you do?

Quick Answer: **122**
Detailed Answer: **125**

- ○ **A.** Run the Windows Vista Program Compatibility Assistant tool
- ○ **B.** Run the Windows Vista Upgrade Advisor
- ○ **C.** Run the Windows Update tool
- ○ **D.** Open the device manager and update its drivers

25. You work as a helpdesk technician for Acme.com. You have a new computer that has Windows Vista Home Basic Edition. You need to be able to watch and record live television feeds and be able to rip DVDs. What do you need to do that is the most cost effective?

Quick Answer: **122**
Detailed Answer: **125**

- ○ **A.** Upgrade the system to Windows Vista Home Premium.
- ○ **B.** Upgrade the system to Windows Vista Business Edition.
- ○ **C.** Upgrade the system to Windows Vista Ultimate.
- ○ **D.** You don't have to do anything. Windows Home Basic edition already has this functionality.

26. What can you use to determine which edition of Windows Vista you have? (Choose the best answer.)

Quick Answer: **122**
Detailed Answer: **125**

- ○ **A.** Task Manager
- ○ **B.** Start Menu
- ○ **C.** Notification Area
- ○ **D.** Welcome Center

27. You are tasked with upgrading computers running Windows XP Pro to Windows Vista Enterprise Edition. You verify the video cards are Windows Display Driver Model (WDDM) compatible. What else do you need to do to support Aero? (Each correct answer presents part of the solution. Choose four.)

Quick Answer: **122**
Detailed Answer: **125**

- ○ **A.** Set the monitor settings to a refresh rate higher than 10
- ○ **B.** Press the Windows Logo Key + Tab
- ○ **C.** Set the resolution to 1280 × 1024 or higher
- ○ **D.** Set Color to 32 bit
- ○ **E.** Set the Theme to Windows Vista
- ○ **F.** Set the Color Scheme to Windows Aero

28. You work as a desktop support technician at Acme.com. You receive a call from a user reporting that she has been using Flip 3D to allow her to work with several folders and applications for a large project. When she loaded a new program, Flip 3D stopped working. What should you do? (Choose the best answer.)

Quick Answer: **122**
Detailed Answer: **125**

- ○ **A.** Add more Random Access Memory (RAM) to the computer
- ○ **B.** Close one application at a time and retry Flip 3D
- ○ **C.** Change the Theme to Windows Vista
- ○ **D.** Replace the card with a card that supports Windows Display Driver Model (WDDM)

29. You have multiple desktop and laptop workstations. What do you need to enable Windows Aero? (Choose the best answer.)

Quick Answer: **122**
Detailed Answer: **125**

- ○ **A.** Ensure that the color depth is set to 16 bit
- ○ **B.** Ensure that the color depth is set to 32 bit
- ○ **C.** Ensure that the screen resolution is set to 800 × 600
- ○ **D.** Ensure that the screen resolution is set to 1280 × 1024
- ○ **E.** Ensure that the monitor refresh rate is greater than 10 hertz
- ○ **F.** Ensure that the theme is set to Windows Vista

30. You work as a support technician at Acme.com. On your desktop, the user interface features of Windows Aero are not being displayed on a system that is running Windows Vista Ultimate edition. You have a 17-inch monitor that supports a refresh rate up to 100 hertz and has a resolution of 1024 × 768. The video card has 32 MB video memory. What do you need to enable the Windows Aero features? (Choose the best answer.)

- ○ **A.** The operating system should be upgraded.
- ○ **B.** The video card should be replaced.
- ○ **C.** The monitor should be replaced.
- ○ **D.** The display theme should be changed.

31. You have a computer running Windows Vista (32-bit). Where are the programs usually stored?

- ○ **A.** C:\Program Files
- ○ **B.** C:\Program Files (x86)
- ○ **C.** C:\Programs
- ○ **D.** C:\Windows\System32

32. You have a computer running Windows Vista (64-bit). Where are the programs usually stored when you install a 32-bit program?

- ○ **A.** C:\Program Files
- ○ **B.** C:\Program Files (x86)
- ○ **C.** C:\Programs
- ○ **D.** C:\Windows\System32

33. You have a computer running Windows Vista (64-bit). Where are the programs usually stored when you install a 64-bit program?

- ○ **A.** C:\Program Files
- ○ **B.** C:\Program Files (x86)
- ○ **C.** C:\Programs
- ○ **D.** C:\Windows\System32

34. What is the name of a pane on the side of the Microsoft Windows Vista desktop where you can keep your gadgets organized and always available?

- ○ **A.** Gadget organizer
- ○ **B.** Windows Sidebar
- ○ **C.** Sync Center
- ○ **D.** Task Bar

35. If you upgrade Windows XP to Windows Vista, where are the previous operating system, user data, and programs saved?

Quick Answer: **122**
Detailed Answer: **126**

- ○ **A.** C:\
- ○ **B.** C:\BAK
- ○ **C.** C:\Windows\System32
- ○ **D.** C:\Windows.OLD

36. What do you call the area on the far right side of the taskbar that includes a clock and group of icons that shows the status of a program or provides access to certain settings?

Quick Answer: **122**
Detailed Answer: **126**

- ○ **A.** Quick Launch Toolbar
- ○ **B.** Notification Area
- ○ **C.** Start Menu
- ○ **D.** Control Panel

37. When you first start Windows XP and log on, what do you call the background that serves as a surface for your work?

Quick Answer: **122**
Detailed Answer: **126**

- ○ **A.** Desktop
- ○ **B.** Notification Area
- ○ **C.** Start Menu
- ○ **D.** Explorer

38. Which version of Windows includes User Account Control (UAC)? (Choose all that apply.)

Quick Answer: **122**
Detailed Answer: **126**

- ○ **A.** Windows XP 32-bit
- ○ **B.** Windows XP 64-bit
- ○ **C.** Windows Vista Home Basic Edition
- ○ **D.** Windows Vista Ultimate Edition

3.2 Given a scenario, demonstrate proper use of user interfaces

- ▶ Windows Explorer
- ▶ My Computer
- ▶ Control Panel
- ▶ Command prompt utilities
- ▶ telnet
- ▶ ping
- ▶ ipconfig
- ▶ Run line utilities
- ▶ msconfig

- ▶ `msinfo32`
- ▶ `Dxdiag`
- ▶ Cmd
- ▶ REGEDIT
- ▶ My Network Places
- ▶ Task bar/systray
- ▶ Administrative tools
- ▶ Performance monitor, Event Viewer, Services, Computer Management
- ▶ MMC
- ▶ Task Manager
- ▶ Start Menu

39. Which of the following is the component that allows you to manage files and directories on a Windows 2000 or Windows XP computer?

- ○ **A.** Control Panel
- ○ **B.** Windows Explorer
- ○ **C.** File Manager
- ○ **D.** Device Manager

Quick Answer: **122**
Detailed Answer: **126**

40. You want to see all of the drives that your Windows XP computer has. Which Windows component should you use?

- ○ **A.** My Computer
- ○ **B.** Control Panel
- ○ **C.** Command Prompt
- ○ **D.** MMC

Quick Answer: **122**
Detailed Answer: **126**

41. On a computer running Windows Vista, what key command can you press from within Windows Explorer to display the menu bar?

- ○ **A.** Ctrl+Alt
- ○ **B.** Shift+Alt
- ○ **C.** Alt
- ○ **D.** Ctrl

Quick Answer: **122**
Detailed Answer: **127**

42. What is the primary utility used to configure the Windows interface?

- ○ **A.** My Computer
- ○ **B.** Control Panel
- ○ **C.** MMC
- ○ **D.** Device Manager
- ○ **E.** Msconfig

Quick Answer: **122**
Detailed Answer: **127**

43. You open the Control Panel. How do you change from Category view to Icon view?

- ○ **A.** Change to Classic view
- ○ **B.** Open the Administrative Tools
- ○ **C.** Open the View menu and select Large Icons
- ○ **D.** Login as an administrator and access the Control Panel

44. How do you remove a software package that you installed on a computer running Windows XP?

- ○ **A.** Open the Control Panel and click Add or Remove Programs
- ○ **B.** Right-click the desktop and click Uninstall a Program
- ○ **C.** Right-click My Computer and click Uninstall a Program
- ○ **D.** Press Ctrl+C and click Uninstall a Program

45. How do you remove a software package that you installed on a computer running Windows Vista?

- ○ **A.** Open the Control Panel and click Uninstall a Program from the Programs section
- ○ **B.** Right-click the desktop and click Uninstall a Program
- ○ **C.** Right-click My Computer and click Uninstall a Program
- ○ **D.** Press Ctrl+C and click Uninstall a Program

46. You have a Windows XP computer. How would you add IIS to Windows XP?

- ○ **A.** Open the Control Panel and click Uninstall a Program. Then click Set Program Access and Defaults.
- ○ **B.** Open the Control Panel and click Uninstall a Program. Then click Add/Remove Windows Components.
- ○ **C.** Right-click My Computer and click Manage.
- ○ **D.** Open the Administrative Tools and click Services.

47. In Windows 2000, where would you optimize virtual memory?

- ○ **A.** Control Panel/Computer Management
- ○ **B.** Control Panel/System/Device Manager
- ○ **C.** Control Panel/System/Performance
- ○ **D.** Control Panel/System/Advanced

48. In Windows XP, what is a shortcut to access the System
Properties without using the Control Panel?

- ○ **A.** Right-click the C drive and click Properties
- ○ **B.** Right-click the taskbar and click Properties
- ○ **C.** Right-click My Computer and click Properties
- ○ **D.** Right-click the desktop and click Properties

49. What command starts the System Configuration Utility?

- ○ **A.** msinfo
- ○ **B.** dxdiag
- ○ **C.** msconfig
- ○ **D.** regedit

50. What utility would you use to disable a program that automatically
starts up during startup?

- ○ **A.** msinfo
- ○ **B.** dxdiag
- ○ **C.** msconfig
- ○ **D.** regedit

51. What utility is used to start the System Information utility?

- ○ **A.** msinfo32
- ○ **B.** dxdiag
- ○ **C.** msconfig
- ○ **D.** regedit

52. You just got a call from your new boss. You need to know how
much memory the computer has and what system drivers are
loaded. What utility should you use to view this information?

- ○ **A.** msinfo32
- ○ **B.** dxdiag
- ○ **C.** msconfig
- ○ **D.** regedit

53. You are trying to play a game but you are having problems. You
want check the status of DirectX. What utility should you use?

- ○ **A.** msinfo32
- ○ **B.** dxdiag
- ○ **C.** msconfig
- ○ **D.** regedit

54. How can you manually change a value in the registry?

    O   **A.** msinfo32

    O   **B.** dxdiag

    O   **C.** msconfig

    O   **D.** regedit

55. Where are the system registry files stored?

    O   **A.** C:\Windows

    O   **B.** C:\Windows\System32

    O   **C.** C:\Windows\Registry

    O   **D.** C:\Windows\System32\Config

56. Which subtree is used to store information about the type of hardware that's installed, drivers, and other system settings?

    O   **A.** HKEY_CLASSES_ROOT

    O   **B.** HKEY_CURRENT_USER

    O   **C.** HKEY_LOCAL_MACHINE

    O   **D.** HKEY_USERS

57. When using the registry editor which of the following keys contains file extension associations?

    O   **A.** HKEY_CURRENT_USER

    O   **B.** HKEY_USERS

    O   **C.** HKEY_LOCAL_MACHINE

    O   **D.** HKEY_CLASSES_ROOT

58. In Windows XP, what happens when you press the Windows key + L?

    O   **A.** Windows XP opens the Start menu.

    O   **B.** Windows XP logs the current user off.

    O   **C.** Windows XP refreshes the desktop.

    O   **D.** Windows XP locks the computer.

59. What keys do you press to access the Windows Security Dialog box in Windows XP?

    O   **A.** Ctrl+Enter

    O   **B.** Ctrl+Alt+Del

    O   **C.** Ctrl+L

    O   **D.** F1

60. What key combination opens the Start menu in Windows XP?

Quick Answer: **122**
Detailed Answer: **129**

- ○ **A.** Ctrl+Esc
- ○ **B.** Alt+Esc
- ○ **C.** Ctrl+Alt+Esc
- ○ **D.** Shift+Esc

61. What keys do you press to switch between applications in Windows XP?

Quick Answer: **122**
Detailed Answer: **129**

- ○ **A.** Alt+Tab
- ○ **B.** Alt+Enter
- ○ **C.** Alt+Ctrl
- ○ **D.** Alt+Ctrl+Del

62. What keys do you press to switch between applications in Windows Vista? (Choose two answers.)

Quick Answer: **122**
Detailed Answer: **129**

- ○ **A.** Alt+Tab
- ○ **B.** Alt+Enter
- ○ **C.** Alt+Ctrl
- ○ **D.** Alt+Ctrl+Del
- ○ **E.** Start+Tab

63. Which Windows utility can be used to automate many routines or periodic functions?

Quick Answer: **122**
Detailed Answer: **129**

- ○ **A.** The Scheduled Tasks tool
- ○ **B.** The Task Manager utility
- ○ **C.** The Device Manager
- ○ **D.** The MSCONFIG utility

3.3 Explain the process and steps to install and configure the Windows OS

- ▶ File systems
- ▶ FAT32 vs. NTFS
- ▶ Directory structures
- ▶ Create folders
- ▶ Navigate directory structures
- ▶ Files
- ▶ Creation
- ▶ Extensions

▶ Attributes

▶ Permissions

▶ Verification of hardware compatibility and minimum requirements

▶ Installation methods

▶ Boot media such as CD, floppy, or USB

▶ Network installation

▶ Install from image

▶ Recover CD

▶ Factory recovery partition

▶ Operating system installation options

▶ File system type

▶ Network configuration

▶ Repair install

▶ Disk preparation order

▶ Format drive

▶ Partition

▶ Start installation

▶ Device Manager

▶ Verify

▶ Install and update device drivers

▶ Driver signing

▶ User data migration—User State Migration Tool (USMT)

▶ Virtual memory

▶ Configure power management

▶ Suspend

▶ Wake on LAN

▶ Sleep timers

▶ Hibernate

▶ Standby

▶ Demonstrate safe removal of peripherals

64. The small unit of storage for an operating system is a

    ○ **A.** Head

    ○ **B.** Cluster

    ○ **C.** Sector

    ○ **D.** Cylinder

Quick Answer: **122**
Detailed Answer: **130**

65. The master boot record holds which of the following?

- ○ **A.** Partition table
- ○ **B.** Volume boot sector
- ○ **C.** File allocation table
- ○ **D.** Root directory

Quick Answer: **122**
Detailed Answer: **130**

66. The top of a file structure tree is which of the following?

- ○ **A.** Partition table
- ○ **B.** Root directory
- ○ **C.** Subdirectory
- ○ **D.** MBR

Quick Answer: **122**
Detailed Answer: **130**

67. How many primary partitions without an extended partition can reside on a basic MBR disk under Windows XP?

- ○ **A.** 1
- ○ **B.** 3
- ○ **C.** 4
- ○ **D.** 128

Quick Answer: **122**
Detailed Answer: **130**

68. What advantages does NTFS have over FAT32 file system? (Choose all that apply.)

- ○ **A.** It supports folder and file permissions.
- ○ **B.** It supports larger partition sizes.
- ○ **C.** It can be accessed and modified using many standard DOS disk utilities.
- ○ **D.** It supports compression, encryption, disk quotas, and file ownership.

Quick Answer: **122**
Detailed Answer: **130**

69. Of the following methods, which two are valid for creating a new folder in Windows Explorer? (Select two answers)

- ○ **A.** Edit, Create, New, Folder
- ○ **B.** File, New, Folder
- ○ **C.** Double-click in Display Window
- ○ **D.** Right-click in Display Window, New, Folder

Quick Answer: **122**
Detailed Answer: **130**

70. On an NTFS volume, which of the following can be used to control the amount of disk space network users can consume?

Quick Answer: **122**
Detailed Answer: **130**

- ○ **A.** Disk Cleanup
- ○ **B.** Security Center
- ○ **C.** Disk Quotas
- ○ **D.** Disk Defragmenter

71. Which of the following uses permissions to control access to network resources?

Quick Answer: **122**
Detailed Answer: **130**

- ○ **A.** FAT
- ○ **B.** FAT32
- ○ **C.** CDFS
- ○ **D.** NTFS

72. What is the native file system for Windows 2000 and Windows XP Professional?

Quick Answer: **122**
Detailed Answer: **131**

- ○ **A.** NTFS4
- ○ **B.** FAT32
- ○ **C.** FAT16
- ○ **D.** NTFS5

73. How many logical drives can be created on a FAT drive?

Quick Answer: **122**
Detailed Answer: **131**

- ○ **A.** 8
- ○ **B.** 23
- ○ **C.** 38
- ○ **D.** 44

74. Which method is used to change file attributes from the Windows Explorer?

Quick Answer: **122**
Detailed Answer: **131**

- ○ **A.** Edit the appropriate Registry entry with RegEdt32
- ○ **B.** Right-click the file and select Properties
- ○ **C.** Highlight the file and choose the Select Options entry from the System Tools menu
- ○ **D.** Highlight the file and choose the Select Options entry from the View menu

75. You want to make a source document you've prepared for your staff a read-only file so that it cannot be altered. Which of the following methods can you use in Windows Explorer to change the file's attributes?

   O   **A.** Edit the appropriate Registry entry for the file using Regedt32

   O   **B.** Right-click on the file, select Properties, and place a check mark in the Read Only check box

   O   **C.** Highlight the file, choose the Select Options entry in the System Tools menu, and select the Read Only option

   O   **D.** Highlight the file, choose the Select Options entry in the View menu, and select the Read Only option

76. Which of the following does Windows 2000 Professional use to start Setup? (Select all that apply.)

   O   **A.** Install

   O   **B.** Winnt32

   O   **C.** Setup

   O   **D.** Winnt

77. You want to upgrade to Windows XP Professional, but you're not sure that your system can support it. What should you do to make sure that the system will support the upgrade?

   O   **A.** Run the HCL.EXE utility from the distribution CD

   O   **B.** Run the ACL.EXE utility from the distribution CD

   O   **C.** Run the Upgrade.exe utility from the distribution CD

   O   **D.** Run the Checkupgradeonly utility from the distribution CD

78. You must do which of the following to perform a clean Windows Vista installation?

   O   **A.** Boot from the Windows Vista installation DVD

   O   **B.** Input a valid product key

   O   **C.** Select a partition on which to install Windows Vista

   O   **D.** All of the above

79. When installing Windows XP Professional, which function key must the technician press to load the drivers for a SCSI hard drive?

○ **A.** F6

○ **B.** F8

○ **C.** F4

○ **D.** F2

80. From what page of the Windows Vista installation can you select the Load Driver option to load a third-party disk driver?

○ **A.** Preparing Your Desktop page

○ **B.** Where Do You Want to Install Vista? page

○ **C.** Select Your Computer's Current Location page

○ **D.** Thank You page

81. To perform an in-place upgrade, from where must you launch Windows Vista setup?

○ **A.** Within Windows

○ **B.** Booted from a CD/DVD

○ **C.** Connect to Microsoft.com

○ **D.** From Windows PE 2.0

82. What is the proper order of operations for preparing a disk drive for use?

○ **A.** Format, partition, run Setup, reboot, load drivers

○ **B.** Partition, format, run Setup, load drivers, reboot

○ **C.** Format, partition, run Setup, load drivers, reboot

○ **D.** Partition, format, run Setup, reboot, load drivers

83. What is the process called when you are assigning part or all of the drives for use by the computer?

○ **A.** Formatting

○ **B.** Modification

○ **C.** Partitioning

○ **D.** None of the above

84. You want to make changes to the hardware. Where should you look to make the changes? (Select all that apply.)

○ **A.** Device Manager

○ **B.** Administrative Tools

○ **C.** Hardware Wizard

○ **D.** None of the above

85. Where do you go to enable Driver Signature Verification in Windows XP Professional?

    ○ **A.** Navigate Start/All Programs/Accessories/System Tools and select the Driver Signing option from the sub-menu

    ○ **B.** Navigate Start/Control Panel/System icon and then select the Hardware tab and click the Driver Signing button

    ○ **C.** Navigate Start/Control Panel/Administrative Tools/Computer Management and select the Driver Signing option from the System Tools snap-in

    ○ **D.** Navigate Start/Control Panel/Add Hardware and click on the Enable Driver Signing option in the Add Hardware Wizard Welcome page

86. Because your company upgraded its PCs to Windows XP Professional, you have encountered numerous problems associated with employees loading manufacturer's drivers for particular equipment they work with. In many cases, the new drivers have created hardware conflicts and operational failures in the systems. What can you do to stop this practice from occurring and to force the employees to use drivers that are known to work with Windows XP?

    ○ **A.** Access the Driver Signing Options page located under the Control Panel, System icon, Hardware tab, Driver Signing button to establish how the system responds when it detects an unsigned driver. Set the option to Substitute.

    ○ **B.** Access the Driver Signing Options page located under the Control Panel, System icon, Hardware tab, Driver Signing button to establish how the system responds when it detects an unsigned driver. Set the option to Warn.

    ○ **C.** Access the Driver Signing Options page located under the Control Panel, System icon, Hardware tab, Driver Signing button to establish how the system responds when it detects an unsigned driver. Set the option to Disable.

    ○ **D.** Access the Driver Signing Options page located under the Control Panel, System icon, Hardware tab, Driver Signing button to establish how the system responds when it detects an unsigned driver. Set the option to Block.

87. What is the default setting for Driver Signing in Windows XP?

Quick Answer: **122**
Detailed Answer: **132**

- ○ **A.** Warn
- ○ **B.** Block
- ○ **C.** Ignore
- ○ **D.** None

88. You are preparing to install a new copy of Windows XP on a network computer in your company. However, the user wants to retain his My Documents, My Pictures, Desktop, and Favorites folders, along with his display properties, mapped network drives, network printers, browser settings, and folder options from his old Windows Me system. What can you do to achieve both goals?

Quick Answer: **122**
Detailed Answer: **132**

- ○ **A.** Access the Windows XP user state migration tool (USMT) to transfer the user configuration settings and files to a clean Windows XP installation without going through the upgrade process.
- ○ **B.** Run the Windows XP Recovery Process utility to move the files to a server on the network and then reinstall them after the operating system installation has been completed.
- ○ **C.** Run the Windows XP Automated System Recovery (ASR) utility to move the files to a server on the network and then reinstall them after the operating system installation has been completed.
- ○ **D.** Run the Windows XP Backup/Restore utility from NTBACKUP to move the files to a server on the network and then reinstall them after the operating system installation has been completed.

89. Which of the following files is used for virtual memory in Windows XP machine?

Quick Answer: **122**
Detailed Answer: **132**

- ○ **A.** PAGEFILE.SYS
- ○ **B.** N386.SWP
- ○ **C.** NTLDR
- ○ **D.** BOOT.SYS

90. In Windows XP, where do you configure the virtual memory settings?

Quick Answer: **122**
Detailed Answer: **132**

- ○ **A.** Open the Control Panel, double-click the System applet, and select the Advanced tab
- ○ **B.** Open the Control Panel, double-click the System applet, and click the Device Manager button

○ **C.** Open the Control Panel, double-click the System applet, and select the Performance tab

○ **D.** Open the Control Panel and double-click the Paging applet.

91. You have two PATA hard drives in a system that keeps getting slower. The system is used to create and manipulate large multimedia files. How can you improve the system's disk drive subsystem performance?

Quick Answer: **122**
Detailed Answer: **132**

○ **A.** Set the virtual memory setting to maximum

○ **B.** Move the system's swap file to the D: drive where there is less traffic and more room to expand

○ **C.** Set the virtual memory setting to variable so that Windows can make the swap file as large as necessary

○ **D.** Set the virtual memory setting to minimum so that the system has to directly interface with the application, eliminating an extra processing step

92. Which power-saving mode provides the best power savings and still permits the computing session to be activated later?

Quick Answer: **122**
Detailed Answer: **133**

○ **A.** Hibernate mode

○ **B.** Suspend mode

○ **C.** Standby mode

○ **D.** Shutdown mode

93. Where would you enable Hibernation on a Windows XP laptop?

Quick Answer: **122**
Detailed Answer: **133**

○ **A.** In Screen Savers in the Control Panel

○ **B.** In the system BIOS

○ **C.** In Power Management in the Control Panel

○ **D.** In Power Options in the Control Panel

94. A salesperson from your company has contacted you asking how she can configure her new notebook PC to go into Hibernate mode to conserve her battery life on long trips. How can she get to the Hibernate configuration page from the Windows XP desktop?

Quick Answer: **122**
Detailed Answer: **133**

○ **A.** Start, All Programs, System Tools, Power Options, Hibernate

○ **B.** Start, Control Panel, Power Options, Hibernate Tab, Enable Hibernation

○ **C.** Start, Control Panel, Power Options, Advanced Tab, Enable Hibernate Support

○ **D.** Start, Settings, Power Options, Hibernate, Enable

95. You have a laptop computer with Windows Vista. You want to
ensure that the laptop is powered off if it is idle for a period of
more than 60 minutes. What should you enable?

- ○ **A.** Standby mode
- ○ **B.** Sleep mode
- ○ **C.** Hibernate mode
- ○ **D.** Screen Saver

96. You want to ensure that your computer can be awakened remotely
from a low power state. What should you include in the computer?

- ○ **A.** NICs that can hibernate
- ○ **B.** NICs with wake-on-LAN capability
- ○ **C.** NICs that can sleep
- ○ **D.** Processors with wake-on-LAN capability

97. All computers running Windows Vista contain a wake-on-LAN–com-
pliant network card. To conserve energy, a corporate policy states
that all computers should be powered off at night. You need to recommend a plan that allows Windows Update installations to run at
night and consume minimal power. You configure the Enabling
Windows Update Power Management to Automatically Wake Up the
System to Install Scheduled Updates option and enable Windows
Updates for all computers. What should you do next?

- ○ **A.** Instruct users to sleep their computers at night
- ○ **B.** Instruct users to hibernate their computers at night
- ○ **C.** Instruct users to shutdown their computers at night
- ○ **D.** Instruct users to leave their computers on at night

98. What power saving mode in Windows Vista saves work and opens
programs to memory?

- ○ **A.** Sleep
- ○ **B.** Hybrid Sleep
- ○ **C.** Hibernate
- ○ **D.** Power-Eco

99. When detaching a removable device from a laptop computer running Windows XP, what would be your first step?

- ○ **A.** Use the Safely Remove Hardware icon to eject the
device
- ○ **B.** Power down the device manually

○ **C.** Use the Add/Remove hardware applet in Control Panel to remove the device

○ **D.** Use Device Manager to disable the device

3.4 Explain the basics of boot sequences, methods, and startup utilities

▶ Disk boot order/device priority

▶ Types of boot devices (disk, network, USB, other)

▶ Boot options

▶ Safe mode

▶ Boot to restore point

▶ Recovery options

▶ Automated System Recovery (ASR)

▶ Emergency Repair Disk (ERD)

▶ Recovery console

100. Which of the following must you do before you can boot from a bootable CD-ROM?

Quick Answer: **122**
Detailed Answer: **134**

○ **A.** Make sure the hard drive is formatted with NTFS

○ **B.** Change the BIOS boot sequence to CD-ROM, A, C

○ **C.** Press the F8 key during the boot sequence

○ **D.** Make a bootable diskette

101. You upgrade the video driver on a Windows XP computer. Now the computer will not boot up properly. What should you do to fix it? (Choose two answers.)

Quick Answer: **122**
Detailed Answer: **134**

○ **A.** Revert to the Last Known Good Configuration

○ **B.** Run the Recovery Console

○ **C.** Start the computer in Safe Mode and roll back the driver

○ **D.** Re-install the operating system.

102. After installing a new network interface card (NIC) driver on a Windows XP computer system, the computer system reboots continuously. What can you do to correct this problem?

Quick Answer: **122**
Detailed Answer: **134**

○ **A.** Reinstall the operating system

○ **B.** Reinstall device drivers for the network interface card (NIC)

○ **C.** Use the Last Known Good Configuration

○ **D.** Remove the network interface card (NIC)

103. Windows Vista will not start after you've installed some software. How can you repair Windows Vista?

- ○ **A.** Boot to the Windows Vista DVD and perform a Startup Repair.
- ○ **B.** Boot into the Windows Recovery Console and type Fixmbr. Reboot Windows Vista.
- ○ **C.** Boot into the Windows Recovery Console and type Fixboot. Reboot Windows Vista.
- ○ **D.** Edit the Boot.ini file and add the Advanced RISC Computing (ARC) path that points to the Windows Recovery Console.

104. What option can you use to repair a master boot record or a volume boot record on a Windows XP computer?

- ○ **A.** Boot to Windows XP and start the Windows Recovery Console
- ○ **B.** Boot with the Windows XP installation CD and start the Windows Recovery Console
- ○ **C.** Boot to Windows PE and start the Windows Recovery Console
- ○ **D.** Edit the Boot.ini file and add the Advanced RISC Computing (ARC) path that points to Windows PE

105. You need to remove a driver that is causing Windows to not boot. What should you do?

- ○ **A.** Access Device Manager to find out more about the issue
- ○ **B.** Access the Display console to change the necessary video card settings, screen resolution, themes and skins, and display adapters
- ○ **C.** Start Windows in Safe Mode and remove the problematic driver
- ○ **D.** All of the above

106. Which of the following Interactive Startup options should you select if you want to start Windows XP using only basic files and drivers, and network connections?

- ○ **A.** Start Windows Normally option
- ○ **B.** Safe Mode option
- ○ **C.** Safe Mode with Command Prompt option
- ○ **D.** Safe Mode with Networking option

107. Which of the following recovery options are available when booting from the Windows XP installation CD?

Quick Answer: **122**
Detailed Answer: **135**

- ○ **A.** Automated System Recovery (ASR)
- ○ **B.** Safe Mode
- ○ **C.** Last Known Good Configuration
- ○ **D.** Emergency Recovery Disk (ERD)

108. What tool is used in Windows 2000 that uses a specially formatted bootable floppy disk that contains information about a particular Windows installation that can be used to restore a computer to a boot state if the registry or other component is damaged?

Quick Answer: **122**
Detailed Answer: **135**

- ○ **A.** Emergency Recovery Disk (ERD)
- ○ **B.** Automated System Recovery (ASR)
- ○ **C.** Recovery Console
- ○ **D.** PE Disk

109. You turn on the computer and it boots to a black screen without loading an operating system. What could cause Windows not to boot from the C drive or the CD/DVD disk?

Quick Answer: **122**
Detailed Answer: **135**

- ○ **A.** You have accidentally installed Linux on top of Windows.
- ○ **B.** The network cable is not connected to the network card.
- ○ **C.** The BOOT.INI file was modified.
- ○ **D.** You have a USB thumb drive connected to the computer.

Quick-Check Answer Key

1. A
2. B
3. B
4. A
5. C
6. C
7. C
8. D
9. D
10. A, B, C and D
11. A, B, C and D
12. A
13. A
14. A, B and C
15. D
16. B and C
17. C
18. A
19. B
20. D
21. B
22. A and B
23. C
24. B
25. A
26. D
27. A, D, E and F
28. B

29. B, E and F
30. B
31. A
32. B
33. A
34. B
35. D
36. B
37. A
38. C and D
39. B
40. A
41. C
42. B
43. A
44. A
45. A
46. B
47. D
48. C
49. C
50. C
51. A
52. A
53. B
54. D
55. D

56. C
57. D
58. D
59. B
60. A
61. A
62. A and E
63. A
64. B
65. A
66. B
67. C
68. A, B, and D
69. B and D
70. C
71. D
72. D
73. B
74. B
75. B
76. B and D
77. D
78. D
79. A
80. B
81. A
82. B

83. C
84. A and C
85. B
86. D
87. A
88. A
89. A
90. A
91. B
92. A
93. D
94. B
95. C
96. B
97. B
98. A
99. A
100. B
101. A and C
102. C
103. A
104. B
105. C
106. D
107. A
108. A
109. D

Answers and Explanations

1. **Answer: A.** The minimum amount of RAM for Windows XP Home and Professional is 64 MB. Per Microsoft's website, it is usually recommended that you have 128 MB or more because 64 MB will limit performance and some features. You should go with a minimum of 512 MB and should consider 1 GB or more if you want decent performance. Therefore, the other answers are incorrect.

2. **Answer: B.** Per Microsoft's website, the minimum amount of RAM to install Windows Vista Home is 512 MB. However, you should plan at least 1 GB as a minimum, and more would give you even better performance. Therefore, the other answers are incorrect.

3. **Answer: B.** Per Microsoft's website, the minimum amount of RAM to install Windows Vista Ultimate is 512 MB. However, they also recommend that you should have at least 1 GB of system memory. Of course, you should consider even more for better performance. Therefore, the other answers are incorrect.

4. **Answer: A.** To install Windows XP, you need a minimum of 1.5 GB. Of course, you will need more for programs and data. Therefore, the other answers are incorrect.

5. **Answer: C.** Per Microsoft's website, you need at least 15 GB of available disk space to install Windows Vista. Of course, you will need much more if you want to install programs and store data. Therefore, the other answers are incorrect.

6. **Answer: C.** Windows XP was originally built for a 32-bit memory bus that will only recognize up to 4 GB of RAM. Therefore, the other answers are incorrect.

7. **Answer: C.** Windows Vista Home Edition (32-bit) is aimed at a system with a 32-bit memory bus that will only recognize up to 4 GB of RAM. Therefore, the other answers are incorrect.

8. **Answer: D.** Windows Vista Home Basic Edition (64-bit) can recognize up to 8 GB of memory. Therefore, the other answers are incorrect.

9. **Answer: D.** X is a reference to the operating system used by some Apple Macintosh computers. Depending on the system hardware and the desires of the user, Windows Vista offers four user interfaces including Basic (Answer A), Windows Classic (Answer B), Standard (Answer C), and Windows Aero.

10. **Answer: A, B, C, and D.** Sidebar with gadgets (Answer A), Internet Explorer 7 (Answer B), Media Player 11 (Answer C), and full support for IPv6 (Answer D) have been added to Windows Vista. Internet Explorer 7 is available as a download for Windows XP. Media Player 11 is available as a download for Windows XP. Windows XP had a test environment only for IPv6. The Sidebar with gadgets is introduced in Windows Vista.

11. **Answer: A, B, C, and D.** Windows Vista introduces many new features that enable users to be more productive (Answer A), make it easier to carry out common tasks (Answer B), provide a more secure desktop environment (Answer C), and a higher level of reliability (Answer D). While its interface and tools make it easier for users to organize, search for, and view information, it is designed to allow users to focus on the most important aspects of their job.

12. **Answer: A.** Vista includes Windows Search (also known as Instant Search or Search as You Type), which is significantly faster (Answer B) and more thorough than before. In addition, search boxes have been added to the Start menu, Windows Explorer, and several of the applications that are included with Vista. Although in Windows Vista the folders structure (Answer C) is slightly different than Windows XP, these changes will not necessarily help you find files faster and will not help you search through emails.

13. **Answer: A.** Windows Aero is a new hardware-based graphical user interface intended to be cleaner and more aesthetically pleasing than those of previous versions of Windows. Therefore, the other answers are incorrect.

14. **Answer: A, B, and C.** Windows Vista Starter, Windows Vista Home Basic, and Windows Vista Home Premium are designed as operating systems for the home, which does not require connecting to a company's Windows domain. Windows Vista Business and Windows Vista Enterprise are aimed specifically at corporations; therefore they can be added to a domain. Windows Ultimate includes everything for home users and business applications, therefore, it allows Windows Vista to be added to a domain.

15. **Answer: D.** The Sidebar is a transparent panel where a user can place Desktop gadgets. Therefore, the other answers are incorrect.

16. **Answer: B and C.** The system requirements specify a minimum of 512 MB of RAM and 20 GB hard drive. The system in the question only has 384 MB of RAM and 15 GB hard drive. The other system requirements include a 1 GHz processor (Answer A) and a super VGA monitor (Answer D), which the system already has. Windows Vista does not require network connectivity but if it is available, it can be used for updates and to communicate with network resources.

17. **Answer: C.** The system requirements specify 15 GB free hard disk space. The system in question only has 8 GB of free disk space. The other system requirements include a 1 GHz processor (Answer A) and 512 MB of RAM (Answer B). The storage for programs (Answer D) is not a requirement to install Windows Vista.

18. **Answer: A.** To have a system dual boot between Windows XP and Windows Vista, you have to install each operating system onto two different partitions. Because Windows XP is already on the first partition, you need to install Windows Vista on the other partition. Therefore, the other answers are incorrect.

19. **Answer: B.** The only edition that can be upgraded to Windows Vista Home Basic edition is Windows XP Home edition. Therefore, the other answers are incorrect.

20. **Answer: D.** You can upgrade to Windows Vista Business from Windows XP Pro, Windows XP Home, Windows XP Media Center, and Windows XP Tablet PC.

21. **Answer: B.** Windows Vista Business Edition (Answer A), Enterprise Edition (Answer D), and Ultimate Edition (Answer C) can support dual processors, but Windows Vista Home Basic and Home Premium cannot.

22. **Answer: A and B.** You can upgrade Windows Vista Starter, Home Basic (Answer B) and Business Editions (Answer A) to Enterprise. You must do a clean install if you want to move from Home Premium (Answer A) and Ultimate Editions (Answer D) to Enterprise Edition.

23. **Answer: C.** When you perform a clean installation of Windows Vista on a hard disk partition that contains an existing Windows installation (assuming you did not reformat the hard disk), the previous operating system, user data, and program files are saved to a Windows.OLD folder. Therefore, the other answers are incorrect.

24. **Answer: B.** When you want to see if a system is compatible with Windows Vista, you should run the Windows Vista Upgrade Advisor. The Windows Vista Program Compatibility Assistant Tool (Answer A) will not check hardware compatibility. The Windows Update tool (Answer C) is used to update Windows, not check compatibility. Updating drivers (Answer D) will not check compatibility.

25. **Answer: A.** The only two versions of Windows Vista that support DVD ripping and the ability to watch TV are Windows Vista Home Premium and Windows Vista Ultimate. Therefore, Windows Vista Business Edition (Answer B) and Windows Home Basic Edition (Answer D) are incorrect. Of course, to be cost effective, Windows Vista Home Premium is less expensive than Windows Vista Ultimate. Therefore, Answer C is incorrect.

26. **Answer: D.** You can quickly see what version of Windows Vista a system is running by looking at the Welcome Center. Therefore, the other answers are incorrect.

27. **Answers: A, D, E, and F.** To enable Windows Aero, you must have set the monitor settings to a refresh rate higher than 10, set Color to 32 bit, set the Theme to Windows Vista, and set the Color Scheme to Windows Aero.

28. **Answer: B.** If an application is not compatible with Windows Aero, it might cause Flip 3D to stop functioning. Adding more RAM (Answer A), changing the theme (Answer C), and replacing the driver (Answer D) will not fix an application that is not compatible with Windows Aero.

29. **Answer: B, E, and F.** For Windows Aero to function, you must have the color depth set to 32 bit, the monitor refresh rate greater than 10 hertz, and the theme set to Windows Vista. Therefore, the other answers are incorrect.

30. **Answer: B.** Because the video card only has 32 MB of video RAM, you need to upgrade the card to one that has at least 64 MB. More memory might be needed if you have a high resolution. You don't have to upgrade Windows Vista (Answer A) because Windows Vista Ultimate already supports Windows Aero. You do not have to replace the monitor (Answer C) because it has a high enough resolution and refresh rate (10 Hertz is the minimum). You might still need to set the theme to Windows Vista (Answer D) and the color scheme to Windows Aero, but you will not be able to do that until you upgrade the video card.

31. **Answer: A.** When you install programs on a 32-bit version of Windows Vista, programs are usually stored in C:\Program Files. Therefore, the other answers are incorrect.

32. **Answer: B.** When you install 32-bit programs on a 64-bit version of Windows Vista, programs are usually stored in C:\Program Files (x86). Therefore, the other answers are incorrect.

33. **Answer: A.** When you install 32-bit programs on a 64-bit version of Windows Vista, programs are usually stored in C:\Program Files. Therefore, the other answers are incorrect.

34. **Answer: B.** Gadgets are easy-to-use mini programs that give you information at a glance and provide easy access to frequently used tools. Windows Sidebar helps you to organize your gadgets. There is no official Gadget Organizer in Windows Vista (Answer A). The Sidebar is the gadget organizer. The Sync Center (Answer C) is a feature of Windows Vista that allows you to keep information in sync between your computer and mobile devices, network servers, and programs that support Sync Center. The Task Bar (Answer D) is at the bottom of the screen and allows you to manage your running programs.

35. **Answer: D.** When you upgrade Windows, the previous version of Windows files will be kept in the C:\Windows.OLD. Therefore, the other answers are incorrect.

36. **Answer: B.** The notification area includes a clock and group of icons, and it is kept on the far right side of the task bar. When you move your cursor to a particular icon, you will see the icon's name or the status of the settings. Double-clicking the notification area usually opens the program or setting associated with it. The Quick Launch Toolbar (Answer A) is usually next to the Start Button and shows little icons you can use to quickly start programs. The Start Menu (Answer C) is a list of shortcuts organized so that you can find a program you want to start. It is accessed by clicking the Start button. The Control Panel (Answer D) is used to configure Windows.

37. **Answer: A.** The desktop is the main screen/graphical space that you see after you turn on your computer and log on to Windows. Like the top of the actual office desk, it serves as a surface for your work. The notification area (Answer B) includes a clock and group of icons, and it is kept on the far right side of the task bar. When you move your cursor to a particular icon, you will see the icon's name or the status of the settings. Double-clicking the notification area usually opens the program or setting associated with it. The Start Menu (Answer C) is a list of shortcuts organized so that you can find a program you want to start. It is accessed by clicking the Start button. Windows Explorer (Answer D) is used to access and manage the folders and files.

38. **Answer: C and D.** User Account Control (UAC), introduced with Windows Vista, is a feature in Windows that can help prevent unauthorized changes to your computer. It is not included with Windows XP (Answers A and B).

39. **Answer: B.** Windows Explorer allows the user to use drag-and-drop techniques and other graphical tools to manage the file system. The Control Panel (Answer A) is a graphical tool that allows you to configure Windows. File Manager (Answer C) is a legacy application used in older Windows to manage files. Device Manager (Answer D) is used to manage your devices.

40. **Answer: A.** When you open My Computer, you will see all drives recognized by the system that have been assigned drive letters. The Control Panel (Answer B) is a graphical tool that allows you to configure Windows. The Command Prompt (Answer C) opens a window where you can perform commands. The Command Prompt is sometimes used to run certain programs or configure certain parts of Windows that cannot be managed with the Windows GUI interface. The Microsoft Management Console (MMC), Answer D, is an interface used by tools included with Windows, such as the Administrative Tools, to configure and manage Windows and its programs. The Computer Management Console is an example of the MMC. If you open the MMC by itself, you will not see the drives that have been assigned. You will first have to add a snap-in.

41. **Answer: C.** To open the menu bar, press the Alt key, which can also be used in combination with a letter or number to perform a function. The Ctrl+Alt key combination (Answer A) does not do anything. Shift+Alt (Answer B) by itself does not do anything. Instead, you have to use Shift+Alt with a letter or number key to perform a function. The Ctrl key (Answer D) can be used with other keys to perform certain tasks or functions.

42. **Answer: B.** The Control Panel is a graphical tool used to configure the Windows environment and hardware devices. It can also be used to access the Administrative Tools and the Device Manager. My Computer (Answer A) allows you to view all of the drives using Windows Explorer. The Microsoft Management Console (MMC), Answer C, is an interface used by tools included with Windows, such as the Administrative Tools, to configure and manage Windows and its programs. The Computer Management Console is an example of the MMC. If you open the MMC by itself, you will not see the drives that have been assigned. You will first have to add a snap-in. The Computer Management Console is an example of the MMC. The Device Manager (Answer D) is used to manage your devices. MSCONFIG is used to control the startup of programs and services.

43. **Answer: A.** While viewing Classic view, the Control Panel will show icons similar to what was found in Windows 2000. Therefore, the other answers are incorrect.

44. **Answer: A.** To cleanly uninstall a program, you need to open the Control Panel. If you are in Standard view, you can click Add or Remove Programs. If you are in Classic view, you can double-click Add or Remove Programs. Therefore, the programs listed in the other answers are incorrect.

45. **Answer: A.** Windows Vista is different from Windows XP in that you would click Uninstall a Program while in Standard view or click Programs or Features while in Classic view. Therefore, the other answers are incorrect.

46. **Answer: B.** To add or remove Windows components including IIS, Indexing Services, and management and monitoring tools, you need to access the Add/Remove programs applet and then click Add/Remove Windows Components. Therefore, the other answers are incorrect.

47. **Answer: D.** You can configure the size and placement of the virtual-memory swap file in Windows 2000 and Windows XP in the Advanced Tab of the System applet in Control Panel. Therefore, the other answers are incorrect.

48. **Answer: C.** When you right-click My Computer and click Properties, you open the System Properties dialog box. This is equivalent to opening the System applet using the Control Panel. Right-clicking the C drive (Answer A) opens the properties for the C drive where you can run tools or rename the volume. Right-clicking the taskbar (Answer B) and clicking properties allows you to configure the task bar properties. Right-clicking the Desktop (Answer D) allows you to configure the Display settings.

49. **Answer: C.** To start the System Configuration Utility, you execute the `msconfig.exe` command. The System Configuration Utility allows you to troubleshoot startup problems, including items loaded with the SYSTEM.INI, BOOT.INI, Services, and Startup. `msinfo32` (not `msinfo`, Answer A) is used to start the System Information utility. The `dxdiag` utility (Answer B) is a DirectX diagnostic tool that can show you what version of DirectX you have and can be used to run a series of tests. `Regedit` (Answer D) is used to access the Windows Registry.

50. **Answer: C.** To start the System Configuration Utility, you execute the `msconfig.exe` command. The System Configuration Utility allows you to troubleshoot startup problems including items loaded with the SYSTEM.INI, BOOT.INI, Services, and Startup. The `msinfo32` (not `msinfo`, Answer A) is used to start the System Information utility. The `dxdiag` utility (Answer B) is a DirectX diagnostic tool that can show you what version of DirectX you have, and it can be used to run a series of tests. `Regedit` (Answer D) is used to access the Windows Registry.

51. **Answer: A.** `Msinfo32.exe` is used to start the System Information utility. It was designed to assist technical support personnel in identifying a PC and its components. The `dxdiag` utility (Answer B) is a DirectX diagnostic tool that can show you what version of DirectX you have and can be used to run a series of tests. The System Configuration Utility (Answer C) allows you to troubleshoot startup problems including items loaded with the SYSTEM.INI, BOOT.INI, Services, and Startup. `Regedit` (Answer D) is used to access the Windows Registry.

52. **Answer: A.** `Msinfo32.exe` is used to start the System Information utility. It was designed to assist technical support personnel in identifying a PC and its components. The `dxdiag` utility (Answer B) is a DirectX diagnostic tool that can show you what version of DirectX you have and can be used to run a series of tests. The System Configuration Utility (Answer C) allows you to troubleshoot startup problems including items loaded with the SYSTEM.INI, BOOT.INI, Services, and Startup. Regedit (Answer D) is used to access the Windows Registry.

53. **Answer: B.** The `Dxdiag.exe` utility is a DirectX diagnostic tool that can show you what version of DirectX you have and can be used to run a series of tests. `Msinfo32.exe` (Answer A) is used to start the System Information utility. It was designed to assist technical support personnel in identifying a PC and its components. The System Configuration Utility (Answer C) allows you to troubleshoot startup problems including items loaded with the SYSTEM.INI, BOOT.INI, Services, and Startup. `Regedit` (Answer D) is used to access the Windows Registry.

54. **Answer: D.** The Registry is the central information database for Windows organized into a tree-structured hierarchy database. Regedit is short for Registry Editor and is the utility that allows you to view and directly edit the registry. `Msinfo32.exe` (Answer A) is used to start the System Information utility. It was designed to assist technical support personnel in identifying a PC and its components. The `Dxdiag.exe` utility (Answer B) is a DirectX diagnostic tool that can show you what version of DirectX you have and can be used to run a series of tests. The System Configuration Utility (Answer C) allows you to troubleshoot startup problems including items loaded with the SYSTEM.INI, BOOT.INI, Services, and Startup.

55. **Answer: D.** The Registry is the central information database for Windows. Several files that make up the registry are stored in `%SystemRoot%\System32\Config`, which is usually `C:\Windows\System32\Config`. In addition, there are registry files stored in the user's profile folder (`%UserProfile%\NTUser.dat` and `%UserProfile%\Local Settings\Application Data\Microsoft\Windows\Userclass.dat`). Therefore, the other answers are incorrect.

56. **Answer: C.** HKEY_LOCAL_MACHINES contains information about the type of hardware installed, drivers, and other system settings. Information includes the bus type, system memory, device drivers, and startup control data. The data in the subtree

remains constant regardless of the user. HKEY_CLASSES_ROOT key (Answer A) contains the file extension associations and OLE information. HKEY_CURRENT_USER (Answer B) is a copy from HKEY_USERS for a specific user and holds the current settings for the user currently logged on. When the user logs off, the settings are copied back to HKEY_USERS (Answer D).

57. **Answer: D.** HKEY_CLASSES_ROOT key contains the file extension associations and OLE information. HKEY_CURRENT_USER (Answer A) is a copy from HKEY_USERS for a specific user and holds the current settings for the user currently logged on. When the user logs off, the settings are copied back to HKEY_USERS (Answer B). HKEY_LOCAL_MACHINES (Answer C) contains information about the type of hardware installed, drivers, and other system settings. Information includes the bus type, system memory, device drivers, and startup control data.

58. **Answer: D.** When you press the Window key + L, you lock Windows. Therefore, the other answers are incorrect.

59. **Answer: B.** To open the Windows Security Dialog box in Windows XP, you press the Ctrl+Alt+Del keys. From the Windows Security Dialog box, you can lock the computer, log off, shut down the computer, change the password, or open the Task Manager. Ctrl+L (Answer C) locks Windows. Ctrl+Esc opens the Start menu. The F1 key (Answer D) is usually used to access help. Ctrl+Enter does not do anything for Windows but might have special meaning to other programs (for example, Ctrl+Enter inserts a page break in Microsoft Word).

60. **Answer: A.** Pressing the Ctrl+Esc key combination pops up the Start menu along with the taskbar in Windows 2000/XP. Alt+Esc (Answer B) can be used to toggle between programs running in Windows. Ctrl+Alt+Esc (Answer C) and Shift+Esc (Answer D) do not do anything for Windows but might have special meaning to other programs running in Windows.

61. **Answer: A.** To switch between programs, you can use the Alt+Tab key combination. You can also use Alt+Esc. Alt+Enter (Answer B) and Alt+Ctrl (Answer C) do not have any special meaning for Windows but might have special meaning for other programs running in Windows. Alt+Ctrl+Del (Answer D) opens the Security Window or the Task Manager or it allows you to log on.

62. **Answer: A and E.** To switch between programs, you can use Alt+Tab, which works in all versions of Windows. Windows Vista also offers Flip 3D, which can be initiated by pressing the Start+Tab keys. To open the Windows Security Dialog box in Windows XP, you press the Ctrl+Alt+Del keys (Answer D). From the Windows Security Dialog box, you can lock the computer, log off, shut down the computer, change the password, or open the Task Manager. Alt+Enter (Answer B) and Alt+Ctrl (Answer C) do not do anything for Windows but might have special meaning for other programs running in Windows. For example Alt+Ctrl+down arrow can invert your screen with some video drivers.

63. **Answer: A.** The Windows utility for scheduling tasks is located under the Control Panel's Scheduled Tasks icon. This utility is used to schedule operating system and application operations so that they start and run automatically. This enables users and technicians to schedule routine tasks, such as backups and defragmentation operations, to occur without a user or technician being involved. Also, these tasks can be scheduled to run at the most convenient times, such as the middle of the night when

no one is using the machine. Tasks can be scheduled to run daily, weekly, monthly, or at prescribed times and dates. The Task Manager (Answer B) is used to view all running programs and processes and allows you to manage those programs and processes, including stopping programs and processes and viewing PC performance. Device Manager (Answer C) allows you to manage devices and drivers. The MSConfig utility (Answer D) allows you to manage the startup of programs and services.

64. **Answer: B.** A cluster, which can be made up of one or more sectors, is the smallest amount an operating system can address. A head (Answer A) is a component of the disk. Usually, you have one head for each side of each platter. A sector (Answer C) is 512 bytes. While it is smaller than a cluster, it is not addressable by the operating system. The Operating system only sees clusters. Cylinders (Answer D) are the concentric circles that are mapped on the platters of a disk.

65. **Answer: A.** The Master boot record, always found on the first sector of a hard drive, tells the system ROM BIOS how the hard drive is divided (master partition table) and which partition to boot from. The volume boot sector (Answer B) holds the boot program. The file allocation table (Answer C) is the index for the FAT/FAT32 file system listing each cluster. The root directory (Answer D) is the first entry in a volume.

66. **Answer: B.** The top of the file structure tree is called the root directory. For example, the top of the C drive would be designed as C:\. The partition tables (Answer A) specify how the disk is divided. The volume boot sector (Answer B) contains instructions of how to boot an operating system from a volume or partition. The Master Boot Record (MBR), Answer D, is the first part of a hard disk that contains the boot program and partition table.

67. **Answer: C.** MBR can support up to four primary partitions or three primary partitions and one extended partition. Therefore, the other answers are incorrect.

68. **Answer: A, B, and D.** The NTFS file system comes from the Windows NT family including Windows 2000, Windows XP, and Windows Vista and Is a more sophisticated file system that has a number of enhancements that set it apart from FAT. It supports larger partition sizes than FAT32. It allows for file-level security to protect system resources and supports compression, encryption, disk quotas, and file ownership. NTFS cannot be accessed by DOS disk utilities (Answer C).

69. **Answer: B and D.** To create a new file or folder, you just need to right-click the empty area of the Display Window, select New, and then select Folder. You can also open the File menu, select New, and then select Folder. Therefore, the other answers are incorrect.

70. **Answer: C.** Disk quotas are used to control the amount of disk space a network user can consume on a single partition or volume. For Windows 2000, XP, and Vista, disk quotas are only available on NTFS partitions/volumes. Disk Cleanup (Answer A) is used to free used disk space. Security Center (Answer B) is used to manage certain features of Windows including the Windows Firewall and Windows Updates. Disk Defragmenter (Answer D) is used to optimize a hard drive by moving files back together.

71. **Answer: D.** NTFS uses permissions to control access to files and folders. FAT (Answer A), FAT32 (Answer B), and CDFS (Answer C) do not have file- or folder-level permissions.

72. **Answer: D.** The Windows 2000 and XP operating systems support several file management system formats, including FAT (Answer A), FAT16, FAT32 (Answer B), CDFS (the compact disk file system is used on CD-ROMs —Answer C), and NTFS4, along with its own native NTFS5 format. Windows Vista uses NTFS V6.0.

73. **Answer: B.** Under the FAT file system, there is room for one primary partition and the extended partition on a hard disk drive. The extended partition can be created on any unused disk space after the primary partition has been established and properly configured. The extended partition can be subdivided into 23 logical drives (the letters of the alphabet minus A, B, and C). Therefore, the other answers are incorrect.

74. **Answer: B.** To change file attributes from Explorer, right-click the desired file, select the Properties option from the pop-up list, move to the General page, and click the desired attribute boxes. Therefore, the other answers are incorrect.

75. **Answer: B.** To change a file's attributes in Windows Explorer, right-click the desired file, select the Properties option from the pop-up list, move to the General page, and click on the desired attribute boxes. Therefore, the other answers are incorrect.

76. **Answer: B and D.** Windows 2000 has two different executables used to start the setup program, depending on the OS you are using to start the install. These executables are WINNT.EXE and WINNT32.EXE. Therefore the other answers are incorrect.

77. **Answer: D.** Before you install Windows XP Professional from the CD, it is recommended that you run the Windows XP version of Checkupgradeonly. This file checks the system for possible hardware compatibility problems and is located on the installation CD under \i386\winnt32. You can also check the Microsoft Windows XP Hardware Compatibility Lists (HCL) page. Therefore, the other answers are incorrect.

78. **Answer: D.** To install Windows Vista, you boot from a Windows Vista installation DVD. You will then choose a partition to install it on and you must provide a valid product key to complete the installation.

79. **Answer: A.** During the early part of installation, you are given the option to press F6 so that you can insert a floppy disk or CD/DVD that contains a SCSI driver. Therefore the other answers are incorrect.

80. **Answer: B.** To load special drivers such as SCSI drivers, you need to select the Load Drivers option from the Where Do You Want to Install Vista? page. Therefore the other answers are incorrect.

81. **Answer: A.** To do an in-place upgrade, you must insert the installation DVD into the drive while Windows is running. Therefore the other answers are incorrect.

82. **Answer: B.** Installing a new operating system on a hard drive has evolved into these five basic steps: Partition the drive for use with the operating system. Format the drive with the basic operating system files. Run the appropriate Setup utility to install the complete operating system. Load all the drivers necessary for the operating system to function with the system's installed hardware devices. Reboot the system to activate all the system components. Therefore, the other answers are incorrect.

83. **Answer: C.** Partitioning is the process of assigning part or all of the drive for use by the computer. Formatting (Answer A) prepares the partition (sometimes referred to as a volume) by creating the file system. There is no official step called modification (Answer B).

84. **Answer: A and C.** While, many hardware changes can be made through the Hardware wizard, it is often easier to use Device Manager, which provides a simple and well-organized method to manage hardware in the system. Administrative Tools give access to many MMC programs, including the Computer Management console.

85. **Answer: B.** Driver Signing is controlled through the Windows 2000/XP Control Panel's System icon. In the System applet, select the Hardware tab and click on the Driver Signing button. The Driver Signing Options page displays. On this page you can establish how the system should react when it detects an unsigned driver. Therefore, the other answers are incorrect.

86. **Answer: D.** The drivers that the employees are downloading are not working with the hardware under the new operating system. Microsoft has a program called Driver Signing that allows hardware manufacturers to verify that their drivers work with given Microsoft operating systems. To prevent the employees from installing drivers that don't work, you need to enforce the use of driver signing to verify drivers before they are installed. On the Windows XP Driver Signing Options page, you can establish how the system should react when it detects an unsigned driver. The Block option does not permit any unsigned drivers to be loaded into the system. Therefore, the other answers are incorrect.

87. **Answer: A.** The Warn setting causes Windows to notify the user when an unsigned driver has been detected. It also produces an option to load or not load the driver. This is the default setting for Driver Signing. Therefore, the other answers are incorrect.

88. **Answer: A.** Windows XP has special tools, called the user state migration tool (USMT), that administrators can use to transfer user configuration settings and files from systems running Windows 9x/Me and Windows NT systems to a clean Windows XP installation. This enables user information to be preserved without going through the upgrade process. The purpose of Recovery tools (Answer B), including the ASR (Answer C), is to recover after a system has failed or files have been deleted, not to migrate users from one system to another. The backup utility (Answer D) is for recovery, not for moving settings over.

89. **Answer: A.** Virtual memory is using disk as RAM. Of course, using the paging file is many times slower than regular RAM. In Windows XP, the paging file called PAGE-FILE.SYS is a virtual memory file that sets aside hard drive space to be used as RAM. Fortunately, it provides more memory by using hard drive space as a temporary storage area. Therefore, the other answers are incorrect.

90. **Answer: A.** To configure virtual memory in Windows XP, you open the control panel and double-click the System applet to open the System Properties. Then Select the Advanced tab. Therefore, the other options are incorrect.

91. **Answer: B.** It is possible to optimize the system's performance by distributing its swap file (PAGEFILE.SYS) space among multiple drives. It can also be helpful to relocate the swap file away from slower or heavily used drives. You should not place the swap file on mirrored or striped volumes. Also, don't create multiple swap files in logical disks that exist on the same physical drive. Setting the virtual memory setting to maximum will not increase performance. Instead of setting the virtual memory to the minimum size or setting it to the maximum (Answers A and D), you should set the minimum and maximum size to the same so that the paging file does not have to shrink or grow. You cannot set the virtual memory to a variable (Answer C).

92. **Answer: A.** Hibernate mode saves the computing session that is stored in RAM to the hard disk and then shuts down the system. When the system is reactivated, the computing session is fully restored into memory and restarted at the place it left off. Standby mode (Answer C) still uses some power to keep the memory alive so that it can quickly come back after the machine has been put in Standby mode. There is no such thing as suspend mode (Answer B). If you Shutdown the computer (Answer D), you will not be able to continue with the current session.

93. **Answer: D.** To access and enable hibernate, you need to open the Power Options properties in the Control Panel. Then click the Hibernate tab and select Enable Hibernation. Therefore, the other answers are incorrect.

94. **Answer: B.** In Windows 2000 and XP, the power management functions are located in the Control Panel under the Power Options icon. These functions include options for configuring hard drive and display shutdown times, standby mode timing, and the hibernate functions. Standby settings are configured under the Power Schemes tab, and the hibernation function is enabled under the Hibernate tab (Enable Hibernate Support in Windows 2000 and Enable Hibernation in Windows XP). Therefore, the other answers are incorrect.

95. **Answer: C.** If a Windows Vista computer hibernates, the system state, along with the contents of the system memory, are saved to a file (Hiberfil.sys) on the hard disk and the computer is shut down. The Hiberfil.sys file will be the same size as the amount of physical memory. No power is required to maintain this state because the data is stored on the hard disk. You can then continue where you left off within a short time. Standby mode (Answer A) still keeps everything in RAM and only maintains enough to keep the content alive. There is no sleep mode (Answer B) in Windows Vista. Enabling the screen saver (Answer D) will not save power.

96. **Answer: B.** Wake on LAN is a technology that allows someone to turn on a network computer remotely by sending a special data packet (called a Magic Packet) to the network adapter. Even if the computer is hibernating, the network adapter is still "listening" on the network, so when the special packet arrives, the network adapter can turn on the computer. It is the NIC that must have the wake-on-LAN compatibility, not the processor (Answer D). You need wake-on-LAN capability, not hibernate (Answer A) or sleep (Answer C).

97. **Answer: B.** If you hibernate the computer, you can send the magic Wake-on-LAN packet to wake up a computer so that you can update the computer. If you shut down the computer (Answer C), you would not be able wake it up. If you have the users leave their computers on at night (Answer D), you will not be saving any power. You could use sleep mode, but hibernate will save more power because sleep mode (Answer A) consumes a little power to keep the contents in RAM active.

98. **Answer: A.** Sleep mode is a power-saving state that saves work and opens programs to memory. To maintain the contents of memory while the computer is in Sleep mode, the system still consumes a small amount of power. The advantage of Sleep mode is that you can continue where you left off, typically within a few seconds. When the machine goes into hibernate (Answer C), it will save all content onto disk and then power off. Different from sleep, hibernate does not keep content in RAM. Hybrid Sleep (Answer B) is a combination of sleep and hibernate. It saves your work to your hard disk and puts your mobile PC into a power-saving state. If you suffer power failure, your data will not be lost. There is no such thing as Power-Eco (Answer D).

99. Answer: A. Any time you have a component that you want to remove from a laptop, you should use the Safely Remove Hardware icon so that it will properly shut down the component before you disconnect it. Therefore, the other answers are incorrect.

100. Answer: B. The BIOS might be set to boot from the hard drive before it tries to boot from the CD-ROM. In this case the boot sequence must be changed to make it possible to boot from the CD-ROM. The F8 key (Answer C) will allow you to enter Safe Mode, VGA mode, or Last Known Good Configuration. Unfortunately, none of those modes will help boot from the CD-ROM. Lastly, having an NTFS-formatted hard drive (Answer A) and creating a bootable diskette (Answer D) will not help your system boot from a CD-ROM disc.

101. Answer: A and C. If you start in Safe Mode, you can roll back the driver. You can also try to boot to VGA mode, which boots to 640×480. You could try the Last Known Good Configuration, but if you have logged on already that most recent logon becomes the Last Known Good Configuration. In addition, if Windows tries to load the driver before you log on, you will not be able to log on. You could try the Recovery Console (Answer B), but it would be much easier and faster to use the Safe Mode and roll back the driver. Re-installing the operating system (Answer D) should be a last resort and should not be necessary in this situation.

102. Answer: C. The Last Known Good Configuration feature is a recovery option that you can use to start your computer by using the most recent settings that worked. The Last Known Good Configuration feature restores registry information and driver settings that were in effect the last time the computer started successfully. Use the Last Known Good Configuration feature when you cannot start Windows after you make a change to your computer, or when you suspect that a change that you just made might cause a problem. For example, you can use this feature if you cannot start Windows after you install a new driver for your video adapter, or if you installed an incorrect driver and have not yet restarted your computer. Reinstalling the device driver for the NIC (Answer B) is not an option because the machine continuously reboots. You could try to remove the network interface card (Answer D) or reinstall the operating system (Answer A), but these are drastic measures and should not be necessary in this situation.

103. Answer: A. Since it will not start, you can try to do a repair. As you boot from the Windows Vista DVD, you will be given a Startup repair option. The ARC paths in the BOOT.INI (Answer D) are found with Windows 2000 and XP machines, not Windows Vista. The Windows Recovery Console (Answers B and C) was found in Windows XP and was replaced by several tools located in the System Recovery Options menu.

104. Answer: B. By default, the Windows Recovery Console is not installed on Windows XP. Therefore, you need to boot to the Windows XP CD. The Windows Recovery Console (Answer A) is available in Windows Vista, not Windows XP. Windows PE (Answer C) does not allow you to start the Windows Recovery Console. Modifying the Boot.ini file (Answer D) will not allow the Windows Recovery Console to load.

105. Answer: C. If you start in Safe Mode, only the drivers and services that are necessary to start Windows are loaded. You can then fix the problem and restart Windows in normal operation mode. If the machine does not boot, you will not be able to use Device Manager (Answer A) or access the display console (Answer B).

106. Answer: D. The Safe Mode with Networking option starts Windows using only basic files, drivers, and network connections. If you start Windows normally (Answer A), all drivers are loaded. Safe Mode without the Networking option (Answer B) will not load the drivers and software for the network connections. Safe Mode with the command prompt (Answer C) does not provide a GUI interface for you to access all the tools that you can access with Safe Mode.

107. Answer: A. ASR is short for Automated System Recovery. It allows you to restore the system disk (usually the C: drive) including the Windows files, all Registry settings, and all user programs and data, so you can recover a completely crashed system. To use this procedure you must be able to boot the Windows XP Pro Setup program from the installation CD-ROM. If you start in Safe Mode (Answer B), only the drivers and services that are necessary to start Windows are loaded. The Last Known Good Configuration (Answer C) feature is a recovery option that you can use to start your computer by using the most recent settings that worked. The Last Known Good Configuration feature restores registry information and driver settings that were in effect the last time the computer started successfully. Use the Last Known Good Configuration feature when you cannot start Windows after you make a change to your computer, or when you suspect that a change that you just made might cause a problem. The Emergency Recovery Disk (ERD), Answer D, is the primary tool that allows you to repair a Windows 2000 computer.

108. Answer: A. The Emergency Recovery Disk (ERD) is the primary tool that allows you to repair a Windows 2000 computer. It has been replaced by the Automated System Recovery in Windows XP. ASR (Answer B) is short for Automated System Recovery. It allows you to restore the system disk (usually the C: drive), including the Windows files, all Registry settings, and all user programs and data, so you can recover a completely crashed system. To use this procedure you must be able to boot the Windows XP Pro Setup program from the installation CD-ROM. The Recovery Console (Answer C) shows you a command prompt so that you can run commands that can be used to diagnose and fix a problem. The PE Disk (Answer D) is a bootable disk used to fix and troubleshoot a range of problems, and it can be used to install Windows.

109. Answer: D. With many systems, if you turn on a computer while the USB thumb drive is connected to a computer, the computer will try to boot from the USB thumb drive. As a result, you usually get a black screen. Windows is most likely still available on the C: drive (Answer A) and the boot.ini has not been modified (Answer C). You just need to remove the USB thumb drive and reboot the computer. The network cable (Answer B) is not a factor unless the computer has been configured to boot from the network.

C H A P T E R   F O U R

Networking

Almost every computer is connected to a network or the Internet. Therefore, you need to understand basic networking concepts and know how to configure network settings on all modern versions of Windows. As you learn more about networking, you will enhance your troubleshooting skills.

This domain for the 220-701 exam counts as 15%. The given objectives for this domain are

- ▶ 4.1—Summarize the basics of networking fundamentals, including technologies, devices, and protocols
- ▶ 4.2—Categorize network cables and connectors and their implementations
- ▶ 4.3—Compare and contrast the different network types

4.1 Summarize the basics of networking fundamentals, including technologies, devices, and protocols

- ▶ Basics of configuring IP addressing and TCP/IP properties (DHCP, DNS)
- ▶ Bandwidth and latency
- ▶ Status indicators
- ▶ Protocols (TCP/IP, NETBIOS)
- ▶ Full-duplex, half-duplex
- ▶ Basics of workgroups and domains
- ▶ Common ports: HTTP, FTP, POP, SMTP, TELNET, HTTPS
- ▶ LAN/WAN
- ▶ Hub, switch, and router
- ▶ Identify Virtual Private Networks (VPN)
- ▶ Basics class identification

Note

The objectives of bandwidth and latency and status indicators are covered by questions in Chapter 9, "Networking" in Part II of this book.

---

1. The protocol used by the Internet is which of the following?

Quick Answer: **159**
Detailed Answer: **160**

   ○ **A.** TCP/IP

   ○ **B.** NetBEUI

   ○ **C.** IPX

   ○ **D.** AppleTalk

2. To connect to a TCP/IP network, you must configure which of the following? (Choose two answers.)

Quick Answer: **159**
Detailed Answer: **160**

   ○ **A.** IP address

   ○ **B.** The gateway

   ○ **C.** The IPX address

   ○ **D.** The subnet mask

   ○ **E.** The DNS server address

3. You have a TCP/IP network with several subnets. You want to be able to communicate with all subnets. What do you need to configure to communicate with these subnets? (Select all that apply.)

Quick Answer: **159**
Detailed Answer: **160**

   ○ **A.** IP address

   ○ **B.** The default gateway

   ○ **C.** The IPX address

   ○ **D.** The subnet mask

   ○ **E.** The DNS server address

4. What needs to be configured for domain and host name resolution?

Quick Answer: **159**
Detailed Answer: **160**

   ○ **A.** IP address

   ○ **B.** The default gateway

   ○ **C.** The IPX address

   ○ **D.** The subnet mask

   ○ **E.** The DNS server address

5. Which of the following must you configure on a computer that must be connected to the Internet? (Choose two answers.)

Quick Answer: **159**
Detailed Answer: **160**

   ○ **A.** The host name of the computer

   ○ **B.** The IP address of the DHCP server

   ○ **C.** The IP address of the default gateway

   ○ **D.** The IP address of the e-mail server

   ○ **E.** The IP address of the DNS server

6. An IP address that you manually assign to a computer is known as which of the following?

- ○ **A.** Dynamic address
- ○ **B.** Revolving address
- ○ **C.** Static address
- ○ **D.** Transfer address

7. What service do you use to automatically assign IP addresses to host computers?

- ○ **A.** DNS
- ○ **B.** WINS
- ○ **C.** MAC
- ○ **D.** DHCP

8. How many bits does an IPv4 address consist of?

- ○ **A.** 16 bits
- ○ **B.** 32 bits
- ○ **C.** 64 bits
- ○ **D.** 128 bits
- ○ **E.** 256 bits

9. How many bits does an IPv6 address consist of?

- ○ **A.** 16 bits
- ○ **B.** 32 bits
- ○ **C.** 64 bits
- ○ **D.** 128 bits
- ○ **E.** 256 bits

10. What is the physical address of a network interface card (NIC) called?

- ○ **A.** SPX address
- ○ **B.** UID
- ○ **C.** IP address
- ○ **D.** MAC address
- ○ **E.** PID

11. You have a computer logged onto Windows XP. You connect a network cable to the network interface card (NIC) and you see a green light that blinks on and off. What does this usually mean?

Quick Answer: **159**
Detailed Answer: **161**

- ○ **A.** Your cable connection is faulty.
- ○ **B.** Your power connection is faulty.
- ○ **C.** You are being affected by EMI.
- ○ **D.** You have network traffic.

12. Which protocol works on top of TCP/IP that runs on most Microsoft networks and is responsible for establishing logical names (computer names) on the network, establishing a logical connection between two computers, and supports reliable data transfer between two computers using the SMB protocol?

Quick Answer: **159**
Detailed Answer: **161**

- ○ **A.** NetBEUI
- ○ **B.** NetBIOS
- ○ **C.** IPX
- ○ **D.** SPX
- ○ **E.** CIFS

13. Which protocol provides reliable, connection-based delivery and is used with many other protocols?

Quick Answer: **159**
Detailed Answer: **161**

- ○ **A.** TCP
- ○ **B.** UDP
- ○ **C.** IP
- ○ **D.** ARP

14. Which transport layer protocol provides connectionless communications and does not guarantee that packets will be delivered?

Quick Answer: **159**
Detailed Answer: **162**

- ○ **A.** TCP
- ○ **B.** UDP
- ○ **C.** IP
- ○ **D.** ARP

15. Which protocol is used primarily for addressing and routing packets between hosts?

Quick Answer: **159**
Detailed Answer: **162**

- ○ **A.** TCP
- ○ **B.** UDP
- ○ **C.** IP
- ○ **D.** ARP

16. Which of the following allows for two devices to communicate at the same time?

- ○ **A.** Simplex
- ○ **B.** Full-duplex
- ○ **C.** Half-duplex
- ○ **D.** Complex

Quick Answer: **159**
Detailed Answer: **162**

17. Which of the following allows for two devices to communicate with each other, but not at the same time?

- ○ **A.** Simplex
- ○ **B.** Full-duplex
- ○ **C.** Half-duplex
- ○ **D.** Complex

Quick Answer: **159**
Detailed Answer: **162**

18. What is sometimes referred to as a peer-to-peer network that has no dedicated server?

- ○ **A.** Workgroup
- ○ **B.** Domain
- ○ **C.** Complex
- ○ **D.** Simplex

Quick Answer: **159**
Detailed Answer: **162**

19. What is a logical unit of computers and network resources that defines a security boundary and uses one database to share its common security and user account information for all computers?

- ○ **A.** Workgroup
- ○ **B.** Domain
- ○ **C.** Complex
- ○ **D.** Simplex

Quick Answer: **159**
Detailed Answer: **162**

20. What provides authentication within a domain?

- ○ **A.** DNS
- ○ **B.** Domain controller
- ○ **C.** WINS
- ○ **D.** SAM

Quick Answer: **159**
Detailed Answer: **163**

21. What port does HTTP use?

- ○ **A.** 21
- ○ **B.** 80
- ○ **C.** 443
- ○ **D.** 110

Quick Answer: **159**
Detailed Answer: **163**

22. What ports does FTP use? (Choose two answers.)

Quick Answer: **159**
Detailed Answer: **163**

   ○ **A.** 20

   ○ **B.** 21

   ○ **C.** 80

   ○ **D.** 443

   ○ **E.** 110

   ○ **F.** 25

23. What port does POP3 use?

Quick Answer: **159**
Detailed Answer: **163**

   ○ **A.** 25

   ○ **B.** 80

   ○ **C.** 443

   ○ **D.** 110

24. What port does IMAP use?

Quick Answer: **159**
Detailed Answer: **163**

   ○ **A.** 25

   ○ **B.** 80

   ○ **C.** 443

   ○ **D.** 110

   ○ **E.** 143

25. What port does HTTPS use?

Quick Answer: **159**
Detailed Answer: **163**

   ○ **A.** 25

   ○ **B.** 80

   ○ **C.** 443

   ○ **D.** 110

   ○ **E.** 143

26. What port does SMTP use?

Quick Answer: **159**
Detailed Answer: **163**

   ○ **A.** 25

   ○ **B.** 80

   ○ **C.** 443

   ○ **D.** 110

   ○ **E.** 143

27. What port does Telnet use?

- ○ **A.** 23
- ○ **B.** 80
- ○ **C.** 443
- ○ **D.** 110
- ○ **E.** 143

28. Which type of network usually has computers connected within a geographical close network such as a room, a building, or a group of adjacent buildings?

- ○ **A.** LAN
- ○ **B.** MAN
- ○ **C.** WAN
- ○ **D.** VAN

29. Which type of network uses long-range telecommunication links to connect the network computers over long distances and often consists of two or more smaller LANs?

- ○ **A.** LAN
- ○ **B.** MAN
- ○ **C.** WAN
- ○ **D.** VAN

30. What is the largest global WAN?

- ○ **A.** Intranet
- ○ **B.** Internet
- ○ **C.** SBC
- ○ **D.** SOHO

31. What is a network called that is based on TCP/IP but belongs to a single organization and is accessible only by the organization's members?

- ○ **A.** Internet
- ○ **B.** Extranet
- ○ **C.** Intranet
- ○ **D.** VAN

32. What is a small network called that is used primarily in home offices that might be part of a larger corporation but remains apart from it?

Quick Answer: **159**
Detailed Answer: **164**

- ○ **A.** Internet
- ○ **B.** Extranet
- ○ **C.** Intranet
- ○ **D.** SOHO

33. What device is a multiport repeater?

Quick Answer: **159**
Detailed Answer: **164**

- ○ **A.** Hub
- ○ **B.** Switch
- ○ **C.** Gateway
- ○ **D.** Router
- ○ **E.** Bridge

34. What device is a multiport bridge?

Quick Answer: **159**
Detailed Answer: **165**

- ○ **A.** Hub
- ○ **B.** Switch
- ○ **C.** Gateway
- ○ **D.** Router
- ○ **E.** Bridge

35. What device connects two or more LANs and shares status and routing information with other such devices?

Quick Answer: **159**
Detailed Answer: **165**

- ○ **A.** Hub
- ○ **B.** Switch
- ○ **C.** Gateway
- ○ **D.** Router
- ○ **E.** Bridge

36. What kind of switch acts as a router based on logical addresses such as IP addresses?

Quick Answer: **159**
Detailed Answer: **165**

- ○ **A.** Gateway
- ○ **B.** Bridge
- ○ **C.** Brouter
- ○ **D.** Layer 3 switch

37. What type of device or software links two different types of networks together?

- ○ **A.** Gateway
- ○ **B.** Bridge
- ○ **C.** Brouter
- ○ **D.** Layer 3 switch

Quick Answer: **159**
Detailed Answer: **165**

38. What is a network made of secured, point-to-point connections across a private network or a public network such as the Internet?

- ○ **A.** SOHO
- ○ **B.** VAN
- ○ **C.** VPN
- ○ **D.** Telnet

Quick Answer: **159**
Detailed Answer: **166**

39. You have a network with 150 computers connected with a hub. What would you suggest as an upgrade that would improve network performance?

- ○ **A.** Wireless network adapters
- ○ **B.** Switches
- ○ **C.** Routers
- ○ **D.** Bridges

Quick Answer: **159**
Detailed Answer: **166**

40. What is used to identify which bits of an IP address are used as the network ID and which bits are used as the host ID?

- ○ **A.** VPN
- ○ **B.** First octet
- ○ **C.** Unicast
- ○ **D.** Subnet mask

Quick Answer: **159**
Detailed Answer: **166**

41. Which of the following is a Class A IP address? (Choose all that apply.)

- ○ **A.** 14.74.67.34
- ○ **B.** 101.34.89.202
- ○ **C.** 175.243.3.1
- ○ **D.** 202.23.53.2

Quick Answer: **159**
Detailed Answer: **166**

42. What is the default subnet mask for a Class A IP address?

   ○   **A.**   0.0.0.0

   ○   **B.**   255.0.0.0

   ○   **C.**   255.255.0.0

   ○   **D.**   255.255.255.0

   ○   **E.**   255.255.255.255

Quick Answer: **159**
Detailed Answer: **166**

43. Which of the following is a Class B IP address? (Choose all that apply.)

   ○   **A.**   14.74.67.34

   ○   **B.**   101.34.89.202

   ○   **C.**   175.243.3.1

   ○   **D.**   202.23.53.2

Quick Answer: **159**
Detailed Answer: **167**

44. What is the default subnet mask for a Class B IP address?

   ○   **A.**   0.0.0.0

   ○   **B.**   255.0.0.0

   ○   **C.**   255.255.0.0

   ○   **D.**   255.255.255.0

   ○   **E.**   255.255.255.255

Quick Answer: **159**
Detailed Answer: **167**

45. Which of the following is a Class C IP address? (Choose all that apply.)

   ○   **A.**   14.74.67.34

   ○   **B.**   101.34.89.202

   ○   **C.**   175.243.3.1

   ○   **D.**   202.23.53.2

Quick Answer: **159**
Detailed Answer: **167**

46. What is the default subnet mask for a Class C IP address?

   ○   **A.**   0.0.0.0

   ○   **B.**   255.0.0.0

   ○   **C.**   255.255.0.0

   ○   **D.**   255.255.255.0

   ○   **E.**   255.255.255.255

Quick Answer: **159**
Detailed Answer: **167**

47. How many hosts can a Class C network support?

  ○ **A.** 62

  ○ **B.** 126

  ○ **C.** 254

  ○ **D.** 510

Quick Answer: **159**
Detailed Answer: **167**

48. What is the binary equivalent of 255?

  ○ **A.** 1000 0000

  ○ **B.** 1111 0000

  ○ **C.** 1111 1110

  ○ **D.** 1111 1111

Quick Answer: **159**
Detailed Answer: **167**

49. What is Class D used for in IP networks?

  ○ **A.** Anycast

  ○ **B.** Unicast

  ○ **C.** Broadcast

  ○ **D.** Multicast

Quick Answer: **159**
Detailed Answer: **167**

50. Which of the following are private network addresses that are not intended to be connected directly to the Internet? (Choose all that apply.)

  ○ **A.** 10.54.43.4

  ○ **B.** 172.16.34.34

  ○ **C.** 183.23.3.4

  ○ **D.** 192.168.4.2

Quick Answer: **159**
Detailed Answer: **167**

51. Which of the following are associated with the 127.0.0.1 address? (Choose all that apply.)

  ○ **A.** Broadcast address

  ○ **B.** Loopback address

  ○ **C.** Multicast

  ○ **D.** localhost

Quick Answer: **159**
Detailed Answer: **168**

52. Which of the following are examples of IPv6 addresses? (Choose all that apply.)

  ○ **A.** 130.23.74.24

  ○ **B.** 255.255.240.0

  ○ **C.** 2001:0db8:85a3:0000:0000:8a2e:0370:7334

  ○ **D.** 2001:db8:85a3:0:0:8a2e:370:7334

  ○ **E.** 2001:db8:85a3::8a2e:370:7334

Quick Answer: **159**
Detailed Answer: **168**

53. Which of the following is a loopback for IPv6? (Choose two answers.)

Quick Answer: **159**
Detailed Answer: **168**

- ○ **A.** 127.0.0.1
- ○ **B.** 0000:0000:0000:0000:0000:0000:0000:0001
- ○ **C.** ::1
- ○ **D.** 255.255.0.1

54. What describes the time between a signal broadcast and the time received at its destination?

Quick Answer: **159**
Detailed Answer: **168**

- ○ **A.** Attenuation
- ○ **B.** Jitter
- ○ **C.** Latency
- ○ **D.** Beaconing

4.2 Categorize network cables and connectors and their implementations

- ▶ Cables
    - ▶ Plenum/PVC
    - ▶ UTP (e.g. CAT3, CAT5/5e, CAT6)
    - ▶ STP
    - ▶ Fiber
    - ▶ Coaxial cable
- ▶ Connectors
    - ▶ RJ45
    - ▶ RJ11

55. Where in a building is the plenum located? (Choose two answers.)

Quick Answer: **159**
Detailed Answer: **168**

- ○ **A.** In the ceilings
- ○ **B.** In the walls
- ○ **C.** In the elevator shaft
- ○ **D.** In the basement

56. What type of cable is a special cable that gives off little or no toxic fumes when burned?

Quick Answer: **159**
Detailed Answer: **168**

- ○ **A.** Riser cable
- ○ **B.** Plenum cable
- ○ **C.** Punch down cable
- ○ **D.** Unshielded twisted pair

57. Plenum cable has which of the following characteristics?

Quick Answer: **159**
Detailed Answer: **168**

- ○ **A.** It has a lower cost than non-plenum cables.
- ○ **B.** It transfers data faster.
- ○ **C.** It is a military version of the cable, which contains more shielding.
- ○ **D.** It meets fire codes.

58. What network cabling has four pairs of wires?

Quick Answer: **159**
Detailed Answer: **168**

- ○ **A.** Coaxial
- ○ **B.** Twisted-pair
- ○ **C.** Fiber optic
- ○ **D.** Twisted optic

59. What network media uses a single copper conductor covered by an insulating layer, which is in turn covered by a conductive mesh and then finally a tough plastic skin?

Quick Answer: **159**
Detailed Answer: **169**

- ○ **A.** Coaxial
- ○ **B.** Twisted-pair
- ○ **C.** Fiber optic
- ○ **D.** Twisted optic

60. What cable uses a glass or plastic core?

Quick Answer: **159**
Detailed Answer: **169**

- ○ **A.** Coaxial
- ○ **B.** Twisted-pair
- ○ **C.** Fiber optic
- ○ **D.** Twisted optic

61. Which cable is the most common in networks?

Quick Answer: **159**
Detailed Answer: **169**

- ○ **A.** UTP
- ○ **B.** STP
- ○ **C.** Coaxial
- ○ **D.** Fiber optic

62. Which of the following best defines when a signal jumps from one wire to an adjacent wire?

Quick Answer: **159**
Detailed Answer: **169**

- ○ **A.** Attenuation
- ○ **B.** Jitter
- ○ **C.** Crosstalk
- ○ **D.** Beaconing

63. What can be done to reduce the noise caused by crosstalk?

Quick Answer: **159**
Detailed Answer: **169**

- ○ **A.** Use twisted pair wiring
- ○ **B.** Use aluminum shielding
- ○ **C.** Use plastic shielding
- ○ **D.** Use a plenum sheath

64. Which of the following has the highest possible throughput?

Quick Answer: **159**
Detailed Answer: **169**

- ○ **A.** STP cable
- ○ **B.** UTP cable
- ○ **C.** Coaxial cable
- ○ **D.** Fiber optic cable

65. Which of the following supports the longest transmission distance?

Quick Answer: **159**
Detailed Answer: **169**

- ○ **A.** Coaxial cable
- ○ **B.** Fiber optic cable
- ○ **C.** UTP cable
- ○ **D.** Wireless

66. Which of the following is not affected by EMI?

Quick Answer: **159**
Detailed Answer: **169**

- ○ **A.** Coaxial cable
- ○ **B.** Fiber optic cable
- ○ **C.** UTP cable
- ○ **D.** Wireless

67. Which of the following Ethernet cable standards supports transmission speeds greater than 200 Mbps?

Quick Answer: **159**
Detailed Answer: **169**

- ○ **A.** CAT4
- ○ **B.** CAT3
- ○ **C.** CAT5
- ○ **D.** CAT6

68. What is the minimum cable rating required for a 1000BASE-TX network?

Quick Answer: **159**
Detailed Answer: **170**

- ○ **A.** CAT3
- ○ **B.** CAT5
- ○ **C.** CAT5e
- ○ **D.** CAT6

69. You have two workstations. Each workstation has a 100BASE-T network card. You want to connect the two workstations directly without the use of a hub or switch. Which cable could you use?

Quick Answer: **159**
Detailed Answer: **170**

- ○ **A.** CAT3 crossover
- ○ **B.** CAT5 crossover
- ○ **C.** CAT3 straight
- ○ **D.** CAT5 straight

70. You want to connect a second router to your core router. What would you use to connect the two routers?

Quick Answer: **159**
Detailed Answer: **170**

- ○ **A.** A patch cable.
- ○ **B.** A crossover cable.
- ○ **C.** A Category 5 cable.
- ○ **D.** Two routers cannot be connected together.

71. Which media type is the MOST susceptible to electromagnetic interference (EMI)?

Quick Answer: **159**
Detailed Answer: **170**

- ○ **A.** Category 5 UTP cable
- ○ **B.** RG-8 coaxial cable
- ○ **C.** Single-mode fiber optic cable
- ○ **D.** Multimode fiber optic cable

72. What is the maximum segment length of a 100BASE-TX cable?

Quick Answer: **159**
Detailed Answer: **170**

- ○ **A.** 25 meters
- ○ **B.** 75 meters
- ○ **C.** 100 meters
- ○ **D.** 182 meters
- ○ **E.** 550 meters

73. The maximum segment length of a CAT5 UTP cable is which of the following?

Quick Answer: **159**
Detailed Answer: **170**

- ○ **A.** 246 feet (75 meters)
- ○ **B.** 656 feet (200 meters)
- ○ **C.** 328 feet (100 meters)
- ○ **D.** 164 feet (50 meters)

74. What would be the best to use when installing a Gigabit Ethernet network?

- ○ **A.** CAT6
- ○ **B.** CAT5e
- ○ **C.** CAT5
- ○ **D.** CAT4

Quick Answer: **159**
Detailed Answer: **170**

75. Which of the following is the connector used for 100Base-T Ethernet cables?

- ○ **A.** RJ-11
- ○ **B.** BNC
- ○ **C.** RJ-58
- ○ **D.** RG-45

Quick Answer: **159**
Detailed Answer: **170**

76. Which connectors does 1000BASE-TX use?

- ○ **A.** MT-RJ
- ○ **B.** RJ-45
- ○ **C.** RJ-11
- ○ **D.** ST

Quick Answer: **159**
Detailed Answer: **170**

77. Which of the following requires a cable with RJ-45 connectors?

- ○ **A.** 10BASE2
- ○ **B.** 10BASE5
- ○ **C.** 10BASE-T
- ○ **D.** 10BASE-FL

Quick Answer: **159**
Detailed Answer: **170**

78. How many pairs of wires are used in an RJ-45 connector?

- ○ **A.** 2
- ○ **B.** 3
- ○ **C.** 4
- ○ **D.** 5

Quick Answer: **159**
Detailed Answer: **170**

79. Which type of a cable uses RJ-45 connectors?

- ○ **A.** RG-58 coaxial
- ○ **B.** RG-59 coaxial
- ○ **C.** Unshielded twisted pair
- ○ **D.** Multimode fiber optic

Quick Answer: **159**
Detailed Answer: **170**

80. What do you use to connect two coaxial cables?

Quick Answer: **159**
Detailed Answer: **170**

- ○ **A.** A BNC terminator
- ○ **B.** A network adapter card
- ○ **C.** A BNC barrel connector
- ○ **D.** A medium attachment unit

81. Which of the following are connectors used with fiber optic cables? (Choose all that apply.)

Quick Answer: **159**
Detailed Answer: **171**

- ○ **A.** ST
- ○ **B.** MT-RJ
- ○ **C.** SC
- ○ **D.** RG-58

82. Which connector is used to replace the SC connectors?

Quick Answer: **159**
Detailed Answer: **171**

- ○ **A.** ST
- ○ **B.** RG-58
- ○ **C.** FC
- ○ **D.** LC

83. Which type of problem is most likely to be caused by increasing cable lengths?

Quick Answer: **159**
Detailed Answer: **171**

- ○ **A.** Attenuation
- ○ **B.** Beaconing
- ○ **C.** Crosstalk
- ○ **D.** Jitter

4.3 Compare and contrast the different network types

- ▶ Broadband
  - ▶ DSL
  - ▶ Cable
  - ▶ Satellite
  - ▶ Fiber
- ▶ Dial-up
- ▶ Wireless
  - ▶ All 802.11 types
  - ▶ WEP
  - ▶ WPA
  - ▶ SSID

▶ MAC filtering

▶ DHCP settings

▶ Bluetooth

▶ Cellular

84. Which of the following is not a modem?

    ○ **A.** ISDN

    ○ **B.** CSU/DSU

    ○ **C.** Cable

    ○ **D.** DSL

Quick Answer: **159**
Detailed Answer: **171**

85. What is the maximum speed of a T1 Internet connection?

    ○ **A.** 1.544 Mbps

    ○ **B.** 2.048 Mbps

    ○ **C.** 44.736 Mbps

    ○ **D.** 274.176 Mbps

Quick Answer: **159**
Detailed Answer: **171**

86. Which of the following is the international telephone system based on copper wires (UTP cabling) carrying analog voice data?

    ○ **A.** PSTN

    ○ **B.** ISDN

    ○ **C.** DS-1

    ○ **D.** DS-3

Quick Answer: **159**
Detailed Answer: **171**

87. Which of the following is a device that enables a computer to transmit data over telephone lines?

    ○ **A.** UART

    ○ **B.** CSA/DSU

    ○ **C.** Cable modem

    ○ **D.** Modem

Quick Answer: **159**
Detailed Answer: **171**

88. What type of jack does an analog telephone line use to connect a phone or modem?

    ○ **A.** RJ-45

    ○ **B.** RJ-11

    ○ **C.** MT-RJ

    ○ **D.** BNC

Quick Answer: **159**
Detailed Answer: **172**

89. What is the speed of standard BRI ISDN?

Quick Answer: **159**
Detailed Answer: **172**

- ○ **A.** 64 Kbps
- ○ **B.** 128 Kbps
- ○ **C.** 256 Kbps
- ○ **D.** 1.544 Mbps

90. To connect a computer to an ISDN line, you would use which of the following?

Quick Answer: **159**
Detailed Answer: **172**

- ○ **A.** Cable modem
- ○ **B.** Terminal adapter
- ○ **C.** Router
- ○ **D.** Access point

91. Which of the following wireless standards has a maximum transmission speed of 54 Mbps? (Choose all that apply.)

Quick Answer: **159**
Detailed Answer: **172**

- ○ **A.** 802.11
- ○ **B.** 802.11a
- ○ **C.** 802.11b
- ○ **D.** 802.11g
- ○ **E.** 802.11n

92. Which of the following wireless standards has a maximum transmission speed of 600 Mbps?

Quick Answer: **159**
Detailed Answer: **172**

- ○ **A.** 802.11a
- ○ **B.** 802.11b
- ○ **C.** 802.11g
- ○ **D.** 802.11n

93. At what radio frequency does an IEEE 802.11g wireless network operate?

Quick Answer: **159**
Detailed Answer: **172**

- ○ **A.** 2.4 GHz
- ○ **B.** 5.0 GHz
- ○ **C.** 5.4 GHz
- ○ **D.** 10 GHz

94. At what radio frequency does an IEEE 802.11a wireless network operate?

Quick Answer: **159**
Detailed Answer: **172**

- ○ **A.** 2.4 GHz
- ○ **B.** 5.0 GHz
- ○ **C.** 5.4 GHz
- ○ **D.** 10 GHz

95. What is the maximum transmission speed supported by IEEE 802.11b?

Quick Answer: **159**
Detailed Answer: **172**

- ○ **A.** 720 Kbps
- ○ **B.** 2 Mbps
- ○ **C.** 11 Mbps
- ○ **D.** 54 Mbps

96. Which of the following would interfere with an IEEE 802.11g wireless network? (Select all that apply.)

Quick Answer: **159**
Detailed Answer: **172**

- ○ **A.** Walls
- ○ **B.** Bluetooth devices
- ○ **C.** Microwave ovens
- ○ **D.** IEEE 802.11a devices

97. What is the maximum transmission speed supported by Bluetooth?

Quick Answer: **159**
Detailed Answer: **172**

- ○ **A.** 720 Kbps
- ○ **B.** 2 Mbps
- ○ **C.** 11 Mbps
- ○ **D.** 54 Mbps

98. Which of the following can be used to connect a WLAN to a LAN?

Quick Answer: **159**
Detailed Answer: **172**

- ○ **A.** Bridge
- ○ **B.** Gateway
- ○ **C.** Modem
- ○ **D.** Access point

99. You can determine the connection speed and signal strength of a wireless network connection on a Windows XP computer by using which of the following?

Quick Answer: **159**
Detailed Answer: **172**

- ○ **A.** Wireless access point
- ○ **B.** Wireless network adapter
- ○ **C.** Wireless NIC properties
- ○ **D.** Wireless connection wizard

100. Which of the following is the best way to prevent unauthorized computers from connecting to a wireless access point?

Quick Answer: **159**
Detailed Answer: **173**

- ○ **A.** Install the wireless access point in a demilitarized zone (DMZ)
- ○ **B.** Install an intrusion detection system (IDS)
- ○ **C.** Configure MAC address filtering on the wireless access point
- ○ **D.** Disable SSID broadcasts on the wireless access point

101. What is a friendly name that identifies a particular 802.11 wireless LAN and is needed to connect to it?

Quick Answer: **159**
Detailed Answer: **173**

- ○ **A.** WEP
- ○ **B.** WPA
- ○ **C.** SSID
- ○ **D.** Ad-Hoc

102. What is the Wireless Encryption Protocol (WEP) standard used for?

Quick Answer: **159**
Detailed Answer: **173**

- ○ **A.** Connecting to wireless access points
- ○ **B.** Security on local area networks
- ○ **C.** Data encryption over IEEE 802.11x networks
- ○ **D.** Privacy on IEEE 802.2 networks

103. Which of the following is a common method of wireless encryption?

Quick Answer: **159**
Detailed Answer: **173**

- ○ **A.** EFS
- ○ **B.** WPA
- ○ **C.** PAP
- ○ **D.** SAP

104. Which of the following is required to set up a secure wireless connection? (Select two answers.)

Quick Answer: **159**
Detailed Answer: **173**

- ○ **A.** The brand and model of the access point
- ○ **B.** The wireless brand being used
- ○ **C.** The SSID of the wireless access point
- ○ **D.** The encryption standard being used

105. When you configure a wireless access point, what is the easiest method to configure a DHCP service to assign IP addresses?

Quick Answer: **159**
Detailed Answer: **173**

- ○ **A.** You need to use static addresses.
- ○ **B.** You need to install a DHCP server on a Windows server.
- ○ **C.** You need to install the DHCP service on a local Windows client.
- ○ **D.** DHCP is built in to the access point and just needs to be enabled and configured.

106. What are the disadvantages of using Satellite Internet Access? (Choose all that apply.)

Quick Answer: **159**
Detailed Answer: **173**

- ○ **A.** High latency
- ○ **B.** Signal loss due to precipitation
- ○ **C.** Limited in certain geographical areas
- ○ **D.** Limited to line of site

Quick-Check Answer Key

1. A	**28.** A	**55.** A and B	**81.** A, B, and C
2. A and D	**29.** C	**56.** B	**82.** D
3. A, B, and D	**30.** B	**57.** D	**83.** A
4. E	**31.** C	**58.** B	**84.** B
5. C and E	**32.** D	**59.** A	**85.** A
6. C	**33.** A	**60.** C	**86.** A
7. D	**34.** B	**61.** A	**87.** D
8. B	**35.** D	**62.** C	**88.** B
9. D	**36.** D	**63.** A	**89.** A
10. D	**37.** A	**64.** D	**90.** B
11. D	**38.** C	**65.** B	**91.** B and D
12. B	**39.** B	**66.** B	**92.** D
13. A	**40.** D	**67.** D	**93.** A
14. B	**41.** A and B	**68.** C	**94.** B
15. C	**42.** B	**69.** B	**95.** C
16. B	**43.** C	**70.** B	**96.** A and C
17. C	**44.** C	**71.** A	**97.** A
18. A	**45.** D	**72.** C	**98.** D
19. B	**46.** D	**73.** C	**99.** C
20. B	**47.** C	**74.** A	**100.** C
21. B	**48.** D	**75.** D	**101.** C
22. A and B	**49.** D	**76.** B	**102.** C
23. D	**50.** A, B, and D	**77.** C	**103.** B
24. E	**51.** B and D	**78.** C	**104.** C and D
25. C	**52.** C, D, and E	**79.** C	**105.** D
26. A	**53.** B and C	**80.** C	**106.** A, B, and D
27. A	**54.** C		

Answers and Explanations

1. **Answer: A.** The most common network protocol used today is the TCP/IP protocol suite, which is used by the Internet. The NetBEUI protocol and IPX protocols are considered legacy protocols. NetBEUI does not allow you to route between networks and IPX was associated with early versions of Novell NetWare. AppleTalk is also considered a legacy network protocol built around Apple computers.

2. **Answer: A and D.** To communicate over a TCP/IP network, the minimum configuration settings are the IP address and the subnet mask. The gateway (Answer B) is only necessary if you need to communicate with hosts that are located on other networks (which means you need to be able to route packets). The DNS Server address (Answer E) is only needed for name resolution. While name resolution is very common, it is not necessary for basic TCP/IP communication. The IPX address (Answer C) is not used with TCP/IP networks.

3. **Answer: A, B, and D.** You need the IP address and subnet mask to communicate with hosts within the same subnet. If you wish to communicate with hosts in the other subnets, you will need to configure the default gateway. The DNS Server address (Answer E) is only needed for name resolution. While name resolution is very common, it is not necessary for basic TCP/IP communication. The IPX address (Answer C) is not used with TCP/IP networks.

4. **Answer: E.** DNS, short for Domain Name Service, is the primary name resolution tool used on a TCP/IP network. When you type in a URL, it will retrieve the address of the web server. The IP address (Answer A) uniquely identifies a host on a network. The default gateway (Answer B) is necessary to communicate with remote networks. It defines the nearest router so that you can route packets. The Subnet mask (Answer D) specifies which bits of your IP address are network bits and host bits. The IPX address (Answer C) is not used in TCP/IP networks.

5. **Answer: C and E.** Besides having an IP address and a subnet mask, which is a minimum to communicate on a TCP/IP network, you must have a default gateway so that it can talk to remote networks and a DNS server to provide name resolution. Host names (Answer A) are configured automatically when you install Windows, so it does not need to be configured. The DHCP server (Answer B) is a server that hands IP addresses to host so that you don't have to manually configure each host. Configuring the IP address of an email server (Answer D) is only necessary if you are sending and retrieving email.

6. **Answer: C.** Static addresses are manually assigned to a host. Because the addresses are manually assigned, they do not change. Dynamic addresses (Answer A) are assigned by a DHCP server and may change. There is no such thing in TCP/IP as a revolving address (Answer B) or a transfer address (Answer D).

7. **Answer: D.** DHCP is short for Dynamic Host Configuration Protocol. It is a network application protocol/service used by devices (DHCP clients) to obtain configuration information for operation in an Internet Protocol network including the IP address, subnet mask, and default gateway. WINS (Answer B) and DNS (Answer A) provide name resolution. DNS, short for Domain Name Service, provides host name to IP address. WINS, short for Windows Internet Name Service (WINS) provides computer name to IP address. Today, WINS is considered a legacy name resolution solution.

MAC (Answer C) is short for Media Access Control, which includes the physical address used when a host communicates on a network. The MAC address is usually burned onto the network card. Much like logical addresses (such as IP addresses), two network cards with the same physical address can exist on the same subnet.

8. **Answer: B.** An IPv4 address consists of 32 bits, divided into four 8-bit groupings called octets. Each octet can range from 0 to 255. Examples include 134.34.64.233 and 12.7.128.3. Therefore, the other answers are incorrect.

9. **Answer: D.** An IPv6 address consists of 128 bits. Different from IPv4, IPv6 is written in hexadecimal format. Therefore, the other answers are incorrect.

10. **Answer: D.** Looking at a low-level view, hosts communicate on a network with a physical address called the MAC address. MAC is short for Media Access Control, which identifies a host on an individual network. To make things easier to understand, we usually assign IP addresses (logical addresses), Answer C, to these devices so that we can organize and manage them. The logical address is then tied to the physical address. SPX addresses (Answer A) are not used in TCP/IP networks. Instead, they are logical addresses usually associated with early Novell NetWare networks. UID (Answer B) is short for User ID, which is usually associated with Linux systems. The PID can be short for Personal ID or process ID; neither of these are defined as part of the networking protocols used with TCP/IP networks.

11. **Answer: D.** When you have a green light that blinks on or off, you are receiving network traffic, which usually means that the cable is connected properly. NICs don't have power connectors (Answer B) and if the power connector for the computer is faulty, the entire computer would not function. EMI (Answer C) is short for electromagnetic interference, which can cause disruption in network traffic. The green lights do not tell us if network traffic is being interrupted or not. If the network cable is faulty (Answer A) and you don't have a network connection, you would not have a blinking green light.

12. **Answer: B.** NetBIOS is short for Network Basic Input/Output System. It is a common protocol found on most Microsoft networks. While it was originally created for IBM for its early PC networks, it was adopted by Microsoft and has since become a de facto industry standard. It uses NetBIOS/computer names to identify computers and uses SMB to share files and folders. The method of encapsulating NetBIOS in TCP and UDP packets is known as NetBIOS over TCP/IP (NBT). NetBEUI (Answer A) is a legacy network protocol. IPX (Answer C) and SPX (Answer D) are legacy transport protocols usually associated with NetWare. CIFS (Common Internet File System) is Microsoft's attempt to rename Server Message Block (SMB), which allows you to do file and print sharing with Windows.

13. **Answer: A.** TCP is short for Transmission Control Protocol. It is one of the core protocols of the Internet Protocol suite, which is commonly referred to as TCP/IP. TCP provides reliable, ordered delivery of a stream of bytes from a program on one computer to another program on another computer. To ensure packets are delivered, it uses acknowledgements. UDP, short for User Datagram Protocol (Answer B), is a transport protocol used in TCP/IP networks that does not use acknowledgements to make sure a packet is delivered. IP (Internet Protocol), Answer C, is the network-level protocol that handles IP addressing. Address Resolution Protocol (ARP), Answer D, is used to translate logical addresses (IP addresses) to physical addresses (MAC addresses).

14. **Answer: B.** UDP is short for User Datagram Protocol (UDP). UDP does not use acknowledgements to ensure data delivery unlike TCP (Answer A), which does. Therefore, UDP is considered unreliable, "best effort" delivery. IP is the network-level protocol that handles IP addressing (Answer C). Address Resolution Protocol (ARP), Answer D, is used to translate logical addresses (IP addresses) to physical addresses (MAC addresses).

15. **Answer: C.** The lowest protocol within the TCP/IP suite is the Internet Protocol (IP), which is primarily responsible for addressing and routing packets between hosts. UDP (Answer B) is short for User Datagram Protocol. UDP does not use acknowledgements to ensure data delivery unlike TCP (Answer A), which does. Therefore, UDP is considered unreliable, "best effort" delivery. Address Resolution Protocol (ARP), Answer D, is used to translate logical addresses (IP addresses) to physical addresses (MAC addresses).

16. **Answer: B.** Full-duplex dialog allows every device to both transmit and receive simultaneously. Today, Ethernet and wireless hosts can communicate using full-duplex. Simplex (Answer A) is communication that is one direction only. A public address (PA) system broadcasts out (one direction). Half-duplex (Answer C) is similar to a Citizen Band (CB) radio or walkie-talkie radio that allows you to communicate with another host, but only in one direction at a time. There is no such thing as complex communications (Answer D) in networking.

17. **Answer: C.** Half-duplex is similar to a Citizen Band (CB) radio or walkie-talkie radio that allows you to communicate with another host, but only in one direction at a time. Full-duplex dialog (Answer B) allows every device to both transmit and receive simultaneously. Today, Ethernet and wireless hosts can communicate using full-duplex. Simplex (Answer A) is communication that is one direction only. A public address (PA) system broadcasts out (one direction). There is no such thing as complex communications (Answer D) in networking.

18. **Answer: A.** A workgroup is a peer-to-peer network with no dedicated server. Instead, each workstation acts as a server (providing services) and workstation (using services). In addition, because there is no dedicated server, typically every computer will have to host its own security database. If you want one user to access another computer, you will have to create accounts on both computers. A domain (Answer B) is usually found on larger Windows networks and defines security boundaries. It uses one database to share its common security and user account information for all computers within the domain. This database is stored within domain controllers. Simplex (Answer D) is communication that is one direction only. A public address (PA) system broadcasts out (one direction). There is no such thing as complex communications (Answer C) in networking.

19. **Answer: B.** A domain is usually found on larger Windows networks and defines security boundaries. It uses one database to share its common security and user account information for all computers within the domain. This database is stored within domain controllers. A workgroup (Answer A) is a peer-to-peer network with no dedicated server. Instead, each workstation acts as a server (providing services) and workstation (using services). In addition, because there is no dedicated server, typically every computer will have to host its own security database. If you want one user to access another computer, you will have to create accounts on both computers. Simplex (Answer D) is communication that is one direction only. A public address (PA)

system broadcasts out (one direction). There is no such thing as complex communications (Answer C) in networking.

20. **Answer: B.** Domain controllers store the security database for domains. Therefore, if you need to authenticate to access a domain resource, you must authenticate with a domain controller. DNS, short for Domain Name Service (Answer A), is used for name resolution and is required for domain controllers to function. DNS translates between host names to IP address. WINS (Answer C) is a legacy name resolution that translates between computer names to IP address. The SAM (Answer D), short for Security Account Manager, is the security database used by Microsoft Windows NT, Windows 2000, and later Microsoft operating systems. Different from a domain, the SAM covers the security for the individual computer.

21. **Answer: B.** HTTP, short for Hypertext Transfer Protocol (HTTP), is an application-level protocol used with web pages. It uses port 80. FTP uses port 20 and 21 (Answer A), HTTPS uses port 443 (Answer C), and POP3 uses port 110 (Answer D).

22. **Answer: A and B.** FTP, short for File Transfer Protocol, is a standard network protocol used to exchange and manipulate files over a TCP/IP network. Port 20 is used to transfer data while port 21 is used for control or commands. HTTP uses port 80 (Answer C) and HTTPS uses port 443 (Answer D). POP3 uses port 110 (Answer E) and SMTP uses port 25 (Answer F).

23. **Answer: D.** POP is short for Post Office Protocol. It is an application-layer Internet Standard protocol used by local email clients to retrieve email from a remote server over a TCP/IP connection. Version 3 (POP3) is the current standard. It uses port 110. SMTP uses port 25 (Answer A) and HTTP uses port 80 (Answer B). HTTPS uses port 443 (Answer C) and Telnet uses port 23 (Answer E).

24. **Answer: E.** Internet Message Access Protocol (IMAP) is used to retrieve, organize and synchronize email messages over a TCP/IP network. It uses port 143. SMTP uses port 25 (Answer A) and HTTP uses port 80 (Answer B). HTTPS uses port 443 (Answer C) and POP3 uses port 110 (Answer D).

25. **Answer: C.** HTTPS is the secure version of HTTP used to display web information. It uses Hypertext Transfer Protocol over TLS/SSL using port 443. When using your browser, the URL will begin with https instead of http. SMTP uses port 25 (Answer A) and HTTP uses port 80 (Answer B). POP3 uses port 110 (Answer D) and IMAP uses port 143 (Answer E).

26. **Answer: A.** SMTP is short for Simple Mail Transfer Protocol (SMTP). SMTP is used to send and route email between mail servers. It uses port 25. HTTP uses port 80 (Answer B) and HTTPS uses port 443 (Answer C). POP3 uses port 110 (Answer D) and IMAP uses port 143 (Answer E).

27. **Answer: A.** Telnet, is short for teletype network. It allows you to execute commands on a remote host. Unfortunately, these commands are broadcast in clear text (unencrypted). Telnet uses port 23. HTTP uses port 80 (Answer B) and HTTPS uses port 443 (Answer C). POP3 uses port 110 (Answer D) and IMAP uses port 143 (Answer E).

28. **Answer: A.** A LAN is short for Local Area Network. It is a relatively small network within a geographically close area. LAN technology is usually very fast when you compare it to networks connected with telecommunication links. WAN (Answer C) is short

for wide area networks. It is used to connect distant sites together using long-range telecommunication links. These telecommunication links are usually slower than LAN links. A MAN (Answer B), short for Metropolitan Area Network, is network technology that usually spans a city. A VAN (Answer D), short for Value-Added Network, is a hosted service offering that acts as an intermediary between business partners sharing standards-based or proprietary data via shared business processes. VANs traditionally transmit data formatted as Electronic Data Interchange, but increasingly they also transmit data formatted as XML or in more specific "binary" formats.

29. **Answer: C.** WAN is short for wide area network. It is used to connect distant sites together using long-range telecommunication links. These telecommunication links are usually slower than LAN links. A LAN (Answer A) is short for Local Area Network. It is a relatively small network within a geographically close area. LAN technology is usually very fast when compared to networks connected with telecommunication links. A MAN (Answer B), short for Metropolitan Area Network, is network technology that usually spans a city. A VAN (Answer D), short for Value-Added Network, is a hosted service offering that acts as an intermediary between business partners sharing standards-based or proprietary data via shared business processes. VANs traditionally transmit data formatted as Electronic Data Interchange, but increasingly they also transmit data formatted as XML or in more specific "binary" formats.

30. **Answer: B.** A global WAN is not owned by any one user or company and can cross national boundaries. The Internet connects millions of computers making it the largest global WAN in the world. An intranet is an organization's internal network (Answer A). The SBC (Answer C) is the name of a corporation, which is not part of AT&T. SOHO (Answer D), short for Small Office/Home Office, is a small network confined within a home.

31. **Answer: C.** An intranet is a TCP/IP network used within an organization. Because it uses the same protocol as the Internet, its websites can look and act like any other website, but they are Isolated by a firewall so that people from outside of the organization cannot see them. The Internet (Answer A) is a global WAN that is not owned by any one user or company and crosses national boundaries. An extranet (Answer B) is an external network that can be accessed from the outside. A VAN (Answer D), short for Value-Added Network, is a hosted service offering that acts as an intermediary between business partners sharing standards-based or proprietary data via shared business processes. VANs traditionally transmitted data formatted as Electronic Data Interchange but increasingly they also transmit data formatted as XML or in more specific "binary" formats.

32. **Answer: D.** SOHO is short for small office/home office. While it is a small network used primarily in home offices, it can be connected to a larger corporation using a virtual private network (VPN). The Internet (Answer A) is a global WAN that is not owned by any one user or company and crosses national boundaries. An extranet (Answer B) is an external network that is allowed access from the outside. An intranet (Answer C) is a TCP/IP network used within an organization. Because it uses the same protocol as the Internet, an intranet's websites can look and act like any other website, but they are isolated by a firewall so that people from outside of the organization cannot see them.

33. **Answer: A.** A hub is a device that works at the physical OSI layer. It is a multi-ported connection point used to connect network devices via a cable segment. Because it is a multiported repeater, whatever signal is sent on one cable is forwarded to all other

ports. Today, a hub is considered a legacy device that has been replaced by switches. A switch (Answer B) is a multiport bridge that can only forward traffic from one port to another. A gateway (Answer C) is hardware and/or software that links two different types of networks by repackaging and converting data from one network to another or from one network operating system to another. A router (Answer D) routes packets between networks. A bridge (Answer E) is a device that connects two LANs and makes them appear as one or is used to connect two segments of the same LAN.

34. **Answer: B.** A bridge (Answer E) works at the data link OSI layer. It connects two LANs and makes them appear as one and it analyzes incoming data packets and will forward the packets if its destination is on the other side of the bridge. A switch is a multiported bridge that builds a table of MAC addresses. When a packet is received, it will look at the header of the packet and only forward the packet to the correct destination port. Because multiple packets can be sent through a switch at the same time, a switch has better performance than a hub. A hub (Answer A) is a device that works at the physical OSI layer. It is a multiported connection point used to connect network devices via a cable segment. Because it is a multiported repeater, whatever signal is sent on one cable is forwarded to all other ports. Today, a hub is considered a legacy device that has been replaced by switches. A gateway (Answer C) is hardware and/or software that links two different types of networks by repackaging and converting data from one network to another or from one network operating system to another. A router (Answer D) routes packets between networks.

35. **Answer: D.** A router works at the network OSI layer. It connects two or more LANs and can be used to connect networks over WAN links. Routers also share status and routing information with other routers so that they can provide better traffic management and bypass slow connections. A hub (Answer A) is a device that works at the physical OSI layer. It is a multiported connection point used to connect network devices via a cable segment. Because it is a multiported repeater, whatever signal is sent on one cable is forwarded to all other ports. Today, a hub is considered a legacy device replaced by switches. A switch (Answer B) is a multiport bridge that can only forward traffic from one port to another. A gateway (Answer C) is hardware and/or software that links two different types of networks by repackaging and converting data from one network to another or from one network operating system to another. A bridge (Answer E) is a device that connects two LANS and makes them appear as one or is used to connect two segments of the same LAN.

36. **Answer: D.** A Layer 3 switch is similar to a router but switches packages based on the logical addresses (Layer 3) such as IP addresses instead of Layer 2 MAC addresses. It is used to configure routing within a LAN but does not provide routing over WAN links. A gateway (Answer A) is hardware and/or software that links two different types of networks by repackaging and converting data from one network to another or from one network operating system to another. A bridge (Answer B) is a device that connects two LANs and makes them appear as one or is used to connect two segments of the same LAN.

37. **Answer: A.** A gateway is hardware or software that links two different types of networks by repackaging and converting data from one network to another network or from one network operating system to another. A gateway can be used at any layer of the OSI reference model, but is usually identified with the upper layers because they must communicate with an application, establish and manage sessions, translate

encoded data, and interpret logical and physical addressing data. A bridge (Answer B) is a device that connects two LANs and makes them appear as one or is used to connect two segments of the same LAN. A brouter (Answer C) acts as a bridge for local traffic and as a router for other packets. A Layer 3 switch (Answer D) switches packages based on the Layer 3 addresses.

38. **Answer: C.** VPN is short for virtual private networking. It creates tunnels to provide secure point-to-point connections across private networks or public networks such as the Internet. Tunneling is a method of transferring data packets over the Internet or other public networks, providing the security and features formerly available on private networks. SOHO (Answer A), short for small office/home office is a small network confined within a home. A VAN (Answer B), short for Value-Added Network, is a hosted service offering that acts as an intermediary between business partners sharing standards-based or proprietary data via shared business processes. VANs traditionally transmitted data formatted as Electronic Data Interchange but increasingly they also transmit data formatted as XML or in more specific "binary" formats. Telnet (Answer D), short for teletype network, is a network protocol used to execute commands on a remote host. Telnet is not a secure connection because authentication and commands are sent in clear text.

39. **Answer: B.** A switch will only forward traffic to its destination port instead of repeating to all ports. Wireless network adapters (Answer A) allow a computer to connect to a network using wireless technology. A hub allows only one host to connect to another host at one time, but a switch allows for multiple connections between hosts at the same time. A router (Answer C) is used to connect two or more networks. A bridge (Answer D) is used to connect two LANS and make them appear as one or is used to connect two segments of the same LAN.

40. **Answer: D.** The subnet mask is used to identify which bits are network bits and which bits are host bits. For example, if you have an IP address of 23.23.54.23 with a subnet mask of 255.255.0.0, 23.23.0.0 is the network address and 0.0.54.23 is the host address. For another example, if you have an IP address of 23.23.54.23 with a subnet mask of 255.255.255.0, 23.23.54.0 is the network address and 0.0.0.23 is the host address. VPN (Answer A) is short for virtual private network. It creates tunnels to provide secure point-to-point connections across private network or public networks such as the Internet. Tunneling is a method of transferring data packets over the Internet or other public network, providing the security and features formerly available on private networks. The first octet (Answer B) is the first eight bits of a 32-bit IPv4 address, which can be used to identify the default class for a classful network. Unicast (Answer C) transmission is the sending of information packets to a single network destination.

41. **Answer: A and B.** A Class A IP address can be identified by looking at the first octet. It will be between 1 and 126. A Class B IP address will be between 128 and 191 (Answer C). A Class C IP address will be between 192 and 223 (Answer D).

42. **Answer: B.** By default, a Class A IP address has a subnet mask of 255.0.0.0, which means the first octet identifies the network ID and the last three octets identify the host ID. The default subnet mask for a Class B network is 255.255.0.0 (Answer C). The default subnet mask for a Class C network is 255.255.255.0 (Answer D). 0.0.0.0 and 255.255.255.255 don't have special meaning for subnet masks.

43. Answer: C. A Class B IP address can be identified by looking at the first octet. It will be between 128 and 191. A Class A IP address can be identified by looking at the first octet. It will be between 1 and 126 (Answers A and B). It should be noted that 127 addresses are reserved for special uses, including the 127.0.0.1 loopback address. A Class C IP address will be between 192 and 223 (Answer D).

44. Answer: C. By default, a Class B IP address has a subnet mask of 255.255.0.0, which means the first two octets identify the network ID and the last two octets identify the host ID. By default, a Class A IP address has a subnet mask of 255.0.0.0 (Answer B), which means the first octet identifies the network ID and the last three octets identify the host ID. The default subnet mask for a Class C network is 255.255.255.0 (Answer D). 0.0.0.0 (Answer A) and 255.255.255.255 (Answer E) don't have special meaning for subnet masks.

45. Answer: D. A Class C IP address can be identified by looking at the first octet. It will be between 192 and 223. A Class A IP address can be identified by looking at the first octet. It will be between 1 and 126 (Answers A and B). A Class B will be between 128 and 191 (Answer C).

46. Answer: D. By default, a Class C IP address has a subnet mask of 255.255.255.0, which means the first three octets identify the network ID and the last octet identifies the host ID. By default, a Class A IP address has a subnet mask of 255.0.0.0 (Answer B), which means the first octet identifies the network ID and the last three octets identify the host ID. By default, a Class B IP address has a subnet mask of 255.255.0.0 (Answer C), which means the first two octets identify the network ID and the last two octets identify the host ID. 0.0.0.0 (Answer A) and 255.255.255.255 (Answer E) don't have special meaning for subnet masks.

47. Answer: C. A Class C network has a subnet mask of 255.255.255.0, which means that the last eight bits are used to identify the host bits. Because there are eight bits available for host bits, there are 2^8 or 256 different combinations. Because 0000 0000 is used to identify the network ID and 1111 1111 is used for broadcast, there are 2^8-2 or 254 available host addresses available. Therefore, the other answers are incorrect.

48. Answer: D. If you convert 255 to binary, it is 1111 1111. 1000 0000 (Answer A) is 128, 1111 0000 (Answer B) is 240, 1111 1110 (Answer C) is 254.

49. Answer: D. Multicast is used to send one packet to multiple computers, reducing the amount of traffic that needs to be transmitted and received. Class D addresses begin with a value between 224 and 239. Anycast (Answer A) is sent to the "nearest" or "best" destination as viewed by the routing topology. Unicast (Answer B) is used to send one packet to a single computer. Broadcast (Answer C) is used to send packets to all hosts.

50. Answer: A, B, and D. Because TCP/IP addresses are growing scarce for the Internet, a series of addresses have been reserved to be used by private networks (networks not connected to the Internet). They are Class A—10.x.x.x, Class B—172.16.x.x to 172.31.x.x, and Class C—192.168.0.x to 192.255.x. If devices need to communicate over the Internet, there needs to be something to translate between private and public network, such as Network Address Translation (NAT). 183.23.3.4 (Answer C) is a public address.

51. **Answer: B and D.** The loopback address and localhost are used to address itself. It is mostly used for testing purposes, including making sure that the TCP/IP protocol is functioning properly. The multicast addresses are addresses ranging from 224–239.

52. **Answer: C, D, and E.** IPv6 addresses are 128-bits long, written in hexadecimal format. 2001:0db8:85a3:0000:0000:8a2e:0370:7334 shows the full address. 2001:db8:85a3:0:0:8a2e:370:7334 omits the leading zeros. The 2001:db8:85a3::8a2e:370:7334 includes a number of consecutive groups of 0 value replaced with two colons (::). The 130.23.74.24 (Answer A) is an IPv4 address and the 255.255.240.0 (Answer B) is a subnet mask.

53. **Answer: B and C.** The loopback address for IPv6 addresses is 0000:0000:0000:0000:0000:0000:0000:0001, which can be abbreviated with ::1. The 127.0.0.1 (Answer A) is the loopback address for IPv4. 255.255.0.0 (Answer D) is a subnet mask.

54. **Answer: C.** Latency is the delay between requesting data and the receipt of a response. In one-way communications such as those used with satellites, it is the time between a signal broadcast and the time received at its destination. Attenuation (Answer A) is the weakening of a signal as it travels along a cable. Jitter (Answer B) is noise on the wire. Beaconing (Answer D) is the process that allows a network (usually Token Ring and FDDI networks) to self-repair network problems. When beaconing is used, the stations on the network notify the other stations on the ring when they are not receiving the transmissions. If there is another ring to communicate, traffic can be re-routed to overcome network problems.

55. **Answer: A and B.** In buildings, the plenum is the space above the ceiling and below the floor that allows air to circulate throughout the workplace. It can also be found in some walls. If there is a fire, the plenum will also circulate toxic fumes generated by burning cables. The plenum is not in the elevator shaft (Answer C) or basement (Answer D).

56. **Answer: B.** A plenum cable is a special cable that gives off little or no toxic fumes when burned. Polyvinyl chloride (PVC) is a common plastic insulation or jacket. Special additives can be added to PVC to make it flame-retardant to meet plenum specifications. A riser cable (Answer A) is used to traverse floors within a building. The punch down cable (Answer C) is normally unshielded twisted-pair cable that is connected to a punch down box. Unshielded twisted-pair cable (Answer D) is the most common cabling used and is used in Ethernet networks.

57. **Answer: D.** A plenum cable is a special cable that gives off little or no toxic fumes when burned. Polyvinyl chloride (PVC) is a common plastic insulation or jacket. Special additives can be added to PVC to make it flame-retardant to meet plenum specifications. Plenum usually costs more than normal cable (Answer A). In addition, it does not transfer data faster (Answer B) and does not have any additional shielding (Answer C) beyond that of normal cable.

58. **Answer: B.** Twisted-pair cabling will have either two pair or four pair of wiring. While twisted-pair cable for phones uses two pair, twisted-pair in networking uses four pair. Coaxial cables (Answer A) have a single copper conductor with an insulating layer and a conductive mesh. Cable television uses coaxial cable. Fiber optic cable (Answer C) uses light transmitted over a glass or plastic core. There is no such thing as twisted-optic cable (Answer D).

59. **Answer: A.** Coaxial cables have a single copper conductor with an insulating layer and a conductive mesh. Cable television uses coaxial cable. Twisted-pair cabling (Answer B) will have either two pair or four pair of wiring. While twisted-pair cable for phones uses two pair, twisted-pair in networking uses four pair. Fiber optic cable (Answer C) uses light transmitted over a glass or plastic core. There is no such thing as twisted optic cable (Answer D).

60. **Answer: C.** Fiber optic cable uses light transmitted over a glass or plastic core. Coaxial cables (Answer A) have a single copper conductor with an insulating layer and a conductive mesh. Cable television uses coaxial cable. Twisted-pair cabling (Answer B) will have either two pair or four pair of wiring. While twisted pair cable for phones uses two pair, twisted-pair in networking uses four pair. There is no such thing as twisted optic cable (Answer D).

61. **Answer: A.** Unshielded twisted-pair (UTP) is the most common network cabling used. It is similar to telephone cabling but uses four pair of wire instead of two. Shielded twisted-pair (STP), Answer B, is cabling similar to UTP but, as the name implies, it includes shielding to protect electromagnetic interference (EMI). Coaxial cable (Answer C) is usually found connecting your cable box. Fiber optic cables (Answer D) are used for long connections and fast connections.

62. **Answer: C.** Crosstalk is when signals induct or transfer from one wire to another. As a result, signals are not as clear as they should be and it might cause interference. Attenuation (Answer A) is the weakening of a signal as it travels along a cable. Jitter (Answer B) is noise on the wire. Beaconing (Answer D) is the process that allows a network (usually Token Ring and FDDI networks) to self-repair network problems. When beaconing is used, the stations on the network notify the other stations on the ring when they are not receiving the transmissions. If there is another ring to communicate, traffic can be rerouted to overcome network problems.

63. **Answer: A.** Twisted wires ensure that the noise is the same on each wire. The common noise is then canceled at each end. The aluminum shielding (Answer B), plastic shielding (Answer C), and plenum sheath (Answer D) will not reduce crosstalk.

64. **Answer: D.** Fiber optic uses light over a plastic or glass core whereas STP, UTP, and coax send electrical signals over a copper core. Light over a plastic or glass core supplies a higher throughput than electrical signals. Therefore, the other answers are incorrect.

65. **Answer: B.** Fiber optic provides the longest transmission distance of up to 10,000 meters. Therefore, the other answers are incorrect.

66. **Answer: B.** Interference occurs when undesirable electromagnetic waves affect the desired signal. Interference can be caused by electromagnetic interference (EMI) produced by large electromagnets used in industry machinery, motors, fluorescent lighting, and power lines. Because fiber optic cable uses light instead of electrical signals, it is not affected by EMI. Because coaxial cable (Answer A) and UTP (Answer C) use electrical signals, they are affected by EMI. In addition, wireless signals (Answer D) can be interrupted with radio waves, which can be generated from EMI.

67. **Answer: D.** CAT6 cable is rated at more than 1000 Mbps. CAT5e cable is rated at up to 1000 Mbps and CAT5 (Answer C) cable is rated at up to 100 Mbps only. CAT3 (Answer B) and CAT4 (Answer A) is rated less than CAT5.

68. **Answer: C.** A 1000BASE-TX network operates at up to 1000 Mbps. The minimum cable rating that can support this speed is CAT5e cable, which is rated at up to 1000 Mbps, and CAT5 cable is rated at up to 100 Mbps only. Therefore, the other answers are incorrect.

69. **Answer: B.** Both workstations' NICs will be physically and electronically the same medium dependent interface (MDI), therefore you need a crossover cable to connect the two. 100BASE-T has a transmission speed of up to 100 Mbps. The minimum twisted-pair, copper cable that can support these speeds is CAT5 cable. Therefore, the other answers are incorrect.

70. **Answer: B.** Because you are going with the same type of port (physically and electrically), you need a crossover cable to connect the two. A patch cable (Answer A) is used to connect a computer to a switch or between a patch panel and a computer. A category 5 cable (Answer C) is a level of UTP cable.

71. **Answer: A.** UTP cable is the most susceptible to EMI while the coaxial cable (Answer B) is close behind. The fiber optic cable (Answers C and D) are not susceptible to EMI.

72. **Answer: C.** 100BASE-TX uses UTP cable with a maximum transmission distance of 100 m. Therefore, the other answers are incorrect.

73. **Answer: C.** Unshielded twisted-pair is rated at 100 meters or 328 feet. Therefore, the other answers are incorrect.

74. **Answer: A.** CAT6 is the cable standard for Gigabit Ethernet and other network protocols and is backward-compatible with CAT5, CAT5e, and CAT3 standards. Some Gigabit Ethernet standards do support CAT5e cables (Answer B). CAT5 (Answer C) and CAT4 (Answer D) cannot be used for Gigabit Ethernet.

75. **Answer: D.** RJ-45 is the eight-pin connector used for data transmission over twisted-pair wiring. RJ-45 (Answer D) is the connector used on 100Base-T Ethernet cables. The RJ-11 (Answer A) is used for connecting telephones. BNC (Answer B), short for British Naval Connector or Bayonet Neill-Concelman Connector, is used to connect coaxial cables. The RJ-58 (Answer C) is not a common connector in networking.

76. **Answer: B.** 1000BASE-TX uses UTP cable with RJ-45 connectors. RJ-11 (Answer C) is used for connecting telephones. MT-RJ (Answer A) and ST (Answer D) connectors are used in fiber optic networks.

77. **Answer: C.** A 10BASE-T cable is either a UTP or an STP cable but today is usually found as UTP. Both these cables use the RJ-45 connections. 10BASE2 (Answer A) and 10BASE5 (Answer B) are coaxial cables. 10BASE-FL (Answer D) uses an optical connector such as ST and SC connectors.

78. **Answer: C.** An RJ-45 connector is used on UTP cable, which consists of four pair of twisted wires. Therefore, the other answers are incorrect.

79. **Answer: C.** RJ-45 connectors are used with UTP and STP cables. RG-58 (Answer A) and RG-59 (Answer B) need BNC connectors. Multimode fiber optic (Answer D) uses a fiber optic connector such as ST, SC, LC, or MT-RJ.

80. **Answer: C.** BNC is short for British Naval Connector or Bayonet Neill-Concelman. It is a type of connector used with coaxial cables, such as RG-58 A/U cable used with a

10BASE2 Ethernet system. A BNC terminator (Answer A) is used to terminate an end of a coaxial so that you do not have the signal bounce back and causing interference. A network adapter card (Answer B) and medium attachment unit (Answer D) would not be used to connect two coaxial cables.

81. **Answer: A, B, and C.** Fiber optic cables use several connectors. The most recognizable connectors are straight tip (ST) and subscriber (SC) connectors. A newer connector called the MT-RJ is similar to the RJ-45 connector. RG-58 (Answer D) is coaxial cable.

82. **Answer: D.** SC is short for subscriber connector (SC). It is slowly being replaced by the LC, which is short for Lucent Connector. LC is sometimes called "Little Connectors." RG-58 (Answer B) is a type of coaxial cable. ST (Answer A), short for Straight Tip, is an older fiber optic connector. The FC connector (Answer C) is another fiber optic connector that is being replaced by SC and LC connectors.

83. **Answer: A.** Attenuation occurs as the strength falls off with distance over a transmission medium. Beaconing (Answer B) is used in Token ring and FDDI networks. Crosstalk (Answer C) is when signals induct or transfer from one wire to another. As a result, signals are not as clear as they should be and it might cause interference. Jitter (Answer D) is noise on the wire. Beaconing is the process that allows a network to self-repair network problems. The stations on the network notify the other stations on the ring when they are not receiving the transmissions.

84. **Answer: B.** CSU/DSU is short for channel service unit/data service unit. It connects a digital carrier line such as the T-series or DDS line. The DSU is a device that performs all error connection, handshaking, and protective and diagnostic functions for a telecommunications line. The CSU is a device that connects a terminal to a digital line that provides the LAN/WAN connection. ISDN (Answer A), cable (Answer C), and DSL (Answer D) are special kinds of modems.

85. **Answer: A.** A T1 line operates at 1.544 Mbps; therefore the other answers are incorrect.

86. **Answer: A.** PSTN is short for public switched telephone network. It is also known as plain old telephone service (POTS). PSTN is the standard telephone service that most homes use. ISDN (Answer B) is short for Integrated Services Digital Network and is a telephone system network based on digital signals instead of analog. DS is short for Digital Signal. The first level, known as DS-1 (Answer C), is a widely used standard in telecommunications in North America and Japan and is also known as a T1, which is rated at 1.544 Mbps. The DS-3 (Answer D) is rated at 44.736 Mbps.

87. **Answer: D.** A modem, short for modulator/demodulator, is a device that enables computers to transmit data over analog telephone lines. A UART (Answer A) is short for universal asynchronous receiver/transmitter. It is a type of "asynchronous receiver/transmitter," a piece of computer hardware that translates data between parallel and serial forms. UARTs are commonly used in conjunction with other communication standards such as EIA RS-232. CSU/DSU (Answer B) is short for channel service unit/data service unit. It connects a digital carrier line such as the T-series or DDS line. The DSU is a device that performs all error connection, handshaking, and protective and diagnostic functions for telecommunications lines. The CSU is a device that connects a terminal to a digital line that provides the LAN/WAN connection. A cable modem (Answer C) allows you to connect a computer to a cable network used by cable television.

88. **Answer: B.** The RJ-11 is a smaller connector than an RJ-45 (Answer A) and uses two pairs of wires to connect a phone to an analog line. MT-RJ (Answer C) is used to connect to a fiber optic network. A BNC (Answer D) is used to connect to a coaxial network.

89. **Answer: A.** The basic rate interface (BRI) uses two bearer (or B) channels, each carrying 64 Kbps. To use BRI services, you must subscribe to ISDN service through a local telephone company or provider. Therefore, the other answers are incorrect.

90. **Answer: B.** A terminal adapter (TA) is like a regular modem but is designed to pass digital signals instead of converting analog to digital signals. A cable modem (Answer A) is used to connect to a cable network used by cable television. A router (Answer C) is used to connect two or more networks. An access point (Answer D) is usually associated with wireless networks.

91. **Answer: B and D.** IEEE 802.11a and IEEE 802.11g have transmission speeds of up to 54 Mbps. IEEE 802.11b (Answer C) supports up to 11 Mbps. The 802.11 (Answer A) represents the various standards for wireless technology.

92. **Answer: D.** The IEEE 802.11n is the newest IEEE 802.11 wireless standard that includes data rates from 54 Mbps to a maximum of 600 Mbps. In addition, 802.11n uses multiple-input multiple-output (MIMO), which uses multiple transmitter and receiver antennas to improve performance. IEEE 802.11a (Answer A) and IEEE 802.11g (Answer C) have transmission speeds of up to 54 Mbps. IEEE 802.11b (Answer B) supports up to 11 Mbps.

93. **Answer: A.** IEEE 802.11b and IEEE 802.11g use the 2.4-GHz frequency band; therefore, the other answers are incorrect.

94. **Answer: B.** IEEE 802.11a uses the 5 GHz frequency band; therefore, the other answers are incorrect.

95. **Answer: C.** IEEE 802.11b has a transmission speed of up to 11 Mbps; therefore, the other answers are incorrect.

96. **Answer: A and C.** Walls interfere with all wireless networks. The more walls you have, the greater the signal loss. Microwave ovens also use the unlicensed 2.4 GHz radio frequency band and could interfere with an IEEE 802.11g wireless network. Bluetooth devices (Answer B) and 802.11a devices (Answer D) use the 5.0 GHz radio frequencies.

97. **Answer: A.** Bluetooth operates at up to 720 Kbps; therefore, the other answers are incorrect.

98. **Answer: D.** A WAP (Wireless Access Point) is the connection point for a wireless network. A bridge (Answer A) is a device that connects two LANs and makes them appear as one or is used to connect two segments of the same LAN. A gateway (Answer B) is hardware or software that links two different types of networks by repackaging and converting data from one network to another or from one network operating system to another. A modem (Answer C), short for modulator/demodulator, is used to connect a computer to a phone line.

99. **Answer: C.** When you open the wireless NIC properties, you can view the speed of the link and the connection strength; therefore, the other answers are incorrect.

100. Answer: C. When you configure MAC addressing filtering, you are configuring which MAC addresses can connect to an access point, which prevents other hosts from connecting. Using a demilitarized zone (DMZ—Answer A) usually means you are connecting to an area that is less secure compared to your internal network. Installing an intrusion detection system (Answer B) only helps you detect if someone is trying to break in; it does not actually prevent someone from breaking in. Disabling SSID broadcast (Answer D) cuts down on authorized use because you have to know the SSID to connect to the network. However, SSID could still be captured with special tools and you can still limit unauthorized access with MAC addressing filtering.

101. Answer: C. Service Set Identifier (SSID) is a friendly name that identifies a particular 802.11 wireless LAN. Unless disabled, a client device receives broadcast messages from all access points within range of advertising their SSIDs. An SSID can be as long as 32 characters. WEP and WPA (Answers A and B) are used for encryption for wireless networks. Ad-hoc (Answer D) networking is a wireless network that does not use access points. Instead the wireless hosts connect directly to each other.

102. Answer: C. Wireless Encryption Protocol (WEP) was one of the early standards used to provide encryption over wireless networks. However, because it is considered a weak solution, it is recommended that you use WPA or WPA2 instead.

103. Answer: B. Wi-Fi Protected Access (WPA) was a solution designed to overcome Wired Equivalent Privacy (WEP) weaknesses. It uses the Temporal Key Integrity Protocol (TKIP), which constantly rotates the keys. It also uses a sequence counter to protect against replay attacks. EFS (Answer A) is short for Encrypted File System. It is used on NTFS volumes to encrypt files and folders. PAP (Answer C) is short for Password Authentication Protocol, where usernames and passwords are not encrypted. SAP (Answer D) is not a wireless encryption.

104. Answer: C and D. To configure a secure wireless connection, you must configure the SSID to connect to the wireless access point and an encryption standard including any passwords or keys to provide encryption. The brand and model and wireless brand is not needed.

105. Answer: D. DHCP, short for Dynamic Host Configuration Protocol, (DHCP), assigns IP configuration information including IP addresses, subnet masks, default gateway, and DNS server address. Therefore, the other answers are incorrect.

106. Answers: A, B, and D. Satellites have a high latency because of the distance it takes for the signal to travel. In addition, precipitation reduces the signal. Finally, satellite signals are limited to line of site. Therefore, buildings or trees could block access. However, the advantage of satellite is that it can be available practically anywhere, including the polar regions.

CHAPTER FIVE

Security

Every time you read websites that focus on technical news, you learn about the importance of security. As much as you hear about security problems with corporations, it is just as important to keep the individual computers secure.

The security domain covers the basics of security and what is needed to secure a system. Its focus is on your understanding of the technology that is available and the advantages and disadvantages of these technologies.

- ▶ 5.1—Explain the basic principles of security concepts and technologies
- ▶ 5.2—Summarize the following security features

5.1 Explain the basic principles of security concepts and technologies

- ▶ Encryption technologies
- ▶ Data wiping/hard drive destruction/hard drive recycling
- ▶ Software firewall
    - ▶ Port security
    - ▶ Exceptions
- ▶ Authentication technologies
    - ▶ User name
    - ▶ Password
    - ▶ Biometrics
    - ▶ Smart cards
- ▶ Basics of data sensitivity and data security
    - ▶ Compliance
    - ▶ Classifications
    - ▶ Social engineering

1. What is the process of transforming information (plaintext or cleartext) using an algorithm (called cipher) to make it unreadable to anyone else except those that know the cipher and key?

    ○   **A.** Decryption

    ○   **B.** Encryption

    ○   **C.** Topping

    ○   **D.** Rights management

Quick Answer: **189**
Detailed Answer: **190**

2. What is a digital code that can be attached to an electronically transmitted message that uniquely identifies the sender?

    ○   **A.** Digital envelope

    ○   **B.** Digital signature

    ○   **C.** Digital certificate

    ○   **D.** Certificate authority

Quick Answer: **189**
Detailed Answer: **190**

3. Which of the following is used primarily to verify the identity of a person or device, authenticate a service, or encrypt files?

    ○   **A.** Digital envelope

    ○   **B.** Digital signature

    ○   **C.** Digital certificate

    ○   **D.** Certificate authority

Quick Answer: **189**
Detailed Answer: **190**

4. What is the entity that issues digital certificates for use by other parties as part of a public key infrastructure (PKI)?

    ○   **A.** Digital envelope

    ○   **B.** Digital signature

    ○   **C.** Digital certificate

    ○   **D.** Certificate authority

Quick Answer: **189**
Detailed Answer: **190**

5. Which type of encryption uses a single key for both encryption and decryption?

    ○   **A.** Symmetric cryptography

    ○   **B.** Asymmetric cryptography

    ○   **C.** Hash function

    ○   **D.** Certificate encryption

Quick Answer: **189**
Detailed Answer: **190**

6. Which type of encryption uses one key for encryption and another key for decryption?

   ○ **A.** Symmetric cryptography

   ○ **B.** Asymmetric cryptography

   ○ **C.** Hash function

   ○ **D.** Certificate encryption

Quick Answer: **189**
Detailed Answer: **190**

7. What is the most widely used digital certificate?

   ○ **A.** X.400

   ○ **B.** X.200

   ○ **C.** X.509

   ○ **D.** LDAP

Quick Answer: **189**
Detailed Answer: **191**

8. What protocol is used to encrypt data being sent over a public network?

   ○ **A.** HTTP

   ○ **B.** Stateful firewall

   ○ **C.** EFS

   ○ **D.** IPsec

Quick Answer: **189**
Detailed Answer: **191**

9. Which of the following can be used to authenticate and encrypt IP (Internet Protocol) traffic?

   ○ **A.** ESP (Encapsulating Security Payload)

   ○ **B.** S/MIME (Secure Multipurpose Internet Mail Extensions)

   ○ **C.** IPsec (Internet Protocol Security)

   ○ **D.** IPv2 (Internet Protocol version 2)

Quick Answer: **189**
Detailed Answer: **191**

10. Your company wants to inexpensively create more secure communications between its remote offices. What is the best recommendation that you can make to management to accomplish this?

   ○ **A.** Implement Remote Access Service (RAS) and modems at each office

   ○ **B.** Encrypt all communications using the MS-CHAP protocol

   ○ **C.** Use VoIP communications

   ○ **D.** Implement a VPN that connects all the offices

Quick Answer: **189**
Detailed Answer: **191**

11. You are ready to donate your corporate computers to charity. What should you do before you donate your computers?

Quick Answer: **189**
Detailed Answer: **191**

  ○ **A.** Wipe your hard drives with special software that over-writes the entire hard drive multiple times

  ○ **B.** Remove your excess RAM

  ○ **C.** Format the RAM

  ○ **D.** Replace the CMOS battery

12. What is one way to completely remove data from a hard disk drive?

Quick Answer: **189**
Detailed Answer: **191**

  ○ **A.** Partition and completely reformat the drive

  ○ **B.** Reinstall the operating system over the existing OS structure

  ○ **C.** Delete all the files on the drive and perform a disk defrag operation

  ○ **D.** Physically destroy the drive's platters with a hammer or acid

13. What is one way to completely remove data from a hard disk drive?

Quick Answer: **189**
Detailed Answer: **192**

  ○ **A.** Reformat the drive

  ○ **B.** Perform a low-level format

  ○ **C.** Run the chkdsk command with the –r option

  ○ **D.** Run a defrag

14. What is one way to completely remove data from a hard disk drive?

Quick Answer: **189**
Detailed Answer: **192**

  ○ **A.** Reformat the drive with Disk Manager

  ○ **B.** Use special software to write 0s and 1s

  ○ **C.** Delete and re-create the partitions

  ○ **D.** Reformat the drive with the format command and the /u option

15. What software, hardware device, or system is designed to prevent unauthorized access to or from a private network or computer?

Quick Answer: **189**
Detailed Answer: **192**

  ○ **A.** Firewall

  ○ **B.** Certificate server

  ○ **C.** AES

  ○ **D.** EFS

16. Which firewall feature blocks a packet based on a protocol?

Quick Answer: **189**
Detailed Answer: **192**

- ○ **A.** Packet filtering
- ○ **B.** Stateful filtering
- ○ **C.** Stateless filtering
- ○ **D.** Signature blocking

17. Which firewall feature blocks a packet based on previous conversations or packets?

Quick Answer: **189**
Detailed Answer: **192**

- ○ **A.** Packet filtering
- ○ **B.** Stateful filtering
- ○ **C.** Stateless filtering
- ○ **D.** Signature blocking

18. Which software included with Windows Vista will automatically block most network services unless it is configured to allow those network services to proceed?

Quick Answer: **189**
Detailed Answer: **192**

- ○ **A.** Windows Defender
- ○ **B.** Chkdsk
- ○ **C.** Scandisk
- ○ **D.** Windows Firewall

19. You have a computer that is part of the corporate domain. You frequently work from home and travel. Which of the following are two wireless security policy items that you should implement to safeguard your data? (Select two.)

Quick Answer: **189**
Detailed Answer: **192**

- ○ **A.** Use an IPSec VPN for remote connectivity
- ○ **B.** Use an HTTPS captive portal
- ○ **C.** Use a personal firewall on this laptop
- ○ **D.** Use a protocol analyzer on this laptop to sniff WLAN traffic for risks
- ○ **E.** Use 802.1X/PEAPv0 to connect to the office network

20. You have a Windows XP computer with SP3. You start a network service but it cannot communicate with a server. What should you do?

Quick Answer: **189**
Detailed Answer: **193**

- ○ **A.** Stop and restart the service
- ○ **B.** Uninstall Service Pack 3
- ○ **C.** Add the port number and name of the service to the Exceptions list in Windows Firewall
- ○ **D.** Reboot the computer

21. Which of the following terms best defines the ability to verify the identity of a user, system, or system element?

Quick Answer: **189**
Detailed Answer: **193**

- ○ **A.** Encryption
- ○ **B.** Hashing
- ○ **C.** Authentication
- ○ **D.** Authorization

22. What is the default authentication method for Windows XP connected to a domain?

Quick Answer: **189**
Detailed Answer: **193**

- ○ **A.** Username and password
- ○ **B.** Username and PIN
- ○ **C.** Username and finger scan
- ○ **D.** Username and smart card

23. Which of the following would be considered a strong password?

Quick Answer: **189**
Detailed Answer: **193**

- ○ **A.** Tsr.34PR
- ○ **B.** Password
- ○ **C.** John.Smith
- ○ **D.** HelloThere

24. For which of the following can biometrics be used?

Quick Answer: **189**
Detailed Answer: **193**

- ○ **A.** Accountability
- ○ **B.** Certification
- ○ **C.** Authorization
- ○ **D.** Authentication

25. Which of the following is not a form of biometrics?

Quick Answer: **189**
Detailed Answer: **193**

- ○ **A.** Finger scan
- ○ **B.** Retina scan
- ○ **C.** Voice recognition
- ○ **D.** PIN

26. Which of the following statements are true? (Choose two answers.)

Quick Answer: **189**
Detailed Answer: **193**

- ○ **A.** You should always use strong passwords.
- ○ **B.** You should change your password often.
- ○ **C.** You should choose passwords that are easy to remember.
- ○ **D.** You should change usernames from time to time.

Quick Check

27. What security service is provided by using a smart card containing a private key when you log onto a workstation?

Quick Answer: **189**
Detailed Answer: **193**

- ○ **A.** Authentication
- ○ **B.** Confidentiality
- ○ **C.** Integrity
- ○ **D.** Non-repudiation

28. One of your customers has research work on his notebook PC that he wants to protect. In the event that the notebook is stolen, he wants more authentication than a simple user name and password login for his PC. What can you recommend that will be easy to implement, will be cost effective, and will adequately protect the information on his notebook?

Quick Answer: **189**
Detailed Answer: **194**

- ○ **A.** Employ an encryption algorithm for login
- ○ **B.** Install a retinal scanner on the PC
- ○ **C.** Employ a Shared Secret login scenario
- ○ **D.** Install a fingerprint scanner on the notebook

29. What type of authentication provides an additional layer of security when memorized passwords are not strong enough?

Quick Answer: **189**
Detailed Answer: **194**

- ○ **A.** Mutual
- ○ **B.** Multi-factor
- ○ **C.** Biometric
- ○ **D.** Certificate

30. Why do social engineering attacks often succeed?

Quick Answer: **189**
Detailed Answer: **194**

- ○ **A.** Strong passwords are not required
- ○ **B.** Lack of security awareness
- ○ **C.** Multiple logins are allowed
- ○ **D.** Audit logs are not monitored frequently

31. In which of the following would an attacker impersonate a dissatisfied customer of a company and request a password change on the customer's account?

Quick Answer: **189**
Detailed Answer: **194**

- ○ **A.** Hostile code
- ○ **B.** Social engineering
- ○ **C.** IP (Internet Protocol) spoofing
- ○ **D.** Man in the middle attack

32. Which of the following is the most effective defense against a social engineering attack?

- ○ **A.** Marking of documents
- ○ **B.** Escorting of guests
- ○ **C.** Badge security system
- ○ **D.** Training and awareness

33. Which of the following attacks are the most common and most successful when network security is properly implemented and configured?

- ○ **A.** Logical attacks
- ○ **B.** Physical attacks
- ○ **C.** Social engineering attacks
- ○ **D.** Trojan horse attacks

34. Which of the following is a characteristic of Mandatory Access Control (MAC)?

- ○ **A.** Uses levels of security to classify users and data
- ○ **B.** Allows owners of documents to determine who has access to specific documents
- ○ **C.** Uses access control lists that specify a list of authorized users
- ○ **D.** Uses access control lists that specify a list of unauthorized users

35. Which of the following access control methods relies on user security clearance and data classification?

- ○ **A.** RBAC (Role-Based Access Control)
- ○ **B.** NDAC (Non-Discretionary Access Control)
- ○ **C.** MAC (Mandatory Access Control)
- ○ **D.** DAC (Discretionary Access Control)

36. Windows uses what kind of security model?

- ○ **A.** RBAC (Role-Based Access Control)
- ○ **B.** NDAC (Non-Discretionary Access Control)
- ○ **C.** MAC (Mandatory Access Control)
- ○ **D.** DAC (Discretionary Access Control)

Quick Check

Quick Answer: **189**
Detailed Answer: **195**

37. You have received a file from your supervisor marked "Confidential—Your Eyes Only." When you save this file to your hard drive, you want to protect it by encrypting it. Where do you set up file encryption in your Windows XP desktop PC?

○ **A.** Select Encryption from the File menu and click Encrypt This File.

○ **B.** Create a new folder, right-click it, and then select the Encrypt option from its Properties menu. Move the file into the encrypted folder.

○ **C.** Right-click the file in Windows Explorer, select Properties, select the Advanced button, and check Encrypt Contents to Secure Data check box.

○ **D.** Navigate to the Control Panel/Administrative Tools/Computer Management console and click the Disk Management option. Then select a drive and choose Encrypt Files on This Drive.

5.2 Summarize the following security features

▶ Wireless encryption

　▶ WEPx and WPAx

　▶ Client configuration (SSID)

▶ Malicious software protection

　▶ Viruses

　▶ Trojans

　▶ Worms

　▶ Spam

　▶ Spyware

　▶ Adware

　▶ Grayware

▶ BIOS Security

　▶ Drive lock

　▶ Passwords

　▶ Intrusion detection

　▶ TPM

▶ Password management/password complexity

▶ Locking workstation

　▶ Hardware

　▶ Operating system

▶ Biometrics

　▶ Fingerprint scanner

38. You entered the wrong WEP (Wired Equivalent Privacy) key into a wireless device. Which of the following symptoms occurs?

Quick Answer: **189**
Detailed Answer: **195**

- ○ **A.** Data can be sent but not received.
- ○ **B.** The network cannot be accessed.
- ○ **C.** Data cannot be sent but can be received.
- ○ **D.** The network can only be accessed using the Service Set Identifier.

39. Which of the following is the most secure?

Quick Answer: **189**
Detailed Answer: **195**

- ○ **A.** WPA
- ○ **B.** WPA2
- ○ **C.** WEP
- ○ **D.** SSID

40. What is the best way to secure a wireless access point from unauthorized wireless connections?

Quick Answer: **189**
Detailed Answer: **195**

- ○ **A.** Install a security firewall
- ○ **B.** Implement biometric access control
- ○ **C.** Reduce the signal strength
- ○ **D.** Disable SSID broadcasts

41. Which of the following preventative maintenance tasks should be performed regularly on a computer that has Internet access?

Quick Answer: **189**
Detailed Answer: **196**

- ○ **A.** Disable the use of cookies
- ○ **B.** Disable all unused features of the web browser
- ○ **C.** Run a virus scan of the hard disk drives
- ○ **D.** Enable the Windows Firewall

42. Which of the following is the most effective method of preventing computer viruses from spreading?

Quick Answer: **189**
Detailed Answer: **196**

- ○ **A.** Require root/administrator access to run programs
- ○ **B.** Enable scanning of email attachments
- ○ **C.** Prevent the execution of .vbs files
- ○ **D.** Install a host-based IDS (Intrusion Detection System)

43. Which of the following is the major difference between a worm and a Trojan horse?

Quick Answer: **189**
Detailed Answer: **196**

- ○ **A.** Worms are spread via email and Trojan horses are not.
- ○ **B.** Worms are self-replicating and Trojan horses are not.

○ **C.** Worms are a form of malicious code and Trojan horses are not.

○ **D.** There is no difference.

44. Which of the following can distribute itself without using a host file?

○ **A.** Virus

○ **B.** Trojan horse

○ **C.** Logic bomb

○ **D.** Worm

Quick Answer: **189**
Detailed Answer: **196**

45. What type of program will record system keystrokes in a text file
and email it to the author, and will also delete system logs every
five days or whenever a backup is performed?

○ **A.** Virus

○ **B.** Back door

○ **C.** Logic bomb

○ **D.** Worm

Quick Answer: **189**
Detailed Answer: **196**

46. What is a piece of code that appears to do something useful while
performing a harmful and unexpected function such as stealing
passwords called?

○ **A.** Virus

○ **B.** Logic bomb

○ **C.** Worm

○ **D.** Trojan horse

Quick Answer: **189**
Detailed Answer: **197**

47. What is the name for a piece of malicious code that has no productive purpose but can replicate itself and exist only to damage
computer systems or create further vulnerabilities?

○ **A.** Logic bomb

○ **B.** Worm

○ **C.** Trojan horse

○ **D.** Virus

Quick Answer: **189**
Detailed Answer: **197**

48. What are the two best methods to protect against viruses on a
Windows XP or Windows Vista computer? (Select two answers.)

○ **A.** Keep the computer updated with the newest security
patches

○ **B.** Rename the Administrator account

○ **C.** Use an up-to-date anti-virus software package

○ **D.** Use NTFS

Quick Answer: **189**
Detailed Answer: **197**

49. What is unsolicited or undesired email called?

- ○ **A.** Worm
- ○ **B.** Trojan horse
- ○ **C.** Virus
- ○ **D.** Spam

Quick Answer: **189**
Detailed Answer: **197**

50. Which of the following strategies provides the best protection from viruses and worms?

- ○ **A.** Change the Administrators account password from the default
- ○ **B.** Make as many people part of the Administrators group as possible
- ○ **C.** Place only as many users as needed in the Admin group
- ○ **D.** Put all the users in the Security group

Quick Answer: **189**
Detailed Answer: **198**

51. How should you protect yourself against spam? (Choose all that apply.)

- ○ **A.** Install spam filtering/blocking software
- ○ **B.** Do not respond to suspicious emails
- ○ **C.** Do not post links to email addresses on websites
- ○ **D.** Install Windows Defender

Quick Answer: **189**
Detailed Answer: **198**

52. What do you call a software package that automatically plays, displays, or downloads advertisements to a computer after the software is installed on it or while the application is being used?

- ○ **A.** Spyware
- ○ **B.** Adware
- ○ **C.** Trojan horse
- ○ **D.** Macro virus

Quick Answer: **189**
Detailed Answer: **198**

53. What is a classification of applications that are annoying or undesirable but are not designed to harm the computer?

- ○ **A.** Blackware
- ○ **B.** Grayware
- ○ **C.** Trojan horse
- ○ **D.** Macro virus

Quick Answer: **189**
Detailed Answer: **198**

54. Which of the following can help protect a computer from being physically accessed by unauthorized personnel?

   ◯   **A.**   Use NTFS

   ◯   **B.**   Use passwords for the BIOS to boot the computer

   ◯   **C.**   Keep the computer under lock and key

   ◯   **D.**   Use share permissions

55. Where would you establish a Supervisory password on a computer that will be installed in an Internet kiosk so that users can access the system but not modify its configuration?

   ◯   **A.**   On the motherboard using jumpers.

   ◯   **B.**   In the BIOS Setup Program.

   ◯   **C.**   In Windows.

   ◯   **D.**   If you set a password in this environment, users will not be able to access the system.

56. What new Windows Vista application prevents the infiltration of spyware into the system?

   ◯   **A.**   Windows Defender

   ◯   **B.**   Windows Firewall

   ◯   **C.**   Windows Security Center

   ◯   **D.**   Automatic Update

57. What additional application, provided by Windows Defender, enables you to monitor details about specific applications running on a Windows Vista computer?

   ◯   **A.**   Windows Defender Plus

   ◯   **B.**   Defender Explorer

   ◯   **C.**   Windows Explorer

   ◯   **D.**   Software Explorer

58. What feature of NTFS encodes the files on a computer so that even if an intruder can obtain a file, he or she will be unable to read it?

   ◯   **A.**   Windows Firewall

   ◯   **B.**   Encrypted File System

   ◯   **C.**   BitLocker

   ◯   **D.**   Windows Malicious Software Removal Tool

59. What is required for BitLocker Drive Encryption to function?

Quick Answer: **189**
Detailed Answer: **199**

- ○ **A.** TPM
- ○ **B.** Digital certificates
- ○ **C.** CA
- ○ **D.** EFS

60. How can you configure the system so that you know if someone has opened a computer?

Quick Answer: **189**
Detailed Answer: **199**

- ○ **A.** Install Windows Defender
- ○ **B.** Enable intrusion detection in the BIOS
- ○ **C.** Install SP2 for Windows XP and SP1 for Windows Vista
- ○ **D.** Add fingerprint dust to the case

Quick-Check Answer Key

1. B	**21.** C	**41.** C
2. B	**22.** A	**42.** B
3. C	**23.** A	**43.** B
4. D	**24.** D	**44.** D
5. A	**25.** D	**45.** C
6. B	**26.** A and B	**46.** D
7. C	**27.** A	**47.** D
8. D	**28.** D	**48.** A and C
9. C	**29.** B	**49.** D
10. D	**30.** B	**50.** C
11. A	**31.** B	**51.** A, B, and C
12. D	**32.** D	**52.** B
13. B	**33.** C	**53.** B.
14. B	**34.** A	**54.** C
15. A	**35.** C	**55.** A
16. A	**36.** D	**56.** A
17. B	**37.** C	**57.** D
18. D	**38.** B	**58.** B
19. A and C	**39.** B	**59.** A
20. C	**40.** D	**60.** B

Answers and Explanations

1. **Answer: B.** Encryption is the process of disguising a message or data in what appears to be meaningless data (cipher text) to hide and protect the sensitive data from unauthorized access. Decryption (Answer A) is the process of converting cipher text back to meaningful data. Rights management (Answer D) is a technology that allows you to store documents that can only be accessed by authorized people. Topping (Answer C) has no meaning when discussing security.

2. **Answer: B.** A digital signature is a digital code that can be attached to an electronically transmitted message that identifies the sender. Like a written signature, the purpose of a digital signature is to guarantee that the individual sending the message really is who he or she claims to be. A digital envelope (Answer A) is a type of security that uses two layers of encryption to protect a message. A digital certificate (Answer C) is an electronic attachment that establishes credentials when doing business or other transactions. It is issued by a certification authority (CA), Answer D. It contains your name, a serial number, expiration dates, a copy of the certificate holder's public key (used for encrypting messages and digital signatures), and the digital signature of the certificate-issuing authority so that a recipient can verify that the certificate is real.

3. **Answer: C.** A digital certificate is an electronic attachment that establishes credentials when doing business or other transactions. It is issued by a certification authority (CA), Answer D. It contains your name, a serial number, expiration dates, a copy of the certificate holder's public key (used for encrypting messages and digital signatures), and the digital signature of the certificate-issuing authority so that a recipient can verify that the certificate is real. A digital signature (Answer B) is a digital code that can be attached to an electronically transmitted message that identifies the sender. Like a written signature, the purpose of a digital signature is to guarantee that the individual sending the message really is who he or she claims to be. A digital envelope (Answer A) is a type of security that uses two layers of encryption to protect a message.

4. **Answer: D.** A certification authority (CA) issues digital certificates that contain a public key and the identity of the owner. The matching private key is not similarly made available to the public, but kept secret by the end user who generated the key pair. A digital certificate (Answer C) is an electronic attachment that establishes credentials when doing business or other transactions. A digital signature (Answer B) is a digital code that can be attached to an electronically transmitted message that identifies the sender. Like a written signature, the purpose of a digital signature is to guarantee that the individual sending the message really is who he or she claims to be. A digital envelope (Answer A) is a type of security that uses two layers of encryption to protect a message.

5. **Answer: A.** Symmetric cryptography uses a single key for both encryption and decryption. It is also known as secret key encryption. Asymmetric cryptography (Answer B) uses one key for encryption and another key for decryption. It is often used as part of a public-key infrastructure. A hash function (Answer C) is a one-way encryption that cannot be converted back to its original value. Digital certificates (Answer D) contain a public key but do not actually perform encryption.

6. **Answer: B.** Asymmetric cryptography uses one key for encryption and another key for decryption. It is often used as part of a public-key infrastructure. Symmetric cryptography (Answer A) uses a single key for both encryption and decryption. It is also

known as secret key encryption. A hash function (Answer C) is a one-way encryption that cannot be converted back to its original value. Digital certificates (Answer D) contain a public key but do not actually perform encryption.

7. **Answer: C.** X.509 is the most widely used digital certificate. It contains information that identifies the user, as well as information about the organization that issued the certificate, including the serial number, validity period, issuer name, issuer signature, and subject/user name. X.400 (Answer A) is an email standard. X.200 (Answer B) is part of the OSI model. LDAP (Answer D) is short for Lightweight Directory Access Protocol. It is a directory service based on X.500. Active Directory is based on LDAP.

8. **Answer: D.** IPsec, short for IP Security, is a set of protocols that can be used to encrypt data that is sent over the Internet. HTTP (Answer A) is the protocol used to display web pages. A stateful firewall (Answer B) analyzes packets sent through a firewall and determines which packets are allowed back in based on previous packets. EFS (Answer C) is short for Encrypted File System (EFS). EFS is used to encrypt folders and files on an NTFS volume.

9. **Answer: C.** IPSec provides secure authentication and encryption of data and headers. IPSec can work in tunneling mode or transport mode. In tunneling mode, the data or payload and message headers are encrypted. Transport mode encrypts only the payload. Encapsulating Security Payload (Answer A) does not exist. S/MIME (Answer B) is used to encrypt email messages. Today's version of IP is IPv4 or IPv6, not IPv2 (Answer D).

10. **Answer: D.** Digital certificates are a major security feature in the Windows 2000, Windows XP, and Windows Vista operating systems. Digital certificates are password-protected, encrypted data files that include data that identifies the transmitting system and can be used to authenticate external users to the network through Virtual Private Networks (VPNs). VPNs use message encryption and other security techniques to ensure that only authorized users can access the message as it passes through public transmission media. In particular, VPNs provide secure Internet communications by establishing encrypted data tunnels across the WAN that cannot be penetrated by others. Remote Access Service (Answer A) is used to provide centralized authentication for remote access. While Remote Access Service can be used to provide VPNs, using modems creates extremely slow links between sites. MS-CHAP (Answer B) is an authentication protocol. VoIP (Answer C), short for Voice over IP, is used to provide phone services over an IP network.

11. **Answer: A.** You need to ensure that all confidential information is removed from the hard drive. Therefore, you need to use special software that writes data throughout the entire disk and overwrites all data including data from previous files. You also can use a special magnet that will erase all data on the hard drive. In addition, you can consider destroying hard drives. The RAM and CMOS memory will not hold confidential information.

12. **Answer: D.** If a hard disk drive is not going to be reused, it should be damaged to the point where it is physically unusable—not just logically unusable. This can involve opening the outer cover of the drive and physically scarring its disk surfaces: scratching the surface with a sharp implement, hammering the disks, or pouring acid on the disk surfaces. Special software and other tools can be used to recover data from disks that have been reformatted (Answer A), files that have been deleted (Answers C), and operating systems that have been reinstalled (Answer B).

13. **Answer: B.** Of the answers available, a low-level format will redraw all of the sectors and tracks. Performing a normal format (considered a high-level format) only erases the file system, but the bits still hold data even though the file allocation table has been erased. With special software, you can still retrieve this data (Answer A). The `chkdsk` command (Answer C) is used to check for disk errors, not to clean a disk. The `defrag` command (Answer D) is used to optimize a hard drive.

14. **Answer: B.** Besides physically destroying the platters, the U.S. Department of Defense (DoD) also approves certain software packages that write all 0s, followed by writing all 1s, followed by writing all 0s on all bits of a platter for making the data unrecoverable. Performing a normal format (considered a high-level format), Answers A and D, or deleting and re-creating partitions (Answer C) will not truly erase the data on the platters.

15. **Answer: A.** A firewall is software, hardware device, or system that prevents unauthorized access to or from a private network or host. All messages or packets entering or leaving through the firewall are examined and the firewall blocks those that do not meet specified security criteria. A certificate server (Answer B) hands out digital certificates. AES (Answer C) is short for Advanced Encryption Standard. It is an encryption standard adopted by the U.S. government and is used by many encryption technologies, including WPA2 wireless encryption. EFS (Answer D) is short for Encrypted File System (EFS). EFS is used to encrypt folders and files on an NTFS volume.

16. **Answer: A.** Packet filtering can block packets based on address or by protocol (based on port number). Stateful filtering filters (Answer B) packets based on previous conversations. Stateless filtering (Answer C) technically is packet filtering, but it is not referred to as such. Signature blocking (Answer D) is a technology that blocks packets based on prerecorded signatures that identify unwanted packets.

17. **Answer: B.** Stateful filtering creates a table of incoming and outgoing packets so that it knows what conversations are taking place. If it sees that you opened an outgoing conversation with a web server, it allows that packet from the web server. If another web server tries to communicate through the stateful firewall or if a web server tries to start a new conversation at a later time, it is blocked because it is not part of the current conversation. Packet filtering (Answer A) can block packets based on address or by protocol (based on port number). Stateless filtering (Answer C) technically is packet filtering, but it is not referred to as such. Signature blocking (Answer D) is technology that blocks packets based on prerecorded signatures that identify unwanted packets.

18. **Answer: D.** Windows Firewall is a packet filtering and stateful firewall. It is included in Windows Vista and Windows XP SP2. Windows Defender (Answer A) is used to detect and block spyware. Chkdsk (Answer B) and Scandisk (Answer C) are used to find and correct disk errors.

19. **Answer: A and C.** To connect to the corporate network while at home or traveling, you should use a VPN connection with IPSec. IPSec encrypts data communicating between the computer and the corporate network. You should also use a personal firewall to protect your computer, especially when you are traveling. Using an HTTPS Captive portal (Answer B) is used to display a special web page that shows before a user can access the Internet. It is usually used for authentication, payment, or to display an acceptable use policy. Unfortunately using an HTTPS Captive portal will not protect your computer. Using a protocol analyzer (Answer D) requires special skills and will only be useful when you are being attacked. 802.1X/PEAP (Answer E) is used for wireless authentication but does not protect you when connecting to other networks.

20. Answer: C. Windows XP SP2 or SP3 include a Windows Firewall. If you need to communicate with a remote host, you need to tell the firewall what to allow to flow through the firewall. Because a firewall is an important tool, you should not uninstall Service Pack 3 (Answer B). Because the firewall is most likely blocking your service, stopping and restarting the service (Answer A), or rebooting the computer (Answer D) will not fix the problem.

21. Answer: C. Authentication is the ability to verify the identity of a user, system, or system element to make sure there is not unauthorized access. Encryption (Answer A) is the process of transforming information (referred to as plaintext) using an algorithm (called cipher) to make it unreadable to anyone except those possessing special knowledge, usually referred to as a key. The result of the process is encrypted information (in cryptography, referred to as ciphertext). A hash function (Answer B) is a one-way encryption that cannot be converted back to its original value. Authorization (Answer D) is the process that verifies a user or other identity can access an object or perform an action.

22. Answer: A. When you use a password to prove who you are, you are proving what you know, which is a username and password. A PIN (Answer B), short for Personal Identification Number, is usually used to access your bank ATM. A finger scan (Answer C), which is part of biometrics, is a form of authentication but is only used on a few computers. Smart Cards (Answer D) are small cards that include a digital certificate or other unique identification to prove who you are.

23. Answer: A. By Microsoft's definition, a strong password is at least seven characters and includes three of the following: uppercase letters, lowercase letters, numerals, and special characters. Password (Answer B) and HelloThere (Answer D) only have upper- and lowercase letters. John.Smith (Answer C) would be a strong password if it did not contain the user's name.

24. Answer: D. Biometrics devices use physical characteristics to identify the user. Therefore, it is used for authentication. Authorization (Answer C) is the process used to verify that a user or other identity can access an object or perform an action. Accountability (Answer A) is used to audit or record actions so that they can be used to prove what was done. Certification (Answer B) is the confirmation that some standard has been achieved.

25. Answer: D. PIN, short for Personal Identification Number, is a password usually based on digits. Finger scan (Answer A), retina scan (Answer B), and voice recognition (Answer C) are based on who you are. These items are part of you.

26. Answers: A and B. You should always use a strong password so that it is more difficult to guess. By Microsoft's definition, a strong password is at least seven characters and includes three of the following: uppercase letters, lowercase letters, numerals, and special characters. You should also change your password often—for example, every 30 to 60 days. You should not choose passwords that are easy to remember because they are easy to guess (Answer C).

27. Answer: A. Smart cards are used for authentication, and in this example the smart card authenticated that the owner of the card was the one authorized to use that particular workstation. Confidentiality (Answer B) makes sure that the message or data is only seen by the people for whom it is intended. Integrity (Answer C) makes sure that the message or data is not changed. Non-repudiation (Answer D) is the ability that ensures that certain actions performed by a person on the network or on a system cannot be denied by that person (in other words, he or she cannot say that he or she did not perform those actions).

28. **Answer: D.** Biometric scanners—including facial-scanning devices, searchable databases, and supporting application programs—are getting significantly more sophisticated. The biometric authentication device most widely used with PCs is the fingerprint scanner. Some manufacturers offer miniature touchpad versions that sit on the desk and connect to the system though a cable and USB connector. Other fingerprint scanners are built into key fobs that plug directly into the USB port. Some manufacturers even build these devices into the top of the mouse. Installing a retinal scanner (Answer B) on the PC is more costly and more difficult to use than the fingerprint scanner. Employing a Shared Secret login scenario (Answer C) or employing a new encryption algorithm (Answer A) does not really make the system more secure.

29. **Answer: B.** When two or more of these access methods are included as a part of the authentication process, you are implementing a multi-factor system. Mutual authentication (Answer A) is a two-way authentication in which the user makes sure the server is also what it says it is. Biometric is a form of authentication based on who you are. It includes finger scan and retinal scan. Digital certificates (Answer D) are authentication based on something you have. The digital certificate has a public key.

30. **Answer: B.** Social engineering is a term used to describe the process of circumventing security barriers by persuading authorized users to provide passwords or other sensitive information. When someone asks for help, people often want to help because they have been in the same situation in the past or they can empathize. If an awareness program is implemented in which employees are made aware of social engineering tactics, the employees are more likely to think about them and be more suspect of an attack when someone asks for a favor. With this knowledge, an employee can make a smarter decision. The other answer options (A, C, and D) are not specifically tied to social engineering attacks.

31. **Answer: B.** Social engineering is a term used to describe the process of circumventing security barriers by persuading authorized users to provide passwords or other sensitive information. Hostile code (Answer A) is creating a time bomb, a form of malware. IP spoofing (Answer C) is an attempt to access a system or to perform phishing by modifying packets that are sent to make them look like they are coming from someplace else. In a man in the middle attack (Answer D) an attacker takes over a conversation to access a system.

32. **Answer: D.** Social engineering is a term used to describe the process of circumventing security barriers by persuading authorized users to provide passwords or other sensitive information. The only preventative measure in dealing with social engineering attacks is to educate your users and staff to never give out passwords and user IDs over the phone, via email, or to anyone who is not positively verified as being who they say they are.

33. **Answer: C.** Social engineering is a term used to describe the process of circumventing security barriers by persuading authorized users to provide passwords or other sensitive information. So when security is successfully implemented, the best method to circumvent that security is by using social engineering because most other attacks are

blocked by the network security. Logical attacks (Answer A), physical attacks (Answer B), and Trojan horse attacks (Answer D) can be prevented, or at least mitigated, when network security is properly implemented and configured.

34. **Answer: A.** MAC is a strict hierarchical mode that is based on classifying data on importance and categorizing it by department. Users receive specific security clearances to access this data. You can think of it as being similar to the military's use of secret and top secret documents. The other answers (B, C, and D) are not characteristic of MAC.

35. **Answer: C.** MAC is a strict hierarchical mode that is based on classifying data on importance and categorizing it by department. Users receive specific security clearances to access this data. You can think of it as being similar to the military's use of secret and top secret documents. Role-Based Access Control (RBAC—Answer A) is based on being assigned to a role, which has permissions. Discretionary Access Control (DAC—Answer D) is based on owners who control access to their objects. For example, if you create a document, you own it. Because you own the document, you can specify who can access the document. Windows uses DAC. Non-Discretionary Access Control (NDAC) does not exist as an access control method.

36. **Answer: D.** Windows permits the owner of an object (such as a process, file, or folder) to manage access control at their own discretion. MAC (Answer C) is a strict hierarchical mode that is based on classifying data on importance and categorizing it by department. Users receive specific security clearances to access this data. You can think of it as being similar to the military's use of secret and top secret documents. Role-Based Access Control (RBAC—Answer A) is based on being assigned to a role, which has permissions. Answer B, Non-Discretionary Access Control (NDAC), does not exist as an access control method.

37. **Answer: C.** Encryption is treated as a file attribute in Windows 2000, Windows XP, and Windows Vista. Therefore, to encrypt a file, you simply need to access a file's Properties page by right-clicking on it and selecting the Properties option from the pop-up menu. Move to the Advanced Attribute window under the General tab and click the Encrypt Contents to Secure Data check box. The other answer options (A, B, and D) do not describe the correct procedure.

38. **Answer: B.** WEP (wired equivalent privacy) requires that both the wireless computer and the WAP (wireless access point) be configured with the same encryption key in order for the two to communicate. If one of the two has the wrong WEP key, communication will not be possible and the network will not be accessible. Therefore, the other answers are incorrect.

39. **Answer: B.** While WPA and WPA2 are considered secure encryption protocols for wireless networks, WPA2 provides strong data protection and network access control, and it provides government-grade security by implementing the AES encryption algorithm and 802.1x-based authentication. AES is short for Advanced Encryption Standard, which is an encryption standard adopted by the U.S. government.

40. **Answer: D.** If you disable SSID broadcasts, the access point will not show up as an available network. Therefore a novice user will not connect to the network if they do not know it exists. Implementing biometric access control (Answer B) is usually implemented on a workstation and not at the access points. Installing a firewall (Answer A)

only blocks certain protocols or certain connections from occurring. Reducing the signal strength (Answer C) limits how far the radio waves can travel but lowering signal strength might cause certain authorized users not to connect.

41. **Answer: C.** Because the Internet is the primary source for virus distribution, you should run a virus scan of your hard drives on a regular basis. Of course, you need to keep your virus scanner up to date. Disabling the use of cookies (Answer A) or certain features of the web browser (Answer B) stops you from using certain websites. Enabling a Windows firewall (Answer D) helps protect your laptop but you most likely get more security by using a virus checker. You normally disable cookies, disable unused features, or enable a firewall once, but you need to run the anti-virus program on a regular basis. Of course, you can usually schedule the anti-virus program to run an automatic scan regularly.

42. **Answer: B.** Viruses are commonly spread through email. Therefore, if you scan all emails and their attachments, you help prevent viruses from spreading. You should not require root or administrator access (Answer A) to run programs because if you run them as root or administrator and you are affected by a virus, it can attack or spread to wherever you have access to. As administrator, you will have access to more data and systems than a standard user. Executing the execution of .vbs files (Answer C) only stops certain files from being executed through your email, but does not stop most viruses, including macro viruses. Installing a host-based IDS system (Answer D) only helps you detect intruders but does not protect against viruses.

43. **Answer: B.** Worms reproduce themselves, are self-contained, and do not need a host application to be transported. The Trojan horse program may be installed as part of an installation process. They do not reproduce or self-replicate.

44. **Answer: D.** Worms are dangerous because they can enter a system by exploiting a "hole" in an operating system. They don't need a host or carry file, and they don't need any user intervention to replicate by themselves. A virus (Answer A) is a program that spreads from computer to computer without your knowledge or permissions and usually does harmful damage. A Trojan horse (Answer B) is a program that enters a system or network under the guise of another program. A Trojan horse might be included as an attachment or as part of an installation program. A logic bomb (Answer C) is a special kind of virus or Trojan horse that is set to go off following a preset time interval or following a preset combination of keyboard strokes.

45. **Answer: C.** A logic bomb is a special kind of virus or Trojan horse that is set to go off following a preset time interval or following a preset combination of keyboard strokes. Some unethical advertisers use logic bombs to deliver the right pop-up advertisement following a keystroke, and some disgruntled employees set up logic bombs to go off to sabotage their company's computers if they feel termination is imminent. A virus (Answer A) is a program that spreads from computer to computer without your knowledge or permission and usually does harmful damage. A back door (Answer B) is an opening left behind on a program that allows a user to bypass the normal security. Worms (Answer D) are dangerous because they can enter a system by exploiting a "hole" in an operating system. They don't need a host or carry file, and they don't need any user intervention to replicate by themselves.

46. Answer: D. Trojan horses can be included as an attachment or as part of an installation program. The Trojan horse can create a back door or replace a valid program during installation. The Trojan horse then accomplishes its mission under the guise of another program. Trojan horses can be used to compromise the security of your system, and can exist on a system for years before they are detected. A logic bomb (Answer B) is a special kind of virus or Trojan horse that is set to go off following a preset time interval or following a preset combination of keyboard strokes. Some unethical advertisers use logic bombs to deliver the right pop-up advertisement following a keystroke, and some disgruntled employees set up logic bombs to go off to sabotage their company's computers if they feel termination is imminent. A virus (Answer A) is a program that spreads from computer to computer without your knowledge or permission and usually does harmful damage. Worms (Answer C) are dangerous because they can enter a system by exploiting a "hole" in an operating system. They don't need a host or carry file, and they don't need any user intervention to replicate by themselves.

47. Answer: D. A virus is a piece of software designed to infect a computer system. The virus might do nothing more than reside on the computer. But a virus might also damage the data on your hard disk, destroy your operating system, and possibly spread to other systems. A logic bomb (Answer A) is a special kind of virus or Trojan horse that is set to go off following a preset time interval or following a preset combination of keyboard strokes. Some unethical advertisers use logic bombs to deliver the right pop-up advertisement following a keystroke, and some disgruntled employees set up logic bombs to go off to sabotage their company's computers if they feel termination is imminent. A virus (Answer D) is a program that spreads from computer to computer without your knowledge or permission and usually does harmful damage. Worms (Answer B) are dangerous because they can enter a system by exploiting a "hole" in an operating system. They don't need a host or carry file, and they don't need any user intervention to replicate by themselves. Trojan horses (Answer C) can be included as an attachment or as part of an installation program. The Trojan horse can create a back door or replace a valid program during installation. The Trojan horse then accomplishes its mission under the guise of another program. Trojan Horses can be used to compromise the security of your system, and they can exist on a system for years before they are detected.

48. Answer: A and C. To best protect against viruses, you must keep your system up-to-date with the newest security patches. You should also use an up-to-date anti-virus software package. Renaming the administrator account (Answer B) and using NTFS (Answer D) will do nothing to protect against a virus.

49. Answer: D. Spam is economically viable because it has virtually no operating costs to send except the management of mail lists. There is more spam than legitimate email. People who create electronic spam are called spammers. Trojan horses (Answer B) can be included as an attachment or as part of an installation program. The Trojan horse can create a back door or replace a valid program during installation. The Trojan horse then accomplishes its mission under the guise of another program. Trojan Horses can be used to compromise the security of your system, and they can exist on a system for years before they are detected. A virus (Answer C) is a program that spreads from computer to computer without your knowledge or permission and usually does harmful damage. Worms (Answer A) are dangerous because they can enter a system by exploiting a "hole" in an operating system. They don't need a host or carry file, and they don't need any user intervention to replicate by themselves.

50. Answer: C. Under general user accounts, the virus and worms cannot gain access to system-level files (admin rights are required for this). Therefore, give as few users as possible administrative rights. Giving too many people administrator rights (Answer B) gives viruses more opportunity to spread from an administrator account. Changing the administrator account password (Answer A) and putting all the users in any specific security group will not protect a system against viruses.

51. Answer: A, B and C. To protect against spam, you should first install spam filtering/blocking software that will help take care of spam before you see it. You should also not respond to suspicious emails. By responding to suspicious email, you will confirm that the email address is valid, which will often lead to receiving more spam. Lastly, do not post your email address on websites so that other people can find them and add them to their mailing lists. Installing Windows Defender (Answer D) will only protect against spyware.

52. Answer: B. Adware is a software program that will play, display, or download advertisements, usually without your consent. Adware comes by visiting certain websites or by being tricked into loading software. Some types of adware are also spyware (Answer A), which collects information about users without their knowledge. A Trojan horse (Answer C) is malware that appears to be a harmless program, but does harm by deleting, modifying, or corrupting files on your computer or performing some other undesirable actions. Some Trojan horse programs can also be adware and spyware. A macro virus (Answer D) is a virus that is hidden within an embedded code usually within a document such as Microsoft Word or Excel.

53. Answer: B. Grayware is a classification of applications designed to be annoying or undesirable but are not as serious as destructive viruses. They can contain spyware, adware, dialers, joke programs, or remote access tools, and they affect the overall performance of your program. A Trojan horse (Answer C) is malware that appears to be a harmless program, but does harm by deleting, modifying, or corrupting files on your computer or performing some other undesirable actions. Some Trojan horse programs can also be adware and spyware. A macro virus (Answer D) is a virus that is hidden within an embedded code usually within a document such as Microsoft Word or Excel. There is no such thing as blackware (Answer A).

54. Answer: C. If you keep a computer under lock and key (in a secure server room or cage), only people with a key can get to it. If you use a BIOS password to boot the computer (Answer B), you will have to provide a password just to boot the computer. While this will prevent someone from booting the computer with a disk that will bypass the operating system security, it is not considered physical security. While NTFS (Answer A) is more secure than FAT32, it will not help protect against physically accessing a computer. For example, a person could boot with a disk or boot with another hard drive and access the content on the hard drive. In addition, share permissions (Answer D) only protect while accessing remote folders, not locally or physically.

55. **Answer: B.** Most BIOSes offer a variety of security options that can be set through the BIOS Setup utility. The Supervisory password option establishes a password that must be used to access the CMOS Setup utility (where the User and Supervisory password options are configured). You cannot configure passwords using jumpers (Answer A). You could use passwords in Windows but because some configuration settings are established in the BIOS setup program (Answer C), some of the configuration options can be changed. The Supervisory password would only be used to prevent the user from accessing the BIOS setup program (Answer D). Of course, you can configure the BIOS setup program that will only boot from the hard drive so that someone cannot insert a disk into the system and boot from that disk.

56. **Answer: A.** Windows Defender is Microsoft's antispyware software product that is included with Windows Vista and is available with Windows XP. Windows Firewall (Answer B) protects against unauthorized access to the computer. Windows Security Center (Answer C) is a new tool added to Windows XP SP2 that allows you to manage Windows updates and firewall. While Automatic Updates (Answer D) help keep a PC secure and it might prevent some spyware, it is not made to catch and stop spyware.

57. **Answer: D.** Windows Defender is Microsoft's antispyware software product that is included with Windows Vista and is available with Windows XP. Software Explorer can allow you to monitor specific applications that are running on Windows. Windows Explorer (Answer C) allows you to manage folders and files in Windows. There are no such things as Windows Defender Plus (Answer A) and Defender Explorer (Answer B).

58. **Answer: B.** EFS is short for Encrypted File System. It is part of NTFS and allows you to encrypt files and folders. If you encrypt a file and another user tries to copy the file to another system, he or she still might not be able to read it. BitLocker Drive Encryption (Answer C) is a full disk encryption that is included with Windows Ultimate and Enterprise edition of Windows Vista. Windows Firewall (Answer A) is used to protect a system from unauthorized access. Windows Malicious Software Remove Tool (Answer D) is used to check for and remove a small range of malware.

59. **Answer: A.** BitLocker Drive Encryption requires a TPM (Trusted Platform Module) be used with Windows Vista to encrypt an entire hard drive. Therefore, if you remove the drive from the system and try to read it in another system, the data could not be read. The TPM is a microchip that is built in to a computer and used to store cryptographic information, such as encryption keys. CA (Answer C), EFS (Answer D), and digital certificates (Answer B) are not needed for BitLocker.

60. **Answer: B.** Some systems have an intrusion detection option in the BIOS. When someone opens a computer, the information will be written and seen in the BIOS. Installing software such as Windows Defender (Answer A) or a Service Pack (Answer C) will not detect if a system has been opened. In addition, using fingerprint dust (Answer D) is a very cumbersome process, and it only works under ideal situations.

CHAPTER SIX

Operational Procedures

The last domain for the 220-701 exam is Operational Procedures. This domain can be divided into two parts. The first part relates to the environment where you work and how you can affect it. The second part deals with how to interact with customers. Remember, you are there to service them; it is not the other way around.

This domain for the 220-701 exam counts as 10%. The given objectives for this domain are as follows:

▶ 6.1—Outline the purpose of appropriate safety and environmental procedures and apply them to a given scenario

▶ 6.2—Given a scenario, demonstrate the appropriate use of communication skills and professionalism in the workplace

6.1 Outline the purpose of appropriate safety and environmental procedures and given a scenario apply them

▶ ESD

▶ EMI

    ▶ Network interference

    ▶ Magnets

▶ RFI

    ▶ Cordless phone interference

    ▶ Microwaves

▶ Electrical safety

    ▶ CRT

    ▶ Power supply

    ▶ Inverter

    ▶ Laser printers

    ▶ Matching power requirements of equipment with power distribution and UPSs

▶ Material Safety Data Sheets (MSDS)

▶ Cable management

    ▶ Avoiding trip hazards

▶ Physical safety

    ▶ Heavy devices

    ▶ Hot components

▶ Environmental – consider proper disposal procedures

1. What type of equipment should be used to minimize the chances of ESD (electrostatic discharge) during normal computer maintenance work?

    ○ **A.** Surge protector

    ○ **B.** Terrycloth towel

    ○ **C.** Wrist strap

    ○ **D.** Screwdriver

Quick Answer: **218**
Detailed Answer: **219**

2. What is the purpose of the antistatic wrist strap?

    ○ **A.** To protect the equipment from electrostatic discharge

    ○ **B.** To protect the technician from injury

    ○ **C.** To place the technician's body at the same electrical potential as the system board

    ○ **D.** To protect technicians working on high-voltage equipment such as power supplies and CRT monitors

Quick Answer: **218**
Detailed Answer: **219**

3. Which of the following is the most effective tool for protecting the PC system from dangerous static buildup?

    ○ **A.** An ESD wrist or ankle strap

    ○ **B.** The safety ground plug at a commercial AC receptacle

    ○ **C.** The ground plane of the system board

    ○ **D.** The chassis ground provided by the brass standoff(s)

Quick Answer: **218**
Detailed Answer: **219**

4. You are going to replace faulty memory within a computer. You shut down the computer. What should you NOT do to avoid ESD? (Choose the best answer.)

    ○ **A.** You should use an ESD mat.

    ○ **B.** You should use an ESD strap.

    ○ **C.** You should touch the ground of the workshop.

    ○ **D.** You should touch the metal case of the power supply that is plugged into a properly grounded outlet.

Quick Answer: **218**
Detailed Answer: **219**

5. Wrist straps will be useful only if which of the following criteria are met? (Choose the best answer.)

Quick Answer: **218**
Detailed Answer: **219**

- ○ **A.** They are plugged into the wrist strap jack.
- ○ **B.** They are clean and make good skin contact.
- ○ **C.** The cord has not been damaged.
- ○ **D.** All of the options provided are correct.

6. In addition to the antistatic wrist strap, which of the following would you use to reduce ESD? (Choose two answers.)

Quick Answer: **218**
Detailed Answer: **219**

- ○ **A.** Use an ESD mat
- ○ **B.** Touch the ground of the workshop
- ○ **C.** Touch the metal case of the power supply that is plugged into a properly grounded outlet
- ○ **D.** Take off your tie and shoes

7. Before opening a static-shielding container or bag that includes an electronic device, you should do which of the following?

Quick Answer: **218**
Detailed Answer: **219**

- ○ **A.** Look inside to see if it is really sensitive
- ○ **B.** Check for paperwork inside the container
- ○ **C.** Ground yourself in an ESD-protected area
- ○ **D.** Call the manufacturer for operating instructions

8. Before transporting an ESD-sensitive device, it must be which of the following?

Quick Answer: **218**
Detailed Answer: **220**

- ○ **A.** Enclosed in a static shielding container or bag
- ○ **B.** Put in a cardboard box
- ○ **C.** Thoroughly cleaned
- ○ **D.** Wrapped in newspaper

9. To prevent ESD, humidity should be kept at least at what percentage when working on a computer?

Quick Answer: **218**
Detailed Answer: **220**

- ○ **A.** 10%
- ○ **B.** 25%
- ○ **C.** 50%
- ○ **D.** 75%

10. Damaging ESD is most likely to occur when which of the following occurs?

Quick Answer: **218**
Detailed Answer: **220**

- ○ **A.** You are working around rubber mats.
- ○ **B.** You are using test instruments on a system.
- ○ **C.** The humidity is low.
- ○ **D.** You unplug a power supply unit.

11. One of your customers has called you because he was attempting to perform a RAM upgrade on his machine when he felt a small snap on his fingertip. Now the system does not start up to the desktop. What should you do in this situation?

Quick Answer: **218**
Detailed Answer: **220**

- ○ **A.** Try to determine the exact damage done and then educate the customer about ESD.
- ○ **B.** Tell the customer it's a lot less expensive to call you in the first place and then install new memory modules in the PC.
- ○ **C.** Tell the customer that he should wear an antistatic wrist strap if he is going to be working on his own equipment. Then replace the system board.
- ○ **D.** Replace the RAM with new modules and install an antistatic mat under the PC.

12. At the office, a number of ceiling fans were installed. Now users are complaining of slow activity on the network. Nothing else has changed on the network. What is the most likely cause of this problem?

Quick Answer: **218**
Detailed Answer: **220**

- ○ **A.** AMI
- ○ **B.** EMI
- ○ **C.** MIB
- ○ **D.** FDM

13. Which of the following can cause EMI? (Choose all that apply.)

Quick Answer: **218**
Detailed Answer: **220**

- ○ **A.** Fluorescent lights
- ○ **B.** Space heaters
- ○ **C.** Industrial motors
- ○ **D.** Radio

14. Magnets can cause which of the following? (Choose two answers.)

Quick Answer: **218**
Detailed Answer: **220**

    ○ **A.** FDM

    ○ **B.** Current

    ○ **C.** EMI

    ○ **D.** AMI

15. What is the most likely cause of wavy images on a CRT monitor?

Quick Answer: **218**
Detailed Answer: **221**

    ○ **A.** Bad memory

    ○ **B.** Viruses

    ○ **C.** EMI

    ○ **D.** Bad motherboard

16. What is used to limit the flow of RFI radiation from the computer?

Quick Answer: **218**
Detailed Answer: **221**

    ○ **A.** The power supply

    ○ **B.** Grounded connector

    ○ **C.** The case

    ○ **D.** Heat sink

17. You have 802.11g network wireless adapters. Every day around lunchtime, wireless users complain of lack of connectivity. What can you do for this problem?

Quick Answer: **218**
Detailed Answer: **221**

    ○ **A.** Replace the WAP with an 802.11b WAP

    ○ **B.** Reduce the RFI around the WAP

    ○ **C.** Configure the wireless workstations and the WAP to operate in ad-hoc mode

    ○ **D.** Connect the WAP directly to the network

18. You have a wireless phone. Every time you get a phone call, you get disconnected from the 802.11g wireless network. What is the problem?

Quick Answer: **218**
Detailed Answer: **221**

    ○ **A.** EMI

    ○ **B.** RFI

    ○ **C.** AMI

    ○ **D.** Power spikes

19. The local weather report indicates that an electrical storm with severe winds is likely to occur in your area overnight. What reasonable precautions should you take to protect your computers?

Quick Answer: **218**
Detailed Answer: **221**

- ○ **A.** Monitor the computers until the storm passes
- ○ **B.** Plug the computers into a surge protector
- ○ **C.** Turn off the computers
- ○ **D.** Unplug the computers

20. What are the voltage levels commonly found in a CRT?

Quick Answer: **218**
Detailed Answer: **221**

- ○ **A.** 250,000V
- ○ **B.** 250V
- ○ **C.** 25,000V
- ○ **D.** 25V

21. Which voltage level is more dangerous—110V AC at 5 amps or 25,000V DC at 5 microamperes?

Quick Answer: **218**
Detailed Answer: **221**

- ○ **A.** The 25,000V level is much more dangerous than the 110V level.
- ○ **B.** Neither are particularly dangerous.
- ○ **C.** Both are extremely dangerous.
- ○ **D.** The 5 amp level is much more dangerous than the 5 microampere level.

22. When would it be inappropriate to use an ESD wrist strap? (Choose two answers.)

Quick Answer: **218**
Detailed Answer: **221**

- ○ **A.** While working on hard disk drives
- ○ **B.** While working on system boards
- ○ **C.** While working on CRT video monitors
- ○ **D.** While working on printers
- ○ **E.** While working on a power supply

23. After you've removed the outer case from a CRT display, what precaution should you take before troubleshooting it? (Choose two answers.)

Quick Answer: **218**
Detailed Answer: **222**

- ○ **A.** Make sure that it's discharged
- ○ **B.** Get clearance from your supervisor
- ○ **C.** Put on an antistatic wrist strap
- ○ **D.** Disconnect the monitor from the AC power source

24. The laser light in a high-quality laser printer is classified as a Class A laser device. What does this rating mean to technicians working on this laser printer?

Quick Answer: 218
Detailed Answer: 222

   ○ **A.** Never shine the light on your skin

   ○ **B.** Never shine the light on any part of your body

   ○ **C.** Never shine the light in your eyes

   ○ **D.** Never touch the light while it is in operation

25. Which type of printer can be a source of electrocution, eye damage, and burns?

Quick Answer: 218
Detailed Answer: 222

   ○ **A.** Laser

   ○ **B.** Dot matrix

   ○ **C.** Inkjet

   ○ **D.** Daisy wheel

26. Which component of a dot matrix printer generates a great deal of heat and can be a burn hazard when working on these units?

Quick Answer: 218
Detailed Answer: 222

   ○ **A.** Paper tray

   ○ **B.** Platen

   ○ **C.** Ribbon

   ○ **D.** Print head

27. What type of device is used to power a laptop using the car's cigarette lighter?

Quick Answer: 218
Detailed Answer: 222

   ○ **A.** UPS

   ○ **B.** Surge processor

   ○ **C.** Capacitance battery

   ○ **D.** Inverter

28. Of the following, which is the most important to keep in mind when choosing an inverter?

Quick Answer: 218
Detailed Answer: 222

   ○ **A.** The amount of power an inverter can supply

   ○ **B.** The amount of surge protection it offers

   ○ **C.** The number of plugs or ports

   ○ **D.** The number of lights

29. You are choosing a UPS to make sure that your computer is protected. What are the two criteria you should choose when selecting the correct UPS? (Choose two answers.)

Quick Answer: **218**
Detailed Answer: **223**

    ○ **A.** The amount of power a UPS can supply

    ○ **B.** The amount of surge protection it offers

    ○ **C.** The number of plugs or ports

    ○ **D.** The amount of time that a UPS can power a PC when AC power is not available

30. A large amount of water is spilt on the floor of the server room. What should you do first?

Quick Answer: **218**
Detailed Answer: **223**

    ○ **A.** Place newspaper over the water

    ○ **B.** Wear rubber soled shoes and mop up the floor

    ○ **C.** Inform the system administrator of this safety hazard

    ○ **D.** Shut down all computers in the server room

31. You are checking a system that has failed when you discover that it failed because one of the power supply wires running to the system board was damaged. How should you handle this situation?

Quick Answer: **218**
Detailed Answer: **223**

    ○ **A.** Cut the wire so it is even with the power supply housing and troubleshoot the system board for possible faults

    ○ **B.** Splice the two ends of the cable together and apply heat-shrink tubing over the repaired area of the wire

    ○ **C.** Cap off the cable using electrical tape

    ○ **D.** Replace the power supply unit

32. Which of the following actions can cause a system board to short out when you change an adapter card?

Quick Answer: **218**
Detailed Answer: **223**

    ○ **A.** Not wearing an antistatic wrist strap

    ○ **B.** The PnP function not being configured properly

    ○ **C.** Placing the adapter card in the wrong type of expansion slot

    ○ **D.** Not removing the power cord from the AC power source

33. What is required for hazardous materials when they change hands?

Quick Answer: **218**
Detailed Answer: **223**

    ○ **A.** Disposal bags

    ○ **B.** Material Safety Data Sheets (MSDS)

    ○ **C.** Red flags

    ○ **D.** OSDF

34. On an MSDS you will not find which of the following?

Quick Answer: **218**
Detailed Answer: **223**

   ◯   **A.** Chemical name

   ◯   **B.** Hazard rating

   ◯   **C.** Safety first measures

   ◯   **D.** Emergency telephone number

35. Which of the following rated fire extinguishers should be used in case of electrical fire?

Quick Answer: **218**
Detailed Answer: **224**

   ◯   **A.** "A-rated" extinguisher

   ◯   **B.** "B-rated" extinguisher

   ◯   **C.** "ABC-rated" extinguisher

   ◯   **D.** None of the answers provided are correct

36. Which of the following fire extinguishers would you use if your computer caught fire?

Quick Answer: **218**
Detailed Answer: **224**

   ◯   **A.** "A-rated" extinguisher

   ◯   **B.** "B-rated" extinguisher

   ◯   **C.** "C-rated" extinguisher

   ◯   **D.** None of the answers provided are correct

37. When you arrive at your workstation, you find three desktop PCs sitting on the floor in front of your workbench. You will have to lift them onto the workbench to work on them. Which of the following describes the correct way to lift a personal computer from the floor?

Quick Answer: **218**
Detailed Answer: **224**

   ◯   **A.** With knees bent, lift with your back

   ◯   **B.** With knees bent, lift with your legs

   ◯   **C.** With knees straight, lift with your back

   ◯   **D.** With knees straight, lift with your arms

38. Which of the following are legitimate ways of disposing of chemical solvents and cans?

Quick Answer: **218**
Detailed Answer: **224**

   ◯   **A.** If they are not listed on the MSDS, dispose of them in your normal trash-disposal system.

   ◯   **B.** Open the containers and allow the liquids to evaporate so that they can be buried.

   ◯   **C.** If your local code calls for it, dispose of the items in a Subtitle-D dumpsite.

   ◯   **D.** Burn them in an acceptable disposal oven.

39. What is the correct procedure for disposing of laptop batteries?

   ○ **A.** Incineration

   ○ **B.** First try to recharge the batteries for reuse

   ○ **C.** Consult the local guidelines for disposing of hazardous material

   ○ **D.** Dispose in a trash can

Quick Answer: **218**
Detailed Answer: **224**

40. What is the recommended method for handling a dead battery?

   ○ **A.** Recycle it

   ○ **B.** Throw it in the trash

   ○ **C.** Burn it in a certified incinerator

   ○ **D.** Recharge it

Quick Answer: **218**
Detailed Answer: **224**

41. What is the recommended method for handling an empty toner cartridge?

   ○ **A.** Recycle it through the original manufacturer

   ○ **B.** Throw it in the trash

   ○ **C.** Burn it in a certified incinerator

   ○ **D.** Turn it in to a licensed computer retailer

Quick Answer: **218**
Detailed Answer: **224**

42. CRT monitors contain which of the following elements that cause their disposal to be considered hazardous?

   ○ **A.** Copper

   ○ **B.** Lead

   ○ **C.** Tin

   ○ **D.** Aluminum

Quick Answer: **218**
Detailed Answer: **224**

43. When disposing of a CRT, you should first do which of the following?

   ○ **A.** Pack it in its original container and dispose of it in the normal garbage

   ○ **B.** Discharge the HV anode and dispose of it in the normal garbage pickup

   ○ **C.** Check applicable local ordinances and dispose of it in accordance with local regulations

   ○ **D.** Smash the CRT's glass envelope with a hammer and dispose of it in a Subtitle-D dumpsite

Quick Answer: **218**
Detailed Answer: **224**

44. When using network cable to connect a computer to a switch, what should you always attempt to prevent a trip hazard? (Choose two answers.)

○ **A.** Use a cable that is short enough that it is lifted off the floor.

○ **B.** Run cables in ceiling or in the walls.

○ **C.** If you need to run cable on the ground, use a cable safety strip.

○ **D.** Remove all cabling and use wireless technology.

6.2 Given a scenario, demonstrate the appropriate use of communication skills and professionalism in the workplace

▶ Use proper language—avoid jargon, acronyms, slang

▶ Maintain a positive attitude

▶ Listen and do not interrupt a customer

▶ Be culturally sensitive

▶ Be on time

    ▶ If late, contact the customer

▶ Avoid distractions

    ▶ Personal calls

    ▶ Talking to co-workers while interacting with customers

    ▶ Personal interruptions

▶ Dealing with a difficult customer or situation

    ▶ Avoid arguing with customers and/or being defensive

    ▶ Do not minimize customers' problems

    ▶ Avoid being judgmental

    ▶ Clarify customer statements

        ▶ Ask open-ended questions to narrow the scope of the problem

        ▶ Restate the issue or question to verify understanding

▶ Set and meet expectations/timeline and communicate status with the customer

    ▶ Offer different repair/replacement options if applicable

    ▶ Provide proper documentation on the services provided

    ▶ Follow up with customer/user at a later date to verify satisfaction

▶ Deal appropriately with customers' confidential materials

    ▶ Located on computer, desktop, printer, etc.

45. A customer complains because she has been on hold for a long time and has been transferred several times. What should you do?

Quick Answer: **218**
Detailed Answer: **225**

- ○ **A.** Apologize for the inconvenience and offer to help her now
- ○ **B.** Give her your home phone number or cellular phone number
- ○ **C.** Tell her the best time to call and tell her to call back
- ○ **D.** Explain how busy you are

46. A customer calls and tells you that the hard drive you just sold him was defective. What should you do?

Quick Answer: **218**
Detailed Answer: **225**

- ○ **A.** Tell the customer to call the manufacturer
- ○ **B.** Call the manufacturer for the customer
- ○ **C.** Tell him you will replace it if he can prove that it is defective
- ○ **D.** Replace the drive

47. A customer calls and complains that the computer you just repaired is still not working properly. What should you do?

Quick Answer: **218**
Detailed Answer: **225**

- ○ **A.** Apologize and explain that it is a different problem than the one you repaired
- ○ **B.** Explain that the customer did something wrong
- ○ **C.** Refer the customer to another repair facility
- ○ **D.** Offer to replace or re-service the computer

48. A customer on the telephone can't understand your directions. What is the one thing that you should not do?

Quick Answer: **218**
Detailed Answer: **225**

- ○ **A.** Ask if there is someone else you can speak to
- ○ **B.** Hang up on him because he can't follow directions
- ○ **C.** Refer him to a customer center
- ○ **D.** Tell him someone will call him back

49. What is the last thing you should do to complete a service call?

Quick Answer: **218**
Detailed Answer: **225**

- ○ **A.** Hand the customer a bill
- ○ **B.** Thank the customer for his or her business
- ○ **C.** Explain why the repair took so long
- ○ **D.** Tell the customer how he or she could have repaired the problem

50. You are talking directly to a customer to try to determine what the issue is. Unfortunately, you do not understand the issue. What should you do next?

Quick Answer: **218**
Detailed Answer: **225**

- ○ **A.** Attempt to fix the problem
- ○ **B.** Allow the customer to repeat the problem once more
- ○ **C.** Ask the customer to go somewhere so that they can't see that you're unsure
- ○ **D.** Restate the problem to the customer

51. When taking a call from a customer what is important for the technician to do?

Quick Answer: **218**
Detailed Answer: **225**

- ○ **A.** Remain in control of the call and gather relevant information from the customer
- ○ **B.** Keep the customer on the line until the problem is resolved
- ○ **C.** Let the customer explain the problem and write down all information given
- ○ **D.** Let the customer explain while you proxy in to their computer and sort out the problem

52. An important thing to remember when helping an angry customer is to do which of the following?

Quick Answer: **218**
Detailed Answer: **225**

- ○ **A.** Remain calm and not make situations personal
- ○ **B.** Complete the job as quickly as possible
- ○ **C.** Report the customer to a supervisor
- ○ **D.** Give the customer a piece of your mind

53. While in a meeting, what do you call it when you structure the way you are listening while observing the speaker's behavior and body language? This method also suspends one's own frame of reference and suspends judgment.

Quick Answer: **218**
Detailed Answer: **226**

- ○ **A.** Active listening
- ○ **B.** Concentration
- ○ **C.** Communicating
- ○ **D.** Verbal communication

54. You are working at a customer site and you get a personal phone call. What should you do?

Quick Answer: **218**
Detailed Answer: **226**

- ○ **A.** Reply to the call by sending a text message
- ○ **B.** Answer the call and speak as briefly as possible
- ○ **C.** Tell the customer that the call has to be answered
- ○ **D.** Ignore the call and let the voicemail answer the call

55. When brainstorming with a group to come up with ideas to solve a problem, what describes the ability to express positive and negative ideas and feelings in an open, honest, and direct way?

Quick Answer: **218**
Detailed Answer: **226**

- ○ **A.** Active listening
- ○ **B.** Concentrating brainstorming
- ○ **C.** Passive communication
- ○ **D.** Assertive communication

56. What should you do if you overhear a confidential conversation with the company CEO?

Quick Answer: **218**
Detailed Answer: **226**

- ○ **A.** Retreat quietly and keep the information in confidence
- ○ **B.** Inform the manager about the conversation
- ○ **C.** Inform the CEO to be careful who is around when having that type of conversation
- ○ **D.** Let the CEO know of your presence

57. What should you do if you are trying to fix a problem, but a customer's child is being disruptive and distracting?

Quick Answer: **218**
Detailed Answer: **226**

- ○ **A.** Talk sternly to the child and tell the child to stop misbehaving
- ○ **B.** Give the child something to play with
- ○ **C.** Refuse to continue working until the child stops misbehaving
- ○ **D.** Ask the customer to remove the child from the work area

58. While working at a customer's home, a fellow co-worker calls you looking for guidance to solve a problem. What should you do?

Quick Answer: **218**
Detailed Answer: **226**

- ○ **A.** Apologize to the customer to take the telephone call
- ○ **B.** Ask the co-worker to call back later and continue working
- ○ **C.** Try to help the co-worker while continuing to work
- ○ **D.** Tell the customer you will be back later and sort out the problem

59. Which of the following techniques is NOT recommended when explaining a repair process to a customer?

Quick Answer: **218**
Detailed Answer: **226**

- ○ **A.** Using visual aids such as graphs and charts
- ○ **B.** Using analogies and examples
- ○ **C.** Using industry jargon or acronyms
- ○ **D.** Limiting the amount of information to what the customer needs to know

60. Which of the following activities are involved in active listening? (Choose three answers.)

Quick Answer: **218**
Detailed Answer: **226**

◯   **A.** Not getting unfocused

◯   **B.** Repeating the customer's key points

◯   **C.** Making written notes about the customer's key points

◯   **D.** Not getting thrown by the customer's demeanor

61. Which of the following are good attributes of an effective customer service person? (Choose two answers.)

Quick Answer: **218**
Detailed Answer: **226**

◯   **A.** Active listening

◯   **B.** Ability to focus on the customer

◯   **C.** Personality

◯   **D.** Analytical skills

62. What is the most important key to handling irate customers?

Quick Answer: **218**
Detailed Answer: **226**

◯   **A.** Remaining calm regardless of the customers' attitudes

◯   **B.** Restating the customers' key points so that they know you are listening to them

◯   **C.** Defending your credibility so that they know they are dealing with a competent professional

◯   **D.** Telling them that you know they are frustrated and leaving them alone until they have a chance to cool down

63. After you inspect a failing printer that is under warranty, you determine that the cause of the problem has been improper use of the machine. When you attempt to explain what has happened with the printer and why it is not covered by the warranty, the customer does not accept your explanation of the situation. What should you do under these circumstances?

Quick Answer: **218**
Detailed Answer: **227**

◯   **A.** Provide the customer with a step-by-step technical explanation of the problem and the warranty's policies.

◯   **B.** Tell the customer that you are leaving because you cannot complete the work without his agreement.

◯   **C.** Agree to disagree with the customer and start working on the problem knowing that your company is going to bill the customer for the work.

◯   **D.** Escalate the discussion to your supervisor.

64. Your customer has been given a specific timeframe for completion of work you are doing. As the deadline approaches, you can tell that the work is not going to be completed on time. What should you do first in this situation?

Quick Answer: **218**
Detailed Answer: **227**

- ○ **A.** Tell the customer the work cannot be done by the deadline and ask the customer for an extension.
- ○ **B.** Call your supervisor to let her know the work will not be done on time.
- ○ **C.** Keep working until the customer checks on your progress.
- ○ **D.** Tell the customer that you can't get the work done on time and that you will keep working until the job is completed.

65. After completing a repair on one of your customer's computers, you discover a folder of pornographic pictures on the computer. What should you do about this discovery?

Quick Answer: **218**
Detailed Answer: **227**

- ○ **A.** Report it to your supervisor
- ○ **B.** Deny access to the user
- ○ **C.** Remove the offensive material from the machine
- ○ **D.** Move the information to a server to secure the network audience

66. When an irate customer begins to use profanity in discussions with you, what action should you take?

Quick Answer: **218**
Detailed Answer: **227**

- ○ **A.** Walk away in protest so that the customer knows you are offended
- ○ **B.** Withdraw from the situation as soon as possible and report the customer to your supervisor
- ○ **C.** Withdraw from the conversation and report the customer to her supervisor
- ○ **D.** Tell the customer you don't appreciate the use of such language and leave her presence

67. On a repair job, the customer asks you for the personal cell phone number of another technician at your company. He says that he knows the other technician and would like to get in touch with him. How should you handle this request? (Select all that apply.)

Quick Answer: **218**
Detailed Answer: **227**

- ○ **A.** Offer to relay the information and have the other person call the customer
- ○ **B.** Give the customer the other technician's number
- ○ **C.** Call the other technician to see if he wants his number released to this person
- ○ **D.** Tell the customer that you do not know the number to avoid any kind of potential problems from giving out the number

68. One of your customers has given you a request for work that is prohibited by your company's written policies. What should you tell the customer?

- ○ **A.** Tell the customer you can't do it; the request is against your company's policies.
- ○ **B.** Tell the customer you will see if there is some allowable alternative that you can offer.
- ○ **C.** Tell the customer to contact your supervisor.
- ○ **D.** Perform the requested work on your own time so that you keep your customer happy without breaking the company's policy.

69. When work is requested that is outside the scope of your company's agreement with the customer, what should you do?

- ○ **A.** Call your supervisor, describe the requested additional work, and proceed as directed.
- ○ **B.** Offer to do the work after hours because this is such an important customer.
- ○ **C.** Refuse the work because it is not part of the scope of work you have been given.
- ○ **D.** Inform the customer that the additional work will cost extra and perform the requested work.

70. While talking with an employee, you notice that he is illegally downloading music on a company computer. What should you do about this?

- ○ **A.** Advise your supervisor
- ○ **B.** Remove the download utility from the machine
- ○ **C.** Tell the user to stop the unauthorized activity
- ○ **D.** Do nothing because this is not your responsibility

71. Which of the following is the best method of training users to operate the new equipment you've just installed?

- ○ **A.** Reading the equipment's documentation to the users and having them highlight the parts they will need after you are gone.
- ○ **B.** Give the users a quick version of the most important points of the equipment's operation, avoiding technical terms whenever possible.
- ○ **C.** Suggest that they purchase an extended training class from your company to ensure that they are fully acquainted with the new device or system.
- ○ **D.** Use their new equipment to show them how it operates.

Quick-Check Answer Key

1. C	**25.** A	**49.** B
2. A	**26.** D	**50.** D
3. B	**27.** D	**51.** A
4. C	**28.** A	**52.** A
5. D	**29.** A and D	**53.** A
6. A and C	**30.** C	**54.** D
7. C	**31.** D	**55.** A
8. A	**32.** C	**56.** A
9. C	**33.** B	**57.** D
10. C	**34.** C	**58.** B
11. A	**35.** C	**59.** C
12. B	**36.** C	**60.** A, B, and D
13. A, B, and C	**37.** B	**61.** A and B
14. B and C	**38.** C	**62.** A
15. C	**39.** C	**63.** D
16. C	**40.** A	**64.** D
17. B	**41.** A	**65.** A
18. B	**42.** B	**66.** B
19. D	**43.** C	**67.** A and C
20. C	**44.** B and C	**68.** B
21. D	**45.** A	**69.** A
22. C and E	**46.** D	**70.** A
23. A and D	**47.** D	**71.** D
24. C	**48.** B	

Answers and Explanations

1. **Answer: C.** Professional service technicians use grounding straps to minimize the chances of electrostatic discharge (ESD) during normal computer maintenance work involving electronic devices. These antistatic devices can be placed around the wrists or ankle to ground the technician to the system being worked on. These straps release any static present on the technician's body and pass it harmlessly to ground potential. Surge protectors (Answer A) are used to protect from power surges, not ESD. Screwdrivers (Answer D) will not dissipate ESD. A terrycloth towel (Answer B) will most likely cause electrostatic discharge.

2. **Answer: A.** Technicians protect the equipment from electrostatic discharge by using grounding strap devices that are placed around the wrists or ankles to ground the technicians to the system being worked on. These straps release any static present on a technician's body and pass it harmlessly to ground potential. It should be noted that you should not use an ESD strap when working on high-voltage equipment because a discharge from the high-voltage equipment (Answer D) could cause harm to the wearer.

3. **Answer: B.** The ground plug on a standard power cable is the best tool for overcoming ESD problems. The ground lead prevents hazardous charge buildups in the circuitry that protects property and life. To avoid damaging static-sensitive computer devices, ground yourself by touching the power supply housing with your finger before touching any components inside the system. This technique works safely only if the power cord is attached to a grounded power outlet. The ESD wrist or ankle strap (Answer A) is to make sure you don't cause ESD while working on an electronic device. The ground plane (Answer C) and chassis ground (Answer D) will only help protect the system board, assuming the system is properly connected to a safety ground plug.

4. **Answer: C.** ESD is short for electrostatic discharge. ESD is generated by friction and is released when two items (including the human body) that have different voltage potentials make contact, which causes electricity to transfer from one object to another. To prevent ESD, you should ground yourself before handling any electronic components. That can be done with a properly grounded ESD mat (Answer A), strap (Answer B), or metal case (Answer D). Of course using an ESD strap (wrist or angle) is the most recommended method.

5. **Answer: D.** Wrist straps are only good if they are first plugged into the wrist strap jack, which should be grounded. It also needs to be clean and make good skin contact. Lastly, the cord needs to be undamaged.

6. **Answer: A and C.** An ESD mat will drain excess charge much like an ESD strap does. In addition, you should touch the metal case while it is plugged into a properly grounded outlet. Touching the ground (Answer B) and taking off your shoes (Answer D) are usually not practical solutions (and shoes don't usually generate ESD).

7. **Answer: C.** Make sure that you are grounded before opening a static-shielding container or bag and before handling any electronic devices. You should always assume electronic devices are sensitive (Answer A). You should not place paperwork inside the container because the paperwork can cause ESD (Answer B). You should call the manufacturer for operating instructions only if you need the operating instructions (Answer D).

8. **Answer: A.** If you need to transport an electronic device, you should enclose it in a static-shielding container or bag. You should not place ESD-sensitive devices in a cardboard box (Answer B) or wrap them in newspaper (Answer D) because both the box and the newspaper can generate ESD. If you decide to clean an electronic device (Answer C), you must take special steps and use special tools to make sure you don't generate ESD.

9. **Answer: C.** Keeping the humidity at 50% or higher will reduce the amount of ESD that is generated. Therefore, the other answers are incorrect.

10. **Answer: C.** ESD is most likely to occur during periods of low humidity. If the relative humidity is less than 50%, static charges can accumulate easily. ESD generally does not occur when the humidity is greater than 50%. Anytime the charge reaches about 10,000V, it is likely to discharge to grounded metal parts. Working around rubber mats (Answer A), using test equipment (Answer B), and unplugging a power supply (Answer D) should not generate damaging electrostatic discharge.

11. **Answer: A.** The snap the customer felt was ESD, and the fact that the system does not operate indicates that damage has occurred with one of the system's integrated circuit devices. All you can do at this point is try to determine the extent of the damage and educate the customer about the causes and effects of ESD. Metal Oxide Semiconductor (MOS) devices are sensitive to voltage spikes and static electricity discharges. The level of static electricity present on your body can be high enough to destroy the inputs of an MOS device if you touch its pins with your fingers (in practice, this level of damage might require multiple electrostatic discharges). Professional service technicians employ a number of precautionary steps when they are working on systems that might contain MOS devices. These technicians normally use a grounding strap that is placed around the wrist or ankle to ground themselves to the system being worked on. These straps release any static present on the technician's body and pass it harmlessly to ground potential.

12. **Answer: B.** Electromagnetic interference (EMI) is an electromagnetic signal released by an electronic device that might disrupt the operation and performance of another device. EMI can be generated by fluorescent lights, space heaters, industrial motors, and heavy equipment. UTP networks are susceptible to EMI, which can be caused by the motors in the ceiling fans. Alternate Mark Inversion (AMI), Answer A, and Frequency Division Multiplexing (FDM), Answer D, are types of signaling. Management Information Base (MIB), Answer C, is a generic term of a database used for some applications.

13. **Answer: A, B, and C.** Electromagnetic interference is an electromagnetic signal released by an electronic device that might disrupt the operation and performance of another device. EMI can be generated by fluorescent lights, space heaters, industrial motors, and heavy equipment. A radio (Answer D) receives radio waves and typically does not generate radio waves.

14. **Answers: B and C.** When you have a current, you have a magnetic field, and when you have a magnetic field, you have a current. In addition, magnets, such as those found in industrial motors, can generate electromagnetic inference (EMI). Answer A—frequency division multiplexing (FDM)—and Answer D—alternate mark inversion (AMI)—are types of signaling.

15. **Answer: C.** Electromagnetic interference is an electromagnetic signal released by an electronic device that might disrupt the operation and performance of another device. EMI can be generated by fluorescent lights, space heaters, microwaves, industrial motors, and heavy equipment. Bad memory (Answer A) causes errors in applications or prevents the computer from booting. A bad motherboard (Answer D) causes errors in applications, prevents the computer from booting, or prevents some devices from being recognized. A virus (Answer B) causes problems with the operating system and data files and might cause your computer to slow or act erratic, for example by generating pop-ups.

16. **Answer: C.** Radio frequency interference (RFI) is unintentional broadcast of signals that interrupt a radio, television, or navigation equipment. Besides protecting the components of a PC, the case also limits the flow of RFI from the computer. The power supply (Answer A) is used to supply clean DC power to the internal components. The heat sink (Answer D) is used to keep the processor cool. The ground connector (Answer B) prevents hazardous charge buildups in the circuitry that protects property and life.

17. **Answer: B.** 802.11g uses the 2.4 GHz range, which is also used by appliances including microwaves. Most likely, during lunch time, people use the microwaves and that interrupts the 802.11g radio signals. Replacing the WAP (Answer A), converting to ad-hoc mode (Answer C), and connecting the WAP directly to the network (Answer D) will not overcome the interference.

18. **Answer: B.** 802.11g uses the 2.4 GHz range. If you check the wireless phone, it is also using the 2.4 GHz range. Therefore, when the wireless phone is transmitting, it is using the same frequencies as your 802.11g wireless network. Answer A, electromagnetic interference (EMI) causes interference or noise on power and data lines and can interrupt PC operations. Alternate mark inversion (AMI), Answer C, is a type of signaling. Power spikes (Answer D) are sudden surges of electricity that can damage electronic components.

19. **Answer: D.** Remove all power cords associated with the computer and its peripherals from the power outlet during thunder or lightning storms. Sudden spikes can still damage a computer even through it is plugged into a surge protector (Answer B) and if the computer is off (Answer C), although the surge protector will protect against most spikes or surges. Of course, monitoring the computer (Answer A) will not help protect the computer.

20. **Answer: C.** Extremely high voltage levels (in excess of 25,000V) might be present inside the CRT housing even up to a year after electrical power has been removed from the unit. Therefore, the other answers are incorrect.

21. **Answer: D.** The 110V AC at 5 amps is much more dangerous than the 25,000V DC at 5 microamperes according to the current-delivering capabilities (5 amps versus 5 microamperes) they create. Therefore, the other answers are incorrect.

22. **Answer: C and E.** Antistatic straps should never be worn while working on higher-voltage components, such as monitors and power supply units. You should wear them when working on hard drives (Answer A), system boards (Answer B), RAM, expansion cards, and printers (Answer D).

23. Answer: A and D. In repair situations, the high-voltage charge associated with video displays must be discharged. This is accomplished by creating a path from the tube's high-voltage anode to the chassis. With the monitor unplugged from the commercial power outlet, clip one end of an insulated jumper wire to the chassis ground of the frame. Clip the other end to a long, flat-blade screwdriver that has a well-insulated handle. While touching only the insulated handle of the screwdriver, slide the blade of the screwdriver under the rubber cup of the anode and make contact with its metal connection. This should bleed off the high-voltage charge to ground. Continue the contact for several seconds to ensure that the voltage has been fully discharged. Note: This should only be done by an electronic technician, but if you feel that you need to open a monitor, be extra, extra careful. You should also not wear an antistatic wrist strap (Answer C) because the strap could carry the charge left inside the monitor through you. You should not have to get clearance from your supervisor (Answer B) unless your company requires such things.

24. Answer: C. The laser light is a hazard to eyesight. Great care should be taken to avoid contact between the laser light and your eyes. Therefore, the other answers are incorrect.

25. Answer: A. Unlike other printer types, the laser printer tends to have several high-voltage, high-temperature, and vision hazards inside it. To get the laser printer into a position where you can observe its operation, you might need to place yourself in potential contact with those areas. Be aware that laser printers can be a source of electrocution, eye damage (from the laser), and burns (from the fuser assembly). A dot matrix printer (Answer B) does contain hot parts that can burn you if you touch them. Because all printers use electricity, even inkjet (Answer C) and daisy wheel (Answer D) printers have the capability to electrocute someone.

26. Answer: D. To exchange the print head assembly, make sure that the print head assembly is cool enough to be handled. These units can get hot enough to cause a serious burn. The other components, paper tray (Answer A), platen (Answer B), and ribbon (Answer C) cannot burn you.

27. Answer: D. An inverter provides AC power (wall outlet) in your car or on a plane so that you can power portal electronic devices such as laptop computers, cell phones, DVD players, MP3 players and digital cameras. An uninterruptable power supply (UPS), Answer A, is a device that provides emergency power via batteries. There is no such thing as a surge processor (Answer B) or capacitance battery (Answer C).

28. Answer: A. The inverter provides AC power in your car or on a plane so that you can power portable electronic devices such as laptop computers, cell phones, DVD players, MP3 players, and digital cameras. When selecting an inverter, you must make sure it can supply enough power (wattage and amperage) to the devices that you are connecting. You should also look at the power requirements of these devices when they start up. You should not use devices with heating elements such as hair dryers or heaters because they draw far more power than an inverter can produce. Although the amount of surge protection (Answer B) and the overloading built-in circuit protection is important, you must make sure it can supply enough power to all of the devices you need. Also keep in mind that your cigarette lighter or similar device can only supply so much power, too. You should consider the number of plugs or ports (Answer C) because you should keep these to a minimum. Lastly, the number of lights (Answer D) is not important.

29. **Answer: A and D.** An uninterruptable power supply (UPS) is a device that provides emergency power via batteries. When choosing a UPS, you must first make sure that it supplies enough power (wattage and amperage) to the devices it is powering. In addition, a UPS cannot power devices indefinitely. Therefore, you need to choose UPS with enough capacity to power its devices as needed and to be able to perform a proper shutdown when necessary.

30. **Answer: C.** The presence of water should always be a cause of alarm and should be corrected. Therefore, you should contact whoever is responsible for building maintenance. You should then move or shutdown any servers (Answer D) or other equipment if the water can cause a problem. You should not place newspaper over the water (Answer A) because that covers it up but does not fix the problem. You should not have to wear rubber-soled shoes (Answer B). If you suspect electricity problems, you should shut off the electricity as needed before doing clean up.

31. **Answer: D.** You should replace the power supply unit. Even if you are very good at soldering and repairing damaged cabling, the condition might have caused damage to the power supply's electronics. Also, the cost of your time to repair and test the unit might exceed the cost of installing a new unit. You should not cut a wire (Answer A), splice wires (Answer B), or cap off the wire (Answer C). These things are normally done by an electronic technician. Instead, it is better to replace the power supply because it would be safer and more cost efficient.

32. **Answer: C.** System boards are fairly sturdy from an electrical point of view. To create a short circuit in one of them, you must get a powered trace connected to a ground trace. The only option that actually accomplishes this is plugging an adapter card into the wrong type of expansion slot and then turning on the system. Although some areas of the system board have electrical energy applied to them even when the system is turned off, the expansion slots are not one of those areas. Therefore, not removing the power cord does not cause a short to occur while the system is turned off. Wearing an antistatic wrist strap (Answer A) reduces ESD when you are working on electronic devices. Of course, ESD can damage the electronic components. PnP (Answer B) stands for plug and play, which means it automatically configures. Therefore, it will not cause a component to short out. Although it is recommended for you to unplug the power from a computer before doing maintenance (Answer D), you should not cause a system board to short out.

33. **Answer: B.** All hazardous materials are required to have Material Safety Data Sheets (MSDS) that accompany them when they change hands. The MSDSs are also required to be on-hand in areas where hazardous materials are stored and commonly used. Disposal bags (Answer A) are not required for all hazardous materials. They also don't require red flags (Answer C) and On Site Disposal Facility (OSDF), Answer D, when changing hands.

34. **Answer: C.** All hazardous materials are required to have Material Safety Data Sheets (MSDS) that accompany them when they change hands. They are intended to provide workers and emergency personnel with procedures for handling or working with that substance in a safe manner, and includes information such as chemical name (Answer A), hazard rating (Answer B), physical data (melting point, boiling point, flash point, and so on), toxicity, health effects, first aid, reactivity, storage, disposal, protective equipment, spill handling procedures, and emergency telephone number (Answer D). It does not contain safety first measures.

35. **Answer: C.** A "C-rated" extinguisher is used for electrical fires. If you don't have a "C-rated" extinguisher that is specifically rated for electrical fires, you can use an ABC-rated extinguisher. Therefore, the other answers are incorrect.

36. **Answer: C.** A "C-rated" extinguisher is used for electrical fires. You can also use an ABC-rated extinguisher. Therefore, the other answers are incorrect.

37. **Answer: B.** Many work-related injuries occur due to improper material handling and lifting techniques. The proper technique for lifting objects is to bend at the knees and lift with your legs, keeping your back straight. In other words, lift with your legs, not with your back! Therefore, the other answers are incorrect.

38. **Answer: C.** Check with your local waste management agency before disposing of them. Some landfills do not accept chemical solvents and cans. In this case, these items must be disposed of in a Subtitle-D dumpsite. You should not just throw them away in the normal trash (Answer A) or throw them in an oven (Answer D). You should never release gases into the air (Answer B).

39. **Answer: C.** Check with your local waste management agency before disposing of them. Because batteries contain hazardous material, you should not dispose of them in a trash can (Answer D). Batteries can explode, so you should not incinerate batteries (Answer A). Although laptop batteries can be recharged (Answer B), they will eventually not hold a charge like they used to or they will not charge at all. In addition, one battery that fits in one model might not fit in another model.

40. **Answer: A.** The desired method of disposal for batteries is recycling because they contain hazardous material. You should not dispose of them in a trash can (Answer B). Batteries can explode, so you should not incinerate batteries (Answer C). Although laptop batteries can be recharged (Answer D), they will eventually not hold a charge like they used to or will not charge at all. In addition, one battery that fits in one model might not fit in another model.

41. **Answer: A.** Laser printer toner cartridges should be refilled and recycled. The preferable method is to return the cartridge to the original manufacturer. However, many third-party refill organizations refill toner cartridges as part of their business. Because toner is considered a hazard material, it should not be thrown in the trash (Answer B) or incinerated (Answer C). Unless the computer retailer is a recycling site (Answer A), they will not have a use for empty toner cartridges.

42. **Answer: B.** Most computer components contain some level of hazardous substances. CRTs contain glass, metal, plastics, lead, barium, and rare earth metals. Therefore, the other answers are incorrect.

43. **Answer: C.** Local regulations concerning acceptable disposal methods for computer-related components should always be checked before disposing of any electronic equipment, such as a CRT display. You should never dispose of them in the normal garbage (Answer A and B) or a non-hazardous subtitle-D dumpsite (Answer D). Remember, monitors contain lead and other hazardous material.

44. **Answer: B and C.** You need to make sure that cables are not in the way to cause a trip hazard. Therefore, you should plan your cable lengths to run in ceilings or in the walls or by using a safety strip (which will protect the cable and reduce the trip hazard). You should not have a cable off the ground because it creates an even greater trip hazard

(Answer A). Wireless technology (Answer D) is not always the best solution due to radio interference, speed, or compatibility.

45. **Answer: A.** An apology can go a long way, especially if you can help her immediately. You should not try to make excuses (Answer D), put the customer on hold, or tell the customer to call back again (Answer C). Giving the customer your home phone number (Answer B) is not acceptable because that is like telling her to call back later.

46. **Answer: D.** As part of good customer service, you should replace the drive immediately so that you get the customer up and running as soon as possible. Therefore, the other answers are incorrect.

47. **Answer: D.** When dealing with customers, your success is based largely on what the customer perceives. Any time that you service a computer, you need to show that the problem is fixed and that the computer is running fine. In this scenario, the customer feels that this has not happened so you should offer to replace or re-service the computer. Therefore, the other answers are incorrect.

48. **Answer: B.** You should almost never hang-up on a customer, especially if the customer cannot understand what you are saying. You might need to take another approach to overcome the confusion. Therefore, the other answers are incorrect.

49. **Answer: B.** Assuming that you have fixed the problem, demonstrated that the problem is fixed, and answered all of the customer's questions, you should always thank the customer for their business. Therefore, the other answers are incorrect.

50. **Answer: D.** Restating the problem to the customer will make sure that both of you agree on what the problem is. The customer can then give more information or correct you as needed. Of course, you might need to have the customer show you the problem again if the customer doesn't agree with your statement of the problem (Answer B). You should not attempt to fix the problem until you understand what the problem actually is (Answer A). Because the customer can give you valuable information, you should not send the customer away (Answer C).

51. **Answer: A.** You need to keep control of the call so that you stay on task. You also need to gather relevant information so that you can figure out the best course of action. You might not necessarily need to keep the customer on the line while you fix the problem, which is often not a quick fix (Answer B). Of course, although you control the call, you should let the customer explain the problem. You don't necessarily need to write down all information, but it is recommended that you record relevant information if you document your work or service calls (Answer C). The problem might not always be on the customer's computer; it might be on a server or with some network device. Therefore, you might not need to proxy in to the customer's computer (Answer D).

52. **Answer: A.** By staying calm and not making the situation personal, you can focus on the problem. This will also prevent the issue from escalating to a higher level of anger and you might be able to calm the customer. This means you shouldn't give the customer a piece of your mind (Answer D). Of course, you want to complete the job as quickly as possible (Answer B), but not at the potential cost of making the situation worse. You should only have to report the customer to your supervisor if the problem cannot be resolved and the customer cannot be satisfied (Answer C).

53. **Answer: A.** Active listening is a way of listening and responding to another person that improves mutual understanding. The listener listens to the speaker fully and repeats, in the listener's own words, what he or she thinks the speaker has said. Therefore, the other answers are incorrect.

54. **Answer: D.** When you are at a customer site, the customer needs to feel that he is important right now, and you need to stay focused on the problem about which you were called. Therefore, you need to ignore the phone call and let the voicemail answer it. Therefore, the other answers are incorrect.

55. **Answer: A.** Active listening allows everyone to communicate their ideas and feelings without fear that they will be persecuted or made fun of. Therefore, the other answers are incorrect.

56. **Answer: A.** Sometimes as an IT technician you have access to confidential information. As a professional, you need to keep the information confidential. Therefore, the other answers are incorrect.

57. **Answer: D.** You are trying to complete a job that might include fixing a problem that affects one or more people. While you need to be calm and professional about everything, you need to talk to the customer about having the child leave the work area so that you can complete your job. You should not try to handle the problem yourself and or give the child something to play with (Answers A and B). You need to get the job done so you should not refuse to work (Answer C).

58. **Answer: B.** You need to let the customer know that she is important. Therefore, you need to tell your co-worker that you will call him or her back later. Therefore, the other answers are incorrect.

59. **Answer: C.** Most customers do not have the technical background to understand industry jargon and acronyms. If you use jargon, you will confuse the customer. Because customers do not have the technical background, you should use visual aids (Answer A), analogies, and examples (Answer B) to explain things, and you should keep the information to a minimum (Answer D).

60. **Answer: A, B, and D.** The art of active listening involves focusing on the customer's comments, repeating key information to let the customer know that you are following what he is saying, and avoiding distractions such as visual or audible activities that draw your attention away from the customer. While making key notes (Answer C) can be useful, it is not necessary for active listening.

61. **Answer: A and B.** One of the attributes that makes a good customer service person is the ability to actively listen to the customer. Real listening means not just hearing what the customer has to say, but trying to pin down what she means. The technique for doing this is called active listening. Using active listening involves focusing on the customer's comments, repeating key information to let the customer know that you are following what she is saying, and avoiding distractions such as visual or audible activities that draw your attention away from the customer. While personality conflicts can cause problems, you can keep the conflict to a minimum by focusing on active listening (Answer A) and focusing on the customer (Answer B).

62. **Answer: A.** When a customer becomes angry, attempt to diffuse the situation. This usually involves letting the customer get pent-up frustrations off his chest by simply

listening to him. The best thing to do is let the customer vent verbal frustrations and not reply to them. It can be very frustrating to let a customer vent without interrupting him, but that is an important part of successfully handling an irate customer. When you do reply, remain calm, speak in a steady voice, and avoid making inflammatory comments. Also try to avoid taking a defensive stance because this signals a conflict point. Realize that criticism given by a customer is generally not personal, and you should not take it personally. Information delivered with an aggressive attitude normally leads to an aggressive or retaliatory response from the customer. Restating the customer's key points (Answer B) is part of active listening. Active listening, defending your credibility (Answer C), telling him you are frustrated, and leaving (Answer D) does not help diffuse the situation.

63. **Answer: D.** If a problem runs beyond the scope of your company's agreement with the customer, take the initiative to move it to the next level of authority. This allows your management to take proper action in deciding how the particular customer should be handled. Therefore, the other answers are incorrect.

64. **Answer: D.** Always notify customers as soon as possible about any appointment changes, service delays, complications, or setbacks that occur. Apologize for the inconvenience and ask how the customer would like to proceed. These things happen to everyone, and your best defenses against customer dissatisfaction are promptness and good communication. Therefore, the other answers are incorrect.

65. **Answer: A.** Pornographic materials on computers fall into the same category as illegal copies of programs. Having such materials on a PC is reason for immediate termination in most companies. If you are exposed to illegal software or pornographic material on a customer's computer, you should report this to your supervisor. If you discover illegal software or pornographic material on one of your company's computers, report it to the proper authority in your organization (provided you are not authorized by your company's policies to handle this situation yourself). Therefore, the other answers are incorrect.

66. **Answer: B.** If the customer is too angry to work through the details with you, conclude the encounter by trying to do, or offer, something to lessen her frustration level. Make certain to follow up as promised. As soon as possible, withdraw from the confrontation and let the situation cool off. Inform your supervisor of the situation as quickly as possible so that you have inside support and so that a plan of relief can be implemented. Therefore, the other answers are incorrect.

67. **Answer: A and C.** Even if you know the other person's number, you should respect his right to privacy and offer to intercede between the customer and other technician. If you have the other technician's number, call it, and arrange the call between the other technician and the customer. If you don't have the number, offer to have the technician call the customer when you see him next. You don't want to give the phone number to the customer (Answer B) until you know it is OK. You should not have to lie (Answer D), and it is likely the customer would not believe you.

68. **Answer: B.** Try never to leave customers hanging without a path to get their problems addressed. If this request cannot be performed under your company's policies, there might be nothing you can offer. However, you should always check to see whether there is some other option available. Therefore, the other answers are incorrect.

69. Answer: A. If a problem runs beyond the scope of your position or your capabilities, take the initiative to move it to the next level of authority. This is also true for requests for work to be performed that are outside your assignment or your company's agreement with the customer. Escalate the request so that management can take proper action in deciding how the particular customer should be handled. Therefore, the other answers are incorrect.

70. Answer: A. If you discover illegal, improper, or pornographic material on one of your company's computers, report it to the proper authority in your organization (provided you are not authorized by your company's policies to handle this situation yourself). Therefore, the other answers are incorrect.

71. Answer: D. The best tool for training users is typically the actual equipment or software they are expected to use. If you are coaching one or two users, it is best to pull up a chair and get to an equal level with them. This allows you to make the training more personable and less formal. Use the documentation that comes with the hardware or software as part of the training process. Point out and mark key topic areas in the documentation that you know the users will need after you're gone. However, do not read the manuals to them; this is an instant cure for insomnia and is very ineffective training. Also be careful to use language that the users can relate to. Use proper terminology. Avoid jargon or industry slang when coaching users.

7

CHAPTER SEVEN

Hardware

The first domain for the 220-702 exam is hardware, which is a continuation of the hardware domain in the 220-701 exam. Different from the hardware domain in the 220-701 exam, the 220-702 exam focuses on installing, configuring, and troubleshooting the hardware components of the PC. Out of the four domains for the 220-702 exam, the hardware domain is the largest and takes up 38%.

The given objectives for this domain of the 220-702 exam are as follows:

▶ 1.1—Given a scenario, install, configure, and maintain personal computer components

▶ 1.2—Given a scenario, detect problems, troubleshoot, and repair/replace personal computer components

▶ 1.3—Given a scenario, install, configure, detect problems, troubleshoot, and repair/replace laptop components

▶ 1.4—Given a scenario, select and use the following tools

▶ 1.5—Given a scenario, detect and resolve common printer issues

1.1 Given a scenario, install, configure, and maintain personal computer components

▶ Storage devices

    ▶ HDD

        ▶ SATA

        ▶ PATA

        ▶ Solid state

    ▶ FDD

    ▶ Optical drives

        ▶ CD/DVD/RW/Blu-ray

    ▶ Removable

    ▶ External

▶ Motherboards

    ▶ Jumper settings

    ▶ CMOS battery

    ▶ Advanced BIOS settings

    ▶ Bus speeds

    ▶ Chipsets

- ▶ Firmware updates
- ▶ Socket types
- ▶ Expansion slots
- ▶ Memory slots
- ▶ Front panel connectors
- ▶ I/O ports
  - ▶ Sound, video, USB 1.1, USB 2.0, serial, IEEE 1394/Firewire, parallel, NIC, modem, PS/2
- ▶ Power supplies
  - ▶ Wattages and capacity
  - ▶ Connector types and quantity
  - ▶ Output voltage
- ▶ Processors
  - ▶ Socket types
  - ▶ Speed
  - ▶ Number of cores
  - ▶ Power consumption
  - ▶ Cache
  - ▶ Front side bus
  - ▶ 32-bit vs. 64-bit
- ▶ Memory
- ▶ Adapter cards
  - ▶ Graphics cards
  - ▶ Sound cards
  - ▶ Storage controllers
    - ▶ RAID cards (RAID array—levels 0,1,5)
    - ▶ eSATA cards
  - ▶ I/O cards
    - ▶ Firewire
    - ▶ USB
    - ▶ Parallel
    - ▶ Serial
  - ▶ Wired and wireless network cards
  - ▶ Capture cards (TV, video)
  - ▶ Media reader
- ▶ Cooling systems
  - ▶ Heat sinks
  - ▶ Thermal compound
  - ▶ CPU fans
  - ▶ Case fans

1. Which of the following determines the master or slave in a system that supports two IDE devices?

Quick Answer: **258**
Detailed Answer: **259**

○ **A.** A twist in the cable

○ **B.** Which device was installed first

○ **C.** The jumper settings

○ **D.** The BIOS

○ **E.** Which drive is connected at the end and which drive is connected in the middle

2. You just installed a second new IDE hard drive in a computer system. However, the system does not recognize the new hard drive. What should be the first thing you check?

Quick Answer: **258**
Detailed Answer: **259**

○ **A.** The BIOS

○ **B.** The cabling

○ **C.** The jumper settings

○ **D.** The drive

3. You have been asked to install a SATA hard drive in a computer that already has a PATA HDD and CD-ROM drive installed. Which cable should you connect the new drive to?

Quick Answer: **258**
Detailed Answer: **259**

○ **A.** The secondary signal cable

○ **B.** The primary signal cable

○ **C.** The 15-pin SATA signal cable

○ **D.** The 7-pin SATA signal cable

4. While installing an IDE device, you find that the cable to connect the IDE device is not keyed. Which of the following should you do? (Select all that apply.)

Quick Answer: **258**
Detailed Answer: **259**

○ **A.** Locate the red stripe on the cable, and connect to the device with the red stripe lining up to pin #1.

○ **B.** Attach the cable any way that fits.

○ **C.** If there is no red stripe, locate the blue stripe on the cable and connect to the device with the blue stripe lining up to pin #1.

○ **D.** Purchase a new cable.

5. When installing an IDE CD-ROM drive on a computer with a single IDE hard drive on the primary chain already configured as master, which of the following would be the best configuration for the CD-ROM drive?

Quick Answer: **258**
Detailed Answer: **259**

- ○ **A.** Master on the secondary IDE controller
- ○ **B.** Slave on the primary IDE controller
- ○ **C.** Master on the primary IDE controller
- ○ **D.** Slave on the secondary IDE controller

6. What is the maximum number of IDE devices that can be installed in an ATX computer?

Quick Answer: **258**
Detailed Answer: **259**

- ○ **A.** 1
- ○ **B.** 2
- ○ **C.** 3
- ○ **D.** 4

7. Which of the following are legitimate PATA drive configuration options? (Select all that apply.)

Quick Answer: **258**
Detailed Answer: **259**

- ○ **A.** Master
- ○ **B.** Cable select
- ○ **C.** ID source
- ○ **D.** Slave

8. Which option must be enabled in the CMOS Setup to support large hard drive sizes and allow the IDE controller to convert the sector/head/cylinder addresses into a physical block address that improves data throughput?

Quick Answer: **258**
Detailed Answer: **259**

- ○ **A.** Type 1
- ○ **B.** Fast-throughput
- ○ **C.** LBA
- ○ **D.** ECHS

9. When installing a SATA hard drive, how many connectors or cables do you have to install?

Quick Answer: **258**
Detailed Answer: **260**

- ○ **A.** 1
- ○ **B.** 2
- ○ **C.** 3
- ○ **D.** 4

10. How many serial ATA drives can you connect to a single data cable?

Quick Answer: **258**
Detailed Answer: **260**

   ○ **A.** 1

   ○ **B.** 2

   ○ **C.** 3

   ○ **D.** 4

11. Which of the following is the SCSI ID number generally recommended for the CD-ROM?

Quick Answer: **258**
Detailed Answer: **260**

   ○ **A.** ID 0

   ○ **B.** ID 5

   ○ **C.** ID 2

   ○ **D.** ID 3

12. How do you configure several SCSI drives connected to a single SCSI chain?

Quick Answer: **258**
Detailed Answer: **260**

   ○ **A.** All the hard drives are terminated and have consecutive IDs of 0, 1, and 2.

   ○ **B.** The chain is terminated and all hard disks have the same ID.

   ○ **C.** Both ends of the chain are terminated and each hard drive has a unique ID.

   ○ **D.** The host adapter is terminated and has a unique ID.

13. Which type of hard drive is based on a daisy chain?

Quick Answer: **258**
Detailed Answer: **260**

   ○ **A.** Parallel ATA

   ○ **B.** Serial ATA

   ○ **C.** SCSI

   ○ **D.** eSATA

14. Which of the following is a task that you have to perform when installing SCSI devices?

Quick Answer: **258**
Detailed Answer: **260**

   ○ **A.** Set the jumpers for master/slave

   ○ **B.** Perform a low-level format on the SCSI drive

   ○ **C.** Assign each SCSI device a unique ID number

   ○ **D.** Set the drive type in the CMOS setup

15. How many pins is a floppy disk drive ribbon cable?

    ○   **A.** 34

    ○   **B.** 40

    ○   **C.** 50

    ○   **D.** 72

Quick Answer: **258**
Detailed Answer: **260**

16. While installing an FDD device, you find that the cable to connect the FDD is not keyed. Which of the following should you do?

    ○   **A.** Locate the red or blue stripe on the cable and connect to the device with the red or blue stripe lining up to pin #1.

    ○   **B.** Attach the cable any way that fits.

    ○   **C.** Locate the red or blue stripe on the cable, and connect to the device with the red or blue stripe lining up to pin #34.

    ○   **D.** Purchase a new cable.

Quick Answer: **258**
Detailed Answer: **260**

17. To reduce the resources used on your computer, you want to disable the serial port. What should you do?

    ○   **A.** Disconnect the serial port from the motherboard

    ○   **B.** Disable the serial port in the BIOS setup program

    ○   **C.** Disable the driver in Windows

    ○   **D.** Uninstall the driver in Windows

Quick Answer: **258**
Detailed Answer: **260**

18. You try to connect a new USB hard drive. Unfortunately, your system does not seem to recognize the drive. What should you do first?

    ○   **A.** Connect the USB devices to a different computer to test the devices

    ○   **B.** Replace the USB cables

    ○   **C.** Verify that USB functionality is enabled in the BIOS setup program

    ○   **D.** Verify that the cables for USB are correctly connected to the motherboard

Quick Answer: **258**
Detailed Answer: **261**

19. Which speeds does the USB 2.0 support?

    ○   **A.** 1.5, 10, and 12 Mbps

    ○   **B.** 1.5, 12, and 480 Mbps

    ○   **C.** 1.5, 10, and 100 Mbps

    ○   **D.** 12, 480, and 5 Gbps

Quick Answer: **258**
Detailed Answer: **261**

20. You have an older PC. You purchase an external USB drive and connect it to the front of your computer. Although the drive gets a light, it is not recognized by the system. What is the problem?

Quick Answer: **258**
Detailed Answer: **261**

- ○ **A.** You need to enable the front USB ports using the BIOS setup program.
- ○ **B.** You need to load the proper Windows driver for the USB ports in the front.
- ○ **C.** You should use the USB located at the back of the system.
- ○ **D.** You need to make sure the front USB ports are connected.

21. Which of the following must you do before you can boot from a bootable CD-ROM?

Quick Answer: **258**
Detailed Answer: **261**

- ○ **A.** Make sure the hard drive is formatted with NTFS
- ○ **B.** Change the BIOS boot sequence to CD-ROM, A, C
- ○ **C.** Press the F8 key during the boot sequence
- ○ **D.** Make a bootable diskette

22. You notice that during POST, the system looks for a second IDE hard drive. What can you do so that it no longer looks for the second hard drive and will boot a little bit faster.

Quick Answer: **258**
Detailed Answer: **261**

- ○ **A.** Disconnect the second hard drive cable from the motherboard
- ○ **B.** Be sure to unload the driver for the second drive
- ○ **C.** Connect a dummy terminator back on the second hard drive connector on the motherboard
- ○ **D.** Disable the hard drive in the BIOS setup program

23. Under what conditions should you update a system's BIOS? (Choose the best answer.)

Quick Answer: **258**
Detailed Answer: **261**

- ○ **A.** Anytime there is an update available
- ○ **B.** When you are installing a new microprocessor
- ○ **C.** When the update has functions that are important to the security or operation of the system
- ○ **D.** When you are installing additional memory modules

24. When a technician upgrades firmware on a motherboard he has to do which of the following?

Quick Answer: **258**
Detailed Answer: **261**

- ○ **A.** Flash the BIOS
- ○ **B.** Replace the CMOS chip
- ○ **C.** Replace the BIOS
- ○ **D.** Reset the CMOS

25. How can hyper-threading be disabled on a 2.8 GHz Pentium 4 system?

Quick Answer: **258**
Detailed Answer: **261**

- ○ **A.** Disable hyper-threading in the system BIOS
- ○ **B.** Disable hyper-threading in Device Manager
- ○ **C.** Disable hyper-threading on the motherboard
- ○ **D.** A Pentium 2.8 GHz CPU does not support hyper-threading

26. When installing a new CPU, what is applied directly to the CPU?

Quick Answer: **258**
Detailed Answer: **261**

- ○ **A.** Cooling liquid
- ○ **B.** Thermal compound
- ○ **C.** A heat sink
- ○ **D.** A fan

27. You work in the U.S. Your company is sending you to Europe to work for an extended period of time. Your desktop PC is being shipped to your new location. What step should you take to prepare your PC for operation in your new location?

Quick Answer: **258**
Detailed Answer: **262**

- ○ **A.** Obtain the correct DC power adapter for the country you are going to visit
- ○ **B.** Download language support and character codes for the country you are going to
- ○ **C.** Change the voltage selector switch position on the power supply
- ○ **D.** Install a native language version of your operating system for the location where you will be working

28. The key to inserting a microprocessor is to do which of the following?

Quick Answer: **258**
Detailed Answer: **262**

- ○ **A.** Make sure to orient the writing on the top of the chip with that of the previous processor
- ○ **B.** Align the notch in the chip with the notch in the socket
- ○ **C.** Reattach the fan unit properly
- ○ **D.** Look for the arrow on the chip and align it with the arrow on the PC board

29. You installed a processor, but realize that the processor is not running at its full speed on your desktop computer. What should you
check?

Quick Answer: 258
Detailed Answer: 262

   ○ **A.** See if the processor is installed properly

   ○ **B.** The speed of the RAM

   ○ **C.** Speed of the front-side bus and the clock multiplier

   ○ **D.** See if the thermal solution is installed properly

30. What technology allows you to link two graphic cards together to
provide scalability and increased performance?

Quick Answer: 258
Detailed Answer: 262

   ○ **A.** Video caching

   ○ **B.** Hyper-VGA

   ○ **C.** SLI

   ○ **D.** Hyper-threading

31. You have been tasked with upgrading the existing RAM in one of
the production room's PCs. What should you consider first before
ordering new RAM for this machine?

Quick Answer: 258
Detailed Answer: 262

   ○ **A.** The PC's current RAM type and speed

   ○ **B.** The speed of the PC's current microprocessor

   ○ **C.** The PC's front-side bus speed

   ○ **D.** The PC's total RAM capacity

32. After you physically install a sound card in a desktop PC's expansion slot, what is the first step in starting up the system?

Quick Answer: 258
Detailed Answer: 262

   ○ **A.** Connect the microphone to the MIC jack

   ○ **B.** Connect the speakers to the speaker jacks of the
sound card

   ○ **C.** Turn on the computer and let Windows detect and
install the correct drivers for the card

   ○ **D.** Plug the computer into the AC power source and turn
it on

33. Which of the following memory modules must be installed in
pairs?

Quick Answer: 258
Detailed Answer: 263

   ○ **A.** 72-pin SIMMs

   ○ **B.** 168-pin DIMMs

   ○ **C.** 184-pin DIMMs

   ○ **D.** 184-pin RIMMs

34. What should you consider when you install a new multimedia device? (Select two answers.)

Quick Answer: **258**
Detailed Answer: **263**

- ○ **A.** The manufacturer of the device
- ○ **B.** The physical dimensions of the device
- ○ **C.** Whether the operating system supports the device
- ○ **D.** The length of the warranty

35. How can you tell the difference between a 32-bit and 64-bit PCI card?

Quick Answer: **258**
Detailed Answer: **263**

- ○ **A.** 64-bit cards include a longer bus connector that includes an additional extension.
- ○ **B.** 64-bit cards include connectors on both sides.
- ○ **C.** 64-bit cards have more, smaller connectors.
- ○ **D.** 64-bit cards have dual-layered connectors.

36. How can you tell the difference between a 3.3 volt PCI card, a 5.0 volt PC card, and a universal PCI card?

Quick Answer: **258**
Detailed Answer: **263**

- ○ **A.** The 3.3 volt, 5.0 volt, and universal PCI cards use different size connectors.
- ○ **B.** The depth of the connectors are different.
- ○ **C.** The 3.3 volt, 5.0 volt, and universal PCI cards use different notches.
- ○ **D.** The 3.3 volt, 5.0 volt, and universal PCI cards are different colors.

37. How can you tell the difference between 1.8 and 2.5 volt 184-pin DIMMs? (Choose the best answer.)

Quick Answer: **258**
Detailed Answer: **263**

- ○ **A.** The 1.8 and 2.5 volt DIMMs are difference sizes.
- ○ **B.** The 1.8 and 2.5 volt DIMMs have different notches.
- ○ **C.** The 1.8 and 2.5 volt DIMM connectors have different depth.
- ○ **D.** The 1.8 and 2.5 volt DIMM are different color.

38. How many physical cores are in the Intel Core i7 processor?

Quick Answer: **258**
Detailed Answer: **263**

- ○ **A.** 1
- ○ **B.** 2
- ○ **C.** 4
- ○ **D.** 8

Quick Check

39. How many cores does the AMD Phenom II processor have? (Choose all that apply.)

Quick Answer: **258**
Detailed Answer: **263**

- ○ **A.** 1
- ○ **B.** 2
- ○ **C.** 3
- ○ **D.** 4
- ○ **E.** 8

40. What type of processor is the Intel Core 2 processor?

Quick Answer: **258**
Detailed Answer: **263**

- ○ **A.** x86
- ○ **B.** x86-64
- ○ **C.** IA-64
- ○ **D.** x32

41. What is the minimum number of disks to support RAID-0?

Quick Answer: **258**
Detailed Answer: **263**

- ○ **A.** 1
- ○ **B.** 2
- ○ **C.** 3
- ○ **D.** 4
- ○ **E.** 8

42. What is the minimum number of disks required to support RAID-1?

Quick Answer: **258**
Detailed Answer: **263**

- ○ **A.** 1
- ○ **B.** 2
- ○ **C.** 3
- ○ **D.** 4
- ○ **E.** 8

43. What is the minimum number of disks required to support RAID-5?

Quick Answer: **258**
Detailed Answer: **263**

- ○ **A.** 1
- ○ **B.** 2
- ○ **C.** 3
- ○ **D.** 4
- ○ **E.** 8

44. You have a computer with a Pentium 4 processor with a PCI graphics card and CRT monitor. How can you improve the display performance?

Quick Answer: **258**
Detailed Answer: **263**

- ○ **A.** Replace the monitor with an LCD screen
- ○ **B.** Replace the graphics card with an AGP graphics card
- ○ **C.** Add more Video RAM
- ○ **D.** Run the computer in VGA mode

45. You want to install more RAM on your computer. How can you determine what type of RAM is needed for the computer?

Quick Answer: **258**
Detailed Answer: **264**

- ○ **A.** Check in Device Manager
- ○ **B.** Look on the label on the computer
- ○ **C.** Open the computer and inspect physical RAM
- ○ **D.** Check Add/Remove Hardware in Control Panel

46. You want to record TV directly from your cable connection onto your computer running Windows Vista. What hardware do you need to grab the video signal to capture the video?

Quick Answer: **258**
Detailed Answer: **264**

- ○ **A.** VGA card
- ○ **B.** Media reader card
- ○ **C.** Scanner card
- ○ **D.** Video capture card

47. After you upgrade a desktop PC by installing a new PC133 DRAM module, you start the system and see that it is still identifying the RAM as PC100. What action should you take to determine why this is occurring? (Choose two answers.)

Quick Answer: **258**
Detailed Answer: **264**

- ○ **A.** Flash the BIOS with the latest updates for this system
- ○ **B.** Check the front-side bus speed of the installed processor
- ○ **C.** Check the installed RAM to make sure it is all PC133 DRAM
- ○ **D.** Check the CMOS Setup to confirm that the system is configured properly for the new RAM

1.2 Given a scenario, detect problems, troubleshoot, and repair/replace personal computer components

- ▶ Storage devices
  - ▶ HDD
    - ▶ SATA
    - ▶ PATA

- ▶ Solid state
- ▶ FDD
- ▶ Optical drives
  - ▶ CD/DVD/RW/Blu-Ray
- ▶ Removable
- ▶ External
- ▶ Motherboards
  - ▶ Jumper settings
  - ▶ CMOS battery
  - ▶ Advanced BIOS settings
  - ▶ Bus speeds
  - ▶ Chipsets
  - ▶ Firmware updates
  - ▶ Socket types
  - ▶ Expansion slots
  - ▶ Memory slots
  - ▶ Front panel connectors
    - ▶ Sound, video, USB 1.1, USB 2.0, serial, IEEE 1394/Firewire, parallel, NIC, modem, PS/2
- ▶ Power supplies
  - ▶ Wattages and capacity
  - ▶ Connector types and quantity
  - ▶ Output voltage
- ▶ Processors
  - ▶ Socket types
  - ▶ Speed
  - ▶ Number of cores
  - ▶ Power consumption
  - ▶ Cache
  - ▶ Front side bus
  - ▶ 32-bit vs. 64-bit
- ▶ Memory
- ▶ Adapter cards
  - ▶ Graphics cards—memory
  - ▶ Sound cards
  - ▶ Storage controllers
    - ▶ RAID cards
      - ▶ eSATA cards
  - ▶ I/O cards
    - ▶ Firewire

- ▶ USB
- ▶ Parallel
- ▶ Serial
- ▶ Wired and wireless network cards
- ▶ Capture cards (TV, video)
- ▶ Media reader
- ▶ Cooling systems
  - ▶ Heat sinks
  - ▶ Thermal compound
  - ▶ CPU fans
  - ▶ Case fans

48. Which of the following could have caused your two new IDE devices, which are installed on the second IDE controller, not to function? (Select all that apply.)

- ○ **A.** Both devices are jumpered as master.
- ○ **B.** The ribbon cable does not have a twist in it.
- ○ **C.** Both devices are jumpered as slave.
- ○ **D.** The red striped cable is connected to pin # 1.

Quick Answer: **258**
Detailed Answer: **264**

49. You have three SCSI drives connected on a single SCSI chain, but none are being recognized by the system. What should you check?

- ○ **A.** Whether all the hard drives are terminated and have consecutive IDs of 0, 1, and 2
- ○ **B.** Whether the chain is terminated and that all hard disks have the same ID
- ○ **C.** Whether both ends of the chain are terminated and that each hard drive has a unique ID
- ○ **D.** Whether the host adapter is terminated and has a unique ID

Quick Answer: **258**
Detailed Answer: **264**

50. After completing the installation of your internal and external SCSI devices that connects to an Adaptec AHA-1542s SCSI adapter, you find that none of the devices works. Which of the following should you do first to try to fix the problem?

- ○ **A.** Disconnect all devices and start over
- ○ **B.** Remove the adapter and replace with a new one
- ○ **C.** Change the SCSI IDs
- ○ **D.** Enable termination on the adapter

Quick Answer: **258**
Detailed Answer: **264**

Quick **Check**

Quick Answer: **258**
Detailed Answer: **264**

51. You have just installed a floppy disk drive. Unfortunately, the drive light never shuts off. What is most likely the problem?

- ○ **A.** The power connector is connected backward.
- ○ **B.** The ribbon cable is connected backward.
- ○ **C.** The ribbon cable is damaged.
- ○ **D.** The floppy disk drive is damaged.

Quick Answer: **258**
Detailed Answer: **264**

52. What is the problem when you insert a floppy disk into a drive, you remove the disk, you insert a second disk, but you still see the content of the first disk when you list the contents of the drive?

- ○ **A.** The power connector is connected backward.
- ○ **B.** The ribbon cable is connected backward.
- ○ **C.** The ribbon cable is damaged.
- ○ **D.** The floppy disk drive is damaged.

Quick Answer: **258**
Detailed Answer: **265**

53. You have a computer where the time is constantly wrong, even though you reset it often. Which of the following should repair the problem?

- ○ **A.** A new system board
- ○ **B.** A hard disk
- ○ **C.** An installation disk to re-install the operating system
- ○ **D.** A new CMOS battery

Quick Answer: **258**
Detailed Answer: **265**

54. You have a computer that is constantly rebooting after a short period of time of being on. What is most likely the problem?

- ○ **A.** An overheating CPU
- ○ **B.** A five-second power failure
- ○ **C.** Insufficient memory
- ○ **D.** A new set of software installed

Quick Answer: **258**
Detailed Answer: **265**

55. You just upgraded a processor and now it overheats. What is most likely the cause of the problem?

- ○ **A.** The CPU was not properly seated.
- ○ **B.** Thermal solution was not applied properly.
- ○ **C.** The thermocouple was not seated.
- ○ **D.** The wrong CPU cable was used.

56. A friend has asked you to check out her PC. She has tried to upgrade its CPU and RAM using a "How To" book purchased at the local bookstore. The system shows no signs of operating except that the power light comes on when you hit the On/Off switch. When you open the system unit, you notice that the fan and heat-sink unit are simply sitting on top of the processor and not locked down. Also the processor sockets locking arm is not clamped down, and the processor is not all the way down in the socket. What should you do first in this situation?

- ○ **A.** Lock the processor securely in place by closing the socket's locking arm
- ○ **B.** Check for thermal grease on the heat sink
- ○ **C.** Check the processor for bent pins
- ○ **D.** Snap the fan/heat sink unit into position and make sure that its power connection is properly attached

57. What are the effects of microprocessor fan failures on the system?

- ○ **A.** The system slows down noticeably.
- ○ **B.** The system displays Excessive Temperature Failure error messages.
- ○ **C.** The system continuously fails and then restarts.
- ○ **D.** The system locks up after a short period of operation.

58. Thermal grease is applied directly to what two components? (Choose two answers.)

- ○ **A.** Motherboard
- ○ **B.** Fan
- ○ **C.** Heat sink
- ○ **D.** Processor

59. Which symptom would the POST not identify?

- ○ **A.** A corrupt CMOS RAM
- ○ **B.** A bad keyboard controller
- ○ **C.** A failed hard drive
- ○ **D.** A RAM memory module that fails at high temperature

60. As you begin to troubleshoot a co-worker's PC, you realize that the power supply fan is not working. What items should you check to determine why this problem has occurred? (Select all that apply.)

Quick Answer: **258**
Detailed Answer: **266**

- ○ **A.** Check to make sure that the system unit's air vents are clear
- ○ **B.** Check the system's CMOS configuration to make sure that the fan circuitry is enabled there
- ○ **C.** Check the external voltage selector switch setting on the back of the power supply unit
- ○ **D.** Check the fan's power connection

61. You hear this ticking inside your computer. While taking a closer look, you realize that the fan that is part of the power supply has failed. What should you do?

Quick Answer: **258**
Detailed Answer: **266**

- ○ **A.** Replace the fan
- ○ **B.** Replace the power supply
- ○ **C.** Replace the case
- ○ **D.** Replace the computer

62. You are called out to troubleshoot a system that doesn't start up and makes a repetitive loud clicking sound when you turn it on. Which component is most likely the cause of these problems?

Quick Answer: **258**
Detailed Answer: **266**

- ○ **A.** The hard disk drive
- ○ **B.** The video adaptor
- ○ **C.** The network adapter card
- ○ **D.** The microprocessor fan

63. Every time you try to put a compact disc in your DVD drive, your machine reboots. What is most likely the problem?

Quick Answer: **258**
Detailed Answer: **266**

- ○ **A.** The processor is not properly seated.
- ○ **B.** The thermal solution was not applied properly.
- ○ **C.** The power supply is not adequate for all of the components running on your PC.
- ○ **D.** The power to the motherboard is not connected properly.

64. What is the best thing to do if your power supply is not functioning?

Quick Answer: **258**
Detailed Answer: **266**

- ○ **A.** Send it to an electrical technician
- ○ **B.** Try to fix it yourself
- ○ **C.** Replace the power supply
- ○ **D.** Replace the computer

65. You have a computer that was working fine one day but the next morning it only gives you one short beep and nothing on the screen. What could be the problem?

Quick Answer: **258**
Detailed Answer: **266**

- ○ **A.** There are loose wires.
- ○ **B.** The monitor isn't working and needs to be replaced.
- ○ **C.** There is a video adapter failure.
- ○ **D.** None of the options provided are correct.

66. Which of the following will NOT cause a memory error?

Quick Answer: **258**
Detailed Answer: **266**

- ○ **A.** Faulty hard drive
- ○ **B.** Faulty RAM chip
- ○ **C.** Power fluctuations
- ○ **D.** Faulty motherboard

67. How can a CD be retrieved from a disabled CD-ROM drive?

Quick Answer: **258**
Detailed Answer: **266**

- ○ **A.** Insert a straightened paper clip into the tray-release access hole in the front panel
- ○ **B.** Press the Open/Close button
- ○ **C.** Eject the disk using the operating system
- ○ **D.** Use a thin knife to gently pry open the door

68. What condition is indicated by the Hard Drive Boot Failure error messages?

Quick Answer: **258**
Detailed Answer: **267**

- ○ **A.** The MBR is missing or corrupt.
- ○ **B.** The drive is not formatted.
- ○ **C.** Operating system files are missing or corrupt.
- ○ **D.** The hard drive signal cable is not attached.

69. What effects does leaving off expansion slot covers after an upgrade have on the operation of the system? (Select all that apply.)

Quick Answer: **258**
Detailed Answer: **267**

- ○ **A.** It permits dust to accumulate in the system unit.
- ○ **B.** It disrupts airflow patterns inside the case.
- ○ **C.** It diminishes the ground potential of the system.
- ○ **D.** It has no discernible effect on the system.

70. Which of the following can cause system overheating? (Select all that apply.)

Quick Answer: **258**
Detailed Answer: **267**

- ○ **A.** Open slot covers in the back panel of the system unit
- ○ **B.** Excessive open space in the system unit case
- ○ **C.** Low humidity conditions
- ○ **D.** High humidity conditions

71. What are the consequences of mixing RAM types and speeds within a system? (Select all that apply.)

Quick Answer: **258**
Detailed Answer: **267**

- ○ **A.** It causes the system to lock up.
- ○ **B.** The system runs slower.
- ○ **C.** Hard-memory errors occur.
- ○ **D.** There is no effect.

72. Which of the following will NOT generate a Hard Disk 0 Failure? (Choose all that apply)

Quick Answer: **258**
Detailed Answer: **267**

- ○ **A.** Power connector is not attached properly.
- ○ **B.** Data cable is not attached properly.
- ○ **C.** Motherboard is faulty.
- ○ **D.** Hard drive is faulty.
- ○ **E.** Keyboard is faulty.

73. When you need to degauss a CRT monitor, you should do which of the following?

Quick Answer: **258**
Detailed Answer: **267**

- ○ **A.** Run the degauss utility in Windows
- ○ **B.** Run an electromagnet across the screen
- ○ **C.** Turn the monitor off for 24 hours
- ○ **D.** Run the degauss routine built into the monitor

74. You attach a hard drive to a four port unpowered USB hub that is connected to a notebook. However, you cannot use the hard drive. What is the likely cause of this problem?

Quick Answer: **258**
Detailed Answer: **267**

- ○ **A.** The hard drive drivers are not installed properly.
- ○ **B.** The hard drive has no USB cable.
- ○ **C.** The hard drive is not formatted.
- ○ **D.** The hard drive requires more power than is available through the USB hub.

1.3 Given a scenario, install, configure, detect problems, troubleshoot, and repair/replace laptop components

▶ Components of the LCD including inverter, screen, and video card

▶ Hard drive and memory

▶ Disassemble processes for proper re-assembly

   ▶ Document and label cable and screw locations

   ▶ Organize parts

   ▶ Refer to manufacturer documentation

   ▶ Use appropriate hand tools

▶ Recognize internal laptop expansion slot types

▶ Upgrade wireless cards and video card

▶ Replace keyboard, processor, plastics, pointer devices, heat sinks, fans, system board, CMOS battery, speakers

75. The correct connection method for an internal laptop hard disk drive would be which of the following? (Choose all that apply.)

   ◯ **A.** SCSI

   ◯ **B.** PATA

   ◯ **C.** IEEE 1394

   ◯ **D.** Firewire

   ◯ **E.** SATA

Quick Answer: **258**
Detailed Answer: **267**

76. You upgrade the memory on your laptop. Now the keyboard does not function, while the touchpad is working. Explain the most likely cause of this by choosing from the following.

   ◯ **A.** The RAM is not seated properly.

   ◯ **B.** The keyboard connector must be replaced.

   ◯ **C.** The RAM type is incorrect.

   ◯ **D.** The keyboard connector is not seated properly.

Quick Answer: **258**
Detailed Answer: **267**

77. A user reports that when he plugged the power adapter cord into a laptop, he saw a spark and now the screen is dim. What would you suspect the cause of this problem?

   ◯ **A.** The power adapter is faulty.

   ◯ **B.** The inverter board is faulty.

   ◯ **C.** The video adapter is faulty.

   ◯ **D.** The laptop has overheated.

Quick Answer: **258**
Detailed Answer: **268**

Quick Check

Quick Answer: **258**
Detailed Answer: **268**

78. You have a laptop with internal wireless capability. Unfortunately, you cannot connect to any wireless network access points. What should you check first?

   ○ **A.** That the latest Service Pack is installed

   ○ **B.** The switch that activates the wireless antenna

   ○ **C.** That the wireless access points are all active

   ○ **D.** That the laptop is equipped with a built-in modem

Quick Answer: **258**
Detailed Answer: **268**

79. Which of the following might cause a permanently distorted image on an LCD screen? (Select all that apply.)

   ○ **A.** Magnets

   ○ **B.** Pressure on the screen

   ○ **C.** Extreme cold

   ○ **D.** Extreme heat

Quick Answer: **258**
Detailed Answer: **268**

80. What is the most common repair for a failed LCD monitor?

   ○ **A.** Replace the signal cable

   ○ **B.** Replace the LCD panel

   ○ **C.** Demagnetize the LCD screen

   ○ **D.** Replace the computer

1.4 Given a scenario, select and use the following tools

   ▶ Multimeter

   ▶ Power supply tester

   ▶ Specialty hardware/tools

   ▶ Cable testers

   ▶ Loop back plugs

   ▶ Anti-static pad and wrist strap

   ▶ Extension magnet

Quick Answer: **258**
Detailed Answer: **268**

81. What meter reading would you expect from an open speaker?

   ○ **A.** 4 ohms

   ○ **B.** Infinite (or a blank display)

   ○ **C.** 8 ohms

   ○ **D.** 0 ohms

82. What should the measured resistance be for a good wire?

Quick Answer: **258**
Detailed Answer: **268**

- ○ **A.** 0 ohms
- ○ **B.** 5 ohms
- ○ **C.** 100 ohms
- ○ **D.** Infinity

83. If you were measuring a wire for connectivity, what resistance should you measure if the wire is broken?

Quick Answer: **258**
Detailed Answer: **268**

- ○ **A.** 0 ohms
- ○ **B.** 5 ohms
- ○ **C.** 100 ohms
- ○ **D.** Infinity

84. Which of the following can be used to check the operation of a network adapter card?

Quick Answer: **258**
Detailed Answer: **268**

- ○ **A.** A cable tester
- ○ **B.** An Ethernet loopback cable
- ○ **C.** A digital multimeter
- ○ **D.** A time domain reflectometer

85. How can you test the output of a power supply?

Quick Answer: **258**
Detailed Answer: **268**

- ○ **A.** Multimeter
- ○ **B.** Loopback plug
- ○ **C.** Battery
- ○ **D.** Capacitor

86. What would you use to measure the output of an AC wall plug?

Quick Answer: **258**
Detailed Answer: **269**

- ○ **A.** Multimeter
- ○ **B.** Loopback plug
- ○ **C.** Battery
- ○ **D.** Capacitor

87. What type of device is commonly used to make checks on a LAN cable?

Quick Answer: **258**
Detailed Answer: **269**

- ○ **A.** OTDR
- ○ **B.** Multimeter
- ○ **C.** Voltmeter
- ○ **D.** Cable tester

88. You have just installed a replacement system board in a customer's PC, and you drop the last screw into the system unit. Which is the best way to retrieve the screw from the system unit?

Quick Answer: **258**
Detailed Answer: **269**

- ○ **A.** Use plastic tweezers
- ○ **B.** Use long needle-nose pliers
- ○ **C.** Use an extension magnet
- ○ **D.** Use a magnetic screwdriver

89. Which of the following is used to attach an RJ-45 connector to a Cat5 cable?

Quick Answer: **258**
Detailed Answer: **269**

- ○ **A.** A multimeter
- ○ **B.** A wire crimper
- ○ **C.** An optical tester
- ○ **D.** A punch down tool

90. Which of the following is used to terminate a Cat5 cable in a wiring closet?

Quick Answer: **258**
Detailed Answer: **269**

- ○ **A.** A multimeter
- ○ **B.** A wire crimper
- ○ **C.** An optical tester
- ○ **D.** A punch down tool

91. Which of the following is used to test for continuity in a copper cable? (Choose all that apply.)

Quick Answer: **258**
Detailed Answer: **269**

- ○ **A.** A multimeter
- ○ **B.** A wire crimper
- ○ **C.** An optical tester
- ○ **D.** Time-domain reflectometer

92. You find an exposed wire inside your computer. What should you do to cover this up?

Quick Answer: **258**
Detailed Answer: **270**

- ○ **A.** Use duct tape
- ○ **B.** Pull the wire out
- ○ **C.** Use black electrical tape
- ○ **D.** Use brown masking tape

1.5 Given a scenario, detect and resolve common printer issues

▶ Symptoms

   ▶ Paper jams

   ▶ Blank paper

▶ Error codes

▶ Out of memory error

▶ Lines and smearing

▶ Garbage printout

▶ Ghosted image

▶ No connectivity

▶ Issue resolution

   ▶ Replace fuser

   ▶ Replace drum

   ▶ Clear paper jam

   ▶ Power cycle

   ▶ Install maintenance kit (reset page count)

   ▶ Set IP on printer

   ▶ Clean printer

93. After printing for several weeks to a local printer the user sudden-ly cannot print any longer. From the following what should the technician check first?

   ○ **A.** The printer cable

   ○ **B.** The paper tray

   ○ **C.** The print drivers

   ○ **D.** All of the above

Quick Answer: **258**
Detailed Answer: **270**

94. You print a test page from the printer but you cannot print a test page from Windows. What should you check first?

   ○ **A.** The device drivers

   ○ **B.** The cable

   ○ **C.** The toner cartridge

   ○ **D.** The paper tray

Quick Answer: **258**
Detailed Answer: **270**

95. After you try to print a numeric error code is displayed on the screen of the printer. To determine the meaning of the code what should you do?

   ○ **A.** Print a test page

   ○ **B.** Consult Microsoft Windows help files

   ○ **C.** Consult the printer's service manual

   ○ **D.** Load the default settings for the printer

Quick Answer: **258**
Detailed Answer: **270**

96. What problem can be caused by a faulty fusing assembly?

Quick Answer: **258**
Detailed Answer: **270**

- ○ **A.** It can cause a worn pickup assembly.
- ○ **B.** The paper comes out with a smudged image, and toner rubs off.
- ○ **C.** It causes a "misfeed" or "paper feed" error.
- ○ **D.** None of the options provided are correct.

97. The usual cause of paper jams in bubble-jet printers is caused through a worn pick up roller. What is the other common cause of paper jams in bubble-jet printers?

Quick Answer: **258**
Detailed Answer: **270**

- ○ **A.** Too much ink on the page
- ○ **B.** The wrong type of paper
- ○ **C.** When more than one page enters the system
- ○ **D.** None of the options provided are correct

98. The term "ghosting" is used when there are light images of previously printed pages on the current page. Which of the following can be the cause of this? (Select two answers.)

Quick Answer: **258**
Detailed Answer: **270**

- ○ **A.** A bad erasure lamp
- ○ **B.** The wrong type of paper
- ○ **C.** A broken cleaning blade
- ○ **D.** Faulty fusing assembly

99. A customer reports that his laptop can no longer print to the wireless IrDA printer after it was relocated. Explain by choosing from the following what the MOST likely cause of this problem would be.

Quick Answer: **258**
Detailed Answer: **270**

- ○ **A.** The printer is more than one meter (three feet) from the laptop.
- ○ **B.** The printer driver has not been set up.
- ○ **C.** The laptop needs to be rebooted.
- ○ **D.** The printer needs to be installed.

100. The letters seem to smear if touched immediately after a document has been printed from a laser printer. From the following options, what is the cause of this condition?

Quick Answer: **258**
Detailed Answer: **270**

- ○ **A.** The toner is running low.
- ○ **B.** The cartridge must be changed.
- ○ **C.** The toner has become desensitized.
- ○ **D.** The fuser is not getting hot enough.

101. What would you check first if an ink jet printer is printing with a horizontal line missing in the middle of each letter?

○ **A.** The paper feed mechanism

○ **B.** The toner cartridge

○ **C.** The print head

○ **D.** The device driver

102. Typically, what is the first test to perform when a printer won't print?

○ **A.** Signal cable-check

○ **B.** Printer self-test

○ **C.** Port loopback test

○ **D.** Configuration check

103. A customer has brought his laser printer into your repair area because it produces a paper feed error when he tries to print a document. Where is the first place to check given this symptom?

○ **A.** The pickup rollers

○ **B.** The compression rollers

○ **C.** The developing rollers

○ **D.** The fuser assembly

104. One of your customers reports that she is getting poor quality output from her color printer. She indicates that the inkjet printer is producing disfigured graphics. What actions should you take to identify the source of this problem? (Select all that apply.)

○ **A.** Calibrate the printer

○ **B.** Install a new print head and ink cartridges

○ **C.** Check the printer's paper thickness settings

○ **D.** Check the wear on the printer's paper-handling mechanisms

105. A laser printer is printing faded text in your documents. The toner cartridge has just been replaced and is not the problem. What is most likely the problem?

○ **A.** A bad primary corona wire.

○ **B.** A bad transfer corona wire.

○ **C.** A bad laser-scanning module.

○ **D.** The rotating drum is not getting completely discharged.

106. You are troubleshooting a laser printer that is producing a Fuser Error message. Which of the following should you do first?

Quick Answer: **258**
Detailed Answer: **271**

- ○ **A.** Replace the fuser assembly.
- ○ **B.** Turn the printer off and on to see whether the error goes away.
- ○ **C.** Replace the paper in the printer.
- ○ **D.** Replace the transfer corona wire.

107. After installing a new printer, you discover that it prints odd characters in places. What should you do to correct this problem?

Quick Answer: **258**
Detailed Answer: **271**

- ○ **A.** Download the latest drivers for this printer from the manufacturer's website.
- ○ **B.** Patch the operating system from the Microsoft Windows Updates site.
- ○ **C.** Download and install updated third-party drivers for this printer.
- ○ **D.** Obtain new flash code from the printer manufacturer to update the printer's firmware.

108. What type of failure would cause your laser printer to start up in an offline condition?

Quick Answer: **258**
Detailed Answer: **271**

- ○ **A.** The offline button has been pressed.
- ○ **B.** The printer's interface cable might be defective.
- ○ **C.** The printer driver is incorrect.
- ○ **D.** The toner cartridge is empty.

109. Your laser printer has started to produce documents that have long white stripes down the length of the page. What type of problem is indicated by this symptom?

Quick Answer: **258**
Detailed Answer: **272**

- ○ **A.** The drum is failing.
- ○ **B.** The fuser is not heating evenly.
- ○ **C.** The conditioning roller has a spot on it.
- ○ **D.** The toner cartridge is not evenly distributing toner.

110. If a standalone printer passes the self-test and the user still cannot print, what else could be the cause of the problem?

Quick Answer: **258**
Detailed Answer: **272**

- ○ **A.** Fuse error
- ○ **B.** Laser error
- ○ **C.** Pickup roller
- ○ **D.** Printer interface

111. For the best quality output from a laser printer, what should you recommend to your customers?

Quick Answer: **258**
Detailed Answer: **272**

- ○ **A.** Use toner cartridges produced by the printer manufacturer
- ○ **B.** Use high-quality toner in a refill cartridge to get good quality and low prices
- ○ **C.** Use only the highest quality printer paper
- ○ **D.** Tell customers to reload their own cartridges so they know that they have high-quality materials to work with

112. A new laser printer in your Hawaiian warehouse is consistently picking up too many sheets of paper. The warehouse is open to the outside atmosphere when large trucks are backed up to its loading docks to load or unload products. What is the most likely cause of this problem?

Quick Answer: **258**
Detailed Answer: **272**

- ○ **A.** Dust from the outside air is defeating the page thickness sensors so that the printer cannot determine the correct thickness of the paper being used.
- ○ **B.** Temperature changes caused by the large doors opening and closing are causing the printer's pickup sensors to incorrectly read the thickness of the paper.
- ○ **C.** Humidity caused by the open atmosphere of the warehouse is causing the pages to stick together so that they cannot be picked up properly by the printer's separation mechanism.
- ○ **D.** The wrong paper setting is being used in the warehouse printer, and a simple adjustment to the tray settings should correct the problem.

113. As part of your company's maintenance agreement with your customers, you have just serviced a customer's three-tray laser printer that has been having paper jam problems. You installed a standard service kit and loaded new paper into all the trays. What steps should you take to complete the job? (Select all that apply.)

Quick Answer: **258**
Detailed Answer: **272**

- ○ **A.** Print test pages from all trays to determine whether the jam problem is still present.
- ○ **B.** Print a registration page to make sure that the print is correctly aligned on the page.
- ○ **C.** Cycle the printer on and off to see whether any errors appear.
- ○ **D.** Have the customer sign off on the job to verify your work.

Quick Check

114. After completing the installation of a new laser printer and walking the user through its operation, you want to establish with the customer a suggested maintenance schedule for the printer. Where are you most likely to find a maintenance schedule for a given laser printer?

Quick Answer: 258
Detailed Answer: 272

   ○ **A.** Under the main access cover where it can be read each time the printer is open for preventative maintenance, upgrading, or repair

   ○ **B.** The printer manufacturer's website

   ○ **C.** The printer's driver page in Windows Device Manager utility

   ○ **D.** The printer's Installation and Service Guide

115. What is the problem caused by when the printer displays "out of memory" message?

Quick Answer: 258
Detailed Answer: 272

   ○ **A.** Printer is too slow.

   ○ **B.** File is too big.

   ○ **C.** Computer is too fast.

   ○ **D.** You are trying to print a color document on a black-and-white printer.

Quick-Check Answer Key

1. C	**30.** C	**59.** D	**88.** A
2. C	**31.** A	**60.** C and D	**89.** B
3. D	**32.** C	**61.** B	**90.** D
4. A and C	**33.** D	**62.** A	**91.** A and D
5. A	**34.** B and C	**63.** C	**92.** C
6. D	**35.** A	**64.** C	**93.** B
7. A, B, and D	**36.** C	**65.** C	**94.** B
8. C	**37.** B	**66.** A	**95.** C
9. B	**38.** C	**67.** A	**96.** B
10. A	**39.** B, C, and D	**68.** A	**97.** B
11. D	**40.** B	**69.** A and B	**98.** A and C
12. C	**41.** B	**70.** A and D	**99.** A
13. C	**42.** B	**71.** A, B, and C	**100.** D
14. C	**43.** C	**72.** E	**101.** C
15. A	**44.** B	**73.** D	**102.** B
16. A	**45.** C	**74.** D	**103.** A
17. B	**46.** D	**75.** B and E	**104.** C and D
18. C	**47.** B and C	**76.** D	**105.** B
19. B	**48.** A and C	**77.** B	**106.** B
20. C	**49.** C	**78.** B	**107.** A
21. B	**50.** D	**79.** C and D	**108.** B
22. D	**51.** B	**80.** B	**109.** D
23. C	**52.** C	**81.** B	**110.** D
24. A	**53.** D	**82.** A	**111.** A
25. A	**54.** A	**83.** D	**112.** C
26. B	**55.** B	**84.** B	**113.** A and D
27. C	**56.** C	**85.** A	**114.** D
28. B	**57.** D	**86.** A	**115.** B
29. C	**58.** C and D	**87.** D	

Answers and Explanations

1. **Answer: C.** You implement the master/slave setting jumpers on the drives. It does not matter what you install first (Answer B), and it does not matter what you set in the BIOS (assuming you configure the BIOS to enable IDE), Answer D. It also does not matter which connector on the ribbon cable you attach to drives. A twist in the cable (Answer A) determines the drive A or drive B for floppy drives.

2. **Answer: C.** You should check jumpers to make sure that one drive is set as the master and other drive is set as the slave. While you can have IDE disabled in the BIOS (Answer A) or the cable (Answer B) might not be connected or connected properly, it is most likely the jumper settings. The last thing you would suspect as the problem is a faulty drive (Answer D).

3. **Answer: D.** Newer system boards provide two or more 7-pin connectors to accommodate Serial ATA (SATA) drives. The flat 7-pin SATA signal cable has four wires used to form two differential signal pairs (A+/A– and B+/B–). The other three wires are used for shielded grounds. The cable is only 0.5-inch wide, which makes cable routing inside the system unit simpler and provides less resistance to airflow through the case. The maximum length for an internal SATA cable is specified as 39.37 inches (one meter). The power cable, not the signal cable, is a 15-pin cable (Answer C). The secondary and primary signal cables are associated with parallel ATA.

4. **Answer: A and C.** When connecting the drives to the controller, you need to make sure that the red stripe or blue stripe is oriented so the wire it represents is connected to pin #1 on the drive and pin #1 on the controller. Therefore, the other answers are incorrect.

5. **Answer: A.** Because the IDE CD-ROM drive is a slower device, it is recommended to place it on the secondary IDE controller. If the CD-ROM is the only device on an IDE controller, it must be configured as the master or stand-alone. Therefore, the other answers are incorrect.

6. **Answer: D.** ATX computer systems have a primary and a secondary IDE channel (parallel ATA). Each channel can support a master and a slave drive. This gives us four drives. Some newer ATX systems that support Serial ATA (SATA) have a single parallel ATA (PATA) IDE channel but will have two or more SATA connectors. Because ATX systems support four parallel ATA drives, the other answers are wrong.

7. **Answer: A, B, and D.** A PATA drive can be configured as the master drive in a single-drive or multidrive system (Answer A) or the slave drive in the same multidrive system (Answer B). It can also be set up for Cable Select (CS) operation, where the system determines its configuration setting (Answer D). There is no ID Source to configure on Parallel ATA (Answer C).

8. **Answer: C.** For larger drives, the Large and LBA modes are used. The LBA mode should be selected if drives support LBA mode. In this mode, the IDE controller converts the sector/head/cylinder address into a physical block address that improves data throughput. The ECHS (or Large mode) option (Answer D) is a generic cylinder/head/sector translation scheme that supports older drive geometries up to 1GB. Today, you almost always auto configure and let the BIOS determine the drive parameters. Type 1 (Answer A) and Fast-throughput (Answer B) are not standard configurations in the BIOS.

9. **Answer: B.** When you install an SATA hard drive, you have to connect two connectors, a power connector (15-pin) and a data connector (7-pin). Therefore, the other answers are incorrect.

10. **Answer: A.** Different from parallel drives, you can only connect one drive to the data cable. Therefore, the other answers are incorrect.

11. **Answer: D.** Every other device can be set to any number as long as it's not in use. It is a recommended practice in the IT community to set the SCSI ID number for CD-ROM drives to 3. Therefore, the other answers are incorrect.

12. **Answer: C.** SCSI drives are connected as a chain (known as a daisy chain). No matter how many drives you connect, each drive must have a unique SCSI ID number and both ends of the chain must be terminated. The end of the chain could be a drive or the controller card. Therefore, the other answers are incorrect.

13. **Answer: C.** Daisy chaining allows one device to connect to another device, which then can connect to another device, making a chain. Legacy SCSI can connect up to seven drives using one controller in a daisy chain. When using daisy chain, the two ends of the chain must be terminated and no other devices should be terminated. Parallel ATA (PATA) can connect two devices on a single cable, but are not considered daisy chain. Serial ATA (SATA) only allows one device per cable. eSATA, short for External SATA, is designed for a single device.

14. **Answer: C.** To properly configure SCSI devices, the ends of the chain(s) must be properly terminated and each device must have a unique ID. Thus once your SCSI devices are correctly connected, you need to assign each device a unique SCSI ID number. Jumpers for master/slave are for parallel IDE drives (Answer A). A low-level format (Answer B) typically does not need to be done on today's drives. Setting the drive types in the CMOS setup on standard desktop PCs are for IDE drives and not SCSI drives (Answer D). A few high-end workstations and servers include SCSI controllers on the motherboards. In these cases, you may configure the SCSI settings within the BIOS, but these are more the exception than the standard.

15. **Answer: A.** Floppy disk drive ribbon cables are 34 pins. Today, floppy disk drive ribbon cables only have two connectors: one to connect to the controller card or motherboard and the second one to connect to the floppy disk drive. In the past, it was common for floppy disk drives to have a middle connector. The cable included a twist that differentiated between drive A and drive B. Because a floppy disk drive cable has 34 pins, the other answers are incorrect.

16. **Answer: A.** When connecting the drives to the controller, you need to make sure that the red stripe or blue stripe is oriented so the wire it represents is connected to pin #1 on the drive and pin #1 on the controller. Therefore, the other answers are incorrect.

17. **Answer: B.** The best way to disable the serial port on a computer is to enter the BIOS setup program and disable the serial port. Disconnecting the serial port from the motherboard only disconnects the port connector but not the port itself (Answer A). Disabling the driver in Windows still uses some resources within Windows (Answer C). If you uninstall the driver in Windows it will only get reinstalled the next time Windows is rebooted (Answer D).

18. **Answer: C.** You can disable USB on a computer within the BIOS setup program. You can then replace the cables (Answer B), open the system, check the cables (Answer D), and try the drive on another system (Answer A).

19. **Answer: B.** USB 2.0 supports 1.5, 12, and 480 Mbps. USB 1.0 supported the original 1.5 Mbps, and USB 1.1 supports 12 Mbps. USB 2.0 supports speeds up to 480 Mbps. USB 3.0 supports up to 5.0 Gbps. Therefore, the other answers are incorrect.

20. **Answer: C.** Although today's newest systems contain USB 2.0 or higher USB ports, some of the older systems mix USB 1.1 ports in the front and USB 2.0 ports in the back. USB 1.1 ports are great for mice and keyboards, but they do not supply as much power or bandwidth as USB 2.0. Therefore, you should try the ports in the back. If this does not work, you might consider external power. You should not have to enable the USB ports using the BIOS setup program (Answer A) or load the Windows drivers (Answer B) because you do have lights on the drive indicating that the USB port is being recognized. In addition, because you have lights, the USB ports are connected in the front (Answer D).

21. **Answer: B.** The BIOS might be set to boot from the hard drive before it tries to boot from the CD-ROM. In this case the boot sequence must be changed to make it possible to boot from the CD-ROM. You do not need to make a bootable diskette (Answer D), although you need to use a bootable compact disc. Pressing F8 (Answer C) displays the advanced boot menu in Windows. It does not matter what file systems a hard drive contains that will affect a bootable compact disc (Answer A).

22. **Answer: D.** Most likely, you have an IDE hard drive and optical disk (CD-ROM or DVD). Therefore, you can disable the other drives so that the computer does not try to identify the non-existent drives during boot up. Disconnecting the cable (Answer A) or unloading the driver (Answer B) does not change anything. Lastly, you cannot connect a dummy terminator (Answer C).

23. **Answer: C.** When a major PC component is upgraded, the system's BIOS (along with any associated BIOS extension devices) should be updated with the latest compatible firmware. Sometimes, the functions include recognizing newer processors (Answer B), fixing processor or motherboard glitches, and recognizing newer memory modules (Answer D). Because the BIOS upgrade can be complicated and can make a system not function properly, you should only do a BIOS upgrade when absolutely needed.

24. **Answer: A.** To add the ability for the motherboard to recognize hardware and to fix some hardware problems, you can update the flash BIOS. To update the flash BIOS, you need to run a special program. Therefore, the other answers are incorrect.

25. **Answer: A.** Hyper-threading is creating two logical processors out of each physical core processor so that it can keep the pipes running at full tilt. To disable hyper-threading, you need to enter the BIOS setup program. It is usually found in Advanced Options menu. Therefore, the other answers are incorrect.

26. **Answer: B.** To make a good thermal connectivity between the processor heat sink (Answer C), you need to apply a thermal compound. A fan (Answer D) is then installed on top of the heat sink. You should never apply cooling liquid to any electronic device (Answer A).

27. **Answer: C.** Change the setting of the 110/220 switch setting on the outside of the power supply. The normal setting for equipment used in the United States is 110VAC. In many other countries, the voltage level is 220VAC 50Hz. Therefore, the other answers are incorrect.

28. **Answer: B.** The notches, beveled-pin patterns, and dots on the various ICs (integrated circuits) are used to identify the location of the IC's number 1 pin. You might also have to check the silkscreen printing around the socket to verify the pin 1 location. The main thing to be sure of when inserting a microprocessor in a socket is to make sure to correctly align the IC's pin 1 with the socket's pin 1 position. Therefore, the other answers are incorrect.

29. **Answer: C.** On some systems when you install processors, you will need to configure the front side bus and the clock multiplier. This used to be done with jumpers on the motherboard in older legacy systems and can be configured within the BIOS setup program. Some systems are auto-configuring, assuming the motherboard supports the new processor. The speed of the RAM (Answer B) should not be a factor, although if you have slow RAM, the system might not run at its full potential. If the processor is not installed properly (for example, if you have it turned 90 degrees), the processor will not fit in the processor socket and will not boot (Answer A). If the thermal solution is not installed properly (Answer D), the processors will most likely overheat and cause erratic behavior such as lock up or reboot.

30. **Answer: C.** SLI is short for scalable link interface, which was developed by NVIDIA. It links two graphics cards together to provide scalability and increased performance by increasing bandwidth and processing power. ATI's competing solution is ATI CrossFire. Video caching (Answer A) will only increase bandwidth. There is no such thing as Hyper-VGA (Answer B). Hyper-threading (Answer D) is technology used in Intel processors that use two logical processors within a single core to keep the processor pipelines full at all times.

31. **Answer: A.** You should never mix memory types when upgrading a system board. If the new memory modules are not technically compatible with the existing memory, the old memory should be removed. Remember that just because the memory modules are physically compatible, this does not mean that they will work together in a system. Mismatched memory speeds and memory styles (registered/unregistered, buffered/nonbuffered, ECC, and so on) can cause significant problems in the operation of the system. These problems can range from preventing bootup to creating simple soft memory errors. You must ensure that the memory type and size you want to install are supported by the system board and that it does not already have the maximum amount of memory installed. The system board's documentation includes information on the type, configuration, and size of memory it will accept. In addition, verify that the memory you want to install is compatible with the memory currently installed on the board. Therefore, the other answers are incorrect.

32. **Answer: C.** At this point in the installation scenario, the power cord can be reconnected to the outlet (it should have been unplugged to install any internal adapter card), and the system can be turned on. Next, the operating system should detect the new sound card and either install the correct drivers or prompt the user for action to install the appropriate drivers for the car. It does not matter if you connect the microphone

(Answer A) or the speakers (Answer B) before or after you load the drivers. Of course, you need to boot Windows and allows Windows to install the driver, not just turn on the computer (Answer D).

33. **Answer: D.** RIMMs are 16-bits wide and must be installed in pairs. SIMMs (Answer A) and DIMMs (Answers B and C) don't have to be installed in pairs.

34. **Answer: B and C.** When you install any multimedia device, you must consider the physical dimensions of the device to make sure that it fits in the computer and whether the operating system supports the device, including having the correct device driver. The manufacturer of the device is not important (Answer A) and the length of warranty (Answer D) does not affect the installation or operations of the device.

35. **Answer: A.** 64-bit connectors are longer and have an additional connector extension. Therefore, the other answers are incorrect.

36. **Answer: C.** The 3.3 volt, 5.0 volt, and universal PCI cards have different notches so that you cannot place the wrong card in the wrong slot. The 3.3 volt, 5.0, and universal PCI card do not differ in size (Answer A), depth (Answer B), or color (Answer D).

37. **Answer: B.** To prevent putting the wrong RAM into a socket, the notches are located in different places. The 1.8 and 2.5 volt are not different sizes (Answer A), do not differ in depth (Answer C), and are not different colors (Answer D).

38. **Answer: C.** The Intel Core i7 has four physical cores and eight logical cores. Therefore, the other answers are incorrect.

39. **Answer: B, C, and D.** Depending on the version, there are either two, three, or four cores in the AMD Phenom II processor. Therefore the other answers are incorrect.

40. **Answer: B.** The Intel Core 2 processor is a 64-bit x86-64 processor that has the capability to run x86 (Answer A) operating systems and applications. It does not share the IA-64 architecture (Answer C), which is used by the Itanium processors. 32-bit applications (sometimes referred to as x32), Answer D, runs on an x86 architecture.

41. **Answer: B.** To support striping (RAID-0), you need to have a minimum of two hard drives. Of course, if you use more disks, you will have more available disk space and generally faster performance.

42. **Answer: B.** In mirroring, one disk is duplicated to another. Therefore, if one fails, you keep on working. To support mirroring (RAID-1), you need to use two disks.

43. **Answer: C.** To support striping with parity (RAID-5), you need to have three hard drives. Similar to RAID-0, you can use additional disks to increase the amount of available disk space.

44. **Answer: B.** The PCI bus is limited to data transfers of 127MBps, the AGP 1x is limited to 266 MBps, and AGP 2x, 4x, and 8x are even faster. Thus the AGP graphics card will provide better performance. Replacing the monitor (Answer A) with an LCD will not increase performance. Adding more video memory (Answer C) gives it the ability to support more color or a higher resolution. Running the computer in VGA mode (Answer D) might speed things up because there is much less to process but many applications and even some operating systems will not function in VGA mode with a resolution of only 640×480 and 16 colors.

45. Answer: C. The only way to determine the type of RAM that is in a computer is to open it up and look at the RAM chips. Therefore, the other answers are incorrect.

46. Answer: D. A TV tuner card is a computer component that allows television signals to be received by a computer. Most TV tuners also function as video capture cards, allowing them to record television programs onto a hard disk. A VGA card (Answer A) is used to display images to your monitor. The media reader (Answer B) is used to read small memory cards such as miniSD or microSD cards found in cameras and telephones. There is no official device called a scanner card (Answer C), but some systems might include a proprietary card to connect to a scanner. Today, scanners usually connect through USB or 1384.

47. Answer: B and C. In some cases, the system may detect the presence of the new RAM modules but not be able to correctly identify them. If the system's front-side bus speed cannot be increased to the maximum capabilities of the RAM modules, the memory type displayed during the POST does not reflect the actual memory type installed. You should never mix memory types when upgrading a system board. If the new memory modules are not technically compatible with the existing memory, the old memory should be removed. Just because the memory modules are physically compatible does not mean they will work together in a system. Mismatched memory speeds and memory styles (registered/unregistered, buffered/unbuffered, ECC, and so on) can cause significant problems in the operation of the system. These problems range from preventing boot-up to limiting the speed of the FSB to the lowest memory speed or creating soft memory errors. You do not need to flash the BIOS (Answer A), and you should not need to check the CMOS Setup program (Answer D) because the RAM speed is usually detected automatically.

48. Answer: A and C. If you have two drives on a bus and both are set to master, neither drive will work because they will be fighting each other for control of the disks. If you have two drives on a bus and both are set to slave, neither drive will work because the disks won't know where to get their instructions from. Only floppy disk cables (Answer B) have a twist in them. Although it's possible that the cable is connected improperly (Answer D), having the jumpers not configured properly is more common.

49. Answer: C. When you connect SCSI devices, both ends of the chain must be terminated and each device must have a unique SCSI ID number. The hard drives do not have to have consecutive IDs (Answer A). SCSI devices cannot use the same SCSI ID (Answer B). The host adapter does not necessarily have to be terminated if it is in the middle of the chain (Answer D). Today, most SCSI devices are auto-terminating.

50. Answer: D. Some legacy adapter cards, such as the Adaptec AHA-1542, still need to have terminators installed. If you set up both internal and external devices and none of them work, try enabling termination on it to see if that fixes the problem. Of course, you should always check connections (Answer A) and check the SCSI unique SCSI IDs (Answer C). Replacing the adapter (Answer B) should be the last thing you should do.

51. Answer: B. When the ribbon cable is connected backward, the drive light never shuts off. In addition, when you insert a floppy disk, it will usually cause the disk to be unreadable. Therefore, the other answers are incorrect.

52. Answer: C. This problem is known as a phantom directory problem. It is caused by a faulty floppy disk cable, specifically, the pin-34 signal is not being transmitted properly, which is the change disk signal. Therefore, the other answers are incorrect.

53. **Answer: D.** If the date and time are always off, the CMOS is not able to keep the internal clock running while the computer is shut off. Therefore, you need to check the CMOS battery because it is what provides power to the real-time clock when the computer is off. If this problem is not fixed after the CMOS battery is replaced, you have to replace the system board (Answer A). You should also check to see if you have any viruses or any software that is changing the time. The hard disk (Answer B) or the operating system (Answer C) have nothing to do with the wrong date and time.

54. **Answer: A.** When the processor overheats, it shuts down to protect itself. Therefore, the other answers are incorrect.

55. **Answer: B.** You need to check the thermal solution. You must make sure that you applied the proper thermal compound and that the heat sink and fan are installed properly. You should also check to make sure that the system (motherboard and thermal solution) is rated for the new processor and that the other fans in the case are working. Also make sure that the fan ports are not being blocked. If the processor is not seated properly (Answer A), the system will not be able to boot. There is no CPU cable (Answer D). The only cable is the power cable to the fan. A thermocouple (Answer C) is used to measure the temperature of an electronic component or surface. Thermocouples are usually located as part of the motherboard and processor so that the system can monitor the system temperature.

56. **Answer: C.** If the processor does not appear to sit completely flush in the socket, remove it before clamping it into place. Check for bent pins that might not be lining up properly with the socket. Also make certain the processor's pin configuration lines up properly with the socket. If you force the processor into the socket, you might break off the pin and ruin the processor. You should not lock the processor by closing the socket's locking arm (Answer A) until you make sure there are no bent pins. You should then check to see if you have the proper application of thermal grease (Answer B) and if the fan and heat sink are installed properly (Answer D).

57. **Answer: D.** If the system consistently locks up after being on for a few minutes, it is a good indication that the microprocessor's fan is not running or that some other heat buildup problem is occurring. The key indicator is that the failure is linked to the time required to heat up and cool down. Although some overheating systems might throttle the system and cause it to be slower (Answer A) in an attempt to produce less heat, if the fan goes out, the system most likely shuts down as the processor becomes way too hot to run. You will most likely not get excessive temperature failure error messages (Answer B). An overheating system (Answer C) usually doesn't repeatedly reboot because it will take some time for the system to cool down before it can operate again.

58. **Answer C and D.** Thermal grease is used to increase thermal conductivity between two components. When installing processors, you have to apply a thermal solution. Thermal grease is placed between the heat sink and processor. It is not placed on the fan (Answer B), which is a mechanical moving part, and you would not place thermal grease directly on a circuit board such as a motherboard (Answer A).

59. **Answer: D.** During the POST, the operation of the microprocessor, RAM, keyboard, hard disk drive, and CMOS RAM are tested. But a RAM chip that fails at high temperatures could not be detected at this stage. A POST could identify a corrupt CMOS RAM (Answer A), a bad keyboard controller (Answer B), and a failed hard drive (Answer C).

60. Answer: C and D. If the power supply's fan is not operational, check the power supply unit. In particular, check for the presence of a voltage level selector switch and make sure it is properly set for the AC supply voltage where you are. If this setting is incorrect, the power supply cannot supply the correct voltage levels to the system's components (Answer C). Also check the fan's power supply connection to make sure that it has not been loosened or disconnected from the system board. The fan must have power to be able to turn (Answer D). If the air vents are not clear (Answer A), heat will not be able to escape, and so it will build up. You cannot enable or disable the fan circuitry in the CMOS Setup program (Answer B).

61. Answer: B. While all of the answers would fix the problem, you should replace the power supply because it is the easiest and most economical solution. You could replace the fan inside the power supply, but these parts are more difficult to obtain and often require an electronic technician instead of a computer technician (Answer A). You can replace the case, including the power supply (Answer C), but this requires you to move all other components to the new case, which can be time-consuming and much more difficult than just replacing the power supply. Lastly, you could replace the computer (Answer D), but this is the most expensive option of all.

62. Answer: A. The loud clicking sound associated with hard disk drive problems is the key to this scenario. This is not a symptom associated with the other components. Start the system and listen for sounds of the hard drive spinning up (a low whine or clicking noise). If there is a loud clicking noise coming from the drive, the drive has lost its alignment and is looking for its starting track. The video adapter (Answer B), network adapter (Answer C), and processor fan (Answer D) do not cause a loud clicking noise.

63. Answer: C. The power supply is overtaxed. Because the DVD drive does not run all the time, when you insert the CD, it is exceeding the limit of the power supply. If the processor is not seated properly (Answer A), the system would not turn on. If the thermal solution is not applied properly (Answer B), the processor would overheat. If the power to the motherboard is not connected properly (Answer D), the system would not boot.

64. Answer: C. It is extremely dangerous to open the case of a power supply. Besides, power supplies are inexpensive, so it probably costs less to replace one than to try to fix it (Answer B), and it is much safer. You can send it to an electronic technician but it is still less expensive to replace it. You don't have to replace the computer (Answer D) when you only have to replace the power supply.

65. Answer: C. A video card failure is indicated by one short beep and no display on the screen. Therefore, the other answers are incorrect.

66. Answer: A. Memory problems can be caused by a faulty RAM chip (Answer B), a faulty motherboard (Answer D), a faulty power supply, and power fluctuations (Answer C). They cannot be caused by a faulty hard drive (Answer A).

67. Answer: A. If the drive is inoperable and there is a CD or DVD locked inside, you should insert a straightened paper clip into the tray-release access hole that is usually located beside the eject button. This releases the spring-loaded tray and pops out the disc. The Open/Close button (Answer B) will not operate and the operating system will not be able to eject a disk (Answer C) if it is disabled. You should not use a thin knife (Answer D) because it can damage the internal workings of the CD-ROM drive.

68. **Answer: A.** A Hard Drive Boot Failure message indicates that the disk's master boot record is missing or has become corrupt. Therefore, the other answers are incorrect.

69. **Answer: A and B.** The missing cover permits dust to accumulate in the system, forming an insulating blanket that traps heat next to active devices and causing components to overheat (Answer A). The missing slot cover interrupts the designed airflow patterns inside the case, causing components to overheat due to missing or inadequate airflow (Answer B). Missing slot covers have no effect on the grounding of the system (Answer C).

70. **Answer: A and D.** The missing cover permits dust to accumulate in the system, forming an insulating blanket that traps heat next to active devices and causing component overheating. It also interrupts the designed airflow patterns inside the case, causing components to overheat due to missing or inadequate airflow (Answer A). High humidity can lead to heat-related problems and failures (Answer D). The open space inside the case should not have any effect (Answer B).

71. **Answer: A, B, and C.** Generally, when you add memory modules to an existing system and the new modules have different speed ratings than the existing modules, at best the system will operate at the speed of the slowest modules (Answer B). However, mixing significantly different RAM types and speeds in a system can also cause the system to lock up (Answer A) and produce hard-memory errors (Answer C). Of course, because the system runs at the slower speed, Answer D is incorrect.

72. **Answer: E.** A Hard Disk Failure, HDD Controller Failure, and similar errors can be caused by an improperly connected drive (Answers A and B), faulty motherboard (Answer C), faulty hard drive (Answer D), and possibly a faulty power supply (specifically the damaged power connector). Therefore, a keyboard (Answer E) has nothing to do with a hard drive error.

73. **Answer: D.** Magnetic fields, such as those generated by stereo speakers, can distort images and cause discoloration of isolated areas on a CRT monitor. Some monitors will have a degauss routine built-in. If your monitor does not have a degauss routine, you need to purchase a special demagnetizing device that is moved over the outside surface of the CRT to eliminate the magnetic fields. Windows does not have a degauss utility (Answer A). You should not use an electromagnet (Answer B) because a magnet most likely caused the problem. Turning off the monitor will not degauss a monitor (Answer C).

74. **Answer: D.** If you connect too many devices to a USB hub, the device will not function because it will not be able to supply enough power to all the devices. Therefore the other answers are incorrect.

75. **Answer: B and E.** Older laptop computers use Parallel ATA and newer laptops use Serial ATA. SCSI drives (Answer A) are usually reserved for high performance workstations and servers. IEEE 1394 (Answer C) and Firewire (Answer D) are used for high speed devices such as video cameras.

76. **Answer: D.** Most likely when you upgrade the RAM, you dislodged the keyboard connector or you did not reconnect the keyboard connector properly. Therefore, the other answers are incorrect.

77. **Answer: B.** The inverter board supplies power to the back light that allows you to see images on the screen. You will have to replace the inverter circuit board. You should still be able to use an external monitor until you can get it repaired. If the power adapter is faulty (Answer A), the entire laptop would not function. If the video adapter is faulty (Answer C), you would not be able to see the dim image. If the laptop was overheated (Answer D), it would most likely operate initially and then lock up.

78. **Answer: B.** Check the obvious. Make sure that the wireless antenna or device is turned on. Because you are having problems with more than one access point (you cannot connect to any wireless network), the problem is most likely isolated to the laptop and not all of the access points (Answer C). A built-in modem (Answer D) is used to connect to telephone lines. A service pack (Answer A) does not help you to connect to a network.

79. **Answer: C and D.** The LCD screen should be shielded from bright sunlight and heat sources. Moving the computer from a cooler location to a hot location can cause damaging moisture to condense inside the housing (including the display). It should also be kept away from ultraviolet light sources and extremely cold temperatures. The liquid crystals can freeze in extremely cold weather. A freeze/thaw cycle might damage the display and cause it to be unusable. Magnets (Answer A) affect LCD screens. Pressure (Answer B) on the screen only temporary distorts the screen unless there is too much pressure that it cracks the screen.

80. **Answer: B.** When an LCD panel fails, the most common repair is to replace the entire display panel/housing assembly. Lads do not need to be demagnetized (Answer C). Replacing the computer (Answer D) is not cost efficient. A signal cable (Answer A) rarely fails.

81. **Answer: B.** If the speaker is defective, the resistance reading should be 0 for an electrical short (Answer D) or infinite for an open circuit. Because it is an open speaker, you should measure infinite. Therefore, the other answers are incorrect.

82. **Answer: A.** If you are testing a wire for connectivity, it should measure 0 ohms indicating that there is no break. If you have a break in the wire, it would measure infinity (Answer D). Anything else indicates a load on the wire (Answers B and C). If you are measuring a wire and nothing else is attached to the wire, there is no load. Therefore, there is some defect with the wire.

83. **Answer: D.** A break in a wire would indicate infinity. A good connection would measure 0 ohms (Answer A). Anything else indicates a load on the wire (Answers B and C). If you are measuring a wire and nothing else is attached to the wire, there is no load. Therefore, there is some defect with the wire.

84. **Answer: B.** You can use an Ethernet loopback cable to make the network adapter think it is attached to a network connection. This cable is made by looping wires from pin 1 to pin 3 and pin 2 to pin 6 of the RJ-45 plug. When the loopback cable is inserted into the Nick's RJ-45 jack, the link light should appear within a few seconds. A digital multimeter is usually used to measure at least voltage and resistance. A cable tester (Answer A) and time domain reflectometer (Answer D) can find problems with cables. An optical time domain reflectometer (Answer C) is used to test fiber cable.

85. **Answer: A.** A multimeter, which includes a voltmeter, can be used to measure the output of power supply. Because a power supply is supposed to output clean DC power, you try to measure DC voltage. Common output voltages should be +3.3, +\-5.0 and

+\-12 volts. A loopback plug (Answer B) is used to test a port by resending an outgoing signal back as the incoming signal. A battery (Answer C) and capacitor (Answer D) are electronic components that provide electricity within a circuit.

86. **Answer: A.** Besides DC voltage, the multimeter can also measure AC voltage. For the United States, you should measure 120 volts AC. A loopback plug (Answer B) is used to test a port by resending an outgoing signal back as the incoming signal. A battery (Answer C) and capacitor (Answer D) are electronic components that provide electricity within a circuit.

87. **Answer: D.** The most efficient way to test a network cable is to use a cable tester to check its functionality. A multimeter includes an ohmmeter that measures resistance of a cable. A cable tester is much more efficient in checking a cable because it can test multiple wires within a cable simultaneously and perform additional test that a multimeter cannot test. A voltmeter (Answer C) measures volts, which cannot be used to test a cable. An optical time-domain reflectometer (OTDR), Answer A, is an optoelectronic instrument used to characterize or test an optical fiber.

88. **Answer: A.** The plastic tweezers are the best tool for retrieving screws and other objects that fall into the system. This tool can save a lot of disassembly/reassembly time when metal objects get loose in the system. Although many computer technicians carry a telescopic or extension magnet (Answer C) in their tool kits for retrieving screws and nuts that get dropped into the system unit or printer, this tool can adversely affect the operation of disk drives and CRT-based monitors. Long needle-nose pliers (Answer B) and screwdrivers are essential in a computer toolkit. However, care needs to be used with magnetic screwdrivers (Answer D) for the reason that was explained with the extension magnet.

89. **Answer: B.** A wire crimper is used to attach RJ-45 connectors to a cable by using pressure to press some kind of metal teeth into the inner conductors of the cable. A multimeter (Answer A) includes a voltmeter and ohmmeter. An optical tester (Answer C) is used to test fiber optic cables. A punch down tool (Answer D) is used to terminate a twisted pair cable into a patch panel or wire closet.

90. **Answer: D.** A cable in a wire closet is terminated by inserting the individual wires into an IDC (insulation displacement connector). IDCs make contact by cutting through, or displacing, the insulation around a single wire. A punch down tool (Answer D) is used to insert the wire in the IDC. A wire crimper is used to attach RJ-45 connectors to a cable by using pressure to press some kind of metal teeth into the inner conductors of the cable. A multimeter (Answer A) includes a voltmeter and ohmmeter. An optical tester (Answer C) is used to test fiber optic cables.

91. **Answer: A and D.** A multimeter is a device that is used to measure voltages and resistances in electronic components. It can also be used to test for continuity in a wire. A continuity test will indicate if there is a break in the wire. A Time-Domain Reflectometer (TDR), which is also called a cable tester, is a device that sends out a signal and measures the time it takes for the signal to return. A break in the cable will cause the signal to return prematurely and will indicate the presence of, and the distance to, a break in the cable. An optical tester (Answer C) is used to test fiber cable. A wire crimper (Answer B) is used to attach RJ-45 connectors to a cable by using pressure to press some kind of metal teeth into the inner conductors of the cable.

92. **Answer: C.** An exposed wire is never good inside an electronic device as it could lead to harm to someone who is working inside the computer, and it could damage components within the computer. Assuming the wire is still performing its function, you should you use black electrical tape to cover the exposed wire by wrapping the tape around the wire. You should not use duct tape (Answer A) or masking tape (Answer D) because these types of tape are not good insulators for the wires that will contain the signals. You should not pull the wire out (Answer B) unless you are going to replace it.

93. **Answer: B.** You should always check the obvious, including checking to see if there is paper in the paper tray and that there is no paper jam. You would then check the printer cable to make sure it is connected. Lastly, you should check the print drivers (Answer C).

94. **Answer: B.** Because the printer is most likely functional, the problem appears to be between the computer and the printer. Therefore, you should check the cable first. Then check the driver to make sure it is installed and pointing to the printer. You should then check the paper tray (Answer D) and toner (Answer C)—which are both highly unlikely causes of the problem—in case you ran out of paper, got a paper jam, or ran out of toner between your two tests.

95. **Answer: C.** The numeric code would be specific to the printer. Therefore, you should consult the printer's service manual. The other answers are incorrect.

96. **Answer: B.** The fusing assembly melts the toner onto the paper. If you have a faulty fusing assembly the text or images on the paper might smudge or the toner might rub off. Therefore, the other answers are incorrect.

97. **Answer: B.** Paper jams in bubble-jet printers are usually due to one of two things: a worn pickup roller or the wrong type of paper. As a result of using the wrong paper or having worn pick up rollers, the printer grabs more than one piece of paper (Answer C). Having too much ink (Answer A) does not cause paper jams or cause the grabbing of more than one sheet of paper at a time.

98. **Answer: A and C.** If the erasure lamps are bad, the previous electrostatic discharges aren't completely wiped away. A broken cleaning blade, on the other hand, causes old toner to build up on the EP drum and consequently present itself in the next printed image. The wrong type of paper (Answer B) might cause paper jams or the grabbing of more than one sheet of paper at the same time. A faulty fusing assembly (Answer D) causes smudged text or images or causes the text and images to be easily rubbed off.

99. **Answer: A.** IrDA is short for Infrared Data Association. IrDA range is about one meter. The other answers would not cause the printer to stop printing if moved.

100. **Answer: D.** The toner is not being melted onto the paper. Therefore, the fuser is not getting hot enough. If toner is running low (Answer A), you see a light image or some text or parts of images don't appear. If the cartridge has to be changed (Answer B) it is because you are low on toner or the cartridge is defective, which causes streaks because the toner is not being released. If the toner is being desensitized (Answer C), you have a problem with the electronic components within the laser, including the corona wire.

101. **Answer: C.** The print head of an ink jet printer has several small spray nozzles that spray ink. If the print head has a single spray nozzle that is clogged, it could cause missing lines in the printed document. A problem with the paper feed mechanism (Answer A) will cause paper jam. Ink jet printers do not use toner cartridges (Answer B). Having the wrong driver or a corrupt driver will not allow you to print at all or will cause garbage to print out. Of course, if you don't have the driver (Answer D) loaded at all, you will not be able to print.

102. **Answer: B.** Nearly every printer is equipped with a built-in self-test. The easiest way to determine whether a printer is at fault is to run its self-test. If the self-test runs and prints clean pages, the printer can be eliminated as a possible source of problems. The port loopback test (Answer C) partially tests the parallel or serial port. You then have to check the configuration (Answer D), including making sure you have the driver loaded and making sure the cable (Answer A) is connected properly.

103. **Answer: A.** Most paper feed errors are related to the paper feed rollers (pickup rollers). Given the symptoms, you first should check the rollers for proper alignment and wear. You can then check the other rollers in the system (Answers B and C). A faulty fuser assembly (Answer D) will cause a temperate error or fuser error.

104. **Answers: C and D.** If the printer's paper thickness selector is set improperly, or the rollers in its paper feed system become worn, the paper can slip as it moves through the printer, which causes disfigured graphics to be produced. Check the printer's paper thickness settings. If they are correct and the print output is disfigured, you need to replace the paper feed rollers. The ink cartridges (Answer B) contain the print head. If you start running out of a particular color, the color might be off or parts of the text or image may be missing. If the printer is not calibrated (Answer A), the image may be off.

105. **Answer: B.** Faint print in a laser printer can be caused by a number of things. If the contrast control is set too low, or the toner level in the cartridge is low, empty, or poorly distributed, the print quality can appear washed out. Other causes of faint print include a weakened corona wire or a weakened high-voltage power supply that drives it. Replace the unit that contains the corona wire. Also replace the high-voltage power supply. The primary corona wire (Answer A) charges the drum before an image is drawn on the drum with a laser. Without the primary corona wire, the toner cannot be attracted to the drum. A bad laser-scanning module (Answer C) will not be able to draw out the image onto the drum. An erase light is used to discharge the drum (Answer D).

106. **Answer: B.** In some cases, turning off the printer, waiting 10 minutes or so, and then turning it back on can clear fuser error messages. If the message continues, remove and reseat the fuser assembly. If this does not correct the error message, troubleshoot or replace the fuser assembly (Answer A) according to the manufacturer's guidelines. Replacing the paper (Answer C) or replacing the transfer corona wire (Answer D) does not affect the operations of the fuser or fuser assembly.

107. **Answer: A.** Drivers delivered with Windows might not be the latest version for a given peripheral device (these drivers were added to Windows when it was created), and they might not support the new printer's current firmware version. Therefore, for a new printer installation, you should always check for driver updates when you have problems. Check the manufacturer's website for newer versions. Patching (Answer B) does not help unless patching includes newer drivers. You should not use third-party drivers (Answer C); you should use the manufacturer's drivers. You do not have to flash the printer's firmware (Answer D) like you do the motherboard BIOS.

108. **Answer: B.** When the printer starts up in an offline condition, there is probably some type of problem with the printer/computer interface that does not allow them to communicate. Disconnect the interface cable to see if the printer starts up in a Ready state. The offline button (Answer A) is used to temporarily pause a printer. If you restart the printer after you pressed the offline button, it usually comes online again. If the toner cartridge is empty (Answer D), the text or images will be light or you will get a message that you are out of toner. If you have the wrong driver (Answer C), your printer will display strange characters or it would print what resembles programming code.

109. **Answer: D.** White lines that run along the length of the page from a laser printer are normally a sign of poorly distributed toner. Remove the toner cartridge and shake it to distribute the toner more evenly. If this does not work, replace the toner cartridge with a new one. The drum will be part of the toner cartridge (Answer A). if the fuser is not heating evenly (Answer B), you will have smudged text or images or the text or image will easily smear. A spot on the conditioning roller (Answer C) will only cause a repeated blank spot, not a line.

110. **Answer: D.** If the printer runs the self-test and prints clean pages, most of the printer has been eliminated as a possible cause of problems. The problem could be in the computer, cabling, or interface portion of the printer. The fuse error (Answer A) indicates a problem with the fuser, which melts the toner onto the paper. The pickup roller (Answer C) grabs the sheets of paper into the laser printer. An error with the pickup roller or a paper jam indicates you are using the wrong type of paper. A laser error means you have a problem with the laser component (Answer B) within the printer that draws the text and images onto the drum.

111. **Answer: A.** Under most circumstances, it is best to recommend products specified by the manufacturer of the product. This typically involves using toner cartridges produced by the printer manufacturer or ones that have been approved by the manufacturer. You should never have a problem using manufacturer-recommended kits and supplies. Toner/cartridge information is usually found in the printer's documentation.

112. **Answer: C.** Using paper that is too heavy or too thick can result in jams, as can overloading paper trays. Similarly, using the wrong type of paper can defeat the separation pad and allow multiple pages to be drawn into the printer at one time. Multiple sheets can move through the printer together, or they might result in a jam somewhere in the printer. In high-humidity environments, paper can absorb moisture from the air and swell up. Also, the moist pages can stick together and cause paper jams. Therefore the other answers cannot be correct.

113. **Answer: A and D.** When you finish any type of printer maintenance, you should always verify the printer's functionality and have the customer sign off on the repair. In this example, you should verify that the printer works correctly from all the trays. You don't have to print a registration page (Answer B) if you printed a test page from each tray. You actually need to test the printer rather than see if the printer detects an error (Answer C).

114. **Answer: D.** Most PC components have recommended maintenance programs and schedules designed by their manufacturers. These schedules are typically available in a device's documentation. You might also be able to obtain the manufacturer's maintenance schedule from its website (Answer B) but this is more doubtful. The printer's driver page (Answer C) does not have any information on maintenance. The printers (Answer A) do not have maintenance schedules written inside the printer.

115. **Answer: D.** Printers almost always ship with enough memory to handle jobs that involve basic text. But if you print large complex graphical documents, your printer could show an "out of memory," "overflow error," or "memory overload" message. Although the printer might be too slow (Answer A), it takes extra time for the printer to process the document. If a computer is too fast (Answer C), the print job will be throttled by the interface through which the computer connects to the printer. Lastly, printing a color document on a black-and-white printer (Answer D) is not a factor because the color will be converted to gray scale.

CHAPTER EIGHT

Operating Systems

The second domain of the 220-702 exam falls in line with the second domain of the 220-701 exam in discussing today's popular Microsoft Windows operating systems, including Windows 2000, Windows XP, and Windows Vista. It makes up 34% of the 220-702 exam. It emphasizes configuring and troubleshooting these Windows operating systems, including tasks such as performing commands at the command prompt and using common Windows tools.

The given objectives for this domain of the 220-702 exam are as follows:

▶ 2.1—Select the appropriate commands and options to troubleshoot and resolve problems

▶ 2.2—Differentiate between Windows Operating System directory structures (Windows 2000, XP, and Vista)

▶ 2.3—Given a scenario, select and use system utilities/tools and evaluate the results

▶ 2.4—Evaluate and resolve common issues

2.1 Select the appropriate commands and options to troubleshoot and resolve problems

▶ MSCONFIG

▶ DIR

▶ CHKDSK (/f, /R)

▶ EDIT

▶ COPY (/A, /V, /Y)

▶ XCOPY

▶ FORMAT

▶ IPCONFIG (/ALL, /RELEASE, /RENEW)

▶ PING (-T, -L)

▶ MD/CD/RD

▶ NET

▶ TRACERT

▶ NSLOOKUP

▶ [command name] /?

▶ SFC

1. What command can you use to start the System Configuration Utility so that you can see what programs start when Windows loads?

   ○ **A.** CHKDSK

   ○ **B.** MSCONFIG

   ○ **C.** IPCONFIG

   ○ **D.** edit

Quick Answer: **304**
Detailed Answer: **305**

2. Which of the following tools allows a user to manage his computer system's configuration?

   ○ **A.** REGEDIT.EXE

   ○ **B.** SCANREG.EXE

   ○ **C.** MSCONFIG.EXE

   ○ **D.** Disk Management

Quick Answer: **304**
Detailed Answer: **305**

3. What command can you execute at the command prompt that will display the folders and files in your current location?

   ○ **A.** CHKDSK

   ○ **B.** LS

   ○ **C.** DIR

   ○ **D.** MSCONFIG

Quick Answer: **304**
Detailed Answer: **305**

4. What command do you use to open a command prompt executed from the RUN option?

   ○ **A.** C:\

   ○ **B.** CMDPROMPT

   ○ **C.** COMMANDPROMPT

   ○ **D.** CMD

Quick Answer: **304**
Detailed Answer: **305**

5. What option would you use to display files using the short names (8.3 format) while using the dir command?

   ○ **A.** /B

   ○ **B.** /C

   ○ **C.** /Q

   ○ **D.** /X

Quick Answer: **304**
Detailed Answer: **305**

6. What option would you use with the `dir` command to pause a long directory listing so that only one screen shows at a time?

Quick Answer: **304**
Detailed Answer: **305**

- ○ **A.** /W
- ○ **B.** /P
- ○ **C.** /B
- ○ **D.** /X

7. What option would you use with the `dir` command to display the listing in alphabetical order?

Quick Answer: **304**
Detailed Answer: **305**

- ○ **A.** /OD
- ○ **B.** /ON
- ○ **C.** /Q
- ○ **D.** /AD

8. What option would you use with the `dir` command to display only subdirectories?

Quick Answer: **304**
Detailed Answer: **306**

- ○ **A.** /OD
- ○ **B.** /AD
- ○ **C.** /B
- ○ **D.** /X

9. What option would you use with the `dir` command to display hidden files?

Quick Answer: **304**
Detailed Answer: **306**

- ○ **A.** /OD
- ○ **B.** /AD
- ○ **C.** /AH
- ○ **D.** /ON

10. What command would you use to check a disk for errors and display a status report?

Quick Answer: **304**
Detailed Answer: **306**

- ○ **A.** FIXDISK
- ○ **B.** CHKDSK
- ○ **C.** CHECKDISK
- ○ **D.** DIR /CH

11. What option would you use to fix disk errors found with the
chkdsk command?

- ○ **A.** /FIX
- ○ **B.** /R
- ○ **C.** /F
- ○ **D.** /FIXDISK

12. What option do you need to use with the chkdsk command that
will locate bad sectors and recover readable information?

- ○ **A.** /FIX
- ○ **B.** /R
- ○ **C.** /SCANDISK
- ○ **D.** /FIXDISK

13. What two commands execute a text editor? (Choose two answers.)

- ○ **A.** NOTEPAD
- ○ **B.** MSCONFIG
- ○ **C.** DIR /E
- ○ **D.** EDIT

14. What command do you use to copy a file from one place to another?

- ○ **A.** DISKCOPY
- ○ **B.** COPY
- ○ **C.** FORMAT
- ○ **D.** SHADOW COPY

15. How do you get a list of the options that can be used with the
COPY command at the command prompt?

- ○ **A.** COPY ?
- ○ **B.** COPY /?
- ○ **C.** COPY *
- ○ **D.** COPY /Help

16. What command would you use to copy test.dll (in your current
location) to the C:\Windows\System32 folder?

- ○ **A.** COPY TEST.DLL C:\WINDOWS\SYSTEM32
- ○ **B.** COPY C:\WINDOWS\SYSTEM32 TEST.DLL
- ○ **C.** COPY TEST.DLL to C:\WINDOWS\SYSTEM32
- ○ **D.** COPY C:\WINDOWS\SYSTEM32 from test.dll

17. What option would you use with the `copy` command to verify whether the file has been copied properly?

- ○ **A.** /A
- ○ **B.** /B
- ○ **C.** /V
- ○ **D.** /N

18. What option do you use with the copy command that copies the text content of the file, stopping when it reaches the End of File (EOF) character.

- ○ **A.** /A
- ○ **B.** /B
- ○ **C.** /V
- ○ **D.** /N

19. You want to copy a group of folders and subfolders—including empty folders—from one place to another in a PC you are working on. You are working from the command prompt, so you need to use the XCOPY command. Which XCOPY switch enables you to perform this operation?

- ○ **A.** XCOPY /s
- ○ **B.** XCOPY /h
- ○ **C.** XCOPY /e
- ○ **D.** XCOPY /CMDLINE

20. You want to copy all files that have a `txt` extension. What command would you use?

- ○ **A.** COPY *txt C:
- ○ **B.** COPY *.TXT C:
- ○ **C.** COPY TXT C:
- ○ **D.** COPY ?.TXT C:

21. What does a switch do when you're using the command line?

- ○ **A.** It turns the command off.
- ○ **B.** It forces the command to perform unrelated tasks.
- ○ **C.** It allows the computer to be overclocked.
- ○ **D.** It widens or narrows the function of the command.

22. Which of the following commands clears the screen when you're using the command line?

- ○ **A.** CLS
- ○ **B.** REM
- ○ **C.** CD
- ○ **D.** DIR

23. Which of the following command-line switches lists the available switches for most command-line utilities?

- ○ **A.** /HELP
- ○ **B.** /*
- ○ **C.** /H
- ○ **D.** /?

24. What Windows XP command-line utility can be used to create and manage disk partitions?

- ○ **A.** FDISK
- ○ **B.** FORMAT
- ○ **C.** DISKPART
- ○ **D.** DISKPERF

25. What command would you use to format a disk so that it can be used by the operating system?

- ○ **A.** CONVERT
- ○ **B.** FORMAT
- ○ **C.** FDISK
- ○ **D.** DISKPART

26. What command would you use to format the D: drive as an NTFS file system?

- ○ **A.** FORMAT D:
- ○ **B.** FORMAT D: /FS:NTFS
- ○ **C.** FORMAT D: /FS
- ○ **D.** FORMAT D: /NTFS
- ○ **E.** FORMAT D: /X

27. What command would you use to perform a quick format that will delete all the files on a volume?

Quick Answer: **304**
Detailed Answer: **307**

   ○ **A.** FORMAT D: /FS
   ○ **B.** FORMAT D: /Q
   ○ **C.** FORMAT D: /VOLUME
   ○ **D.** FORMAT D: /X

28. What option do you use with the copy command that will not prompt you to overwrite an existing file?

Quick Answer: **304**
Detailed Answer: **308**

   ○ **A.** /Y
   ○ **B.** /-Y
   ○ **C.** /V
   ○ **D.** /D

29. What command would you use to delete a file?

Quick Answer: **304**
Detailed Answer: **308**

   ○ **A.** DEL
   ○ **B.** REMOVE
   ○ **C.** CHKDSK
   ○ **D.** EDIT

30. What option do you use with the del command that will prompt you to delete each file?

Quick Answer: **304**
Detailed Answer: **308**

   ○ **A.** /PROMPT
   ○ **B.** /P
   ○ **C.** /Q
   ○ **D.** /F

31. What option would you use with the del command that will delete files from all subdirectories?

Quick Answer: **304**
Detailed Answer: **308**

   ○ **A.** /P
   ○ **B.** /F
   ○ **C.** /S
   ○ **D.** /Q

32. What option would you use with the del command to force the deletion of read-only files?

Quick Answer: **304**
Detailed Answer: **308**

   ○ **A.** /P
   ○ **B.** /F
   ○ **C.** /S
   ○ **D.** /Q

33. What command would you use to view the IP configuration on a Windows computer?

- ○ **A.** CHKDSK
- ○ **B.** NSLOOKUP
- ○ **C.** IPCONFIG
- ○ **D.** MSCONFIG

34. What command would you use to view the DNS servers used by a client?

- ○ **A.** IPCONFIG /ALL
- ○ **B.** IPCONFIG /RENEW
- ○ **C.** IPCONFIG /DNS
- ○ **D.** IPCONFIG /FLUSHDNS

35. You just moved a computer to a different subnet. Now you want to get a new IP address. What command should you execute?

- ○ **A.** MSCONFIG
- ○ **B.** RENEWIP
- ○ **C.** IPCONFIG /RENEW
- ○ **D.** IPCONFIG /ALL

36. What command would you use to release the DHCP addresses assigned to an adapter?

- ○ **A.** MSCONFIG
- ○ **B.** RENEWIP
- ○ **C.** IPCONFIG /RELEASE
- ○ **D.** IPCONFIG /ALL

37. What command would you use to purge the DNS Resolver cache so that it can resolve a different address from the DNS server?

- ○ **A.** IPCONFIG /RELEASE
- ○ **B.** IPCONFIG /RENEW
- ○ **C.** IPCONFIG /REGISTERDNS
- ○ **D.** IPCONFIG /FLUSHDNS

38. You want to test connectivity between a workstation and another host. Which command would you use?

- ○ **A.** PING
- ○ **B.** ARP -a
- ○ **C.** IPCONFIG /ALL
- ○ **D.** WINIPCFG /ALL

39. What command would you use to ping the loopback address?

- ○ **A.** PING 0.0.0.0
- ○ **B.** PING 127.0.0.1
- ○ **C.** PING 192.168.1.122
- ○ **D.** PING 255.255.255.255

40. What command would you use to ping server01?

- ○ **A.** IPCONFIG /SERVER01
- ○ **B.** PING SERVER01
- ○ **C.** ARP -A server01\
- ○ **D.** WINIPCFG /SERVER01

41. What option can you use with the ping command that will make ping keep pinging until you stop it?

- ○ **A.** -T
- ○ **B.** -A
- ○ **C.** -F
- ○ **D.** -W

42. Two computers have the same IP address. What command would you use to help you figure out which two computers are affected?

- ○ **A.** PING
- ○ **B.** ARP -A
- ○ **C.** IPCONFIG /ALL
- ○ **D.** WINIPCFG /ALL

43. What command would you use to create a new folder?

- ○ **A.** CD
- ○ **B.** MD
- ○ **C.** RD
- ○ **D.** DIR

44. What command would you use to remove an empty directory?

Quick Answer: **304**
Detailed Answer: **309**

- ○ **A.** CD
- ○ **B.** MD
- ○ **C.** RD
- ○ **D.** DIR

45. What option would you use with the rd command to remove all subfolders and files in a specified directory?

Quick Answer: **304**
Detailed Answer: **309**

- ○ **A.** /Q
- ○ **B.** /ALL
- ○ **C.** /S
- ○ **D.** /RECURRENT

46. What command would you use to start the server service?

Quick Answer: **304**
Detailed Answer: **309**

- ○ **A.** IPCONFIG SERVER
- ○ **B.** NET START SERVER
- ○ **C.** NET USE SERVER
- ○ **D.** SFS SERVER

47. What command would you use to stop a service?

Quick Answer: **304**
Detailed Answer: **310**

- ○ **A.** NET ST
- ○ **B.** NET STOP
- ○ **C.** NET SHOW
- ○ **D.** NET USE

48. What command would you use to map the G drive to the \\server01\share folder?

Quick Answer: **304**
Detailed Answer: **310**

- ○ **A.** NET START G \\SERVER01\SHARE
- ○ **B.** NET START CONNECT \\SERVER\SHARE
- ○ **C.** NET USE G: \\SERVER01\SHARE
- ○ **D.** NET USE CONNECTTO G: \\SERVER01\SHARE

49. Which of the following commands would you enter at the command prompt in Windows when you want to defragment the C drive?

Quick Answer: **304**
Detailed Answer: **310**

- ○ **A.** DEFRAG C:
- ○ **B.** FDISK
- ○ **C.** SCANDISK
- ○ **D.** CHKDSK C: /F

50. You want to determine which switches for the DEFRAG command you can use to force defragmentation even though the free space on a hard disk is low. What command should you use? (Select all that apply.)

   ○ **A.** DEFRAG /HELP

   ○ **B.** DEFRAG -f

   ○ **C.** DEFRAG /?

   ○ **D.** DEFRAG /H

Quick Answer: **304**
Detailed Answer: **310**

51. Which Windows TCP/IP utility would you use to identify all the connections between source and destination computers?

   ○ **A.** ARP

   ○ **B.** PING

   ○ **C.** NETSTAT

   ○ **D.** TRACERT

Quick Answer: **304**
Detailed Answer: **310**

52. What command can you use to show DNS resolution of a host?

   ○ **A.** IPCONFIG

   ○ **B.** ARP

   ○ **C.** NSLOOKUP

   ○ **D.** NBTSTAT

Quick Answer: **304**
Detailed Answer: **310**

53. Which two TCP/IP utilities display the address of a known remote location?

   ○ **A.** PING

   ○ **B.** NETSTAT

   ○ **C.** IPCONFIG

   ○ **D.** NSLOOKUP

Quick Answer: **304**
Detailed Answer: **310**

54. Which of the following commands or utilities can be used to check the integrity of the system files in Windows XP Professional?

   ○ **A.** SFC /SCANNOW

   ○ **B.** Dr. Watson

   ○ **C.** SFC /SCAN

   ○ **D.** SCANDSK

Quick Answer: **304**
Detailed Answer: **310**

55. What command would you use to delete all files in a folder?

- ○ **A.** DEL ALL
- ○ **B.** DEL *.*
- ○ **C.** RD
- ○ **D.** SFC /ALL

Quick Answer: **304**
Detailed Answer: **310**

56. What command do you use to change to a different folder?

- ○ **A.** CD
- ○ **B.** MD
- ○ **C.** RD
- ○ **D.** CHKDSK

Quick Answer: **304**
Detailed Answer: **311**

2.2 Differentiate between Windows Operating System directory structures (Windows 2000, XP, and Vista)

- ▶ User file locations
- ▶ System file locations
- ▶ Fonts
- ▶ Temporary files
- ▶ Program files
- ▶ Offline files and folders

57. You want to retrieve some files from the Desktop and My Documents folder on a Windows XP computer. Where would you find these folders?

- ○ **A.** C:\Users
- ○ **B.** C:\Documents
- ○ **C.** C:\Documents and Settings
- ○ **D.** C:\Windows\System32

Quick Answer: **304**
Detailed Answer: **311**

58. You want to retrieve some files from the Desktop and My Documents folder on a Windows Vista computer. Where would you find these folders?

- ○ **A.** C:\Users
- ○ **B.** C:\Documents
- ○ **C.** C:\Documents and Settings
- ○ **D.** C:\Windows\System32

Quick Answer: **304**
Detailed Answer: **311**

59. Where should a user create a shortcut to a program so that the program starts automatically for every person that logs into the Windows XP computer?

- ○ **A.** Documents and Settings, Programs, Startup, All Users
- ○ **B.** Documents and Settings, All Users, Start Menu, Programs, Startup
- ○ **C.** Documents and Settings, Programs, All Users, Startup
- ○ **D.** Documents and Settings, All Users, Programs, Startup

60. In Windows 2000, what is the system root folder (or the folder where the bulk of the Windows files are located)?

- ○ **A.** `C:\Windows`
- ○ **B.** `C:\WINNT`
- ○ **C.** `C:\WIN`
- ○ **D.** `C:\WIN2000`

61. In Windows XP and Vista, what is the system root folder (or the folder where the bulk of the Windows files are?

- ○ **A.** `C:\Windows`
- ○ **B.** `C:\WINNT`
- ○ **C.** `C:\WIN`
- ○ **D.** `C:\WIN2000`

62. On a computer running 32-bit Windows XP and Vista, where would you find the program files?

- ○ **A.** `C:\WINNT\System32`
- ○ **B.** `C:\Windows\System32`
- ○ **C.** `C:\Program Files`
- ○ **D.** `C:\Program Files (x86)`

63. On a computer running 64-bit Windows XP and Vista, where would you find the 32-bit program files?

- ○ **A.** `C:\WINNT\System32`
- ○ **B.** `C:\Windows\System32`
- ○ **C.** `C:\Program Files`
- ○ **D.** `C:\Program Files (x86)`

64. On a computer running 64-bit Windows XP and Vista, where would you find the 64-bit program files?

- ○ **A.** `C:\WINNT\System32`
- ○ **B.** `C:\Windows\System32`
- ○ **C.** `C:\Program Files`
- ○ **D.** `C:\Program Files (x86)`

Quick Answer: **304**
Detailed Answer: **312**

65. In what folder would you find the font files for a Windows XP or Windows Vista computer?

- ○ **A.** `C:\Fonts`
- ○ **B.** `C:\Program Files\Fonts`
- ○ **C.** `C:\Windows\Fonts`
- ○ **D.** `C:\Windows\System32\Fonts`

Quick Answer: **304**
Detailed Answer: **312**

66. Where does Windows XP store temporary files?

- ○ **A.** `C:\temp`
- ○ **B.** `C:\windows\temp`
- ○ **C.** `C:\temporary`
- ○ **D.** `C:\users\temp`

Quick Answer: **304**
Detailed Answer: **312**

67. Where does Windows Vista store offline files?

- ○ **A.** `C:\Windows\System32`
- ○ **B.** `C:\Windows\CSC`
- ○ **C.** `C:\Temp`
- ○ **D.** `C:\Windows\Temp`

Quick Answer: **304**
Detailed Answer: **312**

68. A user with a user account named PRegan installs a new program on the C: drive of a Windows XP computer. Where would the installation files be cached during installation?

- ○ **A.** `C:\Documents and Settings\PRegan\Application Data`
- ○ **B.** `C:\Documents and Settings\PRegan\Programs Files\Cache`
- ○ **C.** `C:\Documents and Settings\PRegan\Local Settings\Application Data`
- ○ **D.** `C:\Documents and Settings\PRegan\Local Settings\Temp`

Quick Answer: **304**
Detailed Answer: **312**

69. What folder contains application data, such as user preferences, application state, temp files, and so on, for the PRegan account?

   ○ **A.** `C:\Documents and Settings\PRegan\Application Data`

   ○ **B.** `C:\Documents and Settings\PRegan\Programs Files\Cache`

   ○ **C.** `C:\Documents and Settings\PRegan\Local Settings\Application Data`

   ○ **D.** `C:\Documents and Settings\PRegan\Local Settings\Temp`

2.3 Given a scenario, select and use system utilities/tools and evaluate the results

▶ Disk management tools

▶ DEFRAG

▶ NTBACKUP

▶ Check Disk

▶ Disk Manager

▶ Active, primary, extended, and logical partitions

▶ Mount points

▶ Mounting a drive

▶ FAT32 and NTFS

▶ Drive status

▶ Foreign drive

▶ Healthy

▶ Formatting

▶ Active unallocated

▶ Failed

▶ Dynamic

▶ Offline

▶ Online

▶ System monitor

▶ Administrative tools

▶ Event Viewer

▶ Computer Management

▶ Services

▶ Performance Monitor

▶ Devices Manager

▶ Enable

▶ Disable

▶ Warnings

▶ Indicators

▶ Task Manager

▶ Process list

▶ Resource usage

▶ Process priority

▶ Termination

▶ System Information

▶ System restore

▶ Remote Desktop Protocol (Remote Desktop/Remote Assistance)

▶ Task Scheduler

▶ Regional settings and language settings

70. What command would you use to back up Windows XP?

Quick Answer: **304**
Detailed Answer: **312**

- ○ **A.** BACKUP
- ○ **B.** NTBACKUP
- ○ **C.** WINBACKUP
- ○ **D.** XPBACKUP
- ○ **E.** SDCLT

71. What command would you use to back up Windows Vista?

Quick Answer: **304**
Detailed Answer: **312**

- ○ **A.** BACKUP
- ○ **B.** NTBACKUP
- ○ **C.** WINBACKUP
- ○ **D.** XPBACKUP
- ○ **E.** SDCLT

72. Which Windows 2000 utility is designed to enable administrators to configure drives and volumes located in remote computers?

Quick Answer: **304**
Detailed Answer: **313**

- ○ **A.** Hierarchical Storage Manager
- ○ **B.** Volume Manager
- ○ **C.** FDISK.EXE
- ○ **D.** Disk Management

73. Which Windows-native utilities can be used to partition hard disk drives in Windows XP? (Select all that apply.)

- ○ **A.** FORMAT
- ○ **B.** Disk Management
- ○ **C.** Partition Magic
- ○ **D.** DISKPART.EXE

74. How would you create a dynamic volume in Windows 2000 or Windows XP?

- ○ **A.** Convert a FAT32 volume using the Disk Management tool.
- ○ **B.** Convert a primary volume using the Disk Management tool.
- ○ **C.** Convert a basic volume using the Disk Management tool.
- ○ **D.** Convert an extended volume using the Disk Management tool.

75. After you install an 80GB drive in a desktop PC, only 20GB is displayed when the system is started. No extra disk space is shown in Windows Explorer. How can you make use of the rest of the space on the disk without losing data?

- ○ **A.** Use the Disk Manager utility to partition the rest of the disk space on the drive.
- ○ **B.** Use the Device Manager to recalculate the geometry of the disk to use the additional space on the drive.
- ○ **C.** You must back up the data on the disk and reformat it to include the additional space.
- ○ **D.** You must repartition the drive and start over from the beginning.

76. The GPT disk partitioning style supports volumes up to what maximum size?

- ○ **A.** 18 terabytes
- ○ **B.** 36 terabytes
- ○ **C.** 18 exabytes
- ○ **D.** 36 exabytes

77. Which version of Windows does not support the GPT disk partitioning style?

  ○ **A.** Vista Home Premium

  ○ **B.** Vista Home Basic

  ○ **C.** Windows XP Professional

  ○ **D.** Vista Premium

Quick Answer: **304**
Detailed Answer: **313**

78. Which Windows Vista permissions control the access to files and folders stored on disk volumes formatted with the NTFS file system?

  ○ **A.** NTFS permissions

  ○ **B.** Share permissions

  ○ **C.** Registry permissions

  ○ **D.** Active Directory permissions

Quick Answer: **304**
Detailed Answer: **313**

79. What utility creates an image-based backup in which you can only back up and restore entire drives and is designed to protect against catastrophic failures, such as complete hard drive losses?

  ○ **A.** Total PC

  ○ **B.** Back Up Files Wizard

  ○ **C.** System Backup Utility

  ○ **D.** CompletePC

Quick Answer: **304**
Detailed Answer: **313**

80. How many active partitions can you have on a single hard drive?

  ○ **A.** 1

  ○ **B.** 2

  ○ **C.** 3

  ○ **D.** 4

Quick Answer: **304**
Detailed Answer: **313**

81. You have a single hard disk that is formatted with FAT32 and uses the drive letter C. What command would you use to convert the drive to NTFS without loosing data?

  ○ **A.** `format c: /fs:ntfs`

  ○ **B.** `convert c: /fs:ntfs`

  ○ **C.** `fdisk c: /fs:ntfs`

  ○ **D.** `defrag c: -f:ntfs`

Quick Answer: **304**
Detailed Answer: **314**

82. What is an advantage of using dynamic disk instead of basic disks? (Choose two answers.)

Quick Answer: **304**
Detailed Answer: **314**

- ○ **A.** Dynamic disks will automatically grow and shrink as needed.
- ○ **B.** Dynamic disks will automatically fix errors.
- ○ **C.** You can expand volumes on dynamic disks.
- ○ **D.** You can have unlimited number of volumes on dynamic disks.

83. How can you convert a dynamic disk to a basic disk without losing data using Windows utilities or commands?

Quick Answer: **304**
Detailed Answer: **314**

- ○ **A.** Use the Disk Management console.
- ○ **B.** Use the `diskpart` command.
- ○ **C.** Use the `convert` command.
- ○ **D.** Use the `format` command.
- ○ **E.** It cannot be done.

84. You have a logical drive that is filling up quickly. You want to expand the disk by attaching a volume to one of the folders. What can you do?

Quick Answer: **304**
Detailed Answer: **314**

- ○ **A.** Create a mount point
- ○ **B.** Format the folder
- ○ **C.** Partition the folder
- ○ **D.** Convert the folder to a dynamic folder

85. Where would you look to find out what users have successfully logged on to a computer?

Quick Answer: **304**
Detailed Answer: **314**

- ○ **A.** In the System log
- ○ **B.** In Windows log
- ○ **C.** In the Security log
- ○ **D.** In the Application log

86. What would you use to clear the log when you receive an "error log full" message?

Quick Answer: **304**
Detailed Answer: **314**

- ○ **A.** Event Viewer in Administrative Tools
- ○ **B.** System Restore in System Tools
- ○ **C.** Disk Defragmenter in System Tools
- ○ **D.** Disk Management in Computer Management

87. You see an error message but cannot remember the wording. Where can you see the error again?

Quick Answer: **304**
Detailed Answer: **314**

- ○ **A.** In System Information
- ○ **B.** On the Internet
- ○ **C.** In Event Viewer
- ○ **D.** In My Documents

88. A Windows XP Professional workstation has had problems during operation lately. Which of the following applications enables you to review conflicts and problems that have occurred over time?

Quick Answer: **304**
Detailed Answer: **314**

- ○ **A.** Services and Applications
- ○ **B.** AUTOEXEC.BAT
- ○ **C.** CONFIG.SYS
- ○ **D.** Event Viewer

89. If a computer running Windows XP Professional generates a disk error during the system startup operation, which Event Viewer log file should be checked for the error?

Quick Answer: **304**
Detailed Answer: **315**

- ○ **A.** Application
- ○ **B.** Security
- ○ **C.** System
- ○ **D.** Hardware

90. A user boots into Windows 2000 and receives an error message stating that one or more services did not start. Where can she go to examine which services did not start?

Quick Answer: **304**
Detailed Answer: **315**

- ○ **A.** Device Manager
- ○ **B.** Task Manager
- ○ **C.** Dr. Watson
- ○ **D.** Event Viewer

91. In Windows XP, where can you find a standard set of tools for managing the system's disk drives?

Quick Answer: **304**
Detailed Answer: **315**

- ○ **A.** In the Disk Manager snap-in
- ○ **B.** In the Computer Management Console
- ○ **C.** In the Device Manager utility
- ○ **D.** In the Task Manager utility

92. You must configure a service to start automatically when Windows XP boots up. Which of the following should you use?

Quick Answer: **304**
Detailed Answer: **315**

- ○ **A.** The Computer Desktop applet in Administrative Tools
- ○ **B.** The Services applet in Administrative Tools
- ○ **C.** The Folder Options applet in Control Panel
- ○ **D.** The System applet in Control Panel

93. In Windows Vista, what is a cache of trusted inbox and third-party device drivers that is located on the hard drive of each computer?

Quick Answer: **304**
Detailed Answer: **315**

- ○ **A.** Driver directory
- ○ **B.** Driver store
- ○ **C.** Driver cache
- ○ **D.** Hardware cache

94. In Windows Vista, what is the path where the driver store can be located?

Quick Answer: **304**
Detailed Answer: **315**

- ○ **A.** `%SystemRoot%\System32\DriverStore`
- ○ **B.** `%SystemRoot%\System32\DriverStore\ FileRepository`
- ○ **C.** `%SystemRoot%\System\DriverStore`
- ○ **D.** `%SystemRoot%\System\DriverStore/ FileRepository`

95. Which method can you use to disable a device in Device Manager?

Quick Answer: **304**
Detailed Answer: **315**

- ○ **A.** Select the device and choose Disable from the Action menu
- ○ **B.** Right-click the device and choose Disable from the context menu
- ○ **C.** Open the device's Properties sheet and click the Disable button on the Driver tab
- ○ **D.** All of the options provided are correct

96. What MMC snap-in lists all hardware devices in the computer and indicates problems with hardware identification or driver configuration?

Quick Answer: **304**
Detailed Answer: **315**

- ○ **A.** Device MMC
- ○ **B.** Device Controller
- ○ **C.** Local Device Policy
- ○ **D.** Device Manager

97. When looking at the devices in the Device Manager, what indicates a device that is disabled?

- ○ **A.** Black exclamation point (!)
- ○ **B.** Red X
- ○ **C.** Blue "i"
- ○ **D.** Yellow question mark (?)

98. When looking at the devices in the Device Manager, what indicates a device that is having a problem?

- ○ **A.** Black exclamation point (!)
- ○ **B.** Red X
- ○ **C.** Blue "i"
- ○ **D.** Yellow question mark (?)

99. When looking at the devices in the Device Manager, what indicates a device has been manually configured?

- ○ **A.** Black exclamation point (!)
- ○ **B.** Red X
- ○ **C.** Blue "i"
- ○ **D.** Yellow question mark (?)

100. When looking at the devices in the Device Manager, what indicates an unknown device?

- ○ **A.** Black exclamation point (!)
- ○ **B.** Red X
- ○ **C.** Blue "i"
- ○ **D.** Yellow question mark (?)

101. In Windows Vista, what MMC snap-in provides a real-time view of your computer's performance?

- ○ **A.** Reliability and Performance Monitor
- ○ **B.** Performance Enhancer
- ○ **C.** Task Manager
- ○ **D.** Current Stats

102. What tool displays hundreds of different statistics (called performance counters) and allows you to create a customized graph containing any statistics you choose?

- ○ **A.** Performance Enhancer
- ○ **B.** Task Manager

○ **C.** Performance Monitor

○ **D.** Performance Console

103. What program or utility allows you to view which program is consuming the bulk of your memory or processor?

○ **A.** Device Manager

○ **B.** Task Manager

○ **C.** Computer Management console

○ **D.** Services console

104. What program would you use to terminate a running program?

○ **A.** Device Manager

○ **B.** Task Manager

○ **C.** Computer Management console

○ **D.** Services console

105. What is the proper path to activate the Windows XP System
Restore Wizard?

○ **A.** Start/All Programs/Administrative
Tools/Backup/System Restore

○ **B.** Start/All Programs/Administrative
Tools/System Restore

○ **C.** Start/All Programs/Accessories/System
Tools/System Restore

○ **D.** Start/All Programs/Backup/System
Restore

106. Before installing a new software program on your supervisor's
Windows XP Professional computer, you think it wise to establish
a Restore Point that you can return to in case something goes
wrong with the installation. Where do you set up a Restore Point
in Windows XP Professional?

○ **A.** Control Panel/Administrative
Tools/System Restore

○ **B.** Control Panel/System/System Restore

○ **C.** Start/All Programs/Accessories/System
Tools/System Restore

○ **D.** Control Panel/System/Hardware/Device
Manager/System Restore

107. What allows you to connect to a remote computer, chat with the user, and either view all of the user's activities or take complete control of the system?

- ○ **A.** Remote Assistance
- ○ **B.** Terminal Services
- ○ **C.** Remote Desktop
- ○ **D.** CompletePC

Quick Answer: **304**
Detailed Answer: **317**

108. What administrative feature enables users to access computers from remote locations, with no interaction required at the remote site?

- ○ **A.** Remote Assistance
- ○ **B.** Terminal Services
- ○ **C.** Remote Desktop
- ○ **D.** CompletePC

Quick Answer: **304**
Detailed Answer: **317**

109. What command would you use to start remote desktop?

- ○ **A.** REMDESK
- ○ **B.** MSTSC
- ○ **C.** REMOTE
- ○ **D.** TSC

Quick Answer: **304**
Detailed Answer: **317**

110. In Windows XP, where do you find the Remote Desktop Connections program?

- ○ **A.** Start button, All Programs, Accessories
- ○ **B.** Start button, All Programs, Accessories, System Tools
- ○ **C.** Start button, All Programs, Accessories, Communications
- ○ **D.** Start button, All Programs, Accessories, Accessibility

Quick Answer: **304**
Detailed Answer: **317**

111. In Windows Vista, where do you find the Remote Desktop Connections program?

- ○ **A.** Start button, All Programs, Accessories
- ○ **B.** Start button, All Programs, Accessories, System Tools
- ○ **C.** Start button, All Programs, Accessories, Communications
- ○ **D.** Start button, All Programs, Accessories, Accessibility

Quick Answer: **304**
Detailed Answer: **317**

112. Which of the following Windows XP utilities would you use to view, select, and copy characters from any installed font?

   ○ **A.** Character Map

   ○ **B.** System

   ○ **C.** Accessibility Options

   ○ **D.** Regional and Language Options

Quick Answer: **304**
Detailed Answer: **317**

113. You want to change the time format used on your Windows Vista computer so that you can send it to your European office. What would you use?

   ○ **A.** Date and Time

   ○ **B.** System

   ○ **C.** Accessibility Options

   ○ **D.** Regional and Language Options

Quick Answer: **304**
Detailed Answer: **318**

2.4 Evaluate and resolve common issues

▶ Operational problems

▶ Windows-specific printing problems

▶ Print spool stalled

▶ Incorrect/incompatible driver/form printing

▶ Auto-restart errors

▶ Bluescreen error

▶ System lock-up

▶ Devices drivers failure (input/output devices)

▶ Application install, start or load failure

▶ Service fails to start

▶ Error Messages and Conditions

▶ Boot

▶ Invalid boot disk

▶ Inaccessible boot drive

▶ Missing NTLDR

▶ Startup

▶ Device/service failed to start

▶ Device/program in registry not found

▶ Event viewer (errors in the event log)

▶ System Performance and Optimization

▶ Aero settings

▶ Indexing settings

▶ UAC

▶ Side bar settings

▶ Startup file maintenance

▶ Background processes

114. Which of the following is the first step you should take when several documents are stuck in a print queue and they will not print?

- ○ **A.** Clear the print queue
- ○ **B.** Reboot the user's computer
- ○ **C.** Reboot the printer
- ○ **D.** Restart the print spooler

115. You are troubleshooting a printing problem with your production room's dye sublimation printer. When you examine the print queue of the local printer, you see three files in the print queue but nothing is coming out of the printer. What is first step you should take to correct this problem?

- ○ **A.** Cycle the printer's power on and off until the jam clears.
- ○ **B.** Right-click the printer's icon, click Properties, and then select Details. From this point, select Spool Settings and select the Print Directly to the Printer option to bypass the spooler to get your print job.
- ○ **C.** Delete all the files from the print spooler queue and resend your print job to the printer.
- ○ **D.** Double-click the printer's icon and select the Restart option from the Documents menu.

116. If you receive the "Non-system disk or disk error" message, what issue should you start troubleshooting for?

- ○ **A.** A missing operating system where the computer failed to locate a boot sector with an operating system installed
- ○ **B.** A memory size error
- ○ **C.** A missing or malfunctioning keyboard
- ○ **D.** None of the options provided are correct

117. Which of the following are typical indications of a boot process fail situation?

- ○ **A.** An automatic reboot
- ○ **B.** Complete lock-up
- ○ **C.** A blank screen
- ○ **D.** A blue error screen
- ○ **E.** All of the options provided are correct

118. When you receive a "Kernel file is missing from the disk" error message, which of the following DOES NOT apply?

- ○ **A.** The NTLDR.COM file is missing.
- ○ **B.** The NTLDR.COM file can be copied over from a bootable floppy disk to correct the issue.
- ○ **C.** The NTDETECT.COM file can be copied over from a bootable floppy disk to correct the issue.
- ○ **D.** All statements do not apply.

119. Which of the following would cause a Windows XP system not to boot up? (Select all that apply.)

- ○ **A.** A missing or corrupt NTLDR
- ○ **B.** An accidentally deleted CONFIG.SYS file
- ○ **C.** A missing or corrupt BOOT.INI
- ○ **D.** An accidentally deleted AUTOEXEC.BAT file.

120. You have deployed Windows Vista and Microsoft Windows XP Professional in a dual boot configuration for the developers. You need to ensure that the dual-boot computers start Windows XP Professional by default. What should you do?

- ○ **A.** Convert the hard disk that contains the boot partition to a dynamic disk
- ○ **B.** Convert the hard disk that contains the system partition to a dynamic disk
- ○ **C.** Modify the ARC path for default operating system in the BOOT.INI file
- ○ **D.** Use the BCDEDIT.EXE to set the default entry

121. You download and install an application from the Internet on a computer that runs Windows Vista. When you reboot the computer, a blue screen Stop error is displayed and the user is not able to start Windows Vista. What can you do to fix the problem?

- ○ **A.** Boot to the Windows Vista DVD and perform a Startup Repair.
- ○ **B.** Boot into the Windows Recovery Console and type FIXMBR. Reboot Windows Vista.
- ○ **C.** Boot into the Windows Recovery Console and type FIXBOOT. Reboot Windows Vista.
- ○ **D.** Edit the Boot.ini file and add the Advanced RISC Computing (ARC) path that points to the Windows Vista location.

122. You load a custom video driver from the Internet. You install the driver in the computer and restart the computer. After the restart, the computer performs poorly. You need to change back to what you had before. What is the best way to do this?

- ○ **A.** Use the Device Manager window to roll back the driver for the monitor.
- ○ **B.** Use the Device Manager window to roll back the driver for the graphics card.
- ○ **C.** Delete the VGA.DRV file from the \Windows\System32 folder and restart the computer.
- ○ **D.** Delete any occurrences of Device=video.sys in the Autoexec.nt file in the \Windows\System32 folder.

123. What procedure uninstalls the current driver and reinstalls the previous version, returning the device to its state before you performed the most recent driver update?

- ○ **A.** Retroactive Device Management
- ○ **B.** Roll Back Driver
- ○ **C.** Uninstall Driver
- ○ **D.** Kick Back Driver

124. During the boot process, your computer stalls and produces a blue screen displaying the words NTLDR missing. Which of the following best fixes this problem?

- ○ **A.** Boot to the Advanced Options menu and start the system in Last Known Good Configuration
- ○ **B.** Boot to Safe Mode and run the Roll Back feature from the Device Manager
- ○ **C.** Boot to the Windows distribution CD and use the Recovery Console's FIXMBR command to replace the master boot record (MBR)
- ○ **D.** Boot to Safe Mode and run the MSCONFIG utility

125. Which of the following is the file that guides the Windows 2000/XP boot process?

- ○ **A.** NTIO.SYS
- ○ **B.** NTLDR.EXE
- ○ **C.** NTBOOT.SYS
- ○ **D.** BOOTSECT.DOS

126. What is the purpose of the NTBOOTDD.SYS file in the Windows 2000 operating system?

Quick Answer: **305**
Detailed Answer: **319**

- ○ **A.** It enables SCSI hardware during the Windows 2000 boot process.
- ○ **B.** It detects hardware during the Windows 2000 boot process.
- ○ **C.** It configures PATA hard drives during the Windows 2000 boot process.
- ○ **D.** It creates the Emergency Repair Disk (ERD) during the installation process.

127. You deploy Windows Vista on your computer and discover that kernel32.dll is corrupt. You need to repair kernel32.dll without checking any other system file. Which command should you run?

Quick Answer: **305**
Detailed Answer: **319**

- ○ **A.** SFC /SCANNOW
- ○ **B.** SFC /VERIFYONLY
- ○ **C.** SFC /SCANFILE = C:\WINDOWS\SYSTEM32\ KERNEL32.DLL
- ○ **D.** SFC /VERIFYFILE = C:\WINDOWS\SYSTEM32\ KERNEL32.DLL

128. You upgrade a computer from Microsoft Windows XP Professional to Windows Vista. A user is unable to use the Windows Aero theme. You verify that the computer meets the hardware requirements for Windows Aero. You discover that the problem is due to device driver incompatibility. You need to ensure that the user can use the Windows Aero theme on the computer. What should you do?

Quick Answer: **305**
Detailed Answer: **319**

- ○ **A.** Uninstall the display adapter driver
- ○ **B.** Install an additional display adapter
- ○ **C.** Roll back the display adapter driver to a previous version
- ○ **D.** Update the display adapter driver to Windows Vista Display Driver Model

129. You tried to deploy an application but the application requires more space than was on your C: drive. What can you do to change the location of the temp folder?

Quick Answer: **305**
Detailed Answer: **319**

- ○ **A.** Modify the TEMP environment variable.
- ○ **B.** Add the SET TEMP command to autoexec.nt
- ○ **C.** Move C:\Windows\Temp to the new disk.
- ○ **D.** Move %userprofile%\Appdata\Local\Temp to the new disk.

130. You install a new video adapter on a computer that runs Windows Vista. The video adapter supports the Windows Aero interface. However, the bitmap images appear blurred on the screen. What should you do?

- ◯ **A.** Decrease the hardware acceleration level
- ◯ **B.** Set the Colors drop-down list box to Medium (16 bit)
- ◯ **C.** Set the Screen resolution drop-down list box to 800 × 600
- ◯ **D.** Set the Appearance setting to Windows Vista Basic

131. You accidentally change hardware and service startup settings in the registry on a computer that runs Windows Vista. You cannot successfully restart the computer. What can you do to fix this problem?

- ◯ **A.** Start the computer by using the Enable Low-Resolution Video (640×480) option.
- ◯ **B.** Start the computer by using the Debugging Mode option.
- ◯ **C.** Boot into the Windows Recovery Console and type Fixboot. Reboot Windows Vista.
- ◯ **D.** Start the computer by using the Last Known Good Configuration (advanced) option.

132. Which of the following modes would you use to load only basic files and drivers (mouse, monitor, keyboard, mass storage, base video, default system services, and no network connections) with the requirement that the mode will not save to the last known configuration when you successfully log on?

- ◯ **A.** Recovery mode
- ◯ **B.** Recovery console mode
- ◯ **C.** DOS mode
- ◯ **D.** Safe mode

133. What mode starts Windows in 640×480 mode by using the current video driver (not Vga.sys) that can be used to configure a display when the monitor cannot be seen during the normal startup mode?

- ◯ **A.** Enable VGA mode
- ◯ **B.** Last Known Good Configuration
- ◯ **C.** Debugging mode
- ◯ **D.** Enable Boot Logging

134. What mode starts Windows in 640×480 mode by using the current video driver (not Vga.sys) that can be used to configure a display when the monitor cannot be seen during the normal startup mode?

Quick Answer: **305**
Detailed Answer: **320**

- ○ **A.** Enable VGA mode
- ○ **B.** Last Known Good Configuration
- ○ **C.** Debugging mode
- ○ **D.** Enable Boot Logging

135. You boot Windows normally until the device or driver that is causing a problem either crashes the system or finishes starting up but causes an error message in the Event Log. You then reboot in Safe mode and review the log file named ntbootlog.txt file to view the boot errors. What mode does this describe?

Quick Answer: **305**
Detailed Answer: **321**

- ○ **A.** Enable VGA mode
- ○ **B.** Last Known Good Configuration
- ○ **C.** Debugging mode
- ○ **D.** Enable Boot Logging

136. What methods can you use to back up the entire registry? (Choose two answers.)

Quick Answer: **305**
Detailed Answer: **321**

- ○ **A.** Back up the System State using an NTBackup
- ○ **B.** COPY command
- ○ **C.** Control Panel
- ○ **D.** Use System Restore to create a snapshot

137. Your friend uses Windows Vista and has a handy calendar that came with Windows Vista on his desktop. How can you add the calendar on your desktop?

Quick Answer: **305**
Detailed Answer: **321**

- ○ **A.** Add the Slideshow gadget to Windows Sidebar
- ○ **B.** Install Microsoft Excel from the Office Suite
- ○ **C.** Add the Calendar gadget to Windows Sidebar
- ○ **D.** Launch Windows Meeting Space

138. Which of the following actions writes a new boot sector into the system volume?

Quick Answer: **305**
Detailed Answer: **321**

- ○ **A.** Running the ASR Restore operation
- ○ **B.** Running the Diagnostic Startup option from the Startup tab of the MSCONFIG utility
- ○ **C.** Running the FIXBOOT command from the Recovery Console's command line
- ○ **D.** Running the SYS C: command from the Windows command interpreter

Quick-Check Answer Key

1. B	30. B	59. B	88. D
2. C	31. C	60. B	89. C
3. C	32. B	61. A	90. D
4. D	33. C	62. C	91. B
5. D	34. A	63. D	92. B
6. B	35. C	64. C	93. B
7. B	36. C	65. C	94. B
8. B	37. D	66. B	95. D
9. C	38. A	67. B	96. D
10. B	39. B	68. D	97. B
11. C	40. B	69. C	98. A
12. B	41. A	70. B	99. C
13. A and D	42. B	71. E	100. D
14. B	43. B	72. D	101. A
15. B	44. C	73. B and D	102. C
16. A	45. C	74. C	103. B
17. C	46. B	75. A	104. B
18. A	47. B	76. C	105. C
19. C	48. C	77. C	106. C
20. B	49. A	78. A	107. A
21. D	50. A, C, and D	79. D	108. C
22. A	51. D	80. A	109. B
23. D	52. C	81. B	110. A
24. C	53. A and D	82. C and D	111. A
25. B	54. A	83. E	112. A
26. B	55. B	84. A	113. D
27. B	56. A	85. C	114. D
28. A	57. C	86. A	115. D
29. A	58. A	87. C	116. A

117. E	**123.** B	**129.** A	**134.** A
118. C	**124.** C	**130.** A	**135.** D
119. A and C	**125.** B	**131.** D	**136.** A and D
120. D	**126.** A	**132.** D	**137.** C
121. A	**127.** C	**133.** A	**138.** C
122. A	**128.** D		

Answers and Explanations

1. **Answer: B.** MSCONFIG starts the System Configuration Utility which can show what is in the SYSTEM.INI, WIN.INI and BOOT.INI (although this varies by operating system), what services are configured, and what programs start when Windows is loaded. The CHKDSK command (Answer A) is used to look for and fix disk errors. The IPCONFIG command (Answer C) is used to display the IP configuration. The EDIT command (Answer D) starts a DOS-based text editor.

2. **Answer: C.** The MSCONFIG.EXE tool can be used to manage a computer system's configuration. REGEDIT.EXE (Answer A) is used to modify the Windows registry. SCANREG.EXE (Answer B) is Windows Registry Checker tool found in older versions of Windows. MSCONFIG.EXE (Answer C) is the Windows System Configuration tool used to enable and disable start up programs and services. The Disk Management program (Answer D) is used to manage disks/volumes.

3. **Answer: C.** To display a list of files and subdirectories in a directory, you need to use the dir command at the command prompt. The chkdsk command (Answer A) checks for disk errors. The ls command (Answer B) is used to list files and subdirectories in Linux. msconfig (Answer D) is the Windows System Configuration tool used to enable and disable start up programs and services.

4. **Answer: D.** The CMD command starts a new instance of the Windows command interpreter, which essentially opens a command prompt. The CMDPROMPT (Answer B) and COMMANDPROMPT (Answer C) commands do not do anything. Entering C:\ (Answer A) will open the root folder of the C: drive.

5. **Answer: D.** To display the short names generated for non-8dot3 file names, you should use the /X option with the DIR command. The /B option (Answer A) uses bare format with no heading information or summary. The /C option (Answer B) displays the thousand separator in file sizes. The /Q option (Answer C) displays the owner of the file.

6. **Answer: B.** The /P option pauses after each full screen of information. The /W option (Answer A) is for wide list format. The /B option (Answer C) uses bare format with no heading information or summary. The /X option (Answer D) is used to display the short names generated for non-8dot3 file names.

7. **Answer: B.** The /O option specifies a sorted order. Therefore, when you use /ON, it will sort by name (alphabetical). The /OD option (Answer A) will sort by date and time. The /Q option (Answer C) will display the owner of the files. The /AD option (Answer D) will only show the subdirectories.

8. **Answer: B.** The /A option displays files with specified directories. Therefore, the /AD option displays files with the directory attribute. The /OD option (Answer A) will sort by date and time. The /B option (Answer C) uses bare format with no heading information or summary. The /X option (Answer D) is to display the short names generated for non-8dot3 file names.

9. **Answer: C.** The /A option displays files with specified directories. Therefore, the /AH option displays files with the hidden attribute. The /OD option (Answer A) will sort by date and time. The /AD option (Answer B) displays the files with the directory attribute. The /ON option (Answer D) displays the listing in alphabetical order.

10. **Answer: B.** The CHKDSK command checks a disk and displays a status report. If you execute CHKDSK from a command prompt in the C: drive, it will check the C: drive. If you want to specify the D: drive, you will execute the CHKDSK D:. The FIXDISK (Answer A), CHECKDISK command, (Answer C) and DIR /CH (Answer D) are not valid commands.

11. **Answer: C.** Without the /F option, the CHKDSK command will only look for errors but will not fix them. The /R option (Answer B) locates bad sectors and recovers readable information. The /FIX (Answer A) and /FIXDISK options (Answer D) are not valid.

12. **Answer: B.** The /R option locates bad sectors and recovers readable information. When you execute the /R command, the /F option is implied. The /FIX (Answer A), /SCANDISK (Answer C) and /FIXDISK (Answer D) options are not valid.

13. **Answer: A and D.** To open a DOS-based text editor, you execute the EDIT command. To open a Windows-based text editor, you execute the NOTEPAD command. MSCON-FIG (Answer B) is the Windows System Configuration tool used to enable and disable start-up programs and services. The /E option (Answer C) is not a valid option for the DIR command.

14. **Answer: B.** The COPY command copies one or more files to another location. The DISKCOPY (Answer A) command is used to copy floppy disks. The FORMAT command (Answer C) is used to prepare a volume with a file system. The SHADOW COPY command(Answer D) is a technology used with backups that allows you to back up a volume or files by using a snapshot.

15. **Answer: B.** You can modify the performance of various commands by placing one or more software switches at the end of the basic command. You add a switch to the command by adding a forward slash (/) and one or more letters that define how the command is to be implemented. Placing a question mark after the slash produces a list of switch options that can be used with the command. The ? (Answer A), * (Answer C), and /Help (Answer D) options are not valid options with the COPY command.

16. **Answer: A.** When you use the COPY command, you always follow the command source target format. Therefore the other answers are incorrect.

17. **Answer: C.** The /V option verifies that the new files are written correctly. The /A (Answer A) option indicates an ASCII text file. /B (Answer B) is used to copy a binary file. The /N option (Answer D) uses short filenames.

18. **Answer: A.** The /A option indicates an ASCII text file. The /B option (Answer B) indicates a binary file. /V (Answer C) verifies that new files are written correctly. The /N options (Answer D) use short filenames.

19. **Answer: C.** The XCOPY command copies all the files and directories (except hidden and system files) from the source drive (or location) to the destination drive (or location). The /s switch instructs the XCOPY command to copy directories and subdirectories. Similarly, the XCOPY /e command copies files, directories, and subdirectories, including the empty ones. The /S option (Answer A) does not copy empty folders. The /H option (Answer B) also copies hidden and system files. The /CMDLINE (Answer D) option is not a valid option for the XCOPY command.

20. **Answer: B.** To specify only files that have the txt extension, you use a wildcard for the filename. The * wildcard means all characters. Therefore the other answers are incorrect.

21. **Answer: D.** When you use a switch with the command prompt, it will specify to the command what option or options it is supposed to perform. Therefore, the other answers are incorrect.

22. **Answer: A.** CLS is the command-line utility used to clear the command prompt window. The REM command (Answer B) is short for Remarks. It is used in batch files to disable a line within the batch file from executing. The CD command (Answer C) is used to change directories. The dir command (Answer D) is used to list files and folders.

23. **Answer: D.** /? is the common switch that displays a list of switches that are used with a command. The /HELP (Answer A), /* (Answer B), and /H (Answer C) options are invalid options.

24. **Answer: C.** In Windows XP, the DISKPART command is used to execute disk management tasks from a command line. This includes creating and managing disk partitions. The FORMAT command prepares a disk with a file system. The FDISK command (Answer A) is an older DOS-based command to partition a disk. The DISKPERF command (Answer D) is not a valid command.

25. **Answer: B.** The FORMAT command will format a disk at the command prompt. The convert command (Answer A) is used to convert from FAT or FAT32 to NTFS. The FDISK command (Answer C) is an older DOS-based command used to partition a disk. The DISKPERF command (Answer D) is not a valid command.

26. **Answer: B.** When you format a disk, you most likely need to tell it what file system you want to use. Therefore, you need to specify /FS:NTFS if you want the NTFS file system. Answer A does not specify a specific file system. /FS (Answer C) and /NTFS (Answer D) are invalid options. The /X option (Answer E) forces the volume to dismount first if necessary.

27. **Answer: B.** When you want to perform a quick format that takes only seconds to perform, you can use the /Q option, which quickly erases the file allocation table so that it looks like a new drive. The FORMAT command will operate with just the /FS option (Answer A) or the /VOLUME (Answer C) option. The /X option (Answer D) forces the volume to dismount first if necessary.

28. **Answer: A.** The /Y command suppresses prompting to confirm that you want to overwrite an existing destination file. The /-Y option (Answer B) generates a prompt to
confirm you want to overwrite an existing destination file. The /V option (Answer C)
verifies the new files are written correctly. The /D option (Answer D) allows the destination file to be created decrypted.

29. **Answer: A.** The DEL command is used to delete one or more files. The REMOVE command (Answer B) is an invalid command. The CHKDSK command (Answer C) is used
to find disk errors. Without using the proper switches, the CHKDSK command will
only find errors but will not fix the errors. The EDIT command (Answer D) starts a
DOS-based text editor.

30. **Answer: B.** When you use the /P switch, it prompts for confirmation before deleting
each file. The /Q option (Answer C) specifies quiet mode, which does not ask if it is
okay to delete all files specified when using the global wildcard. The /F option forces
(Answer D) the deleting of read-only files. The /PROMPT option (Answer A) is invalid.

31. **Answer: C.** The /S option deletes specified files from all directories. The /P option
(Answer A) prompts for confirmation before deleting each file. The /F option (Answer
B) forces the deleting of read-only files. The /Q option (Answer D) is quiet mode, which
does not ask if it is okay to delete all files specified when using the global wildcard.

32. **Answer: B.** To force deleting read-only files, you use the /F option. The /P option
(Answer A) prompts for confirmation before deleting each file. The /Q option (Answer
D) is quiet mode that does not ask if it is okay to delete all files specified when using the
global wildcard. The /S option (Answer C) deletes specified files from all subdirectories.

33. **Answer: C.** The IPCONFIG command displays the IP configuration of a Windows
computer, including the current IP address, subnet mask, and default gateway. The
CHKDSK command (Answer A) is used to find and fix disk errors. The NSLOOKUP
command (Answer B) is used to test DNS name resolution. The MSCONFIG command
(Answer D) is used to enable or disable programs and services loaded during bootup.

34. **Answer: A.** To show the IP configuration, including the current IP address, subnet
mask, default gateway, and DNS and WINS servers used by the client, you use the
IPCONFIG /ALL command. The /RENEW option (Answer B) is used to renew the IP
address assigned by a DHCP server. The /FLUSHDNS option (Answer D) is used to
flush the DNS cache of a local machine. The /DNS option (Answer C) is not valid.

35. **Answer: C.** To renew the IP address you need to use the /RENEW option with the
IPCONFIG command. The /ALL option (Answer D) shows the IP configuration
including showing the current IP address, subnet mask, default gateway and DNS and
WINS servers used by the client. The MSCONFIG command (Answer A) is used to
enable or disable programs and services loaded during boot up. RENEWIP (Answer B)
is not a valid command.

36. **Answer: C.** To release the DHCP address assigned to an adapter, you would use the
/RELEASE command. The /ALL option (Answer D) shows the IP configuration,
including the current IP address, subnet mask, default gateway, and DNS and WINS
servers used by the client. The MSCONFIG command (Answer A) is used to enable or
disable programs and services loaded during bootup. RENEWIP (Answer B) is not a
valid command.

37. **Answer: D.** The /FLUSHDNS option purges the DNS Resolve cache from the local host. The /RELEASE option (Answer A) releases the DHCP address assigned to an adapter. The /RENEW option (Answer B) is used to renew the DHCP address lease assigned to a network adapter. The /REGISTERDNS option (Answer C) refreshes all DHCP leases and re-registers the DNS name.

38. **Answer: A.** PING is used to test connectivity between two hosts using the IP address of the remote hosts. The ARP -A command (Answer B) shows the address resolution protocol (ARP) cache. ARP shows the IP to Physical address. The WINIPCFG command (Answer D) is used on Windows 9X. The IPCONFIG /ALL option (Answer C) shows the IP configuration, including the current IP address, subnet mask, default gateway, and DNS and WINS servers used by the client.

39. **Answer: B.** The loopback address is 127.0.0.1. Therefore to ping the loopback, you would ping 127.0.0.1. The other answers are incorrect.

40. **Answer: B.** PING is used to test connectivity between two networked computers using the hostname or the IP address of the remote computer. If the hostname is known, PING first uses DNS to resolve the hostname to its IP address. The ARP command (Answer C) is used to show the address resolution protocol (ARP) cache. ARP shows the IP to Physical address. WINIPCFG (Answer D) is an IP configuration utility found on Windows 9X machines. The IPCONFIG command (Answer A) is used to display IP configuration information. /SERVER01 is an invalid option for the IPCONFIG command.

41. **Answer: A.** The -T option pings the specified host until it is stopped. The -A option (Answer B) is used to resolve addresses to hostnames. The -F option (Answer C) is used to set the Don't Fragment flag in a packet. The -W option (Answer D) is the time-out in milliseconds to wait for each reply.

42. **Answer: B.** The ARP utility is useful for resolving duplicate IP addresses. The ARP -A command displays the local ARP table that lists the IP address to MAC address mappings. The PING command (Answer A) is used to test network connectivity. The IPCONFIG command (Answer C) is used to display IP configuration information. The WINIPCFG command (Answer D) is the IP configuration command for Win9X machines.

43. **Answer: B.** To create a new folder, you use the MD command. CD (Answer A) is short for change directory. The RD command (Answer C) is used to remove an empty folder. The DIR command (Answer D) displays the directory listing.

44. **Answer: C.** To remove or delete a directory you use the RD command. CD (Answer A) is short for change directory. The DIR command (Answer D) displays the directory listing. The MD command (Answer B) is used to create directories.

45. **Answer: C.** Using the /S option with the RD command removes all directories and files in the specified directory in addition to removing the directory itself. In other words, it is used to remove a directory tree. The /Q option (Answer A) is quiet mode, which does not ask whether it is okay to remove a directory tree with the /S option. The /ALL (Answer B) and /RECURRENT (Answer D) options are invalid.

46. **Answer: B.** The NET START command can be used to start any service that is available on a Windows host. The NET USE (Answer C) command is used to map a shared folder to a driver. IPCONFIG SERVER (Answer A) and SFS SERVER (Answer D) are invalid commands.

47. **Answer: B.** The `NET STOP` command can be used to stop a service that is running on a Windows host. `NET ST` (Answer A) and `SHOW` (Answer C) are invalid options. The `NET USE` command (Answer D) is used to map a network drive or folder to a driver letter.

48. **Answer: C.** To map a network drive to the G: drive, you use the `NET USE` command. The `NET START` command (Answers A and B) is used to start services. The `CONNECTTO` option (Answer D) is an invalid.

49. **Answer: A.** The `DEFRAG` command can start the defrag program that optimizes a disk for better performance. The `FDISK` command (Answer B) is used to partition a drive in DOS. The `SCANDISK` (Answer C) and `CHKDSK` (Answer D) commands are used to find and fix disk errors.

50. **Answer: A, C, and D.** `DEFRAG /?`, `DEFRAG /H`, and `DEFRAG /HELP` display a list of switches that are used with the `DEFRAG` command. The list includes the correct switch that allows the technician to force defragmentation even though the free space on the hard disk is low. The `-f` option (Answer B) forces defragmentation of the volume when free space is low.

51. **Answer: D.** The `TRACERT` command is used to test connectivity to a host. Different from `PING`, it shows all connections or hops between the source and destination. The `PING` command (Answer B) is used to test network connectivity. The `NETSTAT` command (Answer C) displays protocol statistics and current TCP/IP network connections. The `ARP` command (Answer A) displays and modifies the IP-to-Physical address translation tables used by Address Resolution Protocol (ARP).

52. **Answer: C.** `NSLOOKUP` allows you to query a DNS server for DNS resolution. For example, if you want to resolve the IP address of a host, you can use type `NSLOOKUP HOSTNAME`. The `IPCONFIG` command (Answer A) is used to display IP configuration information. The `ARP` command (Answer B) displays and modifies the IP-to-Physical address translation tables used by address resolution protocol (ARP). The `NBTSTAT` command is used to resolve NetBIOS names to IP addresses using NBT (NetBIOS over TCP/IP) (Answer D).

53. **Answer: A and D.** `PING` (Answer A) enables you to verify connections to remote hosts. You can use the command to test both the name and IP address of the remote unit. `NSLOOKUP` (Answer D) is a TCP/IP utility found in Windows 2000, Windows XP, and Windows Vista that can be entered at the command prompt to query Internet (DNS) name servers for information about hosts and domains. The `NETSTAT` command (Answer B) displays protocol statistics and current TCP/IP network connections. The `ipconfig` command (Answer C) is used to test DNS name resolution.

54. **Answer: A.** The `SFC` command scans the integrity of all protected system files and replaces incorrect versions with correct Microsoft versions. The `/SCANNOW` option scans integrity of all protected system files and repairs files with problems. The `/SCAN` option (Answer C) only scans but does not repair. Dr. Watson (Answer B) is not a command, but it is a program that is an application debugger. The `SCANDISK` command (Answer D) is used to find and fix disk errors.

55. **Answer: B.** The `DEL` command is used to delete files. To specify all files names and all file name extensions, you use `*.*`. The `all` option (Answer A) with the `DEL` command deletes a file called all. The `RD` command (Answer C) is used to remove empty

folders. The SFC command (Answer D) is used to scan the integrity of all protected system files and replace incorrect versions with correct Microsoft versions.

56. **Answer: A.** The CD command displays the name of the current directory or switches to a new directory. The MD command (Answer B) is used to create a subdirectory. The RD command (Answer C) is used to delete an empty folder. The CHKDSK command (Answer D) is used to find and fix disk errors.

57. **Answer: C.** The Documents and Settings folder on a Windows XP computer has an individual folder for each user who has logged into the computer. Underneath these folders, there is a Desktop and My Documents folder that is mapped for each user as they logged in. The C:\Users folder (Answer A) is similar to C:\Documents and Settings but is found on Windows Vista machines. C:\Windows\System32 (Answer D) is a folder that has many of the Windows system programs. C:\Documents (Answer B) is not a Windows-created folder.

58. **Answer: A.** The C:\Users folder on a Windows Vista computer has an individual folder for each user who has logged into the computer. Underneath these folders, there is a Desktop and Documents folder that is mapped for each user as they logged in. C:\Documents and Settings (Answer C) is similar to the C:\Users folder but is found on Windows XP computers. The C:\Windows\System32 (Answer D) is a folder that has many of the Windows system programs. The C:\Documents (Answer B) is not a Windows-created folder.

59. **Answer: B.** The Documents and Settings folder on a Windows XP computer has an individual folder for each user who has logged into the computer. Underneath these folders, there is a Desktop and My Documents folder that is mapped for each user as they logged in. If you create a shortcut in an individual startup folder, when that person logs on, the program automatically starts for that person. The other answers are not valid.

60. **Answer: B.** For Windows 2000, the default Windows folder is C:\WINNT. The C:\Windows folder (Answer A) is the default Windows folder for Windows XP and Vista. C:\WIN (Answer C) and C:\WIN2000 (Answer D) do not have any special meaning in Windows.

61. **Answer: A.** For Windows XP and Vista, the default Windows folder is C:\Windows. For Windows 2000, the default Windows folder is C:\WINNT (Answer B). C:\WIN (Answer C) and C:\WIN2000 (Answer D) do not have any special meaning in Windows.

62. **Answer: C.** By default, the program files folder is C:\Program Files for a 32-bit version of Windows XP and Windows Vista. By default, the program files folder for 32-bit programs is C:\Program Files (x86) (Answer D) for a 64-bit version of Windows XP and Windows Vista. System32 is a system folder (Answers A and B) that contains many of the programs that make up Windows. By default, Windows XP and Windows Vista use C:\Windows.

63. **Answer: D.** By default, the program files folder for 32-bit programs is C:\Program Files (x86) for a 64-bit version of Windows XP and Windows Vista. By default, the program files folder is C:\Program Files (Answer C) for a 32-bit version of Windows XP and Windows Vista. System32 is a system folder (Answers A and B) that contains many of the programs that make up Windows. By default, Windows XP and Windows Vista use C:\Windows.

64. Answer: C. By default, the program files folder for 64-bit programs is `C:\Program Files` for a 64-bit version of Windows XP and Windows Vista. By default, the program files folder for 32-bit programs is `C:\Program Files (x86)` (Answer D) for a 64-bit version of Windows XP and Windows Vista. `System32` is a system folder (Answers A and B) that contains many of the programs that make up Windows. By default, Windows XP and Windows Vista will use `C:\Windows`.

65. Answer: C. The fonts folder for Windows XP and Windows Vista is `C:\Windows\Fonts`. If you need to add fonts, you typically use an install program or you use the Fonts applet in the Control Panel. Therefore, the other answers are incorrect.

66. Answer: B. By default, Windows uses the `C:\windows\temp` folder to store temporary files. You can sometimes manually clear this out (although some of the files might be in use) or use the disk cleanup utility. Therefore, the other answers are incorrect.

67. Answer: B. Windows XP and Windows Vista store offline files in the `C:\Windows\CSC` folder. By default, Windows uses the `C:\windows\temp` folder (Answer D) to store temporary files. The `C:\Windows\System32` folder (Answer A) is used to store many of the Windows system programs. `C:\Temp` (Answer C) can be a temporary folder for some programs as well as installation files or temporary working files.

68. Answer: D. Each user has a temp folder. When you install something, the installation folders are stored in the `Local Settings\Application Data` folder. All of this is in the user's profile folder, which is located under Documents and Settings. Therefore, the other answers are incorrect.

69. Answer: C. The `C:\Documents and Settings\%username%\Local Settings\Application Data\` folder is used by applications to keep track of application states, temp files, and application-specific data such as a custom dictionary for a word processing program. The `C:\Documents and Settings\PRegan\Application Data` folder (Answer A) stores application-specific data on a per-user basis. The `C:\Documents and Settings\PRegan\Programs Files\Cache` folder (Answer B) is not a valid directory path. The `C:\Documents and Settings\PRegan\Local Settings\Temp` folder (Answer D) is used as a temporary folder for installing a program.

70. Answer: B. To back up Windows XP, you use the Windows Backup program, which can be started by executing the `NTBACKUP` command. To back up Windows Vista, you use the Backup Status and Configuration program, which can be started by executing the `SDCLT` command (Answer E). `BACKUP.EXE` is an old DOS backup program. `WINBACKUP` (Answer C) and `XPBACKUP` (Answer D) do not exist with Windows.

71. Answer: E. To back up Windows Vista, you use the Backup Status and Configuration program, which can be started by executing the `SDCLT` command. To back up Windows XP, you use the Windows Backup program, which can be started by executing the `NTBACKUP` command (Answer B). `BACKUP.EXE` (Answer A) is an old DOS backup program. `WINBACKUP` (Answer C) and `XPBACKUP` (Answer D) do not exist with Windows.

72. Answer: D. The Windows 2000/XP Disk Management utility contains a Dynamic Volume Management feature with a user interface that enables administrators to configure drives and volumes located in remote computers. FDISK.EXE (Answer C) is the DOS utility to partition drives. Hierarchical Storage Manager (Answer A) and Volume Manager (Answer B) do not exist with today's version of Windows.

73. Answer: B and D. In Windows 2000 and Windows XP, you perform the disk partitioning function using the Disk Management utility. You can use this utility to partition drives and see the basic layout of the system's disks. DISKPART.EXE is a Windows XP command-line–based disk-partitioning utility used to establish and manage logical structures on a hard disk drive. It is one of Windows XP's disk management tools. You can access it through the Recovery Console. The FORMAT command (Answer A) is used to prepare a volume with a file system. Partition Magic (Answer C) is a third-party program that allows you to partition a drive. It also allows you to resize a partition.

74. Answer: C. Basic volumes are converted to dynamic volumes using the Disk Management tool (follow the path Start/Run, enter DISKMGMT.MSC into the text box, and then click OK). A basic disk is a physical disk that contains partitions, drives, or volumes created with Windows NT 4.0 or earlier operating systems. Dynamic disks can hold only dynamic volumes (not partitions, volumes, or logical drives). Windows 2000 and XP do not support dynamic volumes on portable computers. Therefore, the other answers are incorrect.

75. Answer: A. During the setup procedure, you normally create only the partition that will hold the operating system. In Windows 2000 or Windows XP, it is more efficient to create any additional partitions using the Disk Management utility after the installation has been completed. You can use the Create a New Partition option if the hard disk has existing partitions but also has free (unpartitioned) space. Windows Explorer does not show unpartitioned space on a drive. Therefore, the other answers are incorrect.

76. Answer: C. The GPT disk partitioning style can support up to 18 exabytes, much larger than MBR. Therefore, the other answers are incorrect.

77. Answer: C. GPT is a disk partitioning style that supports larger hard drives, and is supported only by Windows Vista and newer operating systems. Therefore, the other answers are incorrect.

78. Answer: A. To secure files no matter if they are accessed remotely or locally, you use NTFS permissions. Share permissions (Answer B) only protect a system when they are accessed remotely. The registry permissions (Answer C) are used to protect the registry keys. The Active Directory permissions (Answer D) are used to protect the Active Directory objects such as users, computers, and printers.

79. Answer: D. When you perform a CompletePC, you back up everything including all system files and settings and data files. The other answers are invalid.

80. Answer: A. Because the Active Partition is the partition that first boots, you can only have one marked as Active. After it reads the MBR record and partition table, you can then boot from different operating systems on the different partitions or volumes. Therefore, the other answers are incorrect.

81. **Answer: B.** To convert a FAT or FAT32 volume to NTFS, you should use the CONVERT command. The correct syntax for the CONVERT command is CONVERT *drivelet-ter*: /FS:NTFS. The FORMAT command (Answer A) is used to prepare a drive with a file system. The FDISK command (Answer C) is used to partition a disk using DOS. The DEFRAG command (Answer D) is used to optimize a disk for performance.

82. **Answer: C and D.** Dynamic disks can have an unlimited number of volumes. In addition, except for the system volume, you can expand a volume on dynamic disks using free disk space on the same drive or another drive. Therefore, the other answers are invalid.

83. **Answer: E.** After you convert a basic disk to dynamic disks, you cannot change back without deleting it and re-creating it. Therefore, the other answers are incorrect.

84. **Answer: A.** A mount point allows you to attach a volume to an empty NTFS folder. You can only format a volume, not an individual folder (Answer B). You can only partition a disk, not an individual folder (Answer C). You cannot convert a folder to a dynamic folder (Answer D), only disks.

85. **Answer: C.** Assuming auditing is turned on, the security logs will show you who has logged onto a computer. The system logs can be accessed in the Event Viewer, which can be found as part of the Computer Management console. The system log (Answer A) records system events such as when it was shut down. The application logs (Answer D) records events specific to applications. There is no official Windows log (Answer B). Instead on Windows Vista, the Application, Security, and Systems logs are kept in the Windows Logs folder.

86. **Answer: A.** The Windows logs (including system, application, and security logs) can be viewed in the Event Viewer, which can be found as part of the Computer Management console. System Restore (Answer B) is used to restore the system to a restore point. The Disk Defragmenter (Answer C) is used to optimize a disk for performance. Disk Management (Answer D) is used to manage disks and volumes.

87. **Answer: C.** The Event Viewer shows the Windows logs, including the system logs, application logs, and security logs. The Event Viewer can be found as part of the Computer Management console. The System Information (Answer A) tool is a program to see Windows information, including hardware and software settings. The Internet (Answer B) is only good for finding out what an error message means and how to fix the problem shown by the error message. The My Documents folder (Answer D) is used to store individual documents for a user.

88. **Answer: D.** In Windows 2000 and Windows XP, significant events (such as system events, application events, and security events) are routinely monitored and stored. You can view these events through the Event Viewer utility, enabling you to review conflicts and problems that have occurred over time. This tool is located under the Control Panel/Administrative Tools/Computer Management path. The Event Viewer is also available through the Start/Programs (All Programs in XP)/Administrative Tools/Event Viewer path. The AUTOEXEC.BAT (Answer B) and CONFIG.SYS (Answer C) files were boot files used in Windows 9X. Services and Applications (Answer A) is an invalid option.

89. **Answer: C.** In Windows XP systems, access the Event Viewer utility and expand the System node to view the event log of system events, such as loading the networking services. Even if no Desktop is available, you can restart the system in Safe Mode and access the Event Viewer to use this log to isolate the cause of the error. The Application log (Answer A) displays errors with applications. The Security log (Answer B) displays security information assuming auditing is turned on. There is no hardware log file (Answer D).

90. **Answer: D.** In Windows 2000 systems, access the Event Viewer utility and expand the System node to view the event log of system events, such as loading the networking services. Even if no Desktop is available, you can restart the system in Safe Mode and access the Event Viewer to use this log to isolate the cause of the error. Dr. Watson (Answer C) is an application debugging program. The Device Manager (Answer A) is used to manage hardware devices. The Task Manager (Answer B) is used to manage applications and processes, and it allows you to view overall performance of the system.

91. **Answer: B.** The Computer Management/Storage Console provides a standard set of tools for managing the system's disk drives in Windows XP. This includes the Disk Management, Removable Storage, and Disk Defragmenter snap-ins. Disk Manager (Answer A) was the disk management utility provided in Windows NT versions prior to Windows 2000. The Device Manager (Answer C) is used to manage the hardware devices in Windows. The Task Manager (Answer D) is used to manage applications and processes and allows you to view overall performance of the system.

92. **Answer: B.** You can manage all of your services by opening up the Administrative Tools and accessing the Services applet. If you don't have a direct shortcut to the Administrative Tools, they can be accessed through the Control Panel. The Computer Desktop applet (Answer A) does not exist in Administrative Tools or the Control Panel. The Folder Options applet (Answer C) is used to configure how folders appear in Windows Explorer. The System applet (Answer D) allows you to view the processor and amount of memory, view and configure the computer name, configure Remote Desktop and Remote Assistance and virtual memory settings.

93. **Answer: B.** When a driver has been added to Windows, a copy is kept in the driver store. The driver cache (Answer C) is used in Windows XP machines. The other answers are invalid.

94. **Answer: B.** For Windows Vista, the driver store is located in `C:\Windows\System32\DriverStore\FileRepository`. Therefore, the other answers are invalid.

95. **Answer: D.** There are several ways to disable the device driver. Most people will probably right-click the device and choose Disable. The other methods listed also work.

96. **Answer: D.** The Device Manager console is used to manage devices. It can be accessed through the Computer Management console and by opening System Properties. The other answers are invalid.

97. **Answer: B.** A red "X" indicates a disabled device. A disabled device is a device that is physically present in the computer and is consuming resources, but does not have a protected-mode driver loaded. When looking at the Device Manager, a black exclamation point (!) on a yellow field indicates the device is in a problem state (Answer A). A

blue "i" (Answer C) on a white field on a device resource in Computer Properties indicates that the Use Automatic Settings feature is not selected for the device and that the
resource was manually selected. A yellow question mark (?) (Answer D) indicates an
unknown device, which means you still have to load the proper driver for it to operate.

98. **Answer: A.** When looking at the Device Manager, a black exclamation point (!) on a yellow field indicates the device is in a problem state. A red "X" (Answer B) indicates a
disabled device. A disabled device is a device that is physically present in the computer
and is consuming resources but does not have a protected-mode driver loaded. A blue
"i" (Answer C) on a white field on a device resource in Computer Properties indicates
that the Use Automatic Settings feature is not selected for the device and that the
resource was manually selected. A yellow question mark (?) (Answer D) indicates an
unknown device, which means you still have to load the proper driver for it to operate.

99. **Answer: C.** A blue "i" on a white field on a device resource in Computer Properties indicates that the Use Automatic Settings feature is not selected for the device and that the
resource was manually selected. When looking at the Device Manager, a black exclamation point (!) on a yellow field indicates the device is in a problem state (Answer A). A
red "X" (Answer B) indicates a disabled device. A disabled device is a device that is
physically present in the computer and is consuming resources, but does not have a
protected-mode driver loaded. A yellow question mark (?) (Answer D) indicates an
unknown device, which means you still have to load the proper driver for it to operate.

100. **Answer: D.** A yellow question mark (?) indicates an unknown device, which means
you still have to load the proper driver for it to operate. When looking at the Device
Manager, a black exclamation point (!) on a yellow field indicates the device is in a
problem state (Answer A). A red "X" (Answer B) indicates a disabled device. A disabled device is a device that is physically present in the computer and is consuming
resources but does not have a protected-mode driver loaded. A blue "i" (Answer C) on
a white field on a device resource in Computer Properties indicates that the Use
Automatic Settings feature is not selected for the device and that the resource was
manually selected.

101. **Answer: A.** In Windows Vista, you can access the Reliability and Performance Monitor
to view everything that can possibly affect overall performance of the computer,
including looking at the processor, memory, disk, and network performance. A
Reliability and Performance Monitor (Answer A) can be configured to view real-time
computer performance but must be configured to do so. The Performance Enhancer
(Answer B) and Current Stats (Answer D) do not exist.

102. **Answer: C.** The Performance Monitor (Answer C) allows you to specify what performance values you want to watch using several different views, including a graph. The
Task Manager (Answer B) allows you to see real-world performance quickly. The
Performance Enhancer (Answer A) and Performance Console (Answer D) programs do
not exist.

103. **Answer: B.** The Task Manager will show you overall processor, memory and network
statistics and show you how much each running program is using. The Device
Manager (Answer A) is used to manage hardware devices in Windows. The Computer
Management console (Answer C) is a comprehensive MMC console that includes multiple snap-ins to manage Windows. The Services console (Answer D) is used to manage services running in Windows.

104. Answer: B. The Task Manager will show you overall processor, memory, and network statistics and show you how much each running program is using. You can also right-click an application or process and terminate it. The Device Manager (Answer A) is used to manage hardware devices. The Computer Management console (Answer C) is a comprehensive MMC console that includes multiple snap-ins to manage Windows. The Services console (Answer D) is used to manage services running in Windows.

105. Answer: C. To activate the Windows XP System Restore Wizard, navigate the `Start/All Programs/Accessories/System Tools/System Restore` path and then select the `System Restore` option from the menu. The Welcome screen is displayed. After you confirm the Restore Point, the system conducts the roll-back and the system automatically restarts. Therefore, the other answers are incorrect.

106. Answer: C. To activate the Windows XP System Restore utility, navigate the `Start/All Programs/Accessories/System Tools` path and then select the `System Restore` option from the menu. Therefore the other programs are incorrect.

107. Answer: A. Both Remote Assistance and Remote Desktop (Answer C) are great trou-bleshooting tools that allow you to connect to a computer remotely even when you are not in the same building. However, Remote Assistance allows you to interact with a logged-in user but Remote Desktop cannot interact with a user's session. Terminal Services (Answer B) allows you to use Remote Desktop to connect to a server. Different from Remote Desktop, Terminal Services allows multiple connections at the same time. CompletePC (Answer D) is not a valid program in Windows.

108. Answer: C. Both Remote Assistance (Answer A) and Remote Desktop are great trou-bleshooting tools that allow you to connect to a computer remotely even when you are not in the same building. However, Remote Assistance allows you to interact with a logged in user but Remote Desktop cannot interact with a user's session. Terminal Services (Answer B) allows you to use Remote Desktop to connect to a server. CompletePC (Answer D) is not a valid program in Windows.

109. Answer: B. The command to start the Remote Desktop Connections program is `mstsc`, which is short for Microsoft Terminal Services Console. The other answers are not valid commands in Windows and therefore are incorrect.

110. Answer: C. In Windows XP, Remote Desktop Connections can be launched from the Communications folder under Accessories. Therefore, the other answers are incorrect.

111. Answer: A. In Windows Vista, Remote Desktop Connections can be launched from the Accessories folder. Therefore, the other answers are incorrect.

112. Answer: A. The Character Map allows you to view, select, and copy characters from any installed font. This comes in handy when looking at Greek characters or when looking at special characters such as those found in the Wingdings or Webdings fonts. The System applet (Answer B), accessed from the Control Panel, allows you to view processor and amount of memory, configure virtual memory settings, and enable remote desktop and assistance. The Accessibility Options (Answer C) are used to enable certain features that allow a disabled person to use Windows. Regional and Language options (Answer D) are used to change currency, date, and time settings that are specific to a country or region.

113. Answer: D. You can use the Regional and Language options to configure the date, time, currency, and language options. The Date and Time (Answer A) is used to change the date and time. The System applet (Answer B) accessed from the Control Panel allows you to view processor and amount of memory, configure virtual memory settings and enable remote desktop and assistance. The Accessibility Options (Answer C) are used to enable certain features that allow a disabled person to use Windows.

114. Answer: D. Restart the print spooler by opening the Services console, right-clicking the print spooler service, and selecting Restart. Therefore, the other answers are incorrect.

115. Answer: D. If the printer operation stalls during the printing operation, some critical condition must have been reached to stop the printing process (that is, the system was running but stopped). First, access the print spooler's Document menu and try to restart the printer. If the printer still does not print, delete backed-up spool files (.SPL and .TMP) in the `%SystemRoot%\System32\Spool\Printers` directory. Begin by simply deleting the first print job to determine whether it is the source of the problem. If it is, it's likely that the other print jobs will go ahead and print. Unnecessarily deleting other users' print jobs is poor networking etiquette. Therefore, the other answers are incorrect.

116. Answer: A. When the computer fails to locate a boot sector with an operating system installed on any of its disks you have a missing operating system. Therefore, the other answers are incorrect.

117. Answer: E. Each one of the conditions in options A, B, C, and D point to a failed boot process.

118. Answer: C. When you receive the "Kernel file is missing from the disk" error message, you have an NTLDR file missing or corrupt issue. The `NTDETECT.COM` file deals with hardware detection during startup.

119. Answer: A and C. NTLDR is heavily relied upon during the boot process. If it is missing or corrupted, Windows XP will not be able to boot. The `BOOT.INI` file is required for a successful boot on a Windows 2000 or Windows XP computer. Windows XP does not use the `CONFIG.SYS` file (Answer B) or `AUTOEXEC.BAT` file (Answer D) to boot. The `CONFIG.SYS` and `AUTOEXEC.BAT` files are used on Windows 9X machines.

120. Answer: D. Different from Windows 2000 or Windows XP, in Windows Vista you need to use the `BCDEDIT.EXE` command to change which operating system will load on a dual-boot system. To change the dual boot options in Windows 2000 or Windows XP, you modify the ARC path in the `BOOT.INI` file (Answer C). Converting a disk to dynamic disks (Answers A and B) does not reconfigure a computer for dual-boot.

121. Answer: A. To repair Windows Vista, you can boot from the Windows Vista DVD and perform a Startup repair. The Windows Recovery console (Answers B and C) is used in Windows XP machines. The `BOOT.INI` file (Answer D) is found on Windows 2000 and XP machines.

122. Answer: A. Windows XP and Vista have the capability to roll back drivers. This can be a huge timesaver because many people might not know where the previous drivers were obtained. You would not roll back the driver for the graphics card (Answer B) because you changed the monitor driver, not the graphics driver. You should not have to delete a VGA.DRV file (Answer C) to overcome this problem and you should not have to configure the AUTOEXEC.NT file (Answer D).

123. **Answer: B.** Windows XP and Vista have the ability to roll back drivers. This can be a huge time saver because many people may not know where the previous drivers were obtained before. There is no kick back driver (Answer D) or Retroactive Device Management (Answer A) feature or program in Windows. Uninstalling a driver (Answer C) will not restore a driver to its previous version.

124. **Answer: C.** A Missing Operating System error, such as the Missing NTLDR error message, indicates a problem with the master boot record. In Windows 2000 and XP, you can use the Recovery Console's FIXMBR command to replace the master boot record. The Last Known Good Configuration (Answer A) is used to reset a system to the settings that were good when you last logged on. The Roll Back feature (Answer B) is only good if you installed a wrong or bad driver. The MSCONFIG utility (Answer D) is used to configure programs and services that load during boot up.

125. **Answer: B.** The NT Loader program named NTLDR guides the Windows 2000/XP boot process before the Windows operating system takes control. The NTIO.SYS (Answer A) and NTBOOT.SYS (Answer C) does not exist. The BOOTSECT.DOS (Answer D) is used to dual boot a Windows 9X and DOS operating systems.

126. **Answer: A.** If the Windows system employs a SCSI disk drive, a driver file named NTBOOTDD.SYS must be present in the root directory of the system partition. This condition must also be noted in the BOOT.INI file by placing a numerical ID in its SCSI(x) or MULTI(x) locations. When the operating system encounters the MULTI() designator during the boot process, it relies on the PC's BIOS to support the drive, whereas it refers to the NTBOOTDD.SYS driver file to access the boot partition on the SCSI device when a SCSI() designator is encountered. Therefore, the other answers are incorrect.

127. **Answer: C.** The SFC command will repair Windows System files. If you use the SCANFILE option, you can specify a specific file. The /SCANNOW option (Answer A) is used to scan the integrity of all protected system files and repair files with problems when possible. The /VERIFYONLY option (Answer B) will not repair the files if a problem is found. The VERIFYFILE option (Answer D) will only verify a single file and will not repair the file if a problem is found.

128. **Answer: D.** If your system has the minimum requirements for Windows Aero and you cannot start Windows Aero, you need to update the display adapter driver. You don't want to uninstall (Answer A) the one that you currently have and you should not have to replace your adapter (assuming it is on the compatibility list), Answer B. Rolling back a driver (Answer C) will not replace the driver with a good driver unless you replace a good driver with a bad one.

129. **Answer: A.** By modifying the temp environment variable, you can specify a different drive where you have more disk space. You can use the SET TEMP command to temporarily modify the TEMP variable or you can modify it from within the System properties. Therefore, the other answers are incorrect.

130. **Answer: A.** If you are having some video problems, including blurred images, you can try to decrease the hardware acceleration level. You can also check to see if there is a newer driver available. The other answers are incorrect and will not allow Windows Aero to operate.

131. **Answer: D.** If you cannot log on to a computer because of a configuration change, you should try booting to the Last Known Good Configuration where it will copy a previous registry setting. The Enabling VGA mode (Answer A) is only good if you installed a video driver that does not allow you to boot where you can see the screen. The Debugging mode (Answer B) just saves information to a log on the C: drive. The Recovery Console (Answer C) is only available in Windows XP.

132. **Answer: D.** In Safe Mode, you have access to only basic files and drivers (mouse, monitor, keyboard, mass storage, base video, default system services, and no network connections). To enter Safe Mode, you will enter the Advanced Boot menu by pressing F8 during boot up. The Safe Mode with Networking option, which loads all of the above files and drivers and the essential services and drivers to start networking, or you can choose the Safe Mode with Command Prompt option, which is exactly the same as Safe Mode except that a command prompt is started instead of the graphical user interface. You can also choose Last Known Good Configuration, which starts your computer using the registry information that was saved at the last shutdown. There is no Recovery mode (Answer A), but there is a Recovery Console (Answer B) that you can load. Instead of loading the Windows basic files and drivers, it loads its own files to perform recovery commands. There is no DOS mode (Answer C), although there is a Safe Mode with Command Prompt.

133. **Answer: A.** When you use Enable VGA Mode, Windows starts normally except that it starts Windows in 640×480 mode by using the current video driver (not Vga.sys). This mode is useful if the display is configured for a setting that the monitor cannot display. Safe Mode and Safe Mode with Networking load the Vga.sys driver instead. Last Known Good Configuration option (Answer B) starts Windows by using the previous good configuration. Debugging Mode (Answer C) turns on debug mode in Windows. Debugging information can be sent across a serial cable to another computer that is running a debugger. This mode is configured to use COM2. The Enable Boot Logging option (Answer D) turns on logging when the computer is started with any of the Safe Boot options except Last Known Good Configuration. The Boot Logging text is recorded in the Ntbtlog.txt file in the %SystemRoot% folder.

134. **Answer: A.** When you use the Enable VGA Mode, Windows starts normally except that it starts Windows in 640×480 mode by using the current video driver (not Vga.sys). This mode is useful if the display is configured for a setting that the monitor cannot display. Safe Mode and Safe Mode with Networking load the Vga.sys driver instead. Last Known Good Configuration option (Answer B) starts Windows by using the previous good configuration. Debugging Mode (Answer C) turns on debug mode in Windows. Debugging information can be sent across a serial cable to another computer that is running a debugger. This mode is configured to use COM2. The Enable Boot Logging option (Answer D) turns on logging when the computer is started with any of the Safe Boot options except Last Known Good Configuration. The Boot Logging text is recorded in the Ntbtlog.txt file in the %SystemRoot% folder.

135. **Answer: D.** When you enable boot logging, Windows creates a log file that lists every step processed that is attempted and completed. You can then reboot in to Safe Mode and review the log file named ntbootlog.txt. The log is stored in the %SYSTEMROOT% directory (normally `C:\Windows` or `C:\WINNT` folder). When you use the Enable VGA Mode (Answer A), Windows starts normally except that it starts Windows in 640×480 mode by using the current video driver (not Vga.sys). The Last Known Good Configuration option (Answer B) only starts Windows by using the previous good configuration. Debugging Mode (Answer C) turns on debug mode in Windows. Debugging information can be sent across a serial cable to another computer that is running a debugger. This mode is configured to use COM2.

136. **Answer: A and D.** To back up the entire registry, you can back up the System State which includes the Registry, COM+ Class Registration database and the boot files including the system files. You can also use the System Restore to create a System Restore snapshot. If a problem occurs, you can restore to the previous snapshot without affecting personal information such as documents, history lists, favorites, or emails. The COPY command (Answer B) or Control Panel (Answer C) cannot be used to back up the registry.

137. **Answer: C.** The Sidebar application includes a Calendar gadget. It must be added to the Sidebar, and its opacity is adjustable. The Slideshow gadget (Answer A) displays pictures on the Sidebar. Excel (Answer B) is a spreadsheet application and is not included in Windows Vista. Windows Meeting Space (Answer D) is a peer-to-peer collaboration tool used to share and develop content without server infrastructure; it is not a calendar application.

138. **Answer: C.** The Recovery Console's `FIXBOOT` command writes a new boot sector to the system volume. You can run the Recovery Console from the Windows distribution CD. ASR, short for automatic system recovery (Answer A), can restore the system files such as the NTLDR and BOOT.INI file. The Diagnostic Startup option (Answer B) is used to troubleshoot faulty services or start up programs. `SYS C:` (Answer D) is a legacy command to make a DOS disk bootable.

CHAPTER NINE

Networking

The third domain for the 220-702 exam is networking, which counts for 15% of the exam. Although the networking domain for the 220-701 exam focused on networking technologies and protocols, the networking domain for the 220-702 exam focuses on how to install and configure common network components, including configuring Windows to connect to a network, configuring broadband technology, and configuring wireless access points.

The given objectives for this domain of the 220-702 exam are as follows:

▶ 3.1—Troubleshoot client-side connectivity issues using appropriate tools

▶ 3.2—Install and configure a small office home office (SOHO) network

3.1 Troubleshoot client-side connectivity issues using appropriate tools

▶ TCP/IP settings

  ▶ Gateway

  ▶ Subnet mask

  ▶ DNS

  ▶ DHCP (dynamic vs. static)

  ▶ NAT (private and public)

▶ Characteristics of TCP/IP

  ▶ Loopback addresses

  ▶ Automatic IP addressing

▶ Mail protocol settings

  ▶ SMTP

  ▶ IMAP

  ▶ POP

▶ FTP settings

  ▶ Ports

  ▶ IP addresses

  ▶ Exceptions

  ▶ Programs

▶ Proxy settings

  ▶ Ports

  ▶ IP addresses

  ▶ Exceptions

  ▶ Programs

▶ Tools (use and interpret results)

  ▶ Ping

  ▶ Tracert

  ▶ Nslookup

  ▶ Netstat

  ▶ Net use

  ▶ Net /?

  ▶ Ipconfig

  ▶ telnet

  ▶ SSH

▶ Secure connection protocols

  ▶ SSH

  ▶ HTTPS

▶ Firewall settings

  ▶ Open and closed ports

  ▶ Program filters

1. The computer you are working on is able to contact other systems in the local network using TCP/IP. However, it is unable to contact other systems outside the local network. What is the most likely cause of this problem?

   ○ **A.** There is an IP addressing conflict.

   ○ **B.** The default gateway is not configured properly.

   ○ **C.** The DNS service is not configured properly.

   ○ **D.** The DHCP service is not configured properly.

Quick Answer: **345**
Detailed Answer: **346**

2. After a new segment has been set up on the corporate network, one of the users complains that he can access resources on other network PCs but can't access the Internet. What is the most likely cause of this problem?

   ○ **A.** The subnet mask configuration is incorrect.

   ○ **B.** The TCP/IP protocol is not enabled on this machine.

   ○ **C.** The DHCP service is not working.

   ○ **D.** The gateway address is configured incorrectly.

Quick Answer: **345**
Detailed Answer: **346**

3. What will happen if you configure the incorrect subnet mask?

    ○ **A.** You will not be able to connect to the default gateway.

    ○ **B.** You will not be able to connect to all remote hosts.

    ○ **C.** You will not be able to connect to all local hosts.

    ○ **D.** You will not be able to communicate with some local hosts and/or communicate with some remote hosts.

4. You have been sent to troubleshoot an Internet connectivity problem. When you try to ping the site's FQDN, the site cannot be located; however, you can ping its IP address. What network function should be checked?

    ○ **A.** DNS

    ○ **B.** DHCP

    ○ **C.** WINS

    ○ **D.** FTP

5. After statically assigning an IP address and subnet mask to a Windows XP machine, you try to ping the local adapter's IP address, but you receive a Destination Host Unreachable message. What does this indicate?

    ○ **A.** TCP/IP has not been loaded into the system.

    ○ **B.** The local adapter's IP address has not been initialized.

    ○ **C.** TCP/IP is not working on the gateway device.

    ○ **D.** The default gateway is not functional.

6. You have a Windows Vista computer that cannot connect to the network. When you use the `ipconfig` command, you find the following:

    IP address: 169.254.30.25

    Subnet mask: 255.255.0.0

    What is the problem?

    ○ **A.** The 169.254.30.25 address is the incorrect assigned address.

    ○ **B.** The 255.255.0.0 mask should be 255.255.255.0.

    ○ **C.** TCP/IP needs to be bound to the network interface.

    ○ **D.** The computer could not get an address from the DHCP server.

7. You have a network using an IP proxy that provides Network
Address Translation (NAT). You have implemented IPsec for all
Internet-bound traffic. However, Internet access is now no longer
possible. What is likely the cause of this problem?

- ○ **A.** Network Address Translation (NAT) does not work
  with IPsec.
- ○ **B.** The IP proxy is blocking egress and ingress traffic on
  port 80.
- ○ **C.** The IP proxy is blocking egress and ingress traffic on
  port 1293.
- ○ **D.** The IP proxy is blocking egress and ingress traffic on
  port 8080.

8. You received a message saying that "There is an IP Conflict with
another computer on the network." What problem will this cause?

- ○ **A.** One or both of the computers involved in the conflict
  will not be able to communicate on the network.
- ○ **B.** You cannot communicate with local hosts but you can
  communicate with remote hosts.
- ○ **C.** You cannot communicate with remote hosts but you
  can communicate with local hosts.
- ○ **D.** You cannot access corporate resources but can access
  the Internet.

9. Your internal network is assigned the 10.10.45.XX network
addresses with the subnet mask of 255.255.255.0. You try to
place your web server (address is 10.10.45.10) on the Internet so
that it can be accessed by Internet users. However, users still cannot contact the web server. What is the problem?

- ○ **A.** The subnet mask should be 255.255.0.0.
- ○ **B.** 10.10.45.10 is a private address that cannot be used
  to directly communicate on the Internet.
- ○ **C.** You need to make sure that you define the default
  gateway that is on the Internet.
- ○ **D.** You do not have a working DNS server to translate
  names to IP addresses.

10. If you try to ping the loopback address and nothing happens, what
is most likely the problem?

- ○ **A.** TCP/IP is not working on the local machine.
- ○ **B.** The network cable is bad.
- ○ **C.** The network card is disabled.
- ○ **D.** The NIC in the local machine is defective.

11. Generally, whenever a user tells you that her LAN connection is not working, what is the first thing to check?

    Quick Answer: **345**
    Detailed Answer: **347**

    - ○ **A.** Check the network adapter drivers to see that they are configured properly
    - ○ **B.** Ping a known IP address to see whether the network cable and connectivity are good
    - ○ **C.** Check for the presence of link lights on the back of the NIC
    - ○ **D.** Run `ipconfig` to see whether the local network hardware is functioning

12. Which IP address invokes the TCP/IP loopback test function?

    Quick Answer: **345**
    Detailed Answer: **348**

    - ○ **A.** 127.0.0.1
    - ○ **B.** 10.0.0.1
    - ○ **C.** 169.192.0.1
    - ○ **D.** 172.254.0.1

13. A user has called to report that one of the network's printers previously worked, but now it doesn't. When you inspect the printer, you find that its signal and power cables are all connected properly. You can ping the printer's gateway from the user's computer but cannot ping the printer's IP address. What is the most likely cause of this problem?

    Quick Answer: **345**
    Detailed Answer: **348**

    - ○ **A.** The user has a bad network adapter card.
    - ○ **B.** The user has a corrupt NIC driver.
    - ○ **C.** The local network cable is bad.
    - ○ **D.** The TCP/IP protocol has been disabled on the printer.

14. Which of the following pieces of configuration information is not typically needed to configure an account in an email application?

    Quick Answer: **345**
    Detailed Answer: **348**

    - ○ **A.** DNS server name or IP address
    - ○ **B.** Email account name
    - ○ **C.** SMTP server name or IP address
    - ○ **D.** POP3/IMAP server name or IP address

15. You have an email application and you have problems sending emails, but you don't have any problem receiving email. What is most likely the problem?

    Quick Answer: **345**
    Detailed Answer: **348**

    - ○ **A.** SMTP server name or IP address is incorrect.
    - ○ **B.** POP3 server name or IP address is incorrect.
    - ○ **C.** IMAP server name or IP address is incorrect.
    - ○ **D.** DNS server address is incorrect.

16. You have an email application and you have problems receiving email. What is most likely the problem? (Choose two answers.)

Quick Answer: **345**
Detailed Answer: **348**

- ○ **A.** SMTP server name or IP address is incorrect.
- ○ **B.** POP3 server name or IP address is incorrect.
- ○ **C.** IMAP server name or IP address is incorrect.
- ○ **D.** DNS server address is incorrect.

17. You have enabled the Windows Firewall on a computer running Windows Vista. You try to run an FTP program to access an FTP site to download some files. However, you are unable to connect to the site. What do you think the problem is?

Quick Answer: **345**
Detailed Answer: **348**

- ○ **A.** You need to configure the FTP program with a valid DNS server.
- ○ **B.** You need to configure the Windows Firewall to allow FTP.
- ○ **C.** You need to configure the FTP program with the correct default gateway.
- ○ **D.** You need to map port 20 and 21 to FTP using telnet.

18. When configuring the Windows Firewall, what exceptions can you add? (Apply all that apply.)

Quick Answer: **345**
Detailed Answer: **348**

- ○ **A.** Users
- ○ **B.** Groups
- ○ **C.** Programs
- ○ **D.** Ports

19. How do you specify what computers can communicate through the Windows Firewall?

Quick Answer: **345**
Detailed Answer: **348**

- ○ **A.** You can specify the computer host names in the Exception Properties.
- ○ **B.** You can specify the MAC addresses in the Exception Properties.
- ○ **C.** You can specify the scope to specify IP addresses or subnets.
- ○ **D.** You can specify the computer addresses in the exception.txt file.

20. Your company requires going through a proxy server when browsing on the Internet. What should you do so that you can configure Internet Explorer to browse the Internet?

Quick Answer: **345**
Detailed Answer: **348**

- ○ **A.** Open Internet Options, select the Connections tab, and select LAN settings. Then configure the address of the proxy server and port to use.
- ○ **B.** Open Internet Options and select the Content tab. Specify the address of the proxy server and port to use.
- ○ **C.** Open Internet Options and select the Security tab. Then configure the address of the proxy server and port to use.
- ○ **D.** Open the Windows Firewall and specify the address of the proxy server and port to use.

21. When you enter `ipconfig` in the Run dialog box, you momentarily see a black box followed by an immediate return to the normal desktop screen. What is occurring with this command?

Quick Answer: **345**
Detailed Answer: **348**

- ○ **A.** This is a normal response for running a TCP/IP utility from the Run dialog box.
- ○ **B.** The network adapter is bad. Therefore, there is no information for the `ipconfig` utility to return.
- ○ **C.** The local host is not communicating with the client computer. Therefore, there is no information for the `ipconfig` utility to report.
- ○ **D.** The TCP/IP utility has not been configured on the local machine.

22. What command would you use to renew the DHCP IPv4 addresses?

Quick Answer: **345**
Detailed Answer: **349**

- ○ **A.** `ipconfig`
- ○ **B.** `ipconfig /renew`
- ○ **C.** `ipconfig /renew6`
- ○ **D.** `ipconfig /release_and_renew`
- ○ **E.** `ipconfig /registerdns`

23. What command would you use to flush the DNS cache stored on an individual Windows Vista machine?

Quick Answer: **345**
Detailed Answer: **349**

- ○ **A.** `ipconfig`
- ○ **B.** `ipconfig /renew`
- ○ **C.** `ipconfig /renew6`
- ○ **D.** `ipconfig /registerdns`
- ○ **E.** `ipconfig /flushdns`

24. If you want to show IP addresses and their corresponding MAC addresses, what command would you use?

Quick Answer: **345**
Detailed Answer: **349**

- ○ **A.** `ipconfig`
- ○ **B.** `ipconfig /all`
- ○ **C.** `arp`
- ○ **D.** `ping`
- ○ **E.** `tracert`

25. When you start your networked computer, you receive a Duplicate IP Address error message. What action should you take to remove this error?

Quick Answer: **345**
Detailed Answer: **349**

- ○ **A.** Run `ipconfig/relinquish` from the command prompt
- ○ **B.** Run `ipconfig/renew` from the command prompt
- ○ **C.** Run `ipconfig/all` from the command prompt
- ○ **D.** Run `nslookup/release` from the command prompt

26. Which TCP/IP utility can you use to determine whether the network adapter is receiving an IP address?

Quick Answer: **345**
Detailed Answer: **349**

- ○ **A.** `ping`
- ○ **B.** `tracert`
- ○ **C.** `ipconfig`
- ○ **D.** `nbtstat`

27. What command would you use to get the computer to register itself with the DNS server?

Quick Answer: **345**
Detailed Answer: **349**

- ○ **A.** `ipconfig`
- ○ **B.** `ipconfig/renew`
- ○ **C.** `ipconfig/renew6`
- ○ **D.** `ipconfig/release_and_renew`
- ○ **E.** `ipconfig/registerdns`

28. What command can you use to show network connectivity to a computer on a Windows computer?

Quick Answer: **345**
Detailed Answer: **349**

- ○ **A.** `ipconfig`
- ○ **B.** `arp`
- ○ **C.** `ping`
- ○ **D.** `traceroute`

29. You want to assign an address to a computer that will be available on the Internet and it will have the same address for both IPv4 and IPv6. What kind of address is this?

Quick Answer: **345**
Detailed Answer: **349**

- ○ **A.** A unique private address
- ○ **B.** A multicast local address
- ○ **C.** A site-local address
- ○ **D.** A global unicast address

30. You have a user that works between the Sacramento and New York offices. She currently has a static IP address assigned to her computer. When she is at the Sacramento office, her system has no problem connecting to the network. When she travels to New York, her system cannot connect to the network. What is the problem?

Quick Answer: **345**
Detailed Answer: **350**

- ○ **A.** You need to update the drivers for the network card.
- ○ **B.** You need to assign a Public IPv4 address.
- ○ **C.** You need to run the troubleshooting wizard.
- ○ **D.** Within the TCP/IPv4 Properties dialog box, you need to select the Obtain an IP Address Automatically option.

31. You have two computers with Microsoft Windows XP that have the same IP address, resulting in an IP conflict. Which command can you use to identify the conflicting computers?

Quick Answer: **345**
Detailed Answer: **350**

- ○ **A.** `ping`
- ○ **B.** `arp -a`
- ○ **C.** `ipconfig /all`
- ○ **D.** `winipcfg /all`

32. You cannot reach a website called website1 on your intranet but you can ping the Web server by the host name. What is most likely the problem?

Quick Answer: **345**
Detailed Answer: **350**

- ○ **A.** HTTP on the workstation is down.
- ○ **B.** The DHCP server is down.
- ○ **C.** The DNS server is down.
- ○ **D.** The web server is down.

33. How can a user access a website when his DNS server is down?

Quick Answer: **345**
Detailed Answer: **350**

- ○ **A.** By using the web server's MAC address
- ○ **B.** By using the web server's IP address
- ○ **C.** By using IPsec
- ○ **D.** By using SSL

34. Which TCP/IP utility would you use to identify all the connections between source and destination computers?

Quick Answer: **345**
Detailed Answer: **350**

- ○ **A.** arp
- ○ **B.** ping
- ○ **C.** netstat
- ○ **D.** tracert

35. Which two TCP/IP utilities display the address of a known remote location? (Select two answers.)

Quick Answer: **345**
Detailed Answer: **350**

- ○ **A.** ping
- ○ **B.** netstat
- ○ **C.** ipconfig
- ○ **D.** nslookup

36. What option would you use with the `ping` command to ping a specified host until it stops?

Quick Answer: **345**
Detailed Answer: **351**

- ○ **A.** -t
- ○ **B.** -a
- ○ **C.** -f
- ○ **D.** -w

37. What option would you use with the `ping` command to resolve addresses to host names?

Quick Answer: **345**
Detailed Answer: **351**

- ○ **A.** -t
- ○ **B.** -a
- ○ **C.** -f
- ○ **D.** -w

38. Which of the following causes a mapped drive to disappear from a system when it is shut down and restarted?

Quick Answer: **345**
Detailed Answer: **351**

- ○ **A.** The Reconnect at Login option was not checked when the drive was mapped.
- ○ **B.** The name of the mapped folder has been changed.
- ○ **C.** The path to the mapped folder has changed.
- ○ **D.** The host computer for the mapped folder is turned off.

39. When you are trying to diagnose the cause of networking problems, where do you enter commands to run TCP/IP troubleshooting utilities?

- ○ **A.** At the command prompt
- ○ **B.** On the TCP/IP Properties window
- ○ **C.** In the dialog box that appears when you double-click the tcpip.com file
- ○ **D.** From the dialog box in the Network Neighborhood Control Panel

Quick Answer: **345**
Detailed Answer: **351**

40. Which TCP/IP utility can be used to locate a slow router on a wide area network, such as the Internet?

- ○ **A.** arp
- ○ **B.** tracert
- ○ **C.** netstat
- ○ **D.** ipconfig

Quick Answer: **345**
Detailed Answer: **351**

41. What command would you use to display all incoming and outgoing network connections on a Windows computer?

- ○ **A.** ipconfig
- ○ **B.** tracert
- ○ **C.** netstat
- ○ **D.** nslookup

Quick Answer: **345**
Detailed Answer: **351**

42. What are the two commands you can use to show all routes on a Windows computer? (Choose two answers.)

- ○ **A.** netstat
- ○ **B.** ipconfig
- ○ **C.** tracert
- ○ **D.** route

Quick Answer: **345**
Detailed Answer: **351**

43. What command can you use to display the number of bytes and packets sent and received through an Ethernet network adapter on a Windows computer?

- ○ **A.** netstat
- ○ **B.** ipconfig
- ○ **C.** tracert
- ○ **D.** route

Quick Answer: **345**
Detailed Answer: **352**

44. What command do you use to display all mapped drives on a Windows computer?

Quick Answer: **345**
Detailed Answer: **352**

- ○ **A.** ipconfig
- ○ **B.** ping
- ○ **C.** net use
- ○ **D.** telnet

45. What command can you use to map the Z: drive to the \\ server01\share01 share?

Quick Answer: **345**
Detailed Answer: **352**

- ○ **A.** net z: \\server01\share01
- ○ **B.** ipconfig z: \\server01\share01
- ○ **C.** net use z: \\server01\share01
- ○ **D.** nslookup z: \\server01\share01

46. What command would you use to start a service on a Windows computer?

Quick Answer: **345**
Detailed Answer: **352**

- ○ **A.** net use
- ○ **B.** net go
- ○ **C.** net start
- ○ **D.** start

47. What command is used to execute commands on a remote host?

Quick Answer: **345**
Detailed Answer: **352**

- ○ **A.** net use
- ○ **B.** telnet
- ○ **C.** ping
- ○ **D.** remexec

48. What command can you use to test SMTP connection to a remote mail server?

Quick Answer: **345**
Detailed Answer: **352**

- ○ **A.** net use
- ○ **B.** telnet
- ○ **C.** ping
- ○ **D.** SMTPTest

49. What command would you use to connect to a remote host to execute commands at a command prompt with a secure session?

Quick Answer: **345**
Detailed Answer: **352**

- ○ **A.** telnet
- ○ **B.** SSH
- ○ **C.** ping
- ○ **D.** Stelnet

50. What port does SSH use?

    O **A.** 21

    O **B.** 22

    O **C.** 25

    O **D.** 110

51. What command can you use to display name resolution using a DNS server?

    O **A.** `ipconfig`

    O **B.** `nbtstat`

    O **C.** `telnet`

    O **D.** `nslookup`

52. You cannot add a computer to a domain because it says an RPC server is unavailable. What should you check?

    O **A.** Make sure you are using the correct username and password

    O **B.** Make sure you have the correct DNS server specified for your domain

    O **C.** Make sure that Windows Defender is not blocking the RPC packets

    O **D.** Make sure the domain controllers are up

53. You try to access an HTTPS website, but it will not open. Which of the following could cause HTTPS to fail?

    O **A.** You do not have an assigned digital certificate for the local host.

    O **B.** The date and time are wrong on your local host computer.

    O **C.** You have the incorrect subnet mask in your IP configuration.

    O **D.** You have the wrong default gateway.

54. You try to access an HTTPS website, but it will not open. Which of the following could cause HTTPS to fail?

    O **A.** You need to use the SSH command to create a secure connection with the remote host.

    O **B.** You have damaged or incompatible Internet Explorer settings or you have an incompatible Internet Explorer add-in.

    O **C.** You need to update Internet Explorer.

    O **D.** You have not received the correct DHCP address.

55. You try to connect to your computer using the `telnet` command, but your Windows Vista computer does not respond. What is most likely the problem?

Quick Answer: **345**
Detailed Answer: **353**

- ○ **A.** The Telnet service on the Windows Vista computer is disabled by default.

- ○ **B.** The Telnet service is being blocked by a Windows Defender.

- ○ **C.** You must use SSH when connecting to Windows Vista.

- ○ **D.** You must enable HTTPS when connecting to Windows Vista.

56. You have a computer that is having problems connecting to the network and communicating with the local servers. IP information is configured for your computers using DHCP. You use the `ipconfig/all` command to see the following information:

Quick Answer: **345**
Detailed Answer: **353**

```
Connection-specific DNS Suffix  . :
Description . . . . . . . . . . . : Realtek
RTL8139/810x Family Fast Ethernet NIC
Physical Address. . . . . . . . . : 00-C0-9F-8E-
82-00
Dhcp Enabled. . . . . . . . . . . : No
IP Address. . . . . . . . . . . . : 192.168.3.100
Subnet Mask . . . . . . . . . . . : 255.255.255.0
Default Gateway . . . . . . . . . : 192.168.3.1
DNS Servers . . . . . . . . . . . : 4.2.2.2
```

What is the problem?

- ○ **A.** The wrong IP address is assigned.

- ○ **B.** The wrong subnet mask is assigned.

- ○ **C.** A static address is assigned and, therefore, the computer will not receive an address assigned by a DHCP server.

- ○ **D.** The wrong default gateway is assigned.

3.2 Install and configure a small office home office (SOHO) network

- ▶ Connection types
- ▶ Dial-up
- ▶ Broadband
- ▶ DSL
- ▶ Cable
- ▶ Satellite
- ▶ ISDN
- ▶ Wireless
- ▶ All 802.11

- ► WEP
- ► WPA
- ► SSID
- ► MAC filtering
- ► DHCP settings
- ► Routers/Access Points
- ► Disable DHCP
- ► Use static IP
- ► Change SSID from default
- ► Disable SSID broadcast
- ► MAC filtering
- ► Change default username and password
- ► Update firmware
- ► Firewall
- ► LAN (10/100/1000BaseT, Speeds)
- ► Bluetooth (1.0 vs. 2.0)
- ► Cellular
- ► Basic VoIP (consumer applications)
- ► Basics of hardware and software firewall configuration
- ► Port assignment/setting up rules (exceptions)
- ► Port forwarding/port triggering
- ► Physical installation
- ► Wireless router placement
- ► Cable length

57. What would you use to connect to a Public Switched Telephone Network (PSTN) that supports standard analog signaling?

- ○ **A.** Gateway
- ○ **B.** Router
- ○ **C.** ISDN
- ○ **D.** Modem

Quick Answer: **345**
Detailed Answer: **353**

58. Which of the following protocols establishes the connection for dial-up networking on a computer running Windows?

- ○ **A.** HTTP
- ○ **B.** Telnet
- ○ **C.** PPP
- ○ **D.** SSH

Quick Answer: **345**
Detailed Answer: **353**

59. You have a computer running Windows XP. You open Network Connections and click the Create a New Connection link to configure a dial-up connection to your corporation. Which option would you choose to set up a dial-up connection to your company?

Quick Answer: **345**
Detailed Answer: **353**

   ○ **A.** Connect to the Internet

   ○ **B.** Connect to the Network at My Workplace

   ○ **C.** Set up a Home or Small Office Network

   ○ **D.** Set up an Advanced Connection

60. You have a computer running Windows Vista. You open the Network and Sharing Center and click the Connect to a Network option. Which option would you use to set up a dial-up connection to your company?

Quick Answer: **345**
Detailed Answer: **354**

   ○ **A.** Connect to the Internet

   ○ **B.** Set up a wireless router or access point

   ○ **C.** Set up a dial-up connection

   ○ **D.** Connect to a workplace

61. Which medium can you use to connect a small Office home office (SOHO) computer to an external DSL modem?

Quick Answer: **345**
Detailed Answer: **354**

   ○ **A.** RG-58 coaxial

   ○ **B.** Category 5 UTP

   ○ **C.** Single-mode fiber optic

   ○ **D.** RS-232 serial cable

62. You have a small home network. You connect to the Internet via a DSL router. To protect yourself, you set up filtering on your DSL router. You soon discover that you cannot access Internet sites by domain name but you can by IP address. What is the most likely cause of the problem?

Quick Answer: **345**
Detailed Answer: **354**

   ○ **A.** You have configured your DSL router to block port 80.

   ○ **B.** You have configured your DSL router to block port 53.

   ○ **C.** Your DSL router is not logged in to the ISP.

   ○ **D.** You do not have IP configured on your client machines.

63. You have purchased a cable modem and a straight-through Category 5e patch cable. You connect the cable modem to your computer via a hub that is already connected to your computer. However, your computer is not able to receive a DHCP address from the cable modem. What is the most likely cause of this problem?

Quick Answer: **345**
Detailed Answer: **354**

○ **A.** The cable modem must be directly connected to a computer.

○ **B.** The cable modem requires a crossover cable to connect to the hub.

○ **C.** The cable modem requires an RG-6 coaxial cable to connect to a hub.

○ **D.** The cable modem must use a Category 3 UTP cable to connect to a hub.

64. You use a DSL connection to connect to the Internet. When setting up the network, you connect the DSL modem to the phone outlet using an RJ-11 connector, connect the DSL modem to a router using a CAT5 cable, and plug the DSL modem into a power source. You connect all the PCs to your router using CAT5 cable. You also place line filters on all phone lines and the phone line used for the DSL modem. Unfortunately, none of the PCs can connect to the Internet. What is the most likely solution to this situation?

Quick Answer: **345**
Detailed Answer: **354**

○ **A.** Replace the DSL modem

○ **B.** Remove the line filter for the phone line for the DSL modem

○ **C.** Connect the DSL modem using an RJ-45 connector to the phone outlet instead

○ **D.** Replace the CAT5 cable with coaxial cable

65. A client complains that, after replacing his DSL modem, his home DSL connection isn't working. When you inspect his computer, you notice that none of the lights on the DSL modem are on, and the only two cables that plug into the DSL modem connect via the RJ-11 and RJ-45 connectors. You are able to ping port 127.0.0.1. What is the most likely problem with the DSL?

Quick Answer: **345**
Detailed Answer: **354**

○ **A.** The network interface card (NIC) is improperly set up.

○ **B.** The phone line is not plugged into the DSL modem.

○ **C.** The Ethernet cable is not plugged into the DSL modem.

○ **D.** The power cord is not plugged into the DSL modem.

66. Which device is capable of connecting a computer to a digital data service provided by the local telephone company?

Quick Answer: **345**
Detailed Answer: **354**

○ **A.** V.34 modem

○ **B.** Fax machine

○ **C.** LAN adapter

○ **D.** ISDN adapter

67. You are implementing an ISDN connection to the Internet. How many 64-kbps channels does a BRI ISDN connection support?

Quick Answer: **345**
Detailed Answer: **354**

- ○ **A.** 1
- ○ **B.** 2
- ○ **C.** 3
- ○ **D.** 12

68. A residential customer who has just switched Internet access over to a satellite system has called to find out why she sometimes experiences delays in the satellite system delivering Internet connectivity. How do you explain this delay to the customer?

Quick Answer: **345**
Detailed Answer: **354**

- ○ **A.** Modern satellite systems should not have a delay period.
- ○ **B.** There is a downlink delay time associated with connecting to the satellite source.
- ○ **C.** The dish requires an azimuth correction period to switch to a different satellite.
- ○ **D.** This is due to connection latency caused by additional parties in the communications link.

69. A traveling user needs to access the company's network through a wireless access point when he is in the office. What type of hardware do you recommend?

Quick Answer: **345**
Detailed Answer: **355**

- ○ **A.** An IrDA card
- ○ **B.** An IEEE-1394 adapter
- ○ **C.** An 802.3 adapter
- ○ **D.** An 802.11 adapter

70. A traveling sales member from your company often has meetings with clients on the road. These meetings often occur where there is no Internet access. Unfortunately, the demo that the sales member shows is on the Internet. What type of hardware would you recommend?

Quick Answer: **345**
Detailed Answer: **355**

- ○ **A.** An IrDA card
- ○ **B.** An IEEE-1394 adapter
- ○ **C.** A cellular wireless card
- ○ **D.** An 802.11 adapter

71. A user who travels frequently and works for a customer that employs static IP addresses at the office has called to complain that she cannot connect to the Internet while on the road. She typically stays in motels that offer free Internet connections in the room, but she cannot take advantage of the service. What should you tell her to do?

- ○ **A.** Tell her that she must configure her network connection to automatically obtain an IP address when traveling and then change it back to the static address in her office.

- ○ **B.** Tell her to get a wireless network card.

- ○ **C.** Tell her to wait until her company switches to DHCP.

- ○ **D.** Tell her to set up Automatic Private IP Addressing in the TCP/IP Properties page.

72. You have a wireless network at home that you use to connect your laptop to the Internet. You purchase a new wireless phone. Now, you cannot connect when you are using your wireless phone. What is the problem?

- ○ **A.** You have exceeded the power requirements for the room.

- ○ **B.** Both the wireless card and the wireless telephone are configured to use the same frequency.

- ○ **C.** You need to modify your firewall to allow both to communicate at the same time.

- ○ **D.** You need to connect the wireless card directly into the wireless phone.

73. You have an office located in a building that contains multiple offices. You install a wireless network in one of the offices but users are constantly getting kicked off the network. What can you do to overcome this problem?

- ○ **A.** Make sure each user has a unique MAC address for each interface. Check SSID to make sure it is unique.

- ○ **B.** Change the channels used in the wireless network to make sure they are different from other networks.

- ○ **C.** Change the IP addresses used for private networks so they are unique within the building.

- ○ **D.** Change the authentication password for the wireless access point.

74. Which of the following are NOT valid WEP key lengths?

Quick Answer: **345**
Detailed Answer: **355**

- ○ **A.** 32 bit
- ○ **B.** 40 bit
- ○ **C.** 64 bit
- ○ **D.** 128 bit

75. The computers on the corporate network run Windows Vista. Each computer has a wireless network adapter. You install a wireless router. You need to help ensure the highest possible level of security for your network without using digital certificates. What should you do?

Quick Answer: **345**
Detailed Answer: **356**

- ○ **A.** Configure the access point and clients to use the WPA2-Enterprise security type.
- ○ **B.** Configure the access point and clients to use the Shared security type with WEP encryption.
- ○ **C.** Configure the access point and clients to use the WPA-Personal security type with AES encryption.
- ○ **D.** Configure the access point and clients to use the 802.1x security type with the Protected EAP authentication and WEP encryption.

76. Which of the following should you do when setting up a wireless access point?

Quick Answer: **345**
Detailed Answer: **356**

- ○ **A.** Change the SSID from the default value
- ○ **B.** Disable SSID broadcast
- ○ **C.** Change the default username and password
- ○ **D.** All of the options provided are correct

77. When you install a new wireless point, what should you do to make sure the wireless point runs with minimum problems?

Quick Answer: **345**
Detailed Answer: **356**

- ○ **A.** Update the firmware
- ○ **B.** Disable MAC filtering
- ○ **C.** Enable WEP
- ○ **D.** Enable IEEE 802.5 on the access point

78. What is the typical speed of data transfers for wired, network printers?

Quick Answer: **345**
Detailed Answer: **356**

- ○ **A.** 54 Mbps
- ○ **B.** 10/100/1000 Mbps
- ○ **C.** 24 Mbps
- ○ **D.** 480 Mbps

79. At what speed does 10BaseT run?

- ○ **A.** 10 Mbps
- ○ **B.** 16 Mbps
- ○ **C.** 54 Mbps
- ○ **D.** 100 Mbps

80. What is the speed of Bluetooth 1.0?

- ○ **A.** 1.0 Mbps
- ○ **B.** 2.0 Mbps
- ○ **C.** 3.0 Mbps
- ○ **D.** 4.0 Mbps

81. What is the speed of Bluetooth 2.0?

- ○ **A.** 1.0 Mbps
- ○ **B.** 2.0 Mbps
- ○ **C.** 3.0 Mbps
- ○ **D.** 4.0 Mbps

82. You have to have a Bluetooth-enabled handheld device added to a personal area network (PAN). What do you need to do?

- ○ **A.** Configure the passkey and ensure that the device is discoverable
- ○ **B.** Configure the appropriate wireless security method and ensure that the device is discoverable
- ○ **C.** Turn on Network Discovery and configure the passkey
- ○ **D.** Configure the passkey and ensure that the mobile device is Wi-Fi enabled

83. You have a VoIP application. You call a friend, but the phone call is "patchy." What is the problem?

- ○ **A.** You have to open a port in the firewall.
- ○ **B.** You don't have enough available bandwidth on the network.
- ○ **C.** You have another application that is using the same port as the VoIP application.
- ○ **D.** The cable length is too long between the computer and the switch.

84. What program or network application uses port 80?

- ○ **A.** HTTP
- ○ **B.** SMTP
- ○ **C.** POP3
- ○ **D.** Telnet

Quick Answer: **345**
Detailed Answer: **356**

85. What program or network application uses port 21?

- ○ **A.** HTTP
- ○ **B.** FTP
- ○ **C.** POP3
- ○ **D.** DNS

Quick Answer: **345**
Detailed Answer: **356**

86. What program or network application uses port 443?

- ○ **A.** HTTP
- ○ **B.** FTP
- ○ **C.** HTTPS
- ○ **D.** DNS

Quick Answer: **345**
Detailed Answer: **356**

87. You create a website on your computer that is running Windows XP. You have several computers on your home network, which is protected by a firewall that is built into the access point. What do you need to configure on the firewall so that people from the outside can access your website?

- ○ **A.** You need to enable broadcast on the firewall.
- ○ **B.** You need to configure port forwarding so that HTTP (port 80) traffic is forwarded to your Windows XP computer running IIS.
- ○ **C.** You need to configure authentication for your firewall.
- ○ **D.** You need to configure the Windows XP computer with the default gateway of the firewall.

Quick Answer: **345**
Detailed Answer: **357**

88. What is the maximum cable length for 10BaseT Ethernet?

- ○ **A.** 10 meters
- ○ **B.** 50 meters
- ○ **C.** 100 meters
- ○ **D.** 1000 meters

Quick Answer: **345**
Detailed Answer: **357**

89. Where should you place your wireless access point in a SOHO?

- ○ **A.** It should be placed centrally within the house.
- ○ **B.** You should place it in the closet at the back of the house.
- ○ **C.** You should place it on the ceiling at the front of the house.
- ○ **D.** You should place it on the ground under a bed or in a cabinet.

Quick Answer: **345**
Detailed Answer: **357**

Quick-Check Answer Key

1. B	31. B	61. B
2. D	32. A	62. B
3. D	33. B	63. B
4. A	34. D	64. B
5. B	35. A and D	65. D
6. D	36. A	66. D
7. A	37. B	67. B
8. A	38. A	68. D
9. B	39. A	69. D
10. A	40. B	70. C
11. C	41. C	71. A
12. A	42. A and D	72. B
13. D	43. A	73. B
14. A	44. C	74. A
15. A	45. C	75. A
16. B and C	46. C	76. D
17. B	47. B	77. A
18. C and D	48. B	78. B
19. C	49. B	79. A
20. A	50. B	80. A
21. A	51. D	81. C
22. B	52. B	82. A
23. E	53. B	83. B
24. B	54. B	84. A
25. B	55. A	85. B
26. C	56. C	86. C
27. E	57. D	87. B
28. C	58. C	88. C
29. D	59. B	89. A
30. D	60. D	

Answers and Explanations

1. **Answer: B.** If users can see other local computers in a TCP/IP network but cannot see remote systems on other networks, you might be having routing problems. Determine whether the address for the default gateway (router) listed in the TCP/IP properties is valid. If there is an IP address conflict (Answer A), one of the hosts that has the conflict will not be able to communicate on the network. If DNS service is not configured properly (Answer C), you will not be able to resolve names. If the DHCP service (Answer D) is not configured properly, your hosts will not receive a correct IP address with corresponding subnet mask and default gateway.

2. **Answer: D.** By default, PCs running TCP/IP can communicate only with other computers that are on the same network. If multiple networks are involved, or you are connected to the Internet, you must configure the address of the router (default gateway) on each PC. Therefore, if you cannot access the Internet, but you can access resources on the local area network, the gateway address is most likely configured incorrectly. If the subnet mask is not configured properly (Answer A), you might not be able to communicate with remote and/or local hosts. If the TCP/IP protocol is not enabled on the machine (Answer B), you will not be able to communicate with any host using TCP/IP. If the DHCP service is not working (Answer C), you will not be able to get a dynamic IP address.

3. **Answer: D.** If you did not configure the subnet mask properly, your system has problems determining which hosts are local and which hosts are remote. Therefore, when you try to communicate with a host that thinks it is remote but is really local, it sends its packets to the default gateway. When it tries to communicate with a host that thinks it is local but is really remote, it tries to send its packets directly to the hosts, but the packets will never be sent to the default gateway so that it can be routed to the proper network. Your system is still able to connect to the default gateway (Answer A), but the problem is in determining which hosts are local and which hosts are remote. Your system might be able to connect to some remote hosts (Answer B) and some local hosts (Answer C), depending on what it determines to be local and what it determines to be remote as indicated by the local IP address, remote IP address, and subnet mask. If the system determines that an address is local but it is really remote, it tries to connect directly to the host, but fails to connect. If it calculates that an address is remote but it is really local, it sends packets to the default gateway in an attempt to forward the packets to the remote host.

4. **Answer: A.** To ping the site's FQDN, your DNS must submit a name resolution request to a DNS server. The server searches through its DNS database and, if necessary, through the hierarchical DNS system until it locates the hostname or FQDN that was submitted to it. At this point, it resolves the IP address of the requested hostname and returns it to the client. If DHCP is not working properly (Answer B), you will not receive dynamic IP addresses. If WINS, short for Windows Internet Naming Service, is not functioning, you will not be able to translate from NetBIOS names (computer names) to IP addresses (Answer C). If FTP is not functioning (Answer D), you will not be able to download or upload files.

5. **Answer: B.** The `ping` utility can be used for testing TCP/IP functions. Pinging the local adapter's IP address in a Windows XP machine and receiving a Destination Host

Unreachable message indicates that the adapter's IP address has not been initialized. This is typically due to a bad or disconnected network cable. However, the system will also fail to initialize the adapter's IP address if a duplicate address is assigned. In this case you should receive a notice that a duplicate address exists, and the `ipconfig` utility returns an address of 0.0.0.0 for the adapter. If TCP/IP was not loaded (Answer A), you aren't able to communicate with any hosts using TCP/IP. If TCP/IP is not working on the gateway device (Answer C) or the default gateway is not functioning (Answer D), you aren't able to communicate with any remote hosts.

6. **Answer: D.** When a DHCP server does not respond to a DHCP request, the computer will use Automatic Private IP addressing, which generates an IP address in the form of 169.254.xxx.xxx and the subnet mask of 255.255.0.0. Answers A and B are incorrect because 169.255.30.25 is an address generated by the Automatic Private IP addressing. Answer C is incorrect because TCP/IP is bound to the card or it could not be assigned an IP address.

7. **Answer: A.** Network Address Translation (NAT) is not compatible with IPsec because NAT changes the IP address in the IP header of each packet. IPsec does not allow this and drops the packet. Ports 80 and 8080 are used by HTTP. Port 80 is the default port for HTTP (Answer B), and 8080 (Answer D) is used by many proxy servers to access HTTP. Port 1293 (Answer C) is a port used by IPSec, but the problem is not because it is being blocked; the problem is because of compatibility between NAT and IPSec.

8. **Answer: A.** In most cases when there is a conflict, the first computer is able to communicate but the second computer is not. Of course, you are not able to communicate with both local and remote hosts (Answers B and C) while there is a conflict. In addition, you are not able to communicate with corporate hosts and the Internet (Answer D).

9. **Answer: B.** Private addresses are only valid within a private network and cannot be assigned directly to the Internet. Instead, you have to use Network Address Translation (NAT)—which translates between a public address and a private address—to be able to communicate on the Internet. The default subnet mask for the 10.x.x.x network is 255.255.255.0, but this network has been subnetted and the subnet mask has been modified to 255.255.255.0 (Answer A). The default gateway is probably okay (Answer C) because there is no mention of the server having problems communicating with other internal hosts. Lastly, there is no mention of naming problems (Answer D).

10. **Answer: A.** The TCP/IP loopback test enables you to verify that TCP/IP has been successfully loaded in the local computer. If the test fails to return a reply, the problem is with the installation of TCP/IP on the local machine. If the test responds with a reply, the TCP/IP protocol is installed and functioning correctly. If the network cable is bad (Answer B), the network card is disabled (Answer C) or the NIC is defective (Answer D), you are not able to communicate on the network even at the physical level.

11. **Answer: C.** The first step in troubleshooting local network connectivity is to try to obtain a connection with the network. Check to see that the computer is physically connected to the network and check the activity/status lights on the back plate of the LAN card to determine whether the network recognizes the adapter. If the lights are glowing, the NIC sees network traffic and the connection is alive. If the lights are not glowing, check the adapter in another PC. You should then run IPCONFIG to see the IP configuration (Answer D) and ping a known IP address to test connectivity (Answer B). You can then check the least likely problem—the device driver—last (Answer A).

12. **Answer: A.** You must ping address 127.0.0.1 to perform a loopback test that verifies TCP/IP has been successfully loaded in the local computer. 10.0.0.1 (Answer B) is a private address. 169.192.0.1 (Answer C) and 172.254.0.1 (Answer D) are public addresses.

13. **Answer: D.** Because the user can ping other users or devices on the network, the local network adapter (Answer A), its drivers (Answer B), and its network cable (Answer C) must be good. With TCP/IP disabled, the printer is not able to reply to a ping sent to it.

14. **Answer: A.** When setting up an email account, you must supply the configuration information—that is, email account name (Answer B), password, POP3 server address (Answer D), and SMTP server address (Answer C). Although you need DNS to function on the network in order for email to function, it is not needed to configure an email application.

15. **Answer: A.** Simple Mail Transfer Protocol (SMTP) is used to send emails while Post Office Protocol (POP3), Answer B, and Internet Message Access Protocol (IMAP), Answer C, are used to receive emails. If you configured the address for the DNS server with the wrong address (Answer D), you are not be able to perform name resolution.

16. **Answer: B and C.** Post Office Protocol (POP3) and Internet Message Access Protocol (IMAP) are used to receive emails. Simple Mail Transfer Protocol (SMTP) is used to send emails (Answer A). If you configured the address for the DNS server with the wrong address, you are not able to perform name resolution (Answer D).

17. **Answer: B.** By default, the Windows Firewall blocks all traffic unless you specify that a program or protocol is allowed to go through the firewall. Therefore, you need to allow the FTP program to communicate with the FTP protocol, specifically ports 20 and 21. The FTP programs shouldn't require a DNS server (Answer A) or a default gateway (Answer C) because it uses the IP configuration settings. Telnet (Answer D) is used to connect to a remote host to execute commands at a command prompt. Telnet is not used to map ports.

18. **Answer: C and D.** When you enable Firewall settings and you need to configure exceptions, you can add a program that can communicate through the Windows Firewall or port. You cannot define users (Answer A) and groups (Answer B)

19. **Answer: C.** When you specify the program or port, you can click the Scope button so that you can specify the IP addresses or subnets to allow communications with certain computers. You cannot specify host names (Answer A) or MAC addresses (Answer B). In addition, there is no exception.txt file (Answer D).

20. **Answer: A.** A proxy server is a type of server that makes a single Internet connection and services on behalf of many users. It can also be used to filter requests, increase performance, and increase security. To configure Internet Explorer to use a proxy server, you need to open Internet Options in Internet Explorer, click the LAN settings and specify the address of the proxy server and port. Instead of specifying the address of the proxy server and port number, you can also select Automatically Detect Settings or Automatic Configuration Script, assuming your company uses such a thing. Therefore, the other answers are incorrect.

21. **Answer: A.** This is a normal response for running a TCP/IP utility from the Run dialog box. Because these utilities are troubleshooting tools that return information to the screen, they cannot simply be initiated from the Start/Run dialog box; they must be run from the command prompt. Therefore, the other answers are incorrect.

22. **Answer: B.** To renew IPv4, you have to use the `ipconfig /renew` command. Answer A is incorrect because the `ipconfig` command without any options only displays basic IP configuration information. Answer C is incorrect because the `/renew6` option renews IPv6 IP addresses. Answer D is incorrect because the `/release_and_renew` option does not exist. Answer E is incorrect because the `/registerdns` option is used to get the computer to register itself with the DNS server.

23. **Answer: E.** The command used to flush local cached DNS information is `ipconfig /flushdns`. Answer A is incorrect because the `ipconfig` command without any options only displays basic IP configuration information. Answer B is incorrect because the `/renew` option renews the IPv4 IP addresses. Answer C is incorrect because the `/renew6` option renews IPv6 IP addresses. Answer D is incorrect because the `/registerdns` option is used to get the computer to register itself with the DNS server.

24. **Answer: B.** To show all IP configuration information, you must use the `ipconfig/all` command. Answer A is incorrect because the `ipconfig` command without any options only displays basic IP configuration information. Answer C is incorrect because the `arp` command is used to view and manage IP address to MAC address mappings. Answers D and E are commands used to test network connectivity.

25. **Answer: B.** The `ipconfig` utility can be started with two important option switches: `/renew` and `/release`. These switches are used to release and update IP settings received from a DHCP server. Normally, the `/renew` option works without a preceding `/release` operation. However, this approach sometimes fails, requiring the `/release` operation to be performed first. There is no `/relinquish` option (Answer A) for the `ipconfig` command. The `/all` (Answer C) option shows all IP configuration information, including DNS server addresses. The `/release` (Answer D) option releases the IP address assigned by a DHCP server but does not assign a new one.

26. **Answer: C.** This `ipconfig` command-line utility enables you to determine the current TCP/IP configuration (MAC address, IP address, and subnet mask) of the local computer. It also can be used to request a new TCP/IP address from a DHCP server. The `ping` (Answer A) and `tracert` (Answer B) commands are used to test network connectivity, and the `nbtstat` (Answer D) command is used to troubleshoot NetBIOS name resolution.

27. **Answer: E.** The `/registerdns` option is used to get the computer to register itself with the DNS server. To renew IPv4 (Answer B), you have to use the `ipconfig/renew` command. Answer A is incorrect because the `ipconfig` command without any options only displays basic IP configuration information. Answer C is incorrect because the `/renew6` option renews IPv6 IP addresses. Answer D is incorrect because the `/release_and_renew` option does not exist.

28. **Answer: C.** The two commands that show network connectivity to another computer are the `ping` command and the `tracert` command. Answer A is incorrect because the `ipconfig` command without any options only displays basic IP configuration information. Answer B is incorrect because the `arp` command is used to view and manage IP address to MAC address mappings. The `traceroute` command is found on UNIX and Linux machines. Windows machines use `tracert`.

29. **Answer: D.** If you want an address to be available from the Internet and be the same address for both IPv4 and IPv6, it must have a global address that can be seen on the

Internet. Answer A is incorrect because private addresses cannot be used on public networks such as the Internet. Answer B is incorrect because it has to be a single address assigned to a single computer, not a multicast that is used to broadcast to multiple addresses at the same time. Answer C is incorrect because a local address cannot be seen on the outside.

30. **Answer: D.** Because this person is traveling between two sites, the user needs to have a local address on each site. Therefore, you should let the local DHCP server hand out the addresses when the user connects to each network. Answer A is incorrect because she can connect to one network. Therefore, the driver is working fine. Answer B is incorrect because this means that you are putting this computer directly on the Internet. Answer C is incorrect because running a troubleshooting wizard could be a lengthy process when the solution is simple.

31. **Answer: B.** The arp utility is useful for resolving duplicate IP addresses. The arp -a command displays the local ARP table, which lists the IP address to MAC address mappings. The ping command (Answer A) is used to test network connectivity, and the ipconfig command (Answer C) can be used to show the IP configuration information. winipcfg (Answer D) is the command to show IP configuration for Windows 9x machines.

32. **Answer: A.** Web browsers use HTTP to access websites. If HTTP is down or port 80, which is used for HTTP traffic, is blocked, you won't be able to access the website. If DHCP server is down (Answer B), you most likely have a 169.254.x.x address and you are not able to communicate with network resources. If the DNS server is down (Answer C), you are not able to perform name resolution. Therefore, you most likely are not able to access any host by name. If the web server is down (Answer D), you are not able to ping the server.

33. **Answer: B.** DNS resolves host names to IP addresses. If you use an IP address instead of a host name and you can access the server, you will be informed that a name resolution problem exists. If the name and the IP address do not work, it is a network connectivity problem or you have a problem with the server or a problem with your client. You cannot access a website using MAC addresses (Answer A). MAC addresses are physical addresses assigned to a network adapter. IPsec (Answer C) and SSL (Answer D) are used for encryption.

34. **Answer: D.** The tracert (or traceroute when dealing with UNIX/ Linux machines) utility traces the route taken by packets sent across an IP network. Routers along the path return information to the inquiring system, and the utility displays the host name, IP address, and roundtrip time for each hop in the path. The ping command (Answer B) is also used to test network connectivity but does not show you all of the connections between the source and destination. The arp command (Answer A) is used to display the ARP cache. ARP is short for Address Resolution Protocol, which translates from IP address (logical address) to MAC address (physical address). The netstat command (Answer C) is used to display network statistics, including the routing table for a local Windows host.

35. **Answer: A and D.** ping enables you to verify connections to remote hosts. You can use the command to test both the name and IP address of the remote unit. nslookup (Answer D) is a TCP/IP utility that can be entered at the command prompt to query Internet (DNS) name servers for information about hosts and domains. The

`netstat` command (Answer B) is used to display network statistics including the routing table for a local Windows host. The `ipconfig` command (Answer C) is used to display IP configuration information.

36. **Answer: A.** The `-t` option will ping the specified host until it is stopped. The `-a` option (Answer B) resolves addresses to hostnames. The `-f` option (Answer C) is used to set Don't Fragment flags in packets. The `-w` option (Answer D) is used to set the timeout in milliseconds to wait for each reply.

37. **Answer: B.** The `-a` option resolves addresses to hostnames. The `-t` option (Answer A) pings the specified host until it is stopped. The `-f` option (Answer C) is used to set Don't Fragment flags in packets. The `-w` option (Answer D) is used to set the timeout in milliseconds to wait for each reply.

38. **Answer: A.** The Reconnect at Logon option must be selected in the Map Network Drive page for the drive mapping to be a permanent part of the system. If this option is not selected when the user logs off, the mapped drive information disappears and needs to be remapped for future use. On the other hand, if a red X appears on the icon of a properly mapped drive, it indicates that the drive is no longer available. Its host computer might be turned off (Answer D), the drive might have been removed, or it might no longer be on the same path (Answers B or C). If the drive was mapped to a particular folder and the folder name has been changed (Answer B), the red X also appears.

39. **Answer: A.** TCP/IP troubleshooting utilities are controlled by commands entered and run from the command prompt. Neither the TCP/IP Properties window (Answer B) nor the Network Neighborhood Control Panel (Answer D) give you a place to execute commands. There is no `tcpip.com` file (Answer C).

40. **Answer: B.** The `tracert` utility traces the route taken by ICMP packets sent across the network and displays the hostname, IP address, and round-trip time for each hop in the path. Because the `tracert` report shows how much time is spent at each router along the path, it is helpful to determine where network slowdowns are occurring. The `arp` command (Answer A) is used to display the ARP cache. ARP is short for Address Resolution Protocol, which translates from IP address (logical address) to MAC address (physical address). The `netstat` command (Answer C) is used to display network statistics, including the routing table for a local Windows host. The `ipconfig` command (Answer D) is used to display the IP configuration information.

41. **Answer: C.** `netstat`, short for network statistics, is a command-line tool that displays network connections (both incoming and outgoing), routing tables, and the number of network interface statistics. The `ipconfig` command (Answer A) is a command-line tool that shows IP configuration. The `tracert` command (Answer B) is a command-line tool that shows network connectivity, including all hops between the local host and the remote host. The `nslookup` command (Answer D) is a command-line tool that shows name resolution provided by a DNS server.

42. **Answer: A and D.** `netstat`, short for network statistics, is a command-line tool that displays network connections (both incoming and outgoing), routing tables and the number of network interface statistics. To display routes, use `netstat -r`. The `route` command also shows the routing table on a Windows computer. The `ipconfig` command (Answer B) is a command-line tool that shows IP configuration. The `tracert` command (Answer C) is a command-line tool that shows network connectivity, including all hops between the local host and the remote host.

43. **Answer: A.** `netstat`, short for network statistics, is a command-line tool that displays network connections (both incoming and outgoing), routing tables, and the number of network interface statistics. To display network statistics use `netstat -e`. The `ipconfig` command (Answer B) is a command-line tool that shows IP configuration. The `tracert` command (Answer C) is a command-line tool that shows network connectivity, including all hops between the local host and the remote host.

44. **Answer: C.** The `net use` command with no additional parameters displays all mapped drives, including disconnected mapped drives. The `ipconfig` command (Answer A) is a command-line tool that shows IP configuration. The `ping` command (Answer B) is used to test network connectivity with a remote host. The `telnet` command is used to run commands on a remote host.

45. **Answer: C.** The `net use` command is used to map network drives to a drive letter. The `net` command (Answer A) must have the `use` option to map a drive. The `ipconfig` command (Answer B) is used to display the IP configuration. The `nslookup` command (Answer D) is used to display DNS resolved names.

46. **Answer: C.** The `net start` *servicename* command will start a service on a Windows computer. The `net use` command (Answer A) is used to map network drives. The `net go` (Answer B) and `start` (Answer D) commands do not do anything on a Windows computer.

47. **Answer: B.** The `telnet` command is used to connect to a remote host to execute commands at a command prompt. The `net use` command (Answer A) is used to display mapped drives and to map a drive to a network share. The `ping` command (Answer C) is used to test network connectivity. The `remexec` command (Answer D) does not exist in Windows.

48. **Answer: B.** The `telnet` command can be used to test remote network services. To connect to a remote mail server, you execute `telnet` *hostname* 25, where 25 represents the port used by SMTP. The `net use` command (Answer A) is used to map network drives. The `ping` command (Answer C) is used to test network connectivity. There is no `SMTPTest` command (Answer D) in Windows.

49. **Answer: B.** In Windows, there are multiple third-party applications, such as PuTTY, that allow you to use SSH to connect to a remote host to execute commands in an encrypted session. Telnet (Answer A) connects to a remote host but the packets sent between the local and remote host are unencrypted, including usernames and passwords. The `ping` command (Answer C) is used to test network connectivity. There is no `Stelnet` command (Answer D) in Windows.

50. **Answer: B.** SSH uses port 22. Telnet (Answer A) uses port 23. SMTP (Answer C) uses port 25 and POP3 (Answer D) uses port 110.

51. **Answer: D.** `nslookup`, short for name server lookup, is used to test name resolution from a DNS server. The `ipconfig` command (Answer A) is used to display the IP configuration. The `nbtstat` command (Answer B) is used to show the NetBIOS statistics. The `telnet` command (Answer C) is used to execute commands on a remote host.

52. **Answer: B.** If a system cannot find the RPC server, it is most likely that you are not pointing to the domain DNS servers so that the computer can use the SRV records to find the domain controllers. After you connect to an RPC server, you need a username

and password (Answer A) to be authorized to add a computer to a domain. Windows Defender (Answer C) is used to protect against spyware and is not a firewall. Although your domain controllers might be down (Answer D), it is unlikely that this is causing the problem, especially if your corporation has more than one.

53. **Answer: B.** Authentication and encryption are based on having the correct date and time to make sure that a packet is not replayed in an attempt to break the security of a system. Therefore, you should make sure you have the correct date and time. The remote host needs to have a digital certificate (Answer A), not the local host. If the incorrect subnet mask (Answer C) or default gateway (Answer D) are incorrect, you most likely are not able to connect to other host computers.

54. **Answer: B.** Damaged or incompatible Internet Explorer settings or add-ons might cause problems with accessing HTTPS websites. To reset Internet Explorer settings, you can open Internet Options, click the Advanced tab, and click the Reset button in Reset Internet Explorer Settings dialog box. You do not have to open an SSH command (Answer A) to use HTTPS. You should not have to update Internet Explorer (Answer C) to access HTTPS websites. If you have an incorrect DHCP address (Answer D), you are not able to connect to some hosts.

55. **Answer: A.** Telnet is disabled by default on Windows XP and Vista because when you use Telnet, it is not encrypted. Therefore, if you want to connect remotely to Windows XP or Vista, you need to enable the telnet service. Windows Defender (Answer B) is software used to help protect against spyware. You don't need to use SSH (Answer C) or HTTPS (Answer D) to connect to a computer running telnet.

56. **Answer: C.** When you look at the `ipconfig` command output, you see that the DHCP-enabled setting is "no," which means the address is a static address and not an address assigned by a DHCP server. Therefore, you need to reconfigure the IP configuration to use DHCP instead of a static address. Therefore, the other answers are incorrect.

57. **Answer: D.** A modem can connect two computers over an analog telephone line. A gateway (Answer A) is hardware or software that links two different types of networks by repackaging and converting data from one network to another or from one network operating system to another. A router (Answer B) routes packets between networks. ISDN (Answer C), short for Integrated Services Digital Network, is technology built on digital signals, not analog.

58. **Answer: C.** The PPP protocol is used to establish a connection over point-to-point links, such as dial-up and dedicated leased lines. HTTP (Answer A) is short for Hypertext Transfer Protocol, which is the protocol for web pages. Telnet (Answer B) allows you to connect remotely to a remote host to execute commands at a command prompt. SSH (Answer D) is a secure version of Telnet that allows you to securely connect remotely to a remote host to execute commands at a command prompt.

59. **Answer: B.** To configure dial-up or VPN, you use the Connect to the Network at My Workplace option. The Connect to the Internet option (Answer A) is used to choose an Internet service provider (ISP). The Set up a Home or Small Office Network option (Answer C) is used to create a SOHO, which will share an Internet connection, set up Windows Firewall, share files and folders, and share printers. The Set up an Advanced Connection option (Answer D) is used to connect directly to another computer using serial, parallel, or infrared port.

60. **Answer: D.** To configure dial-up or VPN, you use the Connect to a Workplace option. The Connect to the Internet option (Answer A) is used to set up a wireless, broadband, or dial-up connection to the Internet. The Set up a Wireless Router or Access Point option (Answer B) is used to set up a new wireless network for your home or small business. Use the Set up a Dial-up Connection option (Answer C) to connect through a dial-up connection to the Internet through an Internet service provider (ISPs).

61. **Answer: B.** The computer is connected to the DSL modem with a standard Category 5 UTP cable. An RG-58 coaxial cable (Answer A) is used to connect a cable modem to the cable outlet. Fiber optic cable (Answer C) is only used to connect directly to a fiber optic network. The RS-232 serial cable (Answer D) is used to connect to another device through a PC's serial port.

62. **Answer: B.** When you configured the filtering, you also blocked port 53, which is the port used for DNS. Port 80 (Answer A) is used for HTTP to access websites. If you are not logged into your ISP (Answer C), you are not able to access any websites with name or IP address. If IP is not configured (Answer D) on your machine, you are not able to access any network resources on the Internet.

63. **Answer: B.** To communicate two devices with the same physical and electronic interfaces such as PC-to-PC, switch-to-switch, or switch-to-cable modem, you need to use a crossover cable, not a straight-through cable. Therefore, the other answers are incorrect.

64. **Answer: B.** The DSL service connects with the same line as your telephone. The filters are used to reduce noise on telephones, answering machines, and fax machines caused by the DSL service. If a filter is put on the DSL connection, the Internet connection might not work correctly. The DSL modem connects to your normal phone line. Therefore, it uses an RJ-11 connector, not an RJ-45 connector (Answer C). Cable modems use coaxial cables, and DSL connects to your local network using Cat5 or better Ethernet cables (Answer D). Because the filters seem to be the problem, the DSL modem is probably okay (Answer A).

65. **Answer: D.** DSL modems require an external power source to function. Because you have no lights whatsoever, including the power light, you can easily pinpoint the problem. The NIC is configured properly (Answer A) because you can ping the loopback address of 127.0.0.1. The RJ-11 connection (Answer B) is the phone line, and the RJ-45 (Answer C) is your network connection.

66. **Answer: D.** ISDN is a digital service provided by the local telephone company. The V.34 modem (Answer A) uses the telephone line, but with analog signaling. A fax machine (Answer B) uses the telephone line, but with analog signaling. A LAN adapter (Answer C) cannot be used to connect to the telephone line.

67. **Answer: B.** The BRI ISDN connection supports two 64Kbps channels, giving a total of 128 Kbps bandwidth and allowing two connections at the same time. Therefore, the other answers are incorrect.

68. **Answer: D.** Instead of sending web page requests to a web server on the Internet, the uplink service routes the request to the satellite system's network operation center. The network operation center then requests the desired page from the real web server and returns it to the user through the satellite's downlink. The page request operation can occur only at the speed of the uplink connection, and the additional steps to get

the page to the user might result in a noticeable delay known as latency. Therefore, the other answers are incorrect.

69. **Answer: D.** Wireless network computers use a network interface card (802.11a, b, g, or n adapter card) that has a radio transmitter, receiver, and antenna integrated into the card. Each computer that has a wireless card installed can communicate with other wireless-equipped computers or with the access point. The IrDA card (Answer A) uses infrared technology to connect to other devices that have infrared signaling. The IEEE-1394 adapter (Answer B) is used to connect high-speed devices to a computer. The 802.3 adapter (Answer C) is standard for Ethernet.

70. **Answer: C.** You would recommend a cellular wireless card so that the sales member can access the Internet at all times, even when the customer does not have Internet connection. Because some of the places don't have Internet connections, you will not be able to use 802.11 (Answer D) wireless technology using a network interface card (802.11a, b, g, or n adapter card) that has a radio transmitter, receiver, and antenna integrated into the card. The IrDA card (Answer A) uses infrared technology to connect to other devices that have infrared signaling. The IEEE-1394 adapter (Answer B) is used to connect high-speed devices to a computer.

71. **Answer: A.** The user must learn to reconfigure her network connection to automatically obtain an IP address, subnet mask, gateway address, and DNS address from the host network. DHCP is used to manage these assignments automatically and is particularly convenient when traveling with portable PCs because it automatically obtains DHCP information from network hosts that provide high-speed Internet connections in places such as hotels and airport kiosks. Because the user is connected to a business network in the office, she probably needs to be given administrative rights to change her network configuration. If she acquired a wireless card (Answer B), she would still have the same problem as a wired card. If her company is using static addressing (Answer C), it could be quite some time before the DHCP service becomes available. Automatic Private IP Addressing (Answer D) is used when a client is configured for dynamic addressing via a DHCP server but a DHCP server cannot be found.

72. **Answer: B.** When both devices are being used, it is obvious that they are both using the same frequency, which is causing interference. Therefore, you need to change or replace one of the devices so that each device doesn't use the same frequency. For example, one device should use 2.4 GHz while the other device would use 5.0 GHz. Both devices have sufficient power (Answer A). The firewall does not block frequencies (Answer C). You don't have to connect one device into another device (Answer D) to get them to work together.

73. **Answer: B.** You have a conflict because each wireless access point is using the same frequency and the same channels within the frequency range. You can try to change the channels so that it is different from other wireless networks. It is highly unlikely that you will have the same MAC addresses (Answer A) used within the building, and it is not a password problem (Answer D) because the users can make an initial connection. It is also not a problem with unique IP addresses because each network can use the same private address ranges (Answer C).

74. **Answer: A.** WEP keys can be 40, 64, or 128 bits long, but not 32 bits long.

75. Answer: A. WPA provides strong data encryption. Although WPA-Enterprise requires digital certificates (Answer A), WPA-Personal uses a pre-shared key or password (Answer C). Using a digital certificate is stronger than using a shared security key. WEP encryption (Answers B and D) uses a weak encryption. Therefore, WPA or WPA2 is recommended. WPA uses Temporary Key Integrity Protocol (TKIP) and WPA2 uses Advanced Encryption Standard (AES). WPA2 is slightly stronger than WPA.

76. Answer: D. To make the wireless access point more secure out of the box, you should change the SSID from the default value and the default username and password so that it cannot be easily guessed. You should also disable SSID broadcasts so that the SSID is not seen by all laptops within the range of the wireless access point.

77. Answer: A. You should update the firmware to fix any technical glitches and security holes. You should enable MAC filtering (Answer B) if you want to limit which clients can access the wireless network. You should not use WEP (Answer C) because it has weak encryption. Instead, use WPA or WPA2. IEEE 802.5 (Answer D) is the standard for Token Ring, which has nothing to do with today's access points.

78. Answer: B. A wired network printer is connected to the network through a built-in Ethernet LAN adapter. Therefore, it will use 10 Mbps, 100 Mbps, or 1000Mbps (1Gbps). Therefore, the other answers are incorrect.

79. Answer: A. The 10 in 10BaseT represents the speed. Therefore, 10BaseT runs at 10 Mbps. Therefore, the other answers are incorrect.

80. Answer: A. Bluetooth 1.0, which is used to connect devices to a computer, can run at 1.0 Mbps. Therefore, the other answers are incorrect.

81. Answer: C. Bluetooth 2.0, which is used to connect devices to a computer, can run at 3.0 Mbps, although the practical transfer rate is 2.1 Mbps. Therefore, the other answers are incorrect.

82. Answer: A. When you configure a Bluetooth-enabled handheld device, you need to enable Bluetooth and assign a passkey. Answers B, C, and D are incorrect because they are used to configure a wireless network connection.

83. Answer: B. To use a VoIP, it must be able to send a constant stream of data. If the network bandwidth is fully utilized, your VoIP packets will not be delivered in a timely fashion, which causes the phone call to sound patchy. If the port (Answer A) was blocked, you could not connect at all. It is highly unlikely that you have two applications that are using the same port, which would cause interference between the two applications (Answer C). If the cable length is too long (Answer D), you will have network connectivity problems in general.

84. Answer: A. HTTP uses port 80. SMTP (Answer B) uses port 25, and POP3 (Answer C) uses port 110. Telnet (Answer D) uses port 23.

85. Answer: B. FTP requires ports 20 and 21 to operate. HTTP (Answer A) uses port 80. POP3 (Answer C) uses port 110 and DNS (Answer D) uses port 53.

86. Answer: C. Secure HTTPS (HTTPS) uses port 443. HTTP (Answer A) uses port 80. FTP (Answer B) uses ports 20 and 21. DNS (Answer D) uses port 53.

87. **Answer: B.** When you host network applications through a single firewall on your home network, you can only access a single network application running on a single computer because the firewall cannot differentiate the packets running for that network application for multiple computers. Therefore, when you enable port forwarding, all packets aimed at port 80 on your external IP address will be forwarded to an internal computer. You do not want to enable broadcast (Answer A) because your computer will receive a lot of traffic that will not be blocked. You do not need to configure authentication (Answer C) for the firewall, and you do not need to use the firewall as the default gateway (Answer D).

88. **Answer: C.** Ethernet 10BaseT is limited to 100 meters. Therefore, the other answers are incorrect.

89. **Answer: A.** You should place the wireless access point in the center of the house. Each wall that the wireless signal must pass through reduces the strength of the signal. Placing the wireless access point at the front or back of the house will block less at the front (Answer B) and back (Answer C) of the house because one side will have fewer walls while the other side has more walls. You should only place it under the bed or cabinet (Answer D) if you want to keep it hidden.

10

Security

The last domain for the 220-702 exam is security and comprises 13% of the exam. Much like the last three chapters were extensions of the 220-701 domain objectives, this domain is an extension of the Security domain in the 220-701 exam. Topics include preventing and removing viruses and malware and how to secure the system using different technologies that are available as part of Windows.

The given objectives for this domain of the 220-702 exam are as follows:

▶ 4.1—Given a scenario, prevent, troubleshoot, and remove viruses and malware

▶ 4.2—Implement security and troubleshoot common issues

4.1 Given a scenario, prevent, troubleshoot, and remove viruses and malware

▶ Use antivirus software

▶ Identify malware symptoms

▶ Quarantine infected systems

▶ Research malware types, symptoms, and solutions (virus encyclopedias)

▶ Remediate infected systems

▶ Update antivirus software

   ▶ Signature and engine updates

   ▶ Automatic vs. manual

▶ Schedule scans

▶ Repair boot blocks

▶ Scan and removal techniques

   ▶ Safe mode

   ▶ Boot environment

▶ Educate end user

Quick Check

1. Which of the following does spyware not do?

Quick Answer: **379**
Detailed Answer: **380**

   ○ **A.** Monitors keystrokes in an attempt to retrieve passwords and other private information

   ○ **B.** Changes the default home page to another site

   ○ **C.** Frequently opens pop-up windows

   ○ **D.** Changes the polarity of your monitor, which causes physical damage

   ○ **E.** Slows your machine

2. You have configured Windows Defender on all Microsoft Windows Vista machines on your domain. One user has an accounting application (which comes from a reputable company) that interacts with Microsoft Excel. When the application runs, an alert window opens to give a medium-level warning stating that the software might be spyware. Because you are sure that the application is not spyware, what do you need to do to stop these warnings from appearing? (Select the best answer.)

Quick Answer: **379**
Detailed Answer: **380**

   ○ **A.** Open Windows Defender. Select Tools, Options and configure Windows Defender to ignore medium alert items.

   ○ **B.** Configure Parental Controls to allow this application to run.

   ○ **C.** Open Windows Defender. Select Tools, Options. Under the Advanced options, click Add in the Do Not Scan These Files or Locations area and then browse to the application executable. Click OK.

   ○ **D.** When the warning appears again, click Always Allow.

3. You have a computer running Windows Vista. Every time a user opens Internet Explorer, the home page changes even after it has been manually set to the corporate home page. What should you do?

Quick Answer: **379**
Detailed Answer: **380**

   ○ **A.** Open the Control Panel and remove any programs that do not have any assigned publisher

   ○ **B.** Remove any unfamiliar programs on the Exceptions tab in the Windows Firewall

   ○ **C.** Change the security level for the Internet zone to High in the Internet Options

   ○ **D.** Remove any unfamiliar programs that have the startup type set to Registry: Local Machine

Quick Check

Quick Answer: 379
Detailed Answer: 380

4. You have a computer running Windows Vista. You have a user who is reporting that her machine is extremely slow, even after she reboots the computer. You suspect it is either a virus or spyware. You need to view all programs during startup. What do you do?

- ○ **A.** Open the Control Panel, double-click Services, and view all services that are set to start automatically

- ○ **B.** In Windows Explorer, browse to the Startup folder

- ○ **C.** Open Task Manager and view all applications that are currently running

- ○ **D.** Use Software Explorer to check what programs are loaded during startup

Quick Answer: 379
Detailed Answer: 380

5. You want to run the fastest scan that checks the most common locations where spyware is normally found. Which type of scan would you choose using Windows Defender?

- ○ **A.** Quick Scan
- ○ **B.** Fast Scan
- ○ **C.** Full Scan
- ○ **D.** Custom Scan

Quick Answer: 379
Detailed Answer: 380

6. A mobile user calls you from the road and informs you that his laptop is exhibiting erratic behavior. He reports that there were no problems until he downloaded a poker program from a site that he had never visited before. Which of the following terms describes a program that enters a system disguised in another program?

- ○ **A.** Trojan horse virus
- ○ **B.** Polymorphic virus
- ○ **C.** Worm
- ○ **D.** Peaceful virus

Quick Answer: 379
Detailed Answer: 380

7. What do you call it when an anti-virus software package isolates a file that contains a virus so that you might be able to remove the virus later?

- ○ **A.** Quarantine
- ○ **B.** Isolation mode
- ○ **C.** Boot protection
- ○ **D.** Firewalled

8. If a Windows computer has been infected with a virus, what are the two things you can try to remove the virus? (Choose two answers.)

Quick Answer: **379**
Detailed Answer: **380**

- ○ **A.** Boot the computer in Safe Mode
- ○ **B.** Login as a standard user
- ○ **C.** Perform a clean boot
- ○ **D.** Clear out the quarantine folder

9. You have a Windows XP computer that is connected to your corporate network. You suspect a virus is causing all kinds of problems, including slow and erratic performance. What should be the first thing you do?

Quick Answer: **379**
Detailed Answer: **381**

- ○ **A.** Download the newest security patches from Microsoft
- ○ **B.** Disconnect the computer from the network
- ○ **C.** Reboot the system and go into the BIOS setup program
- ○ **D.** Download the newest antivirus software package

10. What security features found in Windows work with processors to prevent an application or service from executing code from a non-executable memory region?

Quick Answer: **379**
Detailed Answer: **381**

- ○ **A.** PAE
- ○ **B.** Hyper-V
- ○ **C.** DEP
- ○ **D.** Protected mode

11. Where would you disable DEP on a computer running Windows XP with SP3?

Quick Answer: **379**
Detailed Answer: **381**

- ○ **A.** The Boot.ini file
- ○ **B.** The registry
- ○ **C.** System Properties in the Control Panel
- ○ **D.** In the BIOS setup program

12. Where would you disable DEP for an individual program for a computer with Windows XP running SP3?

Quick Answer: **379**
Detailed Answer: **381**

- ○ **A.** The Boot.ini file
- ○ **B.** The processor applet in the Control Panel
- ○ **C.** The system applet in the Control Panel
- ○ **D.** The BIOS setup program

13. You are trying to clean a file that has a virus on a Windows XP machine but you keep getting a message saying the file is in use. What should you do?

Quick Answer: **379**
Detailed Answer: **381**

○ **A.** Restart the computer in VGA mode

○ **B.** Restart the computer in Safe Mode

○ **C.** Boot to the Last Known Good Configuration.

○ **D.** Update the anti-virus program

14. You have a virus that corrupted the Master Boot Record. How can you fix the Master Boot Record?

Quick Answer: **379**
Detailed Answer: **381**

○ **A.** Copy the BOOT.INI file from another computer

○ **B.** Restart the computer in the Recovery Console and execute the `fixmbr` command

○ **C.** Restart the computer in the Recovery Console and execute the `fixboot` command

○ **D.** Select the Repair option in Windows Defender

4.2 Implement security and troubleshoot common issues

▶ Operating systems

▶ Local users and groups: Administrator, Power Users, Guest, Users

▶ Vista User Account Control (UAC)

▶ NTFS vs. Share permissions

▶ Allow vs. deny

▶ Difference between moving and copying folders and files

▶ File attributes

▶ Shared files and folders

▶ Administrative shares vs. local shares

▶ Permission propagation

▶ Inheritance

▶ System files and folders

▶ Encryption (BitLocker, EFS)

▶ User authentication

▶ System

▶ BIOS security

▶ Drive lock

▶ Passwords

▶ Intrusion detection

▶ TPM

15. What group in Windows XP can perform all administrative tasks on the local system? (Choose all that apply.)

Quick Answer: **379**
Detailed Answer: **381**

○ **A.** Administrators

○ **B.** Guests

○ **C.** Power Users

○ **D.** Remote Desktop Users

○ **E.** Users

16. What group in Windows XP or Vista can perform all administrative tasks on the local system? (Choose all that apply.)

Quick Answer: **379**
Detailed Answer: **382**

○ **A.** Administrators

○ **B.** Guests

○ **C.** Power Users

○ **D.** Remote Desktop Users

○ **E.** Users

17. What group in Windows Vista no longer exists unless you upgraded from a Windows XP system?

Quick Answer: **379**
Detailed Answer: **382**

○ **A.** Administrators

○ **B.** Guests

○ **C.** Power Users

○ **D.** Remote Desktop Users

○ **E.** Users

18. What account is disabled by default in Windows XP or Windows Vista?

Quick Answer: **379**
Detailed Answer: **382**

○ **A.** Administrator

○ **B.** Guests

○ **C.** Power User

○ **D.** Remote User

19. Which group contains all user accounts created on a Windows machine?

Quick Answer: **379**
Detailed Answer: **382**

○ **A.** Administrators

○ **B.** Guests

○ **C.** Power Users

○ **D.** Users

20. On Windows Vista, which of the following will UAC prompt for permission or administrative credentials? (Choose all that apply.)

Quick Answer: **379**
Detailed Answer: **382**

- ○ **A.** Change time zone
- ○ **B.** Change power management settings
- ○ **C.** Install fonts
- ○ **D.** Install a device driver
- ○ **E.** Install an application

21. Which of the following is the best method to prevent unauthorized changes to your Windows Vista computer?

Quick Answer: **379**
Detailed Answer: **382**

- ○ **A.** Computer Management Console
- ○ **B.** User Account Control (UAC)
- ○ **C.** Windows Firewall
- ○ **D.** Event Viewer

22. You have configured your children's account on your Windows XP Home computer as a limited account so that they cannot access your financial and personal data. What else will the children not be able to do as members of this group? (Select all that apply.)

Quick Answer: **379**
Detailed Answer: **382**

- ○ **A.** Create additional users
- ○ **B.** Create new folders
- ○ **C.** Delete folders and files
- ○ **D.** Install applications

23. What user group must you be a member of to install a non-hot-swappable device in a Windows XP system?

Quick Answer: **379**
Detailed Answer: **383**

- ○ **A.** Administrators
- ○ **B.** Guest
- ○ **C.** Users
- ○ **D.** Power Users

24. In Windows Vista, what causes the message that asks your permission to continue?

Quick Answer: **379**
Detailed Answer: **383**

- ○ **A.** The Windows Firewall
- ○ **B.** NTFS permissions
- ○ **C.** User Account Control (UAC)
- ○ **D.** Internet Sharing Console

25. You have upgraded several computers from Windows XP Professional to Microsoft Windows Vista Enterprise. You had an accounting application that worked fine in Windows 2000 but does not run fine on Windows Vista. After further research, you find that when the user tries to run the application, it asks for a login. When the accountants enter their usernames and passwords, the application still fails. When you use an administrator user account and password, though, the application works. What is the best solution to fix this problem?

- ○ **A.** Add the user accounts to the local administrator group.

- ○ **B.** Add the user accounts to the domain administrator group.

- ○ **C.** Use Parental Control for the users to access the applications.

- ○ **D.** Right-click the executable and select properties. Use the Application's properties dialog box to run this program as an administrator.

26. Your boss wants you to configure the company's network of computers so that only approved software can be loaded onto company PCs. What can you do to prevent employees from installing their own applications?

- ○ **A.** Create new accounts for all the employees in the Users group and then configure the group to have only Read permissions.

- ○ **B.** Create a new group account for these employees and configure the group with Write and Execute permissions.

- ○ **C.** Create an account for each user, create a special group account, and then move all the user accounts into it. Finally, apply permission settings to the new group account to limit its members to Write permissions.

- ○ **D.** Remove any unauthorized users from the Administrators and Power Users groups and make sure that the Local Administrator and Power Users groups do not contain any Domain User accounts.

27. Your organization is growing, and you need to be able to delegate responsibilities for some network management activities to other members of your team. Which standard Windows group found on Windows XP can you use to grant these employees the ability to manage users and groups that they create without making them administrators?

   ○ **A.** Administrators

   ○ **B.** Backup Administrators

   ○ **C.** Network Configuration Operators

   ○ **D.** Power Users

28. What is the correct order to grant many users with access to the same resources?

   ○ **A.** Create the users, create a group that defines the common needs of the users, and then assign access rights to the group.

   ○ **B.** Create a group that defines the common needs of the users in question, make all the users members of that group, and then assign the group access permissions for the resources they need access to.

   ○ **C.** Assign access permissions to the default Everyone group so that all the users have access to the resources.

   ○ **D.** Assign access permissions to the Guest account so that all the users have access to the resources when they log in to the network.

29. You have many computers that are part of a Windows domain running Windows Vista. Your company decides to have only applications that have been approved by the IT department. You have a handful of users who need to make configuration changes to these applications. However, when they try to make the appropriate changes, they always receive the following error message:

   You need to ensure that *<username>* is able to make configuration changes to *<computer name>*.

   After verifying that these users have administrative access to their computers, what do you need to do to ensure they no longer receive these messages?

   ○ **A.** Add all users to the Power Users group

   ○ **B.** Add all users to the Users group

   ○ **C.** Turn off the Windows Firewall

   ○ **D.** Change the Elevation prompt for administrators in User Account Control (UAC) Admin Approval Mode

30. In Windows Vista, you need to assign a handful of users the ability to install applications without giving administrative permissions. What do you do?

Quick Answer: **379**
Detailed Answer: **384**

   ○ **A.** Make these users part of the local administrator group

   ○ **B.** Turn User Account Control off in the User Accounts Control Panel tool

   ○ **C.** You should configure Parental Controls to block each user from the ability to download unapproved software

   ○ **D.** Configure the user account control not to prompt during software installation in the Security Options section of the Local Security Policy

31. You have several Windows Vista computers to which certain users have to make configuration changes to a handful of applications. Some of the users are reporting that they are getting the following error message while other users do not see this message.

Quick Answer: **379**
Detailed Answer: **384**

You need to ensure that <*username*> is able to make configuration changes to <*computer name*>.

What do you need to do to correct this problem?

   ○ **A.** You need to add the users that see this message to the local administrators group on the computer.

   ○ **B.** The users that see this message have been entering the wrong usernames and passwords.

   ○ **C.** You need to reconfigure the application to run as an administrator instead of a standard user.

   ○ **D.** You need to start the application service on the systems that have the problem.

32. To create local user accounts in Windows Vista, you would use which of the following? (Choose two answers.)

Quick Answer: **379**
Detailed Answer: **384**

   ○ **A.** User Accounts in the Control Panel

   ○ **B.** Computer Management Console

   ○ **C.** Active Directory Users and Computers

   ○ **D.** Users and Groups Administrator console

33. You want to control the permissions of files and directories on an NTFS drive on the network. Which application must you use?

Quick Answer: **379**
Detailed Answer: **384**

   ○ **A.** Windows Explorer

   ○ **B.** Active Directory Users and Computers console

   ○ **C.** Computer management console

   ○ **D.** Disk Administrator console

34. Which of the following file systems is the most secure and the most reliable used by Windows Vista?

- ○ **A.** FAT
- ○ **B.** FAT32
- ○ **C.** NTFS
- ○ **D.** NFS

35. A user can look at the contents of a folder in Windows 2000 but cannot open the files or rename them. What permission does this user have enabled?

- ○ **A.** Read
- ○ **B.** List Folder Contents
- ○ **C.** Read & Execute
- ○ **D.** Modify

36. If you move a shared folder with limited rights to a FAT32 partition, what are the effects on folder permissions?

- ○ **A.** The permissions follow the folder to the new partition.
- ○ **B.** The permissions for the folder are reduced to Read and Write Only.
- ○ **C.** The folder inherits the permissions set on the partition it is being moved to.
- ○ **D.** The established permissions cannot follow the folder to a FAT32 partition.

37. Which NTFS permissions enable you to delete a folder? (Select all that apply.)

- ○ **A.** Full
- ○ **B.** Read
- ○ **C.** Write
- ○ **D.** Modify

38. A Windows XP computer contains a shared folder on an NTFS partition. Which one of the following statements concerning access to the folder is correct?

   ○ **A.** A user who is accessing the folder remotely has the same or more restrictive access permissions than if the user accesses the folder locally.

   ○ **B.** A user who is accessing the folder remotely has less restrictive access permissions than if the user accesses the folder locally.

   ○ **C.** A user who is accessing the folder remotely has the same access permissions as when she accesses the folder locally.

   ○ **D.** A user who is accessing the folder remotely has more restrictive access permissions than if she accesses the folder locally.

39. A Windows Vista computer contains a shared folder on an NTFS partition. Which one of the following statements concerning access to the folder is correct?

   ○ **A.** A user who is accessing the folder remotely has the same or more restrictive access permissions than if she accesses the folder locally.

   ○ **B.** A user who is accessing the folder remotely has less restrictive access permissions than if she accesses the folder locally.

   ○ **C.** A user who is accessing the folder remotely has the same access permissions than if she accesses the folder locally.

   ○ **D.** A user who is accessing the folder remotely has more restrictive access permissions than if she accesses the folder locally.

40. Pat is a member of the manager group. There is a shared folder called DATA on an NTFS partition on a remote Windows Vista computer. Pat is given the Write NTFS permission; the Manager group is given the Read & Execute NTFS permissions; and the Everyone group has the Read NTFS permission to the DATA folder. In addition, Pat, Manager, and Everyone are assigned the shared Contributor permission to the DATA folder. When Pat logs on to the Windows Vista computer that has the DATA folder and accesses the DATA folder directly, what would be Pat's permissions? (Choose all that apply.)

   ○ **A.** Read the files in that folder

   ○ **B.** Write to the files in the folder

   ○ **C.** Execute the files in the folder

   ○ **D.** Delete the files in the folder

   ○ **E.** Have no access to the files in the folder

41. Pat is a member of the manager group. There is a shared folder called DATA on an NTFS partition on a remote Windows Vista computer. Pat is given the Write NTFS permission; the Manager group is given the Read & Execute NTFS permissions; and the Everyone group has the Read NTFS permission to the DATA folder. In addition, Pat, Manager, and Everyone are assigned the shared Read permission to the DATA folder. When Pat logs onto his client computer and accesses the DATA folder, what would be Pat's permissions? (Choose all that apply.)

Quick Answer: **379**
Detailed Answer: **385**

   ○ **A.** Read the files in that folder

   ○ **B.** Write to the files in the folder

   ○ **C.** Execute the files in the folder

   ○ **D.** Delete the files in the folder

   ○ **E.** Have no access to the files in the folder

42. Pat is a member of the manager group. There is a shared folder called DATA on an NTFS partition on a remote Windows Vista computer. Pat is given the Write NTFS permission; the Manager group is giving the Deny All NTFS permissions; and the Everyone group has the Read NTFS permission to the DATA folder. In addition, Pat, Manager, and Everyone are assigned the shared Contributor permission to the DATA folder. When Pat logs onto his client computer and accesses the DATA folder, what would be Pat's permissions? (Choose all that apply.)

Quick Answer: **379**
Detailed Answer: **385**

   ○ **A.** Read the files in that folder

   ○ **B.** Write to the files in the folder

   ○ **C.** Execute the files in the folder

   ○ **D.** Delete the files in the folder

   ○ **E.** Have no access to the files in the folder

43. A client needs to use a custom application on her Windows Vista computer. The custom application saves data to the %program-files%\app1 folder. You install the custom application on her computer. Which of the following actions do you need to ensure that the client can run the custom application? (Choose two answers.)

Quick Answer: **379**
Detailed Answer: **385**

   ○ **A.** Download and install the Windows Vista Upgrade Advisor

   ○ **B.** Run the application with elevated privileges

   ○ **C.** Download and install the Application Compatibility Toolkit (ACT)

   ○ **D.** Modify the NTFS permissions on the %program-files%\app1 folder

44. Which of the following is required to access a network share in an NTFS system?

Quick Answer: **379**
Detailed Answer: **385**

- ○ **A.** Share permissions
- ○ **B.** A password
- ○ **C.** Access rights
- ○ **D.** User permissions

45. You have created an uncompressed file called MyPaper.doc in the Documents folder on an NTFS partition. The Documents folder is not compressed. Now you move the file MyPaper.doc to a compressed folder called TermPaper on a different NTFS partition. Which of the following will occur?

Quick Answer: **379**
Detailed Answer: **386**

- ○ **A.** The file will stay uncompressed.
- ○ **B.** The file will inherit the compression attribute from the target folder.
- ○ **C.** The file will inherit the compression attribute from the target partition.
- ○ **D.** A dialog box will appear, asking you whether you want to compress the file in the target folder.

46. What will occur if you copy a file from one folder to another folder within the same NTFS partition?

Quick Answer: **379**
Detailed Answer: **386**

- ○ **A.** The file will retain its permissions.
- ○ **B.** The file will inherit the permissions of the source folder.
- ○ **C.** The file will inherit the permissions of the target folder.
- ○ **D.** All file permissions will be lost.

47. What will occur if you move a file from one folder to another folder within the same NTFS partition?

Quick Answer: **379**
Detailed Answer: **386**

- ○ **A.** The file will retain its permissions.
- ○ **B.** The file will inherit the permissions of the source folder.
- ○ **C.** The file will inherit the permissions of the target folder.
- ○ **D.** All file permissions will be lost.

48. A user moves a folder from an NTFS partition on his Windows 2000 Server to a shared NTFS folder on a remote Windows 2000 server. What will be the permissions of the moved folder?

Quick Answer: **379**
Detailed Answer: **386**

- ○ **A.** No Access permission
- ○ **B.** Full Access permission
- ○ **C.** The same permissions as its original residing on the user's workstation
- ○ **D.** The same permissions as the folder it was copied to

49. Pat was a member of the Research group. Now he has been reassigned to the Design team. As a result, he needs access to program source files in the \DATA directory on the file server. The Design Administrators group has Full Control permissions to the \DATA directory. The Users group has Read permission, and the Research group has been Denied Access to the \DATA directory. After logging on as a member of the Design group, Pat notices that he still cannot access the files in the \DATA directory on the file server. What is the best way for the Administrator to grant him the required access to the \DATA directory?

Quick Answer: **379**
Detailed Answer: **386**

- ○ **A.** Remove Pat's user account from the Research group
- ○ **B.** Remove Pat's user account from the Research group and the Users group
- ○ **C.** Grant all permissions for the \DATA directory to Pat's user account
- ○ **D.** Add Pat's user account to the Administrators group

50. You have a laptop that has several shared folders. You configure the network location type on the Windows Vista computer as Private to enable you to connect to the main office where you work. You want to ensure that only users with a user account and password on your computer can access your shared folders, including the Public folder. What should you do?

Quick Answer: **379**
Detailed Answer: **386**

- ○ **A.** You need to create a DNS Public entry for a Windows Vista computer.
- ○ **B.** The Public folder sharing option should be turned on in the Network and Sharing Center.
- ○ **C.** The Password Protected Sharing option should be turned on in the Network and Sharing Center.
- ○ **D.** Network discovery should be turned off in the Network and Sharing Center.

51. You have two users who share a computer running Windows Vista Business Edition. Both users are working on a major report, but you don't want one user to access the other user's data files. What should you do?

Quick Answer: **379**
Detailed Answer: **386**

- ○ **A.** Give each the appropriate NTFS permissions to the other's My Documents folder
- ○ **B.** Have the users log in with the same account
- ○ **C.** Instruct these users to store the report in the public folder
- ○ **D.** Instruct these users to log out as themselves and log in as the other user to access the report

52. You have shared a couple of folders on your Windows Vista computer. Unfortunately, they are not visible on anyone's network map so that users can find the shares easily. What is most likely the problem?

- ○ **A.** You need to enable the Network Discovery service.
- ○ **B.** You did not give the appropriate share permissions to the Everyone group.
- ○ **C.** You did not give the appropriate NTFS permission to the Everyone group.
- ○ **D.** You need to make sure there is a DNS entry in the DNS server for the Windows Vista computer.

53. After receiving an NTLDR Is Missing message on a Windows 2000 Professional system, you boot the machine using the Windows distribution CD kit and gain access to the system's Recovery Console. When you examine the contents of the drive, you do not see the NTLDR file in the root directory. You suspect that the file is not apparent because it is a hidden system file. Which of the following actions enables you to change the attributes of the file so that you can verify its presence?

- ○ **A.** Restart the system in Safe Mode, access the Windows Explorer, right-click the C: drive, select Properties from the pop-up list, move to the General page, and click the desired attribute box.
- ○ **B.** Run the `attrib -r -s -h c:\ntldr` command from the command line.
- ○ **C.** Restart the system in Safe Mode, access the Windows Explorer, click the View menu, select the Folders entry, click the View tab, and check the Show All Files box.
- ○ **D.** Run the `attrib +r +s +h c:\ntldr` command from the command line.

54. You want to give a source document you've prepared for your staff a read-only file attribute so that it cannot be altered. Which of the following methods can you use in Windows Explorer to change the file's attributes?

- ○ **A.** Edit the appropriate Registry entry for the file using Regedt32.
- ○ **B.** Right-click the file, select Properties, and place a check mark in the Read Only check box.
- ○ **C.** Highlight the file, choose the Select Options entry in the System Tools menu, and select the Read Only option.
- ○ **D.** Highlight the file, choose the Select Options entry in the View menu, and select the Read Only option.

55. You have been called because one of your customers wants to encrypt a folder on her drive. However, when she accesses the folder's properties, there is no option to encrypt it. Why might this be?

Quick Answer: **379**
Detailed Answer: **386**

- ○ **A.** The folder is located on a FAT partition.
- ○ **B.** The customer does not have adequate permissions to change the attributes of this folder.
- ○ **C.** The folder has been marked as Read Only.
- ○ **D.** The folder is inheriting its attributes from the partition it is installed in.

56. A Windows XP Professional customer asks you to show him how to set up file and folder encryption to protect his private information on his disk drive. How do you do this?

Quick Answer: **379**
Detailed Answer: **387**

- ○ **A.** Click on the Encrypt option of the drive's Properties menu and choose Encrypt Files on This Drive
- ○ **B.** Tell the user that file and folder encryption is performed automatically on NTFS5 disks
- ○ **C.** Click the Encrypt Contents to Secure Data check box in the folder's Advanced Attributes window
- ○ **D.** Click on the Encrypt option of the drive's Properties menu and choose Encrypt Folders on This Drive

57. You have configured BitLocker Drive Encryption on a computer, which has a Trusted Platform Module (TPM) installed. Unfortunately when Windows Vista starts, a TPM error is displayed and the user cannot access the data on her computer because it is encrypted. What should you do?

Quick Answer: **379**
Detailed Answer: **387**

- ○ **A.** Restart the computer and enter the recovery password at the BitLocker Driver Encryption Recovery Console.
- ○ **B.** Restart the computer and login as the local administrator
- ○ **C.** Disable the TPM component in the BIOS and reboot the computer
- ○ **D.** Open the TPM management console

58. Your boss wants to protect the laptops if they get stolen. What would you do? (Choose the best answer.)

Quick Answer: **379**
Detailed Answer: **387**

- ○ **A.** Make sure that all volumes are using NTFS file system
- ○ **B.** Implement BitLocker
- ○ **C.** Implement IP Security (IPsec) for all network communications
- ○ **D.** Implement Encrypted File System (EFS) on key data files

59. Which of the following is not a requirement for BitLocker?

Quick Answer: **379**
Detailed Answer: **387**

- ○ **A.** A computer with a TPM

- ○ **B.** A computer with only one large NTFS volume

- ○ **C.** A computer that has a compatible BIOS with TPM

- ○ **D.** A USB flash drive if your system does not have TPM

60. One of your customers has research work on his notebook PC that he wants to protect. In the event that the notebook is stolen, he wants more authentication than a simple username and password login for his PC. What can you recommend that will be easy to implement and cost effective, and will adequately protect the information on his notebook?

Quick Answer: **379**
Detailed Answer: **387**

- ○ **A.** Employ an encryption algorithm for login

- ○ **B.** Install a retinal scanner on the PC

- ○ **C.** Employ a Shared Secret login scenario

- ○ **D.** Install a fingerprint scanner on the notebook

61. An employee returns to the company after being gone for several months. She cannot remember her last password. How do you get her back to work?

Quick Answer: **379**
Detailed Answer: **387**

- ○ **A.** Email the employee her password

- ○ **B.** Call her with it

- ○ **C.** Default to the company policy

- ○ **D.** Make up a password for her

62. When you start up your PC at the beginning of your workday and try to log in to the network server, you receive a "The system could not log you on" error message. You have logged in to this server several times before, so which of the following could be the cause of this message? (Select all that apply.)

Quick Answer: **379**
Detailed Answer: **387**

- ○ **A.** You have mistyped your username or password.

- ○ **B.** The network server is down, so you cannot be authenticated.

- ○ **C.** You have been locked out by the network's password policy.

- ○ **D.** Your network's NSLOOKUP server is not available.

63. Which protocol type is used specifically for authenticating users in a credit-card-based e-commerce setting?

   ○ **A.** HTTP

   ○ **B.** IMAP

   ○ **C.** SSL

   ○ **D.** SMTP

Quick Answer: **379**
Detailed Answer: **388**

64. Which remote access authentication provides two-way authentication that requires both the server and the client to authenticate?

   ○ **A.** PAP

   ○ **B.** CHAP

   ○ **C.** MS-CHAP

   ○ **D.** MS-CHAPv2

Quick Answer: **379**
Detailed Answer: **388**

65. Which remote access authentication is the least secure because the username and password are sent in clear text?

   ○ **A.** PAP

   ○ **B.** CHAP

   ○ **C.** MS-CHAP

   ○ **D.** MS-CHAPv2

Quick Answer: **379**
Detailed Answer: **388**

66. What dial-up authentication protocol is an industry standard that uses a challenge response with a one-way hash algorithm?

   ○ **A.** PAP

   ○ **B.** CHAP

   ○ **C.** MS-CHAP

   ○ **D.** MS-CHAPv2

Quick Answer: **379**
Detailed Answer: **388**

67. Which authentication protocol is needed for smart cards?

   ○ **A.** CHAP

   ○ **B.** MS-CHAP

   ○ **C.** MS-CHAPv2

   ○ **D.** EAP

Quick Answer: **379**
Detailed Answer: **388**

Quick Check

Quick Answer: **379**
Detailed Answer: **388**

68. You need to ensure that all the Windows XP computers in the company authenticate with other computers on your corporate domain by using Kerberos. Which action should you perform?

- ○ **A.** Upgrade all the computers to Windows Vista.
- ○ **B.** Join all the computers to the corporate domain.
- ○ **C.** Configure the local policy on each computer to reject NTLM responses.
- ○ **D.** You don't have to do anything. Windows XP uses Kerberos by default, whether it is part of a domain or not.

Quick-Check Answer Key

1. D	24. C	47. A
2. D	25. D	48. D
3. D	26. D	49. A
4. D	27. D	50. C
5. A	28. B	51. C
6. A	29. D	52. A
7. A	30. D	53. B
8. A and C	31. A	54. B
9. B	32. A and B	55. A
10. C	33. A	56. C
11. A	34. C	57. A
12. C	35. B	58. B
13. B.	36. D	59. B
14. B	37. A and D	60. D
15. A	38. D	61. C
16. A	39. A	62. A, B, and C
17. C	40. A, B, C, and D	63. C
18. B	41. A and C	64. D
19. D	42. A	65. A
20. D and E	43. B and D	66. B
21. B	44. A	67. D
22. A and D	45. B	68. B
23. A	46. C	

Answers and Explanations

1. **Answer: D.** Spyware cannot physically damage a computer. It can, however, capture information as you type it in, change the default home page, generate pop-up Windows and slow your machine. Therefore, Answers A, B, C, and E are incorrect.

2. **Answer: D.** When you know that a program is not spyware, click Always Allow so that it stops thinking the software is spyware. Answer A is incorrect because you don't want to ignore the other programs. Answer B is incorrect because Parental Controls do not function on domains. Answer C is incorrect because Answer D is the better answer.

3. **Answer: D.** If you use Software Explorer (part of Windows Defender), you can remove any program that executes during startup. Many spyware programs include those that change home pages and load themselves automatically during startup. Therefore, you should remove any programs that you don't recognize. Answer A is incorrect because not all programs will be shown in the Add/Remove programs. Answer B is incorrect because there is no indication that it is communicating with the outside world, and using the firewall would not stop the spyware program from changing the home page. Answer C is incorrect because changing the security level would have no effect because the spyware program is already on the machine.

4. **Answer: D.** Because the computer is slow even after reboot, the spyware program must load every time the computer is rebooted. Therefore, it has to be loaded during startup. Answer A is incorrect because spyware is not typically loaded as a service. Answer B is not the best answer because most startup programs are specified in the registry, not the startup folder. Answer C is incorrect because if you use Task Manager to stop the program, the program will still reload after you restart the computer.

5. **Answer: A.** Quick Scan will check all places that you normally would find spyware, including those that execute during startup. Answer B is incorrect because a Fast Scan does not exist. Answer C is incorrect because full scans are much more thorough scans but take much longer. Answer D is incorrect because you would then need to manually specify where to search for spyware.

6. **Answer: A.** A Trojan horse virus appears, to the user, to perform a desirable function but, in fact, it facilitates unauthorized access to the user's computer system. A polymorphic virus (Answer B) is a virus that changes often to keep it from being detected. A worm (Answer C) is malware that spreads and utilizes the resources of a computer, slowing the computer down. There is no classification called Peaceful virus (Answer D).

7. **Answer: A.** If an anti-virus software package cannot remove a virus from a file, it can be configured to delete the file or to quarantine the file. When a file is quarantined, it is copied to a special folder (usually named quarantined). Isolation mode (Answer B), Boot protection (Answer C), and Firewalled (Answer D) are not terms used with anti-virus software.

8. **Answer: A and C.** Often, you cannot remove a virus if it is loaded in memory. Therefore, you need to boot the computer in Safe Mode or perform a clean boot before you can remove the virus so that certain programs are not loaded. If the virus has infected your computer, you might need to be an administrator (Answer B) to remove it. Lastly, files that are in the quarantine folder (Answer D) have already been isolated and therefore should not be the source of the virus.

9. **Answer: B.** Because you are connected to the network and you think it is infected with a virus, you should disconnect it from the network so that the virus does not spread to other computers. It is important to download the newest security patches (Answer A) and newest antivirus software package (Answer D), but do this only after the virus is removed. Rebooting and going into the BIOS setup program (Answer C) will not help you remove the virus.

10. **Answer: C.** Data Execution Prevention (DEP) is a security feature included in Windows XP with SP2 and Windows Vista intended to prevent an application or service from executing code from a non-executable memory region. This helps prevent certain exploits that store code via a buffer overflow. Hyper-V (Answer B) is an Intel technology that creates two logical processors on each physical core in an attempt to keep the pipelines full at all times. PAE (Answer A), short for Physical Address Extension, is technology that allows 32-bit Windows to access more than 4 GB of physical memory. Protected mode (Answer D) is a mode used in processors that allows the operating system to use virtual memory, paging, and multitasking.

11. **Answer: A.** Data Execution Prevention (DEP) is a security feature included in Windows XP with SP2 and Windows Vista that is intended to prevent an application or service from executing code from a non-executable memory region. This helps prevent certain exploits that store code via a buffer overflow. To disable DEP, modify the Boot.ini file. You cannot disable DEP using the registry (Answer B), System Properties (Answer C), or the BIOS Setup Program (Answer D).

12. **Answer: C.** Data Execution Prevention (DEP) is a security feature included in Windows XP with SP2 and Windows Vista that is intended to prevent an application or service from executing code from a non-executable memory region. To enable or disable for an individual application, you open the System Properties, access the Advanced System Settings, select Settings in the Performance session, and click the Data Execution Prevention tab. You cannot configure individual programs using the Boot.ini file (Answer A) or BIOS setup program (Answer D), and there is no Processor applet in the Control Panel (Answer B).

13. **Answer: B.** If you reboot the computer into Safe Mode, Windows only loads the essential files needed to start Windows. You can then use the anti-virus software package to clean the virus. If you restart the computer in VGA mode (Answer A), your screen will turn to 640×480 resolution, but all the other service and programs still load. The Last Known Good Configuration (Answer C) only undoes the most recent change. Updating the anti-virus software (Answer D) will not help because the file cannot be cleaned because it is in use, not because the program does not know what do with the file.

14. **Answer: B.** The Master Boot Record contains the partition table and a volume boot sector. The `fixmbr` command executed from the Recovery Console will fix a corrupted fix Master Boot Record (MBR). Copying the Boot.ini file (Answer A) from another computer will not fix an MBR and executing the `fixboot` command (Answer C) will only repair the Windows boot sector on the system partition. There is no Repair option in Windows Defender (Answer D), Microsoft's anti-spyware program.

15. **Answer: A.** Members included in the Administrators group can perform all administrative tasks on the local system. By default, the built-in Administrator account is a member of the Administrators group. The guest account (Answer B) is used to give temporary

access to a system but has minimum rights and permissions. The Power Users group (Answer C) can create and modify local user accounts on the computer, share resources, and install drivers for legacy software. They do not have full administrative permissions. Remote Desktop Users (Answer D) are granted the right to log on locally through a Remote Desktop Connection. Users (Answer E) can perform tasks for which they have been assigned permissions.

16. **Answer: A.** Members included in the Administrators group can perform all administrative tasks on the local system. By default, the built-in Administrator account is a member of the Administrators group. The guest account (Answer B) is used to give temporary access to a system, but has minimum rights and permissions. The Power Users group (Answer C) has some but not all the user rights of the Administrator accounts, including creating and modifying local user accounts on the computer, sharing resources, and installing drivers for legacy software. They do not have full administrative permissions. Remote Desktop Users (Answer D) are granted the right to log on locally through Remote Desktop Connection. Users (Answer E) can perform tasks for which they have been assigned permissions.

17. **Answer: C.** The Power Users group has some, but not all, of the user rights that Administrator accounts have. In Windows Vista, the Power Users Group has been simplified and the Power Users group no longer exists unless you upgrade from Windows XP. The other groups exist in both Windows XP and Windows Vista.

18. **Answer: B.** To help keep Windows secure, the guest account is disabled because it is meant to be used as an anonymous login with minimum access. The Administrator account (Answer A) is not disabled. There are no Power User (Answer C) or Remote User (Answer D) accounts.

19. **Answer: D.** The Users group contains all Windows accounts created on a Windows computer. When a computer is added to the domain, Windows adds Domain users to the local Users group. By default, the Administrators group (Answer A) only contains the Administrator user account. The Guests group (Answer B) only contains the Guest user account. By default, the Power Users group (Answer C) does not contain any accounts.

20. **Answer: D and E.** Installing a device driver and installing an application require administrative permissions. Therefore, UAC prompts you to make sure it is something that you want to do. Answers A, B, and C are incorrect because standard users can do this.

21. **Answer: B.** User Account Control is used to prevent unauthorized changes to the computer. Answer A is incorrect because the Computer Management Console is used to manage the computer, including managing volumes, using the Event Viewer, and managing local users and groups. Answer C is incorrect because the Windows Firewall helps block unwanted packets from getting to your computer. Answer D is incorrect because the Event Viewer looks at warning and error messages and the security logs.

22. **Answers: A and D.** Windows XP Home does not provide the variety of account options found in Windows 2000 or XP Professional. Windows XP Home provides only Limited and Administrative rights options for controlling access to system resources. When a user is given a Limited account, she is enabled to access programs already installed on the computer but cannot install software or hardware components or change her account name or type. The user cannot create a new user because this activity is relegated to computer administrators. Therefore, the other answers are incorrect.

23. Answer: A. In Windows XP, the administrator has been given tools that can be used to limit what the user can do to any given resource. Non-hot-swappable devices, such as local printers, cannot be added to Windows 2000 or Windows XP systems without Administrator permissions. In a Domain environment, members of the Print Managers group can normally add printers to the system. Likewise, members of the Local Users group can add network printers to the system. All these capabilities are based on the default permission settings for these groups; with the exception of the Administrators group, the capabilities of these groups can be modified through Group Policy settings. Guests (Answer B), Users (Answer C), and Power Users (Answer D) cannot install non-hot-swappable devices.

24. Answer: C. The User Account Control asks for permission to continue when you are performing tasks that require you to be an administrator to ensure that you really want to complete the tasks. Answer A is incorrect because the Windows Firewall prevents unwanted packets from the outside. Answer B is incorrect because NTFS permissions help protect the files on an NTFS volume. Answer D is incorrect because there is no such thing as an Internet Sharing Console.

25. Answer: D. To configure legacy applications to run under Windows Vista, you can right-click an executable and open the Properties dialog box. From there, you can specify what environment to run under and, if necessary, specify if the application can run under an administrator account. It is not recommended to give all users who need access to this application administrator accounts (Answers A and B) because they could cause other security problems. Parental Control (Answer C) is not included in Windows Vista Enterprise.

26. Answer: D. By default, only members of the Administrators and Power Users groups have the ability to install applications in a Windows domain. Members of other Windows groups do not have this ability unless they are given it by a Group Policy or inherit it through a group association. Therefore, the other answers are incorrect.

27. Answer: D. Power Users is a special group that has permissions to perform many management tasks on the system but does not have the full administrative privileges of the Administrator account (Answer A). Power Users can create and manage users and groups that they create. Also, they do not have access to files and folders on NTFS volumes unless they are granted permissions to them through other sources. There are no members in this group when it is created. Backup Operators, not Backup Administrators (Answer B) give the ability to backup and restore all files. The Network Configuration Operators (Answer C) allow you to change the network configuration.

28. Answer: B. The most efficient method of assigning large groups of users access to the same resources is to (1) create the group, (2) make all users a member of the group, and (3) assign the group access permissions to the resource. Therefore, the other answers are incorrect.

29. Answer: D. The message is generated by the User Account Control, which you can configure by using local or group policies. Answer A is incorrect because the Power Users group is left behind from Windows 2000 and XP for backward compatibility. Answer B is incorrect because all standard user accounts should already be a member of the Users group. Answer C is incorrect because turning off the firewall would not get rid of the message.

30. **Answer: D.** You need to edit the Local Security Policy to not prompt during installs by disabling the Detect Application Installations and Prompt for Elevation setting. This will allow applications to be installed without prompting for the administrative credentials. Answer A is incorrect because you don't want to give administrative permission. Answer B is incorrect because turning off User Account Control will stop protecting the system. Answer C is also incorrect because Parental Controls cannot be used when a computer is connected to a domain.

31. **Answer: A.** Some users are not having the problem but other users do. Therefore, you need to focus on what is different between the two groups of users—in this case you need to add the users who are having the problem to the administrator group. Answer B is incorrect because if they were using the wrong usernames and passwords, they would not get logged into the system. Answer C is incorrect because if the application runs as a standard user, it would affect all users. Answer D is incorrect because there is no such thing as the application service.

32. **Answer: A and B.** The Control Panel User accounts and the Computer Management Console, specifically under Users and Groups, are used to add and manage user accounts. Answer C is incorrect because Active Directory Users and Computers console is used to manage domain user accounts. Answer D is incorrect because the Users and Groups Administrator console does not exist.

33. **Answer: A.** Folders and files and their NTFS permissions are managed by the Windows Explorer. Answer B is incorrect because Active Directory Users and Computers console is used to manage the user and computer accounts within Active Directory, not NTFS permissions. Answer C is incorrect because the Computer Management Console, which includes the disk administrator, can be used to look at the Event Viewer, to examine the status of the disks, and to manage the file system volumes, but it has nothing to do with NTFS permissions. Answer D is incorrect because the Disk Administrator has nothing to do with NTFS permissions.

34. **Answer C.** NTFS is the only one that provides security features, such as encryption and NTFS permissions and the ability to use transaction tracking to keep the file system reliable. Answers A and B are incorrect because they do not offer the features just mentioned for NTFS. NFS (Answer D) is a file system used in UNIX/Linux machines and is not supported by Windows Vista as a file system.

35. **Answer: B.** When users of a Windows 2000 system complain that they can see files in a folder but cannot access any of the files, they might have been assigned the List Folder Contents permission at the folder level. The List Folder Contents permission enables users only to view the contents of the folder, denying them all other permissions, including Read and Execute. The Read permission (Answer A) means they can open the files. The Read & Execute permission (Answer C) can read and execute executable files. The Modify permission (Answer D) means they can read and execute files, list folder contents, modify the contents of files, and change attributes.

36. **Answer: D.** When files and folders from an NTFS partition are moved to a FAT partition, their NTFS attributes and security features are lost. Even moving files between different NTFS partitions on different drives can change the security level of the files. Migrating NTFS data to a partition that has lower permission levels than the original partition causes the data to inherit the lesser permissions of the target folder. Therefore, the other answers are incorrect.

37. **Answer: A and D.** The Modify permission enables users to modify and delete the file and to perform all the activities associated with the Read, Write, and Read & Execute permissions. The Full Control permission enables the user or group to take ownership of the file and to change its permissions, as well as perform all the other activities possible with all the other permissions. The Read permission (Answer B) only allows you to open and read a file. The Write permission (Answer C) allows you to write and change a file.

38. **Answer: D.** When you combine NTFS and Share permissions, the most restrictive permissions are applied. Therefore, the other answers are incorrect.

39. **Answer: A.** When you access a computer remotely through the share, you include the share permissions and the NTFS permissions which can both restrict access. When you access the local folder directly, only the NTFS permissions apply. Therefore, they could have the same or more restrictive access if both are applied. Answers B and C are incorrect because if the user is accessing it remotely, their share permissions may be further restricted. Answer D is incorrect because the share and NTFS permissions combined also give the same access rather than more restrictive access.

40. **Answer: A, B, C, and D.** When you combine the NTFS permissions assigned to Pat and to the Manager group that Pat is a member of, Pat can read, write, execute, and delete the files in the folder. When you access a folder directly on a local computer, Share permissions do not apply.

41. **Answer: A and C.** When you combine the NTFS permissions assigned to Pat and to the Manager group that Pat is a member of, Pat can read, write, execute, and delete the files in the folder. However, the Read share permission only allows the user to read and execute the files, blocking writing and deleting when going through the shared folder. Answers B and D are incorrect because the Read permission blocked the Write and Delete permissions.

42. **Answer: A.** Pat is a member of the Managers group. Because Deny All NTFS permissions has been granted to the Managers group, it blocks all permissions for Pat. Answers B, C, and D are incorrect because no access permissions always wins. Answer E is incorrect because permissions are assigned.

43. **Answer: B and D.** If you run the application with elevated privileges or manually give NTFS permissions, the user will be able to run the program. Installing a Windows Vista Upgrade Advisor (Answer A) and Application Compatibility Toolkit (Answer C) will not overcome the problem; it will only point out incompatible applications.

44. **Answer: A.** In Windows, the administrator has the tools to limit what the user can do to any given file or directory. This is accomplished through two types of security permissions: share permissions and NTFS permissions. The sharing function is implemented at the computer that hosts the folder or resource (resources are devices capable of holding or manipulating data). To access the shared remote resource, the local operating system must first connect to it. After the connection has been established, the level of access to the resource is controlled by the share or NTFS permissions (or a combination of the two) configured (or inherited) for the resource. Therefore, the other answers are incorrect.

45. Answer: B. When you copy a file to a different NTFS, the file is new to the partition. As a result, it will inherit the attributes of the target folder. Therefore, the other answers are incorrect.

46. Answer: C. When you copy the file from one folder to another folder within the same NTFS partition, it creates a brand new file in that folder. Therefore, it inherits the permissions of the target folder. Therefore, the other answers are incorrect.

47. Answer: A. Because you are moving the file, it only changes the file allocation table to indicate the new location. Therefore, it will retain the same permissions that it had before. The other answers are incorrect.

48. Answer: D. When you are moving a folder to a different NTFS partition, it is a new file to that NTFS partition. Therefore, it will receive the permissions of the target folder. The other answers are incorrect.

49. Answer: A. When giving NTFS permissions, a Deny permission always wins out. Therefore, you will need to remove Pat from the Research group so that he no longer has the Deny permission. Therefore, the other answers are incorrect.

50. Answer: C. For other users to access your shared folders, including the public folder, you need to enable the Password Protected Sharing option. Answer A is incorrect because this scenario mentioned any problem with name resolution. Answer B is incorrect because the Public Folder sharing option would not affect the other shared folders. Answer D is needed for Link Layer Topology Discovery (LLTD).

51. Answer: C. One place to store the report is in the public folder where they both can have access to it. Answers A, B, and D are not the best answer because they do not provide a secure environment where one user cannot look at the data files of another user.

52. Answer: A. To view the computer using the network map, you need to have the Link Layer Topology Discovery (LLTD) operational. Therefore, you need to have the Network Discovery service. Answers B and C are incorrect because Share and NTFS permissions have nothing to do with a computer showing on the network map. Answer D is incorrect because there is no indication that there is a name resolution problem.

53. Answer: B. From the command prompt environment, you can use the `attribute` command to verify that the hidden system files have been successfully copied to the disk (that is, `attrib -r -s -h c:\ntldr` to make it visible and to remove its read-only, system, and hidden status). The `attrib +r +s +h c:\ntldr` command (Answer D) will enable the read-only, system, and hidden attributes. Using the `attrib` command is quicker than restarting the entire system (Answer C). In addition, you should not change the attributes of the C: drive from the Properties page (Answer A).

54. Answer: B. To change a file's attributes in Windows Explorer, right-click on the desired file, select the Properties option from the pop-up list, move to the General page, and click on the desired attribute boxes. Therefore, the other answers are incorrect.

55. Answer: A. It is a good security move to convert any FAT or FAT32 partitions to NTFS so that the stronger NTFS and share permissions can be used to provide stronger control over access to data on the drive. This also allows you to use the NTFS encrypting file system to protect files on the drive. When a file is moved from an NTFS partition to a FAT partition, the NTFS-specific attributes are discarded. Therefore, the other answers are incorrect.

56. Answer: C. Encryption is treated as a file attribute in Windows. Therefore, to encrypt a file, you need to access its properties page by right-clicking it and selecting its Properties option from the pop-up menu. Move to the Advanced area under the General tab and click the Encrypt Contents to Secure Data check box. You cannot encrypt an entire drive (Answers A and D), and files and folders are not automatically encrypted on NTFS5 (Answer B).

57. Answer: A. When you get a TPM error, you need to restart the computer and enter the recovery password in the recovery console. Answer B is incorrect because you cannot log in as any user because of the TPM error. Answer C is incorrect because disabling the feature in BIOS will not decrypt the disk. Answer D is incorrect because it will not be able to open the TPM management console.

58. Answer: B. Because BitLocker encrypts the entire drive, it is the best solution. Answer A is incorrect because you can connect a stolen hard drive to another system that has another operating system and bypass much of the security on the stolen drive, including those set by NTFS permissions. Answer C is incorrect because IPSec is used to encrypt data being transmitted over the network. Answer D is incorrect because EFS is made only to encrypt data files, not system files.

59. Answer: B. You need to have two NTFS volumes, not one. Answers A, C, and D are correct because they are requirements for BitLocker.

60. Answer: D. Biometric scanners are getting significantly more sophisticated—including facial-scanning devices, searchable databases, and supporting application programs. However, the biometric authentication device most widely used with PCs is the fingerprint scanner. Some manufacturers offer miniature touchpad versions that sit on the desk and connect to the system through a cable and USB connector. Other fingerprint scanners are built into key fobs that plug directly into the USB port. Some manufacturers even build these devices into the top of the mouse. Changing the encryption algorithm (Answer A) for login is a complicated process. A fingerprint scanner (Answer B) is easier and less expensive than a retinal scanner. Using a Shared Secret login (Answer C) would be less secure.

61. Answer: C. In matters of security, such as handling of passwords, you should always fall back on the company's policies to protect the company, its employees, its proprietary information, its intellectual properties, and yourself. Therefore, the other answers are incorrect.

62. Answer: A, B, and C. Access to network accounts is based on your user account name and password, which the network asks for each time you log on. Forgetting or misspelling either item results in your being denied access to the network. Password entries are typically case sensitive, so forgetting to properly capitalize key characters or having the Caps Lock key engaged prevents the system from authenticating you and providing access. On the other hand, if the network server is down, there is no component in the network to authenticate you and log you in. Finally, if you violate one of the network's established password policies, you might be locked out and prevented from logging in for a predetermined amount of time. There is no such thing as a NSLOOKUP server. A DNS server would provide name resolution, and you can use the `nslookup` command to help troubleshoot name resolution problems.

63. **Answer: C.** The Secure Sockets Layer (SSL) protocol is used to authenticate organizations or e-commerce servers on the Internet and to encrypt/decrypt messages using a security process called public-key encryption. Most e-commerce transactions are protected under SSL. HTTP (Answer A) is a web protocol that is not secure. IMAP (Answer B) and SMTP (Answer D) are protocols for email.

64. **Answer: D.** Of these protocols, only MS-CHAPv2 provides two-way authentication where both the server and client authenticate each other. Therefore, the other answers are incorrect.

65. **Answer: A.** PAP is short for Password Authentication Protocol. It is a simple protocol that sends the username and password in clear text and therefore is not recommended. The other authentication protocols do not use clear text.

66. **Answer: B.** CHAP is short for Challenge Handshake Authentication Protocol. It does not send the username and password across the network. Instead, it uses a challenge response with a one-way hash algorithm. It is an industry standard protocol that can be used to authenticate non-Windows-based clients. PAP (Answer A) sends the username and password in clear text. MS-CHAP (Answer C) and MS-CHAPv2 (Answer D), created by Microsoft, improve on CHAP by including a password change mechanism.

67. **Answer: D.** EAP is short for Extensible Authentication Protocol. It is an extension of PPP that provides support for other authentication mechanisms, such as smart cards. This authentication protocol requires the presence of a PK infrastructure (PKI). CHAP (Answer A), MS-CHAP (Answer B), and MS-CHAPv2 (Answer C) are popular remote access protocols.

68. **Answer: B.** Kerberos is the primary authentication protocol used on today's Windows domains. You don't need to upgrade Windows XP to Windows Vista (Answer A) and you don't have to configure the local policies (Answer C) to activate this feature. For Windows to automatically use Kerberos, it must be part of the domain. Therefore, Answer D is not correct.

FREE Online Edition

Your purchase of **CompTIA A+ 220-701 and 220-702 Practice Questions Exam Cram** includes access to a free online edition for 45 days through the Safari Books Online subscription service. Nearly every Exam Cram book is available online through Safari Books Online, along with more than 5,000 other technical books and videos from publishers such as Addison-Wesley Professional, Cisco Press, Que, IBM Press, O'Reilly, Prentice Hall, and Sams.

SAFARI BOOKS ONLINE allows you to search for a specific answer, cut and paste code, download chapters, and stay current with emerging technologies.

Activate your FREE Online Edition at
www.informit.com/safarifree

> **STEP 1:** Enter the coupon code: NVEFREH.

> **STEP 2:** New Safari users, complete the brief registration form.
> Safari subscribers, just log in.

If you have difficulty registering on Safari or accessing the online edition, please e-mail customer-service@safaribooksonline.com